HEA

YOU AND YOUR
FAMILY TREE

A Contemplative Approach to
Personal and Generational Healing

Updated First Edition

Father Christopher Ngozi Onuoha

May you who read and pray through this book be filled
with the sanctifying grace of the Holy Spirit;
may you be clothed in the Mantle of grace and intercession
of Mary, the holy Mother of God;
and may you experience the healing power of the
Precious Blood of the Victorious Lamb of God,
Jesus Christ.

Amen! Amen! Amen!

Nihil Obstat Rev. Matthew J. Gutowski, S.T.L.,
Censor Librium, Archdiocese of Omaha, August 1, 2015.

Nihil Obstat and Imprimatur are official declarations of the Church that a book or publication is free from doctrinal or moral error. No implication is meant that those who granted these declarations agree with the content, ideas or statements expressed.

To contact the author by email:

familyprayerministry3@gmail.com
Or visit: *www.familyprayerministries.org*

Cover art and design by Mat Thackray

Printed and bound in the United States of America

Softcover, ISBN: **9781719240871**

Dedication

To
Saint Raphael the Archangel
Medicine of God

to
Saint Michael the Archangel
Prince of the Heavenly Armies

to
Saint Gabriel the Archangel
Herald of the Incarnation

to
The Holy Angels who minister and protect us

and to
The Queen of the Holy Angels
The Blessed Virgin Mother, Mary

and in gratitude to
The Most Blessed Trinity for the Holy Angels

The *Anima Christi*

Soul of Christ, sanctify me
Body of Christ, save me
Blood of Christ, inebriate me
Water from the side of Christ, wash me
Passion of Christ, strengthen me
O good Jesus, hear me
Within Thy wounds hide me
Suffer me not to be separated from Thee
From the malignant enemy defend me
In the hour of my death call me
And bid me come to Thee
That with Thy saints and with Thy angels
That I may praise Thee
Forever and ever.

Amen.

Family Prayer Ministry of the Holy Spirit

Prayer to Saint Raphael the Archangel

Saint Raphael the Archangel, Medicine of God
Revered friend and intercessor of those in need
Healer of the blind, terror of demons
Accompany us in our life's journey here
Guard us to our salvation in the next

Bring healing and freedom to us from God
To praise and glorify Him as our Father
Protect and deliver us we humbly pray,
From all temptations and bondage of the devil

Oh Saint Raphael, Guardian and defender of families
Obedient messenger of God Most High
Assist us that our fiat to God be firm
To carry our crosses daily and follow Jesus
In perfect surrender to His most holy will
For the greater praise and glory of God,
For the salvation of souls.

Amen.

Scripture citations are taken from the *New American Bible* (NAB) unless otherwise stated.

Other Bible versions cited and their abbreviations:

AMP	Amplified Bible
ESV	English Standard Version
GNT	Good News Translation
GW	God's Word Translation
NET	New English Translation
NIV	New International Version
NJB	New Jerusalem Bible
NKJV	New King James Version
NLT	New Living Translation
NRSV	New Revised Standard Version

The books of the Bible cited and their abbreviations:

Old Testament		New Testament	
Gen	Genesis	Mt	Matthew
Ex	Exodus	Mk	Mark
Num	Numbers	Lk	Luke
Deut	Deuteronomy	Jn	John
Josh	Joshua	1 Jn	1 John
Jdg	Judges	Rom	Romans
1 Sam	1 Samuel	1 Cor	1 Corinthians
1 Kgs	1 Kings	2 Cor	2 Corinthians
2 Kgs	2 Kings	Phil	Philippians
1 Chron	1 Chronicle	Jam	James
2 Chron	2 Chronicle	Gal	Galatians
Tob	Tobit	1 Pet	1 Peter
Jdt	Judith	2 Pet	2 Peter
Esth	Esther	Heb	Hebrews
1 Mac	1 Maccabees	1 Tim	1 Timothy
2 Mac	2 Maccabees	2 Tim	2 Timothy
Job	Job	Rev	Revelation
Ps	Psalm		
Prov	Proverbs		
Eccl	Ecclesiastes		
Wis	Wisdom		
Sir	Sirach (Ecclesiasticus)		
Song	Song of Solomon		
Is	Isaiah		
Jer	Jeremiah		
Lam	Lamentation		
Eze	Ezekiel		
Dan	Daniel		
Hosea	Hosea		
Mal	Malachi		

Acknowledgments

The writing of this book *Healing You and Your Family Tree* was a collective effort. I thank all whose contributions made it possible.

My thanks go to the Archbishop of Omaha, George J. Lucas, who gave me his blessings to conduct the Family Healing Retreats during my ministry at Saint Cecilia Cathedral Parish in the Archdiocese of Omaha, and for approving the publication of this book, which is a fruit of those retreats. His questions challenged me to research the subject of this book more thoroughly.

I truly cherish the input of Msgr. William S. Whelan. He read the manuscript and offered corrections and suggestions; his appraisal of it spurred me on with confidence. He constantly hinted on the relevance of the contemplative and transformative potential of this work for all who would use it as intended. His endorsement for the book spoke his heart.

My thanks to Fr. Roberto Marie Ike, whose insightful corrections and suggestions helped me to rewrite some ideas for greater accuracy. I appreciate his endorsement of this work.

My gratitude goes out to all who volunteered to proof read this book and offered valuable insights and corrections. Especially, I thank Beth Flug, who read most of the manuscript. She was always available to help when I ran into hitches along the way. She spoke of the high relevance of the theme for our families today. Deb Neberman put her editing skills to work; she provided helpful corrections and insights. Maris Bentley was the first to proof the chapters. Mat Thackray designed the book cover. Yolanda Bello produced two artworks in this book, shared her experiences and offered useful suggestions. Tom and Maria Engesser proofed and typed my hand-written notes. Their endorsement of the book is based on their unique experience of God's miraculous power in their lives. I thank them for sharing their testimony and for their valuable contributions. They were a source of inspiration and encouragement to me personally.

I am grateful to the members of the House of Prayer and Evangelization (H.O.P.E.) Ministry Prayer Group at Saint Cecilia Cathedral Parish, Omaha, for their prayerful support as I took on the writing of this project; together we shared our faith in Jesus Christ.

I thank Margaret Schlientz for inviting me to attend the Healing and Exorcism Conference in Mundelein Seminary in 2011. There I gained more insight and knowledge on the ministry of deliverance and exorcism. I was highly inspired by the presentations.

My thanks go to Fr. Matthew Gutowski for his painstaking review of this work so it correctly reflects the true theology, in faith and morals, taught by the holy Catholic Church. On behalf of the Archbishop, and with his permission, he granted the *Nihil Obstat*.

I also thank my fellow former members of the Intercessors of the Lamb hermit Priests, Brothers and Sisters, and Lay Companions throughout the world. With them I learned, lived and shared the charism of Contemplative Communal Intercession and Spiritual Warfare. We were a community dedicated to living Jesus Christ and His Cross. In the difficult period following the inevitable suppression of the community, we suffered, cried, laughed, persevered, praised and worshipped together under the fatherly care of Archbishop George J. Lucas. You all are part of the inspiration for this book. For the faith we lived; the love we received; for the community life we shared; and for the charism that was our lifestyle together, I say, thank you!

In gratitude to all, I pray: Glory be to Jesus Christ; honor to the Blessed Virgin Mary.

Book Recommendations

In reviewing *Healing You and Your Family Tree,* I found it most helpful in understanding the theology of intergenerational healing. This is an area which has remained mysterious to me and to many other priests. It seems to me that Fr. Onuoha has exemplified as clearly as anything I have read the theological basis for intergenerational healing. He bases much of his theory on Fr. John Hampsch's reliable theology.

Father Christopher Onuoha shows how the intergenerational traits or tendencies which remain after Baptism can be healed by prayers offered in the name of Jesus Christ. These prayers, especially by priests, can heal these proclivities towards vice and sin. I found his research reliable and logical. His use of Scripture as the basis of his beliefs about intergenerational healing is particularly apt.

– Msgr. William S. Whelan

In an age of scientific inquiry, where many people assume science is better than philosophy, and philosophy better than theology, there is a need to revisit our many obvious experiences that are not readily verifiable by science, but are hugely relevant to life. What *Healing You And Your Family Tree* does is remind us of the importance of dealing with the many trials of life that have been greatly ignored in the so-called scientific age. A genuine experience of truth does not ignore the complimentary importance of science, philosophy (logic) and theology. I encourage the reader to suspend his/her prejudices and read *Healing You And Your Family Tree.* The reader may discover insights that will help him/her face the truth about one's identity and the role of faith in dealing with personal and generational struggles.

–Fr. Roberto Marie Ike

The message of this book is at once both powerful and life transforming; we experienced both. It promises hope for all God's people who struggle with bondage. We attended the Family Healing Retreats and read the book; and we experienced transforming renewal. Our biggest grace is the blessing of a son, Mark, as the fruit of Jesus' ministry of freedom through Fr. Christopher. *Healing You And Your Family Tree* is a powerful resource for spiritual awakening and combat readiness for anyone in personal or generational struggles. We highly recommend that your family read and pray through *Healing You And Your Family Tree,* and if possible attend the healing conference. We pray that you be blessed as we were.

–Tom, Maria and Mark Engesser

Table of Contents

Part I

Chapter 1–6   Understanding the Concepts

Part II

Chapters 7–13   The Primary Open Doors to Bondage

Part III

Chapters 14–18 The Secondary Open Doors to Bondage

● ● ●

Part IV

Chapters 19–20   Celebrating Healing

Figures and Charts

Appendices

Introduction

The reality of bondage

I was motivated to write this book because of my personal experience with generational bondage. I realized how easily the distress of bondage can potentially disrupt one's spiritual life. We can deal with the trials of bondage from a place of true spiritual strength in us, if only we can access that place within. It is the place of our true identity, where God and I are one. It is the place where I am loved and in love; it is the place of intimacy and freedom where I am at home in myself and with God who loves me.

Jesus said we must be born again from above by water and the Holy Spirit, if we are to enter the Kingdom of God (Jn 3:3–8). Saint Paul insists that we, the baptized, must be led by the Holy Spirit. Ignorance in the face of the trials of bondage can cause disruptions in our spiritual lives. We often get confused and distressed and desolate, and we lack peace.

Such was my experience. If we knew precisely what our problems were, we would be effective in directing our attention and efforts to finding a solution; we would take effective measures to resolve them. But if we don't, we may look in the wrong places, which may cause us unnecessary suffering. We may waste time and energy complaining, blaming and condemning ourselves and others for our problem. We may even blame God for what He is not responsible for, or blame ourselves for what we are not responsible for, or blame others for what they are not responsible for.

The trials of bondage are not beyond God's power to resolve. Bondage occurs because God permits it; He does so for our greater good. He alone is able to bring good out of evil. Bondage can be a blessing in disguise. The suffering of bondage may seem like going through a dark tunnel with no hope of escape. But we can be assured there is always light at the end of the tunnel. In Saint Peter's words: "after you have suffered for a little while, the God of all grace who called you to his eternal glory in Christ will himself restore, confirm, strengthen, and establish you" (1 Pet 5:10, NET). Let's look at the suffering of bondage through the lens of the Letter to the Hebrews 12:3–8, as God's discipline. We read that God treats us as His children; His discipline is our training in endurance. Every good father disciplines his child. A child without discipline in which all have a share, ceases to be a child, and is an illegitimate one. Jesus endured so much hostility from us sinners so that we may not grow weary and become fainthearted. None of us has resisted and struggled against sin to the point of shedding blood. But Jesus did so for our sake. Faced with the trials of bondage, we must look onto our crucified Jesus and be strong; it is by His wounds that we are freed and healed. Jesus is our light and strength; the risen Jesus is our glory, He who once was slain, now lives forever. He became a curse for us that we might be released from all bondage. Bondage may feel like a death experience, but Saint Francis of Assisi said: "It is in dying that we are born to eternal life." Thanks be to God, Jesus Christ has conquered death and the grave. Alleluia!

Perseverance in trials

The Letter to the Hebrews encourages us to endure our trials as discipline, because God treats us as sons and daughters. Our earthly fathers disciplined us to prepare us to face the challenges of life. Every discipline, at the time it is given, is like a bitter pill when swallowed; it is painful and uncomfortable. But when we accept and surrender and are trained by it, in due time, it bears the "peaceful fruit of righteousness" in us (Heb 12:7–11). We become stronger, wiser, and more matured spiritually. It unites us more deeply with the Crucified Lord. God allowed the saints to go through trials, bondage, temptations, and persecutions; the same trials we face daily. For our good, the Lord permits these trials to test the quality of our faith, which is more valuable than fire-tried gold that does not last. The true faith will bring praise and honor and glory to Jesus Christ when He returns to reward His saints (1 Pet 1:7). My best definition of a saint is: *a saint is a sinner who never stopped trying.* God allows all our sufferings to bring us into deeper purification, so that all the corruption and false belief systems in us would be purged from us. Indeed, we must be purged! And we are being purged!

When I was a seminarian, I began to experience an unusual interior distress that I did not understand. I brought this regularly to spiritual direction and Confession, but I had no relief. I found no one knowledgeable in generational issues to help me. I informed my superiors in my community, the Intercessors of the Lamb. They prayed and discerned and relayed to me what they were getting in prayer. My unusual experiences seem to have some generational origin, as well as pre- and post- natal open doors to spiritual contamination, from the effects of the pagan culture of my ancestral tribe, the Igbos in Nigeria, and the "ritual of protection" that natives were sometimes subjected to. These situations compromised in me the wholeness, life and wellbeing, and the peace promised to believers by the Gospel of Christ. My unusual experiences were the result of multiple contaminations beyond my control.

Getting to the root

I was totally ignorant of the underlying issues when the effects of bondage began to manifest in my seminary formation. I was mystified by them, and in my search for answers, I met with Monsignor John Esseff, a priest of the Diocese of Scranton, who had been my spiritual director while attending the Seminarian Summer Program of the Institute for Priestly Formation (IPF) in Omaha, Nebraska. He made me understand clearly that I was under some generational bondage. He advised me to conduct an investigation into my family tree. So, I travelled to Nigeria for this purpose, and I was surprised at the findings I briefly stated above. I became aware of situations in my family tree I did not know before that were affecting me. These revelations in themselves were healing for me. They gave me hope and confidence, and I gained the knowledge that empowered me for prayer and for spiritual battle. I resolved to do battle and intercede for my ancestry.

In the years that followed, I spent long hours in silent prayer and self-reflection, asking from the Holy Spirit the light to see what I needed to see. Gradually, I began to receive confirmations that the root of my experiences was indeed in my family tree. I talked to Jesus about them, and He has walked with me in my struggle.

I wrote this book also because I believe the evil one is using the media to attack families and propagate lies and falsehood. Books have been written that falsify the true teachings of Christianity, and these have created much confusion in the faith of believers. The lies contained in these books corrupt and erode our Christian and Catholic faith and values. They create tension in hearts and minds, and constitute a threat to, and a disruption in the spiritual life of families.

Pope Emeritus Benedict XVI, while Prefect of the Congregation for the Doctrine of the Faith (CDF), said in a letter regarding the book, Harry Potter—a fiction series featuring elements of the occult, that it corrupts and poisons authentic Christian beliefs and the faith of young people, who are called to holiness by Jesus Christ. It desensitizes Christians to the dangers of evil that confront us daily. The Christian life calls us to attain the holiness of Christ, which is opposed to worldly values.

Truth as solid foundation

Our families deserve to know the truth that is Christ; and through this knowledge, to enjoy freedom and peace in our hearts, families and relationships. Only the truth of Christ can lead to this end. Only the truth sets us free. There is no compromise or relativism in the truth. We either believe truths or we believe lies; there are no gray areas in God. No one experiences the true freedom of Christ who believes half-truths and half-lies. Falsehoods and lies are poisons that gradually and surely kill the true faith, especially in young people who will lead the Church of tomorrow. Only the truth of God's Word can arm young people to conquer the prince of this world, the father of lies and the evil spirit of deception (1 Jn 2:14; Jn 8:44).

Some families may be going through sufferings that, in my experience, are not necessary. Jesus did not suffer and die necessarily (Lk 24:26), so that we may undergo unnecessary suffering. His suffering and death were necessary in order that we might be freed from unnecessary bondage. He became sin, so that we might be made righteous (2 Cor 5:21). Jesus invites us to come to Him with our burdens, and to experience His rest and peace (Mt 11:28). Our unnecessary sufferings would melt away if we pray correctly and effectively according to the mind of Christ. God is far greater than all our problems. He is our victory; He is everything.

If we fail to understand the reason for our suffering, we may believe and act wrongly. We may even believe that God is responsible for our problems, when in truth He is not. God is love! God is good! God cares! God loves us more than we love ourselves. How can He cause us unnecessary suffering? God reminds us that if we who are sinners and wicked can give the children we love good gifts, "how much more will the Father in heaven give the Holy Spirit to those who ask him?" (Lk 11:13).

I knew a family that was going through unnecessary suffering. The mother of a few months old baby boy, who was born deaf, told me her baby was born deaf, because God did not want him to hear bad news. Sadly, she believed and accepted this situation as God's will. But that did not sound right to me! How could God be so mean as to deny this innocent boy the sense of hearing? The truth is that God gave us ears to hear the word of life, and thereby be saved. God sent His Son, Jesus Christ, into the world so that all who believe in Him, and all who listen to Him, might have life. This is why we have ears: to hear the Good News and be saved. Paul says that faith comes by hearing God's word (Rom 10:17). On the Mount of Transfiguration, God the Father spoke saying: "This is my beloved Son. Listen to him" (Mk 9:7). Isaiah 50:4 reads: "Morning after morning he opens my ear that I may hear," so that we do not rebel.

Bringing hope to families

This book is also written to bring hope to those in personal or generational bondage in any form. Jesus our Good Shepherd is in our midst. He rose from the dead to lead us to springs of living water. He came to set captives free from bondage. When Jesus came, He went about doing good works. He raised Lazarus from the dead after four days in the tomb. He worked mighty deeds in Palestine, as recorded in the Scriptures; He wants to do the same for us, for our family tree, and for our world.

The Family Healing Retreats bring hope to families and all God's people. No one is excluded from the touch of Christ, who raises the dead, sets prisoners free, heals the sick, and delivers those held captive by demons. Healing happens when we cooperate with our Lord Jesus, and allow Him to love us the way we are. In this regard, the consent and ascent of our intellect and free will are important—this is faith. Our free will is the open door to bondage. It is also the open door to God's grace, healing and freedom. It all depends on which door we choose to open: to sin and disobedience, or to freedom and obedience to God. God desires we "choose life" (Deut 30:19), healing, freedom and love and live.

Oh my Jesus, forgive us our sins, save us from the fires of Hell,
lead all souls to Heaven,
especially those who are most in need of Thy mercy.[1]

Self-knowledge needed

My experiences in spiritual direction and retreat ministry have led me to include chapter 4, which treats the important subject of self-knowledge. It is one of the core chapters of this book. Most of our problems are rooted in a deep lack of self-knowledge. I would encourage the reader to take this chapter particularly seriously. Self-knowledge will equip us with the tools we need to deal effectively with bondage situations calmly without panic. Self-knowledge will help us to remain peaceful and open to do God's will, even in times of adversity and desolation. It will strengthen us against paralyzing fears that alienate us from God. God's love dispels all fear (1 Jn 4:18). When we are in touch with our true selves, we are not afraid of the crosses that God permits in our lives. Self-knowledge will empower us to intercede effectively and fruitfully for our family trees. We are ambassadors of Christ, who was sent by the Father (Jn 20:21; 17:18), and who in turn has sent us (Jn 20:21). We are also ambassadors of our ancestors, because we represent them now. As such, our prayers benefit them, because of our connection with them in Christ. We want to represent Christ well here before we join Him in Heaven. We also want to represent our ancestors well here in the hope that we all may have eternal fellowship with the Son and with the Father. God desires this, and He helps us with His grace to attain it.

Be a contemplative

I place strong emphasis in this book on the contemplative approach. This approach makes possible, easy and fruitful the encounter with God who alone heals us. To God, all things are possible. Contemplation creates the interior opening that disposes us to receive all that God desires to give for our well-being and happiness. Contemplation is a call in which our response must always be, "Speak Lord, your servant is listening." It demands the receptive attitude of listening, waiting and availability. As a flower that is open to the Sun receives all the rays and benefits of the Sun, so we should be open to the Son to receive life from the Son (see page 250, Jn 5:21). Saint John of the Cross says, "Human effort does little more than dispose one for divine action."[2]

Why this book on contemplative healing?

Healing is both a spiritual and a physical experience that embraces the contemplative and the active dimensions of our lives, that is, the receiving and giving, the Marian and the apostolic charisms. The fundamental approach in this important work is to bring the two aspects into a working relationship, for the purpose of experiencing healing in Christ. Without the contemplative, we cannot have the active; without the receiving from the Spirit, there is nothing to give from the Spirit. We must first be filled: receptive and be healed, before we can give and be instruments of healing for others. We cannot give what we do not have. Practically speaking, no one gives out of emptiness.

Family healing is a journey of faith in Christ

Family healing is a faith journey. Pope Saint Clement I said, "God's blessing must [always] be our objective, and the way to win it our study."[3] Faith disposes us to receive God's blessing. The journey of faith is one of liberation; God bringing us, as it were, out from that place of bondage to the Promised Land where milk and honey flow. What God is about to do for our families, He already made known through the prophets. He freed us from the power of darkness so that we may belong now to the Kingdom of Christ, His Son. There we shall worship Him without fear in holiness and righteousness all the days of our life (Col 1:13; Lk 1:74).

Family healing is a journey of "let my people go" from the clutches and bondage of "Pharaoh" and the "Egyptians," to the freedom of the Promised Land, of living in God's fulfilling and amazing grace as His children. The faith-response disposes us to listen to all the instructions of the Lord. It is a response that witnesses to the mighty plagues from the Mighty hand of God, which breaks the enemy stronghold to set the captives free.

In the Scriptures, Israel's bondage in Egypt lasted 430 years. Their deliverance did not happen overnight. It began in a most unsuspecting way. Pharaoh's daughter found the deliverer of God's suffering people, as a baby boy in a papyrus basket floating on the river side. He was raised up in Pharaoh's household, hidden in God's quiver for the appointed time. This child, Moses, was to be God's instrument of liberation for His people who were under the yoke of slavery (Ex 2).

Jesus likewise came into this world to liberate us from the bondage of Satan, sin and death. He was born in a most unsuspecting way, in a manger, wrapped in swaddling clothes in the silence of Christmas night. He came as light into the darkness, but the darkness did not overcome Him; His own people to whom He was sent did not receive Him (Jn 1:5, 11). Those who receive Him He empowered to be His children. On them He fulfills God's plan of salvation. He frees them from the bondage of this world and the emptiness it offers.

Renew our commitment to cherish, honor and defend the family

The family instituted by God faces grave threats in our world today. Before the Synod on the Family in October 2014 in Rome, Pope Francis, while addressing fifty-two thousand faithful at the Charismatic Renewal Convocation—*Renewal in the Spirit,* at the Rome's Olympic Stadium said: "Families are the domestic church where Jesus grows in the love of a married couple, in the lives of their children. This is why the devil attacks the family so much."[4] He further explained that the evil one hates the family, and ceases every opportunity to try to destroy it. He tries to make love disappear from the family.[5] The Pope then enjoined all the faithful to "… pray to the Lord [Jesus] and ask him to protect the family in the crisis with which the devil wants to destroy it."[6] We know that the evil one uses the instrumentality of human agents inside and outside the Church for these hateful and destructive attacks. It uses false doctrine, distortion, lies, half-truth, deceit, and various strategies to corrupt the faith and families. This is why Saint Ignatius of Antioch, in a letter to the Ephesians, warned:

> Make no mistake, my brothers: those who corrupt families will not inherit the kingdom of God. If those who do these things in accordance with the flesh have died, how much worse will it be if one corrupts through evil doctrine the faith of God for which Jesus Christ was crucified? Such a person, because he is defiled, will depart into the unquenchable fire, as will anyone who listens to him.[7]

Much faith needed

Faith in Jesus is the interior disposition necessary to receive the Father's healing and freedom. Jesus is God's Anointed Son. He spent His earthly life doing good works, freeing captives and healing the oppressed, because God's power was in Him. Liberation from bondage frees us to fulfill the Father's blessing to increase and multiply and to fill the earth. In this way we become the source of joy and fulfillment for our brothers and sisters. This is our particular call and charism as Christians. This book is written to help us receive the abundant life promised us by the Good Shepherd of our souls, so that our joy might be complete.

So we cannot sit idly by while Satan destroys the most beautiful creation of God-Man, by leading him astray. We must act against it. We must be prepared to enter enemy territory and claim back what it has stolen from us. The situation calls for spiritual combat, and we cannot shy away from the challenges of combat. Pope Saint Leo XIII calls us to this combat; he said Catholics are born for combat. We are faced with a culture of death that threatens to destroy the civilization of love. This culture manifesting in different forms, shows itself in the grave hatred for human nature, as shown in its manifestations: human trafficking, modern-day slavery and sex trades, euthanasia, wars, population control, hunger, abortion, suicides, homosexuality, fornication, sexual immorality and all impure acts, abuse of the body, violence, lying, deception, falsification, and all shades of evil.

To prepare us for this combat, I have included chapter 5: "Understanding Basic Spiritual Warfare." We are not called to be exorcists. We are called to be saints, and saints do battle. Yes! We are the Church Militant. Earthly life is a warfare from which we cannot run away. The greatest and most effective weapon we have for combat is our union with Jesus Christ, the holy One of God. To engage successfully in spiritual warfare, it is necessary that we pray with the Psalmist that the gates of holiness be opened to us (Ps 118:19–20). We must choose to live and become holy. To do so, we need to grow in humility, love and perseverance. We must mature in love and respect for ourselves and others. Do we see ourselves as God's gift to ourselves and to others, and others as God's gift to us? See how Jesus appreciates us before the Father: "Father, they are your gift to me. I wish that where I am they also may be with me, that they may see my glory that you gave me" (Jn 17:24).

Effective prayer is the key

Because we speak of faith and act in faith, we must also speak of prayer. Faith in Jesus Christ is a supernatural gift. We received supernatural faith at Baptism. Prayer is the language of supernatural faith. For effective prayer to occur through faith, we need silence and solitude. For spiritual receptivity, and for any active and fruitful ministry to happen, since apart from works our faith is dead, prayer in the Spirit is necessary. Our primary vocation is to live lives in the Holy Spirit.[8] Living an intense and authentic spiritual life prepares us to receive healing, deepens our relationship with God, and ensures our salvation. This means that any obstacles that hamper our prayer life, degrade our relationship with God, and so must be removed. Whatever blocks our openness to receive God is bondage. It is important then that we identify these blocks in us, where possible, and allow Jesus to work with us to resolve them.

Empower families with tools to identify and pray against bondage

The family is under attack by enemies that often hold it captive. Fr. César Truqui believes there are demons that specialize in attacking families. He warned that things that harm the family, such as divorce, are the things that please the devil.[9] In the Book of Tobit 3:8, the evil demon Asmodeus, in Hebrew means "destroyer," killed the seven husbands of the virgin Sarah before their marriages could be consummated. It is believed that "God allowed the demon to slay these men because they entered marriage with unholy motives."[10] But the pious and young Tobias, God-fearing and acting on the instruction of the Archangel Raphael, who expelled the wicked Asmodeus from Sarah, was able to marry her peacefully. The exemplary chastity and temperance of Tobias and Sarah protected them from the attack and bondage of the wicked demon. This teaches our world an example of how to live peaceful fruitful marriages and holy family life. It is also presented as a "motive to chasten man's lust and sanctify marriage,"[11] which God desires for all married couples.

The treatment of the different open doors to bondage in families constitutes most of the chapters of this book, but they are not necessarily the most important. The most important chapters deal with our relationship with God. Union with God is the ultimate goal of the spiritual life which this book addresses. This union which happens in freedom and holiness shields our families from demonic attacks and consequent bondage. It is important that we know how to recognize the open doors to these attacks and the bondage that can result from them in our lives and family. This will help protect our families from unnecessary suffering. Generational or personal bondage is situated and felt in a human person as a discomfort or limitation of freedom; so, it is significant. The open doors to bondage will be treated comprehensively in two main sets: the "Primary Open Doors" and the "Secondary Open Doors."

The primary open doors are the Seven Capital sins (chapters 7–13); while the "Secondary Open Doors" (chapters 14–18) are essentially complications of the "Primary Open Doors." Sin is the common denominator in all the open doors, and the first sin ever committed was pride (Chapter 9). It is the basis of all other sins. Sin, which is disobedience, compromises of our relationship with God. These open doors are discussed to provide us with the tools we need for discernment when we are faced with bondage. Bondage can potentially plunge us into spiritual disarray, so it is important to understand their dynamics in us.

In discussing each of the capital sins, I made sure to suggest potent weapons for waging war against them and to reclaim our freedom. We can fight with the weapons the Holy Spirit gave us at our Baptism, the Isaiah Gifts. Our ammunition also includes the Seven Words of Our Lord on the cross, followed by a component of the Armor of God, which as Christian soldiers, we acquire as we grow daily in holiness. Lastly, we have the weapon of our Blessed Mother's Seven Sorrows. Her Fiat to God has made her powerful, the Almighty has done great things for me... all generations will call me blessed (Lk 1:48–49). She is our unfailing intercessor before her Son, Jesus, for all God's children in their need. She is the Mediatrix of All Graces, Mother of the Redeemer and Mother of Mercy. In her Canticle of Praise to the Blessed Trinity, the Blessed Virgin prays for the healing of all our generations. Her prayer is both an invitation and a fulfillment: "from now on will all generations will call me blessed." In accepting her as the Lord's humble handmaid, we enter into her effective intercession for our generations, because "His mercy is from generation unto generation to them that fear Him" (Lk 1:50). In the Memorare we pray:

Remember, O most gracious Virgin Mary, that never was it known that anyone who fled to thy protection, implored thy help, or sought thy intercession was left unaided. Inspired with this confidence, I fly unto thee, O Virgin of virgins, my mother; to thee do I come, before thee I stand, sinful and sorrowful. O Mother of the Word Incarnate, despise not my petitions,
but in thy clemency hear and answer me. Amen.

Powerful resource for prayer, spiritual growth and spiritual warfare

Often we go to prayer, even before the Blessed Sacrament, with our novels, spiritual books, magazines and church bulletins, because we feel bored by prayer; as if our Eucharistic Lord begins His nap the moment He sees us come into His presence to pray. We busy ourselves with many distractions: read away our prayer time, play games, text and answer phone calls, and we end our prayer time not realizing the reason we came to pray, which is to encounter God who waits to love and speak and embrace us in His merciful love. This book draws our attention to what to look for when we pray, and how to dispose ourselves for authentic prayer. It gives guidelines to help us listen more attentively to God in our hearts, and to engage God in the dialogue of prayer. In prayer we listen and ask questions and share our hearts: thoughts, feelings and desires. We listen to the Father and hear Him do what He does best for us His beloved children, allowing us to hear His voice. In this way we grow in friendship with Jesus, and experience the companionship of the Holy Spirit.

This book does not aim to make us exorcists, by no means. But as Christians we must realize that together with Jesus we are spiritual warriors for the salvation of souls. Contained in these pages are principles for daily spiritual warfare. In it, we learn how to recognize the tactics of our enemy, the demons, and the weapons needed to fight them. We learn strategies of warfare and how to protect ourselves, where possible, because bondage often presents us with situations of spiritual warfare.

Knowing our identity and mission as Christians will help us remain faithful to Jesus' call to follow Him, as His disciples, and so attain perfection through faith in Him. To follow Jesus more closely and love Him more dearly and confidently, we need to discern God's voice in the many affective movements of our hearts. We need discernment in the Church today, so we can recognize the voice of the Good Shepherd calling and leading His sheep in truth to restful pastures in the Father's house.

Most Holy Trinity, Father, Son and Holy Spirit, I adore Thee profoundly. I offer Thee the most precious Body, Blood, Soul and Divinity of Jesus Christ, present in all the tabernacles of the world, in reparation for the outrages, sacrileges, and indifferences by which He is offended. By the infinite merits of the Most Sacred Heart of Jesus and the Immaculate Heart of Mary,
I beg Thee for the conversion of poor sinners.[12]
Amen.

Part I

Chapters 1–6

Understanding the Concepts

Glory be to Jesus; honor to Mary and Joseph!

Chapter 1

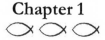

The Contemplative Approach

But his delight is in the law of the Lord, and in His law he meditates day and night (Ps 1:2, NKJV).

The fruitful approach to healing

This book approaches generational and personal healing from the contemplative dimension. This approach helps us grow in the faith needed to receive the healing God has for us. This approach requires that we be generous to the demands of the interior life lived out in deep prayer, in an atmosphere of silence, where we listen to the voice of the Lord. This approach calls for a personal relationship with the Lord Jesus who shows us how to be like God. "The simple truth is that the human soul can only flourish spiritually only by cultivating a contemplative quality."[13] The contemplative approach is a decision; it is not an idea or a play on imagination. It means that we must commit some time for, first exterior silence, and nurture interior quiet. Contemplation does not happen by chance; it requires a disciplined, conscious and sustained effort to practice silent prayer, to be with and journey with God.

A man brought his young son who was in bondage to unclean spirits to Jesus' disciples. But they were not able to set the boy free because of their lack of faith. At this failure, Jesus exclaimed: "O faithless generation, how long shall I be with you? How long shall I bear with you? Bring him to Me" (Mk 9:19, NKJV).

Jesus began the process of healing the boy by seeking background information: "How long has this been happening to him?" "Since childhood," the boy's father said. He went on to detail the bondage and its manifestations. The disciples, amazed at the ease with which Jesus freed the boy, asked Him, "Why could we not cast it out?" He said to them, "This kind can come out by nothing but prayer and fasting" (Mk 9:28–29, NKJV).

This response of Jesus introduces us to the contemplative approach to healing. It is the prayer-of-faith approach. The disciples had not yet learned from Jesus how to receive in prayer. They had not yet learned to pay attention to Jesus' words and actions. They had not yet learned Jesus' prayer of intimacy with the Father. They were not yet familiar with the prayer of abandonment to the Father. Jesus said He could not do anything on His own. He does only what He sees and learns from the Father (Jn 8:28). Learning from God involves interior silence and listening, so that we can recognize the voice of the Good Shepherd, and receive eternal life (Jn 10:27–28). Contemplation enriched and propelled Jesus' life and ministry; it is built on four main pillars of *prayer, penance, silence and solitude.*[14]

For a contemplative person, every suffering is a participation in the mystery of God. He/she sees things as God sees them. That person is like the eagle which flies high up in the sky (high ground) and sees everything clearly. A contemplative is not rash in action or decision making, but always waits for God's timing in all things.

The Blessed Virgin Mary is the contemplative *par excellence*. She is full of grace. She pondered God and His Word (Lk 1:29; 2:19, 51), and received divine light and sanctity in doing so. She sees as God sees, and because she is open, she receives without limits. Her will is in union with Divine Will. In her faith, she believed that nothing was impossible for God. Contemplatives imitate the Virgin Mary. They see bondage and suffering as means of growing in holiness. They unite their pain and distress with the suffering of Jesus to save the world. Through contemplation, we can shake off the dust of sin, and ascend to God's throne. It is an opportunity and a way to loosen the bonds from the neck of captive daughter Zion (Is 52:2).

When we have the contemplative spirit or the surrendered attitude, we give God the freedom to be God in our lives. We let go, and let God. Mary chose the contemplative approach as she sat at the feet of Jesus and listened to His Word (Lk 10:39). This gave Jesus the freedom to love her as God. God's ordinary actions are miracles to us human beings. God loves to work miracles because that is His nature. He is a Miracle Worker. A contemplative does not complain or grumble, because such an attitude blocks and resists God's love and actions in the soul. Contemplatives accept all things and endure all things. They learn to persevere in every situation. They are God's children beyond reproach, and they shine like the stars in a world enveloped in darkness (Phil 2:15).

The contemplative approach safeguards us against illusions and deceptions, because it gives us God's perspective on things. God alone is able to bring good out of evil. Contemplation helps us to unmask and expose hidden lies in us and make us transparent and pure of heart. A contemplative cannot hide behind shadows, as the Psalmist reminds us:

Where can I go from your Spirit? Where can I flee from your presence? If I go up to the heavens, you are there; if I make my bed in the depths, you are there. If I rise on the wings of the dawn, if I settle on the far side of the sea, even there your hand will guide me, your right hand will hold me fast. If I say, "Surely the darkness will hide me and the light become night around me," even the darkness will not be dark to you; the night will shine like the day, for darkness is as light to you (Ps 139:7–12, NIV).

Healing happens when God pours Himself out in love. We are receptors and channels of God's healing love. Obedience must underlie our response to God's call and presence. Obedience is at the heart of Jesus' relationship with the Father. The sin of the world that the Lamb of God came to take away (Jn 1:29), is disobedience. This is why Jesus reminds us, "The world must know that I love the Father and that I do just as the Father has commanded me" (Jn 14:31). Jesus lived a life of deep interior connectedness with the Father. He lived the following four dimensions of the contemplative approach.

Silence

Silence is God's language. The one who contemplates dwells in interior silence, and you may call it "digital silence." Contemplation happens in the silence. Silence is a state of mind and heart that fosters communion and union with God. It is more than simply not speaking; it is qualitative and active. We are called to enter the living silence of God's presence in our pilgrim journey. Saint John Paul II holds up for our imitation the Blessed Mary who, "by her words and her silence the Virgin Mary stands before us as a model for our pilgrim way."[15] He also said, "The *Magnificat* is followed by *silence: nothing is said to us* about the three months that Mary stayed with her kinswoman Elizabeth. Yet perhaps we are told the most important thing: that *goodness works quietly,* the power of love is expressed in the unassuming quietness of daily service."[16]

Only silence has the capacity to replenish our inner spirit and keep a deeper layer of soul open to truth. "The presence of some silence in our day has the effect of drawing us to a more generous attentiveness."[17] We listen better in silence, but more importantly, the greater impact of silence is in the quality of our eyes. "A more selfless act of attention permeates our perception of reality as we live a day." "We are attracted... to the silence that resides at the heart of all reality and all events."[18] Especially, it brings us mystically in touch with the silence of creation, and of the redemption, and even now draws us close to the mystical silence of the Triune God as He reveals Himself in our world. There may be noise and turmoil, and even a surface turbulence, "but a love of silence conveys a deeper truth. It allows us to sense that God is present with His secret gaze upon all that occurs in every day."[19]

God says, "Be still and know that I am God" (Ps 46:10). In this silence God wants to be known and experienced. There, He wants to reveal Himself to us. This God who dwells in eternal silence wants to speak to our hearts. Drawn to us and ravished by love, He says, "I will allure her into the desert, and there speak to her heart" (Hos 2:16). It is the "she" in us that receives God's self-emptying presence. In this receptivity of the heart—listening, we experience healing and life. For this reason the Father desires and invites us to listen to His beloved Son (Mk 9:7).

When Jesus went into the temple and knocked down the tables of those who were selling and buying there (Mk 11:15–17), He was teaching us that we have to keep our interior life clean and quiet. He was teaching us about inner silence of the heart. Saint Paul reminds us that our body is God's temple (1 Cor 6:19) where God is reverenced and worshiped. Jesus wants God's temple in us to be a house of prayer where God is adored in spirit and in truth. He said, "When you pray go into your inner room, close the door, and pray to your Father in secret" (Mt 6:6). It is in this 'secret' silence that we worship God in spirit and in truth. The Father seeks those who worship Him this way. In this inner room we listen and receive God's life (Is 55:3). It is in the silence that the sheep learns to recognize the voice of the Good Shepherd (Jn 10:3–4; 14–16). It is there that we know ourselves and are known by God.

The Lord began to teach me about the value of listening in this interior place when I joined the Intercessors of the Lamb. I was charged with caring for five sheep. It was initially a disgusting experience for me. I thought, "This was not why I joined religious life." But since religious life demands obedience and a generous gift of self in love to God, I later accepted this responsibility, and I was at peace serving the sheep like Jesus.

When I first got to the sheep barn, I was surprised that all the sheep ran away. They did not run away when the brother I was taking over from came into the barn. When he was there, the sheep would come to him; he called each sheep by name, and they responded. But when I tried it, they either ran away or stayed far off. This was amazing to me. When I asked him why they ran away from me, he directed me to read John chapter 10. It was then I realized the sheep did not recognize my voice, because I was a stranger to them. It took many more weeks for all that to begin to change. I began to appreciate Jesus' words: "My sheep hear my voice, I know then and they follow me" (Jn 10:27). The sheep "will never follow a stranger… they will run away from him because they do not recognize a stranger's voice" (Jn 10:5, NIV).

Jesus' hidden life in Nazareth for thirty years is a powerful sign that we should take silence seriously in our lives. Without the silence of formation, there will be no silence of surrender. The mature silence of Nazareth led to the sacrificial and redemptive silence of Calvary—Jesus' total surrender even to death on the Cross. Like a sheep He was led to the slaughter, and He did not open his mouth (Is 53:7). The silence of Calvary gave birth to the silence of the empty tomb that speaks so powerfully that Jesus is alive. By this silent surrender, our redemption in Christ Jesus is accomplished. All the silence find their meeting point in the silence of the Eucharistic presence. This expectant silence kindles a holy fire that must burn in the heart of the Christian for effective and fruitful evangelization. In this silence, we are united to the contemplative heart of Mary of Nazareth who calls us into the silence to "do whatever he tells you" (Jn 2:5). Only then can we drink fully of the New Wine of Pentecost for the life of the world.

Prayer

Authentic life-giving prayer happens in the silence, that is, prayer offered in spirit and truth, which God seeks, and which allows us to dwell in His presence. It drives us to seek union with, and to be like God. Prayer is to a Christian what water is to fish. Prayer is life itself, and a way of life. It is a way of being. Through it, we engage God with our whole heart, and allow His presence to absorb our maximum attention. This is prayer of the heart—to allow our whole being to be absorbed, to rest and be in the Father.

Prayer is God's gift; it is also an art to be learned. Eli taught Samuel to pray: "Speak, Lord, your servant is listening" (1 Sam 3:9, 10). When the Lord calls us by name to prayer, we say, "Speak, Lord, your servant is listening." Let us imitate the Apostles and ask: "Lord, teach us to pray" (Lk 11:1). We learn how to pray by watching how Jesus prays in the Scriptures. The purpose and the core of prayer is to experience intimacy with God. Intimacy leads to union and transformation into His Divine likeness. In intimacy, pure faith grows; the old man is cast aside and conversion to the "new man" takes place. I learned a simple song about Jesus, the Man of prayer:

Prayer is the key, prayer is the key
Prayer is the master key
Jesus started with prayers and ended with prayers.
Prayer is the master key.[20]

The Holy Mass is the most powerful prayer ever prayed by anyone on this earth. At Mass Jesus prays with His life on the Cross for us. It is the prayer of Jesus' whole life summed up as one. Jesus prayed with the heart in His priestly prayer (Jn 17). He speaks from the heart to the Father. Jesus does only what He hears from the Father (Jn 5:30). At Mass, we celebrate the entire prayer life of Jesus and His total self-sacrifice to the Father, His prayer of surrender and thanksgiving.

As we are drawn more and more into the prayer of Jesus, the goal of prayer becomes union with God. Jesus invites us into this union with Him through prayer. Like a branch on the vine, He says, "Remain in me, as I remain in you" (Jn 15:4, 7), so that whatever you ask for in My Name will be done for you. This is why the early Church Father, Tertullian, strongly stated that, "Prayer is the only thing that can conquer God."[21] Jesus wants us to learn how He relates with the Father. He said when we pray, to "go into your inner room, close the door, and pray to your Father in secret" (Mt 6:6). In this 'inner room' we learn to pray as the Spirit teaches us.

The Lord showed Saint Teresa of Avila the dynamics of prayer in her seven mansions of the *Interior Castle*. The inner room comprises the stages of growth in the interior life as we seek union with God. It is God who carries us through the mansions as we progress in prayer. If we do not resist God on this journey, we will arrive quickly and safely home. We must surrender to the daily trials of this journey. It is a journey inward to self-discovery; to know God who is love.

We must shed all the false images, concepts and beliefs we have of God. These worldly beliefs which have been fed into us are opposed to God's values. We are vulnerable to false beliefs about reality from the moment of our conception, and throughout our prenatal and postnatal life. These false beliefs do influence us negatively and manifest through our thoughts, feelings, words and actions. Whenever we get in touch with these false beliefs, we should talk to Jesus about them in prayer.

Authentic prayer will reveal the extent of self-love that is rooted in us. We will realize how self-centered we are. In this journey in the inner room, we move from falsehood to truth, selfishness to selflessness, and from self-centeredness to God-centeredness.

Prayer should be for us a daily discipline, allowing the Holy Spirit to teach us and bring us into a deeper prayer experience of God, as we are further purified of all false beliefs. The Spirit comes to help us in our weakness. He intercedes for us with groanings that only God understands (Rom 8:26). When we have learned to surrender and have become truly poor, then our prayer for our daily bread will catch God's ears (Mt 6:11). He gives us not only our daily bread as He promised, but also His Spirit in the intimacy of His love (Lk 11:13; Jn 4:10).

Time of prayer is God's time. God's agenda, not ours, must be the priority and focus of our prayer time. Authentic prayer will always call us to acquire the open disposition of a child's heart, which wants to be taught by God and imitate the meek and humble of Heart of Jesus (Mt 11:29).

God's Heart is rich and wants to reveal and pour out His treasures on those who desire to receive them. "I will give you treasures out of the darkness, and riches that have been hidden away, That you may know that I am the LORD, the God of Israel, who calls you by your name" (Is 45:3). In addition to revealing Himself and His plans, God also reveals hidden, painful and unresolved memories, so they can be healed and bear holy fruits for the Kingdom. The Letter to the Hebrews encourages us to make strong our drooping hands and weak knees, so that what is deformed in us may be restored whole (Heb 12:11–13).

It happens that sometimes we are simply not ready to face ourselves in that space of silent prayer. So we fail to see the hidden but present parts of us where we may be held in bondage. We run from this kind of prayer experience, and we run around from place to place looking for someone who will wave a magic wand over us and solve all our problems without effort. We may find ourselves skipping spiritual direction or not taking it seriously, or not praying. We put up resistance to spiritual directors who want to help us experience God's love. We may even lash out and get angry at them and blame others for our problems. Or we may choose to keep ourselves too busy as an escape tactics to avoid facing the realities inside of us. Busy-ness about many things except that which most deepens our intimacy with God takes over our lives. This slothful attitude kills genuine prayer life, and we can remain in deep spiritual darkness without knowing it.

When Jesus said, "This kind can only come out through prayer" (Mk 9:29), He is speaking of the prayer that moves us from brokenness to wholeness, captivity to freedom, oppression to liberation, sinfulness to holiness, division to unity, woundedness to wholeness, and being a sinner to being a saint. This is the prayer of the servant of the Lord, the prayer of the handmaid of the Lord. It is the courageous prayer of fiat, the prayer response of Mary of Nazareth: "Let it be done to me according to your word" (Lk 1:38). This kind of prayer changes history for good, because hearts are renewed. Without it, there is no fruitful evangelization, and the Church will remain in the dark.

Solitude

Jesus loved silence and solitude. It was a way of life for Him. Scripture recounts that after a long day's ministry, Jesus says to His apostles: "Come away by yourselves to a deserted place and rest a while" (Mk 6:31). They all entered a boat and departed to a deserted place. Matthew the Evangelist tells us that at the death of John the Baptist, Jesus "withdrew to a deserted place by himself" (Mt 14:13). On another occasion, Jesus sent His disciples off in a boat, and after dismissing the crowd climbed the mountain to be with God in prayer till it was evening (Mt 14:23). Jesus was fond of rising early before dawn to be alone in prayer (Mk 1:35).

By these examples, Jesus teaches us the value of solitude. A one-on-one time with God is necessary to sustain a healthy spiritual life. Solitude is a place of intimacy, and a place of purification and transformation. It is the place where new life is received, since we have to be born again from above to enter the Kingdom of God (Jn 2:3).

Jesus longed for solitude, because He encountered the Father there. In solitude, He lived in and with the Father, and received the Father's love. Jesus assured His disciples before His Passion, "I am not alone, the Father is with me" (Jn 16:32). Jesus makes us understand that the problem of loneliness is not caused by the absence of people around us, but the absence of God in our lives. When we are filled with worldly things, and not with God, we are lonely. Jesus wants us to experience solitude just as He did. For this reason, He said: "when you pray, go to your inner room, close the door, and pray to your Father in secret" (Mt 6:6).

This inner room is the furnace where we are changed. In that inner room the Holy Spirit removes from our hearts all the lies and falsehood buried deep in us that confuse and complicate our lives. In this place of aloneness with God, only the truth prevails; there is no room for lies. It was in this inner room that Peter heard Jesus ask: "Simon, son of John, do you love [*agape*] me more than these?" And Peter replied, "Yes, Lord, you know that I love [*filio*] [22] you" (Jn 21:15). Peter could not give what he does not yet have—a self-less and sacrificial love. Peter was faced with the truth about himself and he could not deny it. It is in this desert solitude that Moses encountered God in the burning bush, and was changed. There he got to know his true identity, and received his mission to lead God's people out of slavery.

Silence is the ramp that leads to solitude, and solitude is the furnace of change. The journey to change and transformation requires that we constantly pay attention and listen to the voice of the Father who sees in the secret and repays us. God is the one who brings us into that place of solitude so that He can speak to our hearts (Hos 2:6). Solitude is not about us—what we want or what we are thinking and doing. Solitude is all about God and what He is doing and wants to do in our souls to bring us peace and fullness of life. It is a place of receptivity, a place to rediscover our true baptismal identity as God's children—chosen and precious. This rediscovery of self is always a struggle. It is a struggle between the flesh and the spirit (Gal 5:17), and between light and darkness in us. It is a struggle in which light always overcomes the darkness (Jn 1:5); and the spirit always subdues the flesh to produce its golden fruits: love, joy, peace, patience, kindness, generosity, faithfulness, gentleness, and self-control (Gal 5:22–23).

Solitude is that inner place where we must choose to go, so that we may die to the false-self in us. It was there God says to the Moses in us: Take off your sandals from your feet, the place you stand is holy ground (Ex 3:5,

NIV). It is a fight we must fight, and we cannot afford to lose; or else the false self will dominate our lives and we can be held in perpetual bondage to perfectionism, false religion, and addictions, etc. We must persevere in this struggle knowing that we are not alone. The weapon to win this struggle is surrender. We must learn to surrender knowing that the battle belongs to the Lord.

Also in solitude, we come face-to-face with our arch enemy, the devil. It comes with its temptations as it did to Jesus. After Jesus had fasted for forty days and forty nights, the devil tempted Him to rely only on Himself and not on God. The evil one does the same to us; it comes to tell us that we can rely on ourselves, that we are in control and don't need anyone to help us, that we don't need God, that everything is okay, and that we can save ourselves. To accept the devil's plan is to fall into the sin of pride and presumption. If unchecked, this attitude can derail our relationship with God and ruin our hope for salvation.

Since solitude is the place of encounter, it is also the place of conversion and healing. It is a place where, in our weakness, the Holy Spirit comes to our aid. He helps us receive what we lack, and He intercedes for us (Rom 8:26). As we come face-to-face with ourselves in truth, we are drawn to change. We want to surrender to Jesus so He can wash our feet. Then we can have communion with Him. Solitude is the place where we can always return to taste and see that the Lord is truly and always good. In solitude we can taste the sweetness of the cross.

Penance

Love is the motivating force behind the contemplative pillar of Penance. Fruitful penance is always the work of the Holy Spirit. The primary mission of the Spirit is to produce Jesus in us. He does so in His mystical union with the Blessed Virgin Mary, His spouse. He does this by His purifying and sanctifying graces as He empties us of all that is not of God. Penance is poverty of body and spirit, by which we are released from all that holds us back from giving the greater love, the love in us that lays down its life for one's friend (Jn 15:13). Because we are flesh-spirit beings, penance has both exterior and interior dimensions. We need to mature in both to attain the perfection to which we are called by Jesus.

Our faith walk is to learn the way of perfect love—the *Via Dolorosa*. Jesus invites those who want to follow Him to deny themselves, pick up their crosses, and follow Him along the *Via Dolorosa*. Jesus asks, "What profit is there for one to gain the whole world yet lose or forfeit himself?" (Lk 9:23–25). He made this teaching clearer when He said, "Unless a grain of wheat falls into the earth and dies, it remains just a single grain; but if it dies, it bears much fruit. Those who love their life lose it, and those who hate their life in this world will keep it for eternal life" (Jn 12:24–25, NRSV). The penance that bears much spiritual fruit is that which unites us the most to the Cross of Jesus Christ. This union takes place daily in the choices we make, and in the lifestyles we live.

A penitential lifestyle serves to empty us of unhealthy self-love, which blocks the action of grace in us. Penance brings us into conformity with the Suffering Servant, our Crucified Lord. Often we are too attached to ourselves; we want things done our way, and we want to control how things should be. We even want to control other people's lives. These symptoms are signs of serious danger in the spiritual life. If they are left unchecked, these could lead us to fatal spiritual head-on-collision.

As sinners, we cannot on our own power empty ourselves of self. Only God is able, by His own power as God, and empty Himself of Self. He does so because of His love for us, so that our joy might be complete and that we might enjoy abundant life. God has no attachments that limit Him from pouring Himself out. He poured Himself out in giving us His only Son—Jesus Christ—who Paul says emptied Himself in taking the form of a slave, not regarding His equality with the Father as something to hold unto (Phil 2:6–7). Jesus' intimate knowledge of the Father, and His total surrender in humility empowered Him to lay His life down on His own (Jn 10:18). There is strength in humility. Jesus had full possession of the "I" of His being.

We need God's grace to empty ourselves of self so that we can grow in conformity to Christ's humility. To attain this, we should invoke the Holy Spirit daily. He will work with us to help us understand our faults and grow in self-knowledge, so that we can surrender and allow God to eradicate our sins, and the limitations they impose on us. He will cure our sinful tendencies and negative dispositions that limit our freedom and hold us as slaves within ourselves. Cardinal Mercier composed the following prayer of submission to the Holy Spirit. He said this submission to the Holy Spirit is the secret of sanctity:

O Holy Spirit, soul of my soul, I adore You.
Enlighten, guide, strengthen, and console me.
Tell me what I ought to do and command me to do it.
I promise to be submissive in everything You ask of me,
and to accept all that You permit to happen to me.
Only show me what is Your will,
and give me the grace to do it.

Jesus said He is the true vine and His Father is the vine grower. The branch that bears fruit the Father prunes making it bear more fruit (Jn 15:1–2). By the fruit we bear, we glorify God and become Jesus' disciples (Jn 15:8). We, who love and follow Jesus, must be pruned. Penance prunes us. The pruning process happens in stages, similar to the stages of growth in the interior life: the purgative stage, the illuminative stage, and the unitive stage (or ways).

Beginners in the spiritual life start off with great enthusiasm, with a determined goal to be perfect. But they first must pass through the *purgative way*. They want to conquer the world without effort. They want to reach the height of perfection without being humiliated. They have a drive to love God and avoid serious sin. This drive makes them embrace many sacrifices, some of which may be extreme. They are generous and faithful in keeping the Commandments. These efforts are all commendable, but they are purely personal efforts to achieve personal goals. Because they are impressed with their efforts, they talk much about them at the slightest opportunity. Generally, the things of God are sweet and appealing, such as the Cross, martyrdom, and becoming a great saint. But often their commitment is superficial and they have no roots yet. These souls represent the seed sown on the path. They hear God's word but make no effort through prayer and fasting and study and meditation to understanding it. The evil one then comes and steals what was sown in their heart (Mt 13:19). Their motivations are not based on reality, even though they may have good intentions. For them, it is all about personal achievement.

Spiritual writers say that many people do not go beyond this stage, because the enemy preys on them especially if they rely on themselves and do not have spiritual directors. The purgative stage is similar to the first class of Ignatius' three classes of people, that is, people who talk a lot but do not practice with perseverance. Most of their actions are rooted in self-love. The Lord is attentive to these souls. He bestows graces on them for deeper growth in His love. He never leaves us orphans, because He is the good Teacher of the way of perfection. He gently shows us our pride and the self-motivation behind our desires and actions. In this way, He prepares us for the next stage, the illuminative way.

The *illuminative way* is the way of light. It is marked by a burning desire to do God's will. The pilgrims on this way have gone beyond the basics. They are conscious of the operation of sin in their interior. They can recognize the presence of the seven capital sins within them. Faithfulness to prayer will be the anchor and sustenance for pilgrims at this stage, so that they may receive the necessary light to see the darkness hiding beneath the surface. As the pilgrim begins to experience the conversion process, the initial consolations of the purgative way begin to give way to dryness. As the Father begins to prune the branches, some level of struggle sets in, and the pilgrim may taste the loneliness of Christ in the Garden of Olives. We need perseverance in the purification process so that the transformation and renewal of our hearts bears fruit.

As the purification process continues and sin is uprooted, we begin to detach from worldly things. We begin to see the emptiness of creatures, the vanity of worldly things, and the nothingness of riches. We decrease our emphasis on spiritual favors as our desires become more and more purified. But the roots of self-love may still remain a struggle as we pursue perfection. The light given at this stage helps us to make informed choices in conformity to the Divine Will. We may hear Jesus address us in these words: "If you love me, keep my commandments" (Jn 14:15). He may ask us, "What are you looking for?" (Jn 1:38). Or He may say, "If you wish to be perfect, go sell all you have... then come and follow me" (Mt 19:21). The pilgrim at this stage is ready to enter transforming union.

We experience a deeper purification of our desires in the *unitive way* as we become more like Jesus. We become more dependent on God, and are surrendered to Him in all things. We acquire Jesus's interior receptivity attitude: "A son cannot do anything on his own, but only what he sees his father doing" (Jn 5:19). As we allow God more freedom in us, we become freer and more peaceful. We first seek God's mind before we make decisions, knowing that God cares for us to the minutest detail. We do not choose and act and then tell God. Rather, we choose that which God had first chosen for us. Our lives become aligned to God's will and we have the mind of Jesus. Our Blessed Mother lived in this Divine Will as she gave her Fiat in the Annunciation of the Archangel Gabriel: "May it be done to me according to your word" (Lk 1:38). Pilgrims at this stage represent the seed sown on rich soil, that is, those who hear God's word and understand it, and bear fruit a hundred fold (Mt 13:23).

Jesus lived in total surrender to the Father: "Father... not my will but yours be done" (Lk 22:42). When we live a baptismal and priestly forgiveness, we experience the peace of God that is beyond understanding. Unconditionally forgiving those who have hurt us can be penitential, but we must remember that Jesus, who commands us to forgive, will always be there to help us forgive. Forgiveness is not an option. To forgive is to love as Jesus loves. When we can freely forgive others, we experience healing and new life; and we become instruments of God's healing graces for others. In the unitive stage of penance, we willingly accept suffering for the sake of Jesus. We do not complain when humiliated, knowing that humiliation is the exercise of humility. We become totally indifferent to created things and do not prefer health to sickness, riches to poverty, honor to dishonor, and a long life to a short life. Our core desire at this stage is focused on what is more conducive to the end for which we are created.[23]

We need the help of the Holy Spirit to fruitfully make this contemplative journey inwards to that place of aloneness with God. It is a decision we must make. "People naturally shrink from anything that brings them face to face with themselves—which is exactly what the spiritual life does."[24] We need courage and considerable honesty "to face even the superficialities of life, but if one is obliged to take a good straight look at what lies under the surface, and particularly at what lies deep within oneself, one winces and runs a mile. Far greater honesty and courage is required to remain and face the facts."[25] When we do, the fruit will always be beautiful and blessed; it will always be *Jesus*.

Goal of family prayer ministry

God desires healing for our families

God desires our health and freedom so we can worship Him in spirit and in truth. God demanded from Pharaoh of Egypt the freedom of the family of Israel. He sent Moses to tell Pharaoh to release His people from the slavery that prevents them from worshipping Him (Ex 7:16). God desires our physical and spiritual freedom so that we can praise and worship Him with our whole heart and our whole soul and so possess the peace and joy of Christ. Saint Ignatius of Loyola teaches that, "Man is created to praise, reverence, and serve God our Lord, and by this means to save his soul."[26] This principle has application in our families.

The human family, modeled on the Holy Trinity, is created to praise, reverence, and serve God and by so doing, secures the salvation of families. Salvation history is about God laboring to knock down the gates of bronze and break the iron bars (Ps 107:16) that are holding His people in bondage, and limiting their freedom to worship. Family freedom should be the cherished ideal for all family generations. It should be a land of the new creation, the land of the free. It should be a land flowing with milk and honey; not a land of misery and pain, violence and division, and anger and death. It is for the good life that we are created.

God blessed Adam and Eve and empowered them: "Be fertile and multiply; fill the earth and subdue it…" (Gen 1:22, 28). He charged them to have dominion over all creation. The family is central to God's plan of eternal happiness for His people. God is love, and He wants to be in love with us. Love is relationship. The family is the place where God's love flourishes.

This book seeks to bring this about—one family at a time. It is written to inspire families to wake up to this ideal, and to provide opportunity for healing the family through faith in Jesus Christ. It is written to foster family communion with the Trinity. Toward this end, I regularly conduct the *Family Healing Retreats* to help families experience God's healing touch. For this to be achieved, much prayer is needed.

The Incarnation is the unique character of Christian spirituality. In the Incarnation, God who first loved us enters into our human experience to be in relationships with us. He loved us by sending His Son, Jesus; so that by believing in Him, we may obey and imitate Him, and so have life eternal (Jn 3:16). When we accept this gift of God's Son, we receive the power to become His family (Jn 1:12). Jesus says that those who belong to His family are those who do the Father's will. They are His brother and sister, and mother (Mt 12:50). Jesus does not want to be alone; He does not want us to be alone either (Gen 2:18).

A genuine and loving family experience drives loneliness away, because God's love drives out loneliness. He desires to give each family member a unique experience of His love. Only in this love do we discover our personal and family identity and mission. It is in this love that we are healed. It is in the family that the image and likeness of God is either fostered or distorted. A child comes to know and love God, and receives the full complement of His love through the father and the mother. When a child is deprived of this complementary love of father and mother, the spiritual and physical well-being of that child is compromised and impaired. This impairment may manifest in some form as the child matures to adulthood.

It is important to know that sickness, misery, fear, sin, and death; and other desolation experiences can adversely impact our spiritual lives, i.e. our relationship with God. This in turn can limit our inner freedom as God's children. Freedom, health, wholeness, peace and joy, and consolation experiences, do on the other hand foster and promote a healthy self-image and deepen our relationship with God. For those who are suffering, Jesus comes with good news. He comes to say to the captives – **be set free.** He comes to restore sight to blind people and to release the oppressed (Lk 4:18) and to untie the bound and let them go (Jn 11:43). Jesus comes to share with families the good news that God is love, mercy, forgiveness, redemption, salvation, and fullness of life.

Jesus heals families

Jesus did not simply announce the arrival of God's Kingdom on earth. He witnessed to it by His actions: "But if I drive out demons by the Spirit of God, then the kingdom of God has come upon you" (Mt 12:28, NIV).

He confirmed this by saying, "My Father is at work until now, so I am at work" (Jn 5:17). Luke the Evangelist tells the amazing story of how Jesus freed a woman from bondage while teaching on the Sabbath. The woman was bent over, and crippled by a spirit for eighteen years. Her bondage made her, "completely incapable of standing erect." Jesus said to her, "Woman, you are set free of your infirmity" (Lk 13:10–12). "Completely incapable of standing erect," is Scripture's way of saying that this woman's uprightness before God was a problem. Satan had taken away her freedom and put her in bondage. Her relationship with God was impaired for unknown reasons.

Maybe we or our families are in a similar situation. We do not hear God in our prayer; we do not see His beauty and glory in our lives; God's mighty power is not visible in our lives. Or maybe we are confused and feel imprisoned inside ourselves. Our relationships are not working; we can't get married; we can't keep a job or get one; we feel blocked and suspect we are under some spiritual attack; we feel we have failed. Maybe we lack healthy self-worth, or we have a sense that something is not just right. These situations may give us a bad taste of what a good life really is. Maybe the abundant life Jesus promised is so far an illusion. We must remember that Jesus, who raised the dead, cleansed lepers, cast out demons from possessed people, and freed the woman under the bondage of Satan and restored her identity and dignity, said He will be with us. This Jesus remains the same yesterday, today and forever. To all, God says through Isaiah:

> Do you not know? Have you not heard? The Lord is the everlasting God, the Creator of the ends of the earth. He will not grow tired or weary, and his understanding no one can fathom. He gives strength to the weary and increases the power of the weak. Even youths grow tired and weary, and young men stumble and fall; but those who hope in the Lord will renew their strength. They will soar on wings like eagles; they will run and not grow weary, they will walk and not be faint (Is 40:28–31, NIV).

Jesus performed many signs for which the people glorified and praised God. Luke says that when Jesus healed the paralytic, "At once the man got up in front of them all, took the bed he had been lying on, and went home, praising God" (Lk 5:25, GNT). On another occasion, Jesus healed ten lepers, and one of them, aware of God's favor, glorified Him, and humbled himself at the feet of Jesus in thanksgiving (Lk 17:15–16). Jesus wants to do for us what He did for these people.

Family called to conversion in Christ

This book aims to promote family conversion by creating opportunities for Jesus' healing to be experienced. Saint Pope John Paul II calls us to this family conversion when he said:

> To the injustice originating from sin—which has profoundly penetrated the structures of today's world—and often hindering the family's full realization of itself and of its fundamental rights, we must all set ourselves in opposition through a conversion of mind and heart, following Christ Crucified by denying our own selfishness: such a conversion cannot fail to have a beneficial and renewing influence even on the structures of society.[27]

The Saint continues, "What is needed is a continuous, permanent conversion which, while requiring an interior detachment from every evil and an adherence to good in its fullness, is brought about concretely in steps which lead us ever forward."[28]

In our age when our families are heavily attacked by the evil forces of this world, we must work to strengthen our families in the Lord. Jesus prayed that they all may be one. Together, we must work for this unity by our prayers and holy deeds.

The family in God's plan of salvation

Family as protection against evil

Family life serves to protect against the infiltration of evil, especially against demonic attacks and bondage. Love is the cement that bonds family life together. The family is the forum where love is first experienced: received and shared. When this is not the case, the evil one gains entry into family life and inflicts suffering and bondage. Many species of animals: such as buffalos, elephants, deer, and so on, live in herds as a defense tactic against predators. If a member of the group separates itself from the flock, it is vulnerable to attack and can be preyed upon. The goal of the enemy is always to isolate its target in order to destroy it.

Similarly, when a family member isolates himself/herself from the protection guaranteed by God within the family dynamics, that person becomes easy prey to the evil one. This is why when Jesus freed the Gerasene demoniac, He asked him to go to his home (his family) and tell of the mighty works of God (see Lk 8:39).

Demons cannot love, and so they cannot genuinely operate as family. The only time demons mimic family life is when they target and try to isolate a soul so as to separate it from God. In order to emphasize this power of family, Jesus always sent His disciples out on missions in twos to every town and village that He intended to visit. He encouraged them to stay in the same house or family, as they minister (Lk 10:7).

Family life has its origin and receives its breath from the Trinity—the Father, and the Son, and the Holy Spirit. The Trinity gave us the Holy Family of Jesus, Mary, and Joseph as the model of all human families. Because the family is both a divine and human institution; our identity as father, mother, child (son or daughter), and brothers and sisters derive from it. It is within the family that we learn to relate in love, and mature in love. If the distinction between these identities is blurred in a child, future relationships for that child may be difficult and life may remain unfulfilled. More importantly, such a person may lack interior peace. The balanced and healthy meaning we have of this life begins and matures within the context of family relationships. Outside of the family, the world has no meaning and there is no meaningful relationship of love that protects, heals and satisfies.

The late Sister Zoe, my professor of Church History at Kenrick School of Theology (Kenrick-Glennon Seminary), was fond of saying, "Nothing falls out from the sky." Indeed, nothing falls out from the sky. We all came into this world through the first human family of Adam and Eve whom God blessed saying, "Be fertile, increase and multiply, subdue the earth." No one simply falls out from the sky, in spite of the advances in science and technology. The human family needs to be preserved, as established by God, for society to flourish and attain the holiness to which it is called.

Obedience guarantees protection for family life. Jesus knows His sheep, because they obey Him. He gives them eternal life, and they will never perish (Jn 10:27–28). We belong to Jesus' family as His mother, brothers and sisters, when we do God's will (Mt 12:50). We are protected as His family when we listen and obey His voice. We become Jesus' friends when we obey His commands (Jn 15:11). Jesus assures us that we are secure in His hands. He is one with the Father; and the Father is greater than all, and we have nothing to fear (Jn 10:28).

Human sinfulness with its wide ranging consequences has made families vulnerable to demonic attacks and destabilization, leading to various forms of bondage. The evil one is reckless and relentless in attacking families, because of the good that family life holds for everyone born into this world. The culture of death has taken a heavy toll on our families, which are the nuclei of society. This culture manifests itself essentially in the moral issues of our day: abortion, contraception, family breakdowns in divorce and separation, lack of communication, premarital sex, homosexuality, and pornography among others. These evils do not foster healthy family life as envisioned by the Creator. The mission of the evil one is to steal, slaughter and destroy when he gains entry into our families through one or more of the open doors that will be discussed later in Parts II and III of this book. Such entry of the evil one due to compromise of free will inflicts bondage on the family. This bondage in turn maybe transmitted to subsequent generations.

This book will help to foster healing in our families by being a resource for educating our families. Ignorance is a powerful tool in the hands of the enemy. Scripture says, "My people perish for want of knowledge!" (Hos 4:6). Even in our civil language we say that ignorance is no excuse for breaking the law. As long as the enemy succeeds in keeping us in the dark, it has control over our lives and can treat us as its puppets.

Socrates, the ancient philosopher, shouts out to us, "Man know thyself." Jesus wants us to know, because knowledge is power. He wants us to walk in the light and be a light for the world. "O house of Jacob, come, let us walk in the light of the LORD!" (Is 2:5). Jesus said, "Walk while you have the light, so that darkness may not overcome you" (Jn 12:35). Once we have light we are empowered to evict the enemy from our families and close the doors to their entry in the power of Jesus' name. This book promotes the ministry of light and freedom in the Holy Spirit. *Healing You and Your Family Tree* is closely linked to the Family Healing Retreats that I conduct wherever it is needed. It is a ministry of the new covenant in the Holy Spirit which brings healing and reconciliation with God from within. It is a ministry of God's mercy for His people, bringing hope to those in discouragement and despair.

The contemplative approach gives us God's perspective on things. It helps us to be open to the presence and readiness of God to human situations. John says that the Savior came to His own people, but they did not receive Him (Jn 1:11), because they were blinded to the truth. But the people of humble disposition always receive the truth. They recognize the divine in unlikely people and situations. God hides His mysteries from the wise and learned people, but He opens them to the childlike (Lk 10:21).

Zacchaeus was able to recognize the Christ in Jesus of Nazareth, but the religious leaders did not. Zacchaeus had the interior contemplative disposition which the religious leaders lacked. Zacchaeus entered a contemplative moment when he climbed the sycamore tree. He paid attention to the presence and words of Jesus of Nazareth, and gained the invitation to the Lord's banquet in his own house. He and his household were healed and saved.

We are called to climb this spiritual high ground, in the contemplative approach with Zacchaeus, carrying our bondage to Jesus. In this interior place, we are called to slow down and pay attention to the presence and words of Jesus. If we experience any of the bondages that will be described in this book, we should prayerfully turn to Jesus as we investigate them. We ask the patience, light and wisdom of the Holy Spirit to discern what needs to be done. As always, recourse to a spiritual director is highly encouraged in discerning God's will.

Scriptures and questions for self-reflection and journaling

1) Isaiah 50:4
2) Hosea 2:6
3) John 10:27

✗ Do I keep silent and allow Jesus to speak to me?

✗ Can I recognize the voice of Jesus speaking in my heart?

✗ Do I take quiet time for prayer daily: time to slow down and reflect in silence, and acknowledge my being in Christ, and to pay attention to my heart and listen?

✗ Where do I tend to focus when I am in prayer: my problems; myself; others; or God? Who is in control in my prayer?

✗ Is my prayer a dialogue (talking to God and God talking to you) or a monologue (talking to myself)? Since a fruitful relationship of prayer is always a dialogue with God, is our attention on God?

Chapter 2
✕ ✕ ✕

Fundamental Truths

Through all generations your truth endures; fixed to stand firm like the earth (Ps 119:90).

The following truths are fundamental and are the bases for the discussions related to healing persons and families in this book. These truths form the building blocks of our faith in Christ, as well as the beliefs which hold the teachings together. Only the truth and belief in the truth can bring us true inner freedom and healing.

God is First Principle
The existence of God is the supreme and most fundamental of all truths. God as first principle is that from which all other reality proceeds. When I was in my twenties, I grappled with the question of the existence of God. How did God come to be? I simply could not understand how a being can exist without a beginning or end. I read and prayed and researched on this subject, all to no avail. I questioned, and no one was able to help me resolve this key question. I concluded in the midst of my search that I would believe and accept as absolutely true, all that the Church believes, lives and teaches as truths about God until proved otherwise. The Triune God is a mystery, and the human mind is not equipped to fully and completely understand mysteries.

All creation reveals the truth of God's existence. God's existence is not someone's idea, but the truth that holds all other truths together. There is a design to the universe. There is a purpose to this life.

Saint Augustine of Hippo has taught that we must first believe before we understand. Saint Anselm of Canterbury had the motto: *fides quaerens intellectum*, meaning, "faith seeking understanding." Thomas Aquinas proposed five proofs of the existence of God. The Letter to the Hebrews tells us that faith is necessary to please God. Anyone who comes to God must first believe His existence (Heb 11:6).God has to be revealed to be known. In Christ Jesus, God has fully revealed Himself to us; He has nothing more to reveal or say. We are certain that in Christ, we are at this moment God's beloved children. What we shall be beyond now we do not know, but when it is revealed, we shall be like Him, for we shall see Him as He is (1 Jn 3:12).

The mystery of the human person at creation, upon deep reflection, reveals evidence of God's existence. If we are good, there must be Perfect Goodness. We desire happiness, therefore God must be Perfect Happiness. Proofs have been advanced, and continue to be advanced which show the compatibility of science and creation. I came across this quote, probably attributed to Saint Thomas Aquinas, which said: "For those who believe, no explanation is necessary; for those who do not believe, no explanation is possible." There are allowable theological opinions on the matter of science versus creation.

The existence and the knowledge of God based on faith is a revealed truth. However, God "can be known with certainty from created reality by the light of human reason (cf. Rom 1:20) (DV 6)." This teaching of Paul in Romans 1:19–21, is reaffirmed at Vatican Council I (December 8, 1869 to October 20, 1870) by Pope Pius IX, and repeated by Pope Saint John Paul II in his General Audience.[29] Sacred Scriptures contains all that God has revealed about Himself. Christian doctrine teaches that God is a Trinity of Persons: Father, Son and Holy Spirit. This God is love; He loves me unconditionally and cares personally for me. We are children of God called to live in freedom as God does.

The four last things

Every human being is faced with four unavoidable options, which Traditional Catholic theology calls, the Four Last Things: Death, Judgment, Heaven and Hell. These are recommended for our reflection and meditation. Meditation on these truths will help give meaning and purpose to our lives.

Death

Sacred Scripture affirms that we are destined to die once, and then be judged (Heb 9:27; 2 Cor 5:10; Heb 4:13; 1 Pet 4:5). The Church treasures the incorrupt bodies of many Saints: John Mary Vianney, Padre Pio of Pietrelcina, Bernadette Soubirous, Thérèse of Lisieux, and many others. For these saints, as for all the dead, their immortal souls have separated from their mortal bodies. Death is the result of original sin committed by Adam and Eve, and *contracted* by all humanity.[30] Only the Most Blessed Virgin Mary was exempt from the stain of original sin. Blessed Pope Pius IX, in the Dogmatic Bull, *Ineffabilis Deus*, of December 8, 1854, said:

We declare, pronounce, and define that the doctrine which holds that the most Blessed Virgin Mary, in the first instance of her conception, by a singular grace and privilege granted by Almighty God, in view of the merits of Jesus Christ, the Savior of the human race, was preserved free from all stain of original sin, is a doctrine revealed by God and therefore to be believed firmly and constantly by all the faithful.

Death is not a permanent state, but a transition. Jesus promised and revealed the resurrection of the body by His words (Jn 6:39–40, 44, 54; 11:25), as well as by the event of His Paschal Mystery (Lk 24, Mt 28:6). Paul also preached the resurrection of the body on the last day, and prayed that he might experience it himself (Phil 3:11).

Judgment

Paul says that after death we will be judged by Christ, after which we will receive our reward according to the merits of our deeds in this world: good or evil. The evil doers, Jesus said, will go "to eternal punishment, but the righteous to eternal life" (Mt 25:46; cf. 2 Cor 5:10; Rom 14:10). The judgment referred to here is the last judgment, which will occur when Jesus returns to judge the living and dead (Acts 10:42; 2 Tim 4:1; 1 Pet 4:5). Jesus spoke of this imminent and unavoidable event in His preaching: "Do not marvel at this, for an hour is coming when all who are in the tombs will hear his voice and come out, those who have done good to the resurrection of life, and those who have done evil to the resurrection of judgment" (Jn 5:28–29, ESV). Scripture teaches that Jesus will come in His glory with the Angels. Seated on His throne, He will separate the sheep to His right and the goats to His left. He will say to those on His right, "Come, you who are blessed by my Father; take your inheritance, the kingdom prepared for you since the creation of the world" (Mt 25:34, NIV). To those on His left, He will command to depart into the eternal flames reserved for the devil and the demons (Mt 25:41).

Catholic doctrine also holds that there is a particular judgment which occurs immediately after death.[31] At death, the immortal soul separates from the body, and its eternal destiny is decided by the just judgment of God.[32] Scripture lends evidence that there is "an immediate retribution after death and thereby clearly imply a particular judgment" (see Acts 1:25; Rev 20:4–6; 12–14).[33] Jesus said to the penitent thief, "Today you will be with Me in Paradise" (Lk 23:43, NKJV). Christ's story about Lazarus and The Rich Man (Dives), which illustrates the fate of the just and the sinner, shows them receiving their immediate reward soon after death (Lk 16:19–31).[34] It follows that the event of the particular judgment will not change the outcome of the last judgment at the second coming of Jesus. Patristic evidence from the writings of Saint Augustine and Saint Ephraem support this teaching of the early Church on particular judgment.[35]

Heaven

Heaven is the state of the beatific vision, when we shall see God face-to-face. John says that we are God's children now, but the fullness of who we are will be revealed in Heaven. It is then "we shall be like him, for we shall see him as he is" (1 Jn 3:2). This is why the Father sent His Son, so that those who believe in Him, who listen and obey Him, may receive eternal life. The whole purpose of our earthly life is to prepare for Heaven. Heaven is the state of eternal and experiential knowledge, praise, love and adoration of God, and of Jesus Christ, whom He sent (Jn 17:3). To help us attain it, our Lord gave us the Sacraments, and challenges us to become like the Father in perfection (Mt 5:45; Rev 3:5).

Hell

Hell is the state of eternal separation from God. Scripture says that at the judgment of the nations, Jesus would say to those on His left, those who failed in the love of neighbor: "Depart from me, you who are cursed, into the eternal fire prepared for the devil and his angels" (Mt 25:41, NIV). The Church's teaching upholds the "existence of hell and its eternity." It says that, "Immediately after death the souls of those who die in a state of mortal sin descend into hell, where they suffer the punishment of hell, 'eternal fire.' The chief punishment of hell is eternal separation from God, in whom alone man can possess the life and happiness for which he was created and for which he longs."[36]

Body and soul

"The human person created in the image and likeness of God, is a being at once [body and soul] corporeal and spiritual."[37] They are truly one. Sacred Scripture speaks of this in a symbolic language when it says that God created man in His image and likeness using clay from the ground. He breathed into him and gave him life (Gen 2:7). Man in his entirety is willed into existence by God.[38] The "soul" in Scripture usually refers to the human person.[39] It can also mean the inmost aspect of man; that which is of greatest value in him, and that by which he is most especially in God's image. "Soul" signifies the spiritual principle in man.

The Church teaches that, "The human body also shares in the dignity of 'the image of God:' it is a human body precisely because it is animated by a spiritual soul, and it is the whole human person that is intended to became, in the body of Christ, a temple of the Holy Spirit."[40] Saint John Paul II writes, "According to Genesis, 'body' means the visible aspect of man and his belonging to the visible world."[41] In speaking of Paul's teaching of the hope that comes from the mystery of the redemption of our body (Rom 8:23), John Paul II said in his General Audience of July 21,

1982, that the body's redemption has both an anthropological and a cosmic dimension. This redemption is the object of our hope, which was first implanted in our hearts immediately after the first sin in Genesis 3:15. The redemption of the body is connected with this hope, as Paul says, "we have been saved" (Rom 8:24).[42] Through this hope traced back to man's beginning, our body's redemption has its anthropological dimension: the redemption of man. This hope radiates also "on all creation, which from the beginning was bound to man and subordinated to him (cf. Gen 1:28–30). This redemption of the body is therefore the redemption of the world: the cosmic dimension."[43]

The Church re-affirms this unity of soul and body in her teaching on The Dignity of the Human Person in the Second Vatican Council (1962–1965) document, *Gaudium et Spes,* when it said: "Though made of body and soul, man is one."[44] We are not allowed to despise our bodily life. Rather, we are obliged to regard it as good and honorable, because God created it. He will raise it up on the last day. By his interior qualities, man is superior to the whole sum of physical things.[45]

> He plunges into the depths of reality whenever he enters into his own heart; God, Who probes the heart, awaits him there; there he discerns his proper destiny beneath the eyes of God. Thus, when he recognizes in himself a spiritual and immortal soul, he is not being mocked by a fantasy born only of physical or social influences, but is rather laying hold of the proper truth of the matter.[46]

This unity is so profound that one has to consider the soul to be the "form" of the body, that is, it is because of its spiritual soul that the body made of matter becomes a living, human body; spirit and matter, in man, are not two natures united; rather, their union forms a single nature.[47] In Holy Scripture, we read, "Did he not make one being, with flesh and spirit...?" (Mal 2:15). As stated earlier, the soul is that which is of most value in man. By it, man is most especially in God's image. Because of this unity, it follows that whatever affects the soul affects the body. Conversely, whatever affects the body affects the soul also. Pain of the soul is experienced in a real way in the flesh, and physical pain can put us in spiritual distress. Hence, Saint Ignatius of Loyola speaks of spiritual consolation and desolation. Both body and soul form one single person.

Scripture says: "God is spirit" (Jn 4:24). Our truest identity is rooted in that by which we are most like Him: the spiritual—our faculties of intellect and will. Our Lord Jesus calls us to the perfection of the Heavenly Father. This call expressed in the universal call to holiness at Baptism, is rooted more in our spiritual likeness to God, who alone is Holy. Through our bodies in union with our souls, we grow in virtue onto the likeness of God. Also through our bodies united with our souls, we separate ourselves from God by sin.

In assuming human nature at the Incarnation, the only Begotten Son of God shares in the body-soul experience of our human nature, so that we may share the experience of His divine nature through the flesh. Ontologically speaking (i.e., in the true sense of what human nature is), the human nature of Jesus Christ is the fullness, the perfection, of our human nature as God created it to be. Because of the Incarnation, it is impossible for God to pass us by in our human suffering and misery. Jesus said, "Everything that the Father gives me will come to me, and I will not reject anyone who comes to me" (Jn 6:37).

The Apostle Peter encourages us in these words: "Cast all your worries upon him because he cares for you" (1 Pet 5:7). This explains why over 70 percent or more of the public ministry of Jesus of Nazareth dealt with healing, deliverance and exorcism in the course of His preaching the Kingdom of God. Truly, God cares! Jesus said He came to free captives and release prisoners. Scripture testifies that Jesus' ministry was successful. People reached out and touched Him, because power from His body healed them *all*[48] (Lk 6:19).

Free will: the game changer

God gave us the gift of free will so we can choose Him as our ultimate Good. We exercise our free will to choose either the good or the bad. Set before us are fire and water; whichever we choose, we stretch forth our hand. "Before man are life and death, whichever he chooses shall be given him" (Sirach 15:16–17; Deut 30:15–19). It is totally up to us what we choose, and our choices have consequences. To help us understand and discern the different spiritual movements in our hearts so we can make right decisions, Saint Ignatius of Loyola gives us two basic rules:

The first rule says that for people who commit one mortal sin after another, the bad spirits (Satan, demons, and evil-minded people); to keep them sinning more and more tempts them with apparent pleasures.[49] "He fills their imagination with sensual delights and gratifications."[50] The good spirit (Holy Spirit, Angels, and good-minded people), will use a way different from the one above. Using the light and power of reason, He will sting their conscience and fill them with remorse for their sins.[51]

The second rule says that in those who are truly striving to grow in perfection as the Lord desires, by purifying their souls in rejecting sin so that they can serve God better, normally, the evil spirit will harass with anxiety to discourage and prevent them from advancing.[52] The good spirits on the other hand will "give courage, strength, consolation, tears, inspiration and peace, by making all easy, by removing obstacles so that the soul goes forward in doing good."[53]

Make a note of the beginnings in these two rules: in rule one, people who commit one mortal sin after another; and in rule two, people who are growing in perfection, purifying their souls in rejecting sin.

What the good spirits or the evil spirits do depend on the free choice a person makes: choosing one mortal sin after another, or choosing to grow in perfection by purifying their souls and rejecting sin. Salvation is a choice. Freedom is a choice. Holiness is a choice. Sin is a choice. Bondage is a choice. Heaven or Hell is a choice we must make. None of these are forced on us, and people do not stumble into Heaven or Hell. Paul says that we have been pre-destined by God for salvation (Eph 1:3–7). God will not force salvation on us, because He will not force our consent; evil spirits cannot force our consent either. We have to freely choose whom to serve, God or Satan. Jesus said it is not possible to serve two masters. We must hate one and love the other, but not the two at the same time. We either choose to serve God or mammon (Mt 6:24). Joshua made the wise choice when he declared: "As for me and my household, we will serve the Lord" (Josh 24:15).

Our baptismal identity as children of God

By Baptism, we are God's adopted sons and daughters through the grace of the Holy Spirit. John says it most beautifully: "See what love the Father has bestowed on us that we may be called the children of God. Yet so we are... Beloved, we are God's children now" (1 Jn 3:1–2). This grace is made possible by the sacrifice of Jesus Christ on the Cross. By our baptism in Christ we share in Divine life, and have become temples of the Holy Spirit. By our Baptism we share in the three fold offices of Jesus Christ, as Priest, Prophet and King. This identity we have received from God. It cannot be taken away from us or changed by anyone, not even by ourselves. We are marked for all eternity as God's beloved children. The Holy Spirit bears witness to this truth that we are God's children (Rom 8:16).

Priest

By Baptism, we are a royal priesthood, by which we are called to offer spiritual sacrifices acceptable to God through the one Priesthood of Jesus Christ (1 Pet 2:5, 9). Priesthood exists to take away sin (Heb 9:26). Hence Jesus, the Lamb of God, who was slain and still lives, has purchased us for God by His Blood by taking away the sin of the world (Jn 1:29; Rev 5:9). The hallmark of the priesthood: the common priesthood of the baptized and the ordained priesthood, is victimhood. The cross is central to our identity as priests. For this reason Jesus said: Deny yourself; Take up your cross; and follow Me (Mt 16:24). We exercise our priesthood in daily victimhood.

Prophet

Prophets are men and women of the desert, whose role essentially is to listen to God's voice, and speak only what He commands. They do not say what they think or what the president or some person or group tells them. Jesus is God's Prophet who teaches us how to communicate with Him. Authentic God-fearing prophets avoid the poisonous secular and worldly media as sources of saving truth. Prophets pray, discern, weep, adore, fast, suffer, and obey. A true prophet has trained spiritual ears to listen to the Good Shepherd's voice (Jn 10:27; Lk 9:35; Num 12:4; Jer 26:2, 42:4), who calls His sheep by name.

King

Kings weld power, and they speak and act with authority. Kings fight and rule. Jesus demonstrated great power and authority. He is the Universal King of kings and Lord of lords. Jesus is King of Heaven and earth by right and by conquest. His Blessed Mother is Queen of Heaven and earth by grace, and we are kings and queens by participation in Christ's Kingship.

Jesus' Kingdom is not of this world (Jn 18:36); His Kingdom consists principally in the interior of man[54] (Lk 17:21, NIV). The kingdom of this world belongs to the devil (1 Jn 5:19). Jesus fought and defeated Satan, sin and death. The highest kingly authority that can ever be exercised in this world is the authority to set people free from sin for salvation, to save them and to give them peace (Lk 1:68). This authority was exercised by Jesus. Our baptismal authority comes from Jesus. By it we belong to God, and our kingdom is not of this world also. With Jesus, we are to fight spiritual battles to drive out the ruler of this world (Jn 12:31; 16:11), and to give people an experience of salvation by preaching repentance from sin.

These three powers or offices that we share with Jesus through Baptism are oriented toward the salvation of souls. They find their fullest expression in the Eucharist, which is our very life and the reason we exist. It is the reason Jesus Christ came, to be Eucharist for the life of the world. We live now a Eucharistic life in memory of Jesus, the Bread of life. As I have done for you, you also should do (Jn 13:15); "Do this in memory of Me" (Lk 22:19).

Source of our identity

Identity comes through relationship. We are related to God the Father as sons and daughters through His Son, Jesus Christ. It is in Christ that we are reborn through water and the Holy Spirit to be the children that we now are. The Father desires that we enter fully into the possession of our identity. Saint Teresa of Avila says that most of our problems in the spiritual life are rooted in lack of knowledge of who we are. Our deepest healing therefore is realized when we are able to see ourselves as the Father sees us.

Our identity does not come from what we do, how we look, how much we know, where we come from, how much money or things we own. Our identity does not depend on the authority we have, or the amount of influence we exercise over others, or other peoples' opinion of us, or the temporal offices we occupy, however high they may be. It does not come from the church ministries we perform in whatever capacity. Our identity does not come from us.

The identities derived from these sources mentioned above are false, and can cause us to be prideful, rebellious, and self-willed; these lead to death. When faced with the trials of life, the identities we have built on these false and sandy foundations (Mt 7:24) will all collapse, and we shall be left empty and confused inside. The various experiences of our lives can affect the way we perceive ourselves. If we see ourselves the way God sees us, we grow in healthy self-worth. If we see ourselves differently from the way God sees us, we have a distorted and negative self-worth. These two identity scenarios reveal themselves in the ways we think, feel, speak, and act.

Our identity has been defined and given to us by God. Scripture says, "God created man in his image; in the divine image he created him; male and female he created them" (Gen 1:27). Scripture also says that, we have been chosen by God before the foundation of the world, to be holy and blameless, and destined for adoption as children through Jesus Christ as is the will of God (Eph 1:4–5, 11, ESV).

This grace of identification with the Father through Christ inserts us deeply into the saving mission of Jesus and the ministry of the Holy Spirit. Our Baptism comes with a great responsibility. By it, we are called to proclaim the truth of the Gospel message, and to intercede with Jesus to set captives free and reconcile souls to the Father. The power at work in our baptism is the power of the risen Christ who gave His life to ransom us from the kingdom of darkness. Baptism orients us to the supernatural life of Heaven. Paul reminds all the baptized to look to the things of heaven; not things of earth. Our baptism defines our identity and mission. When we know our identity, we know our mission as well, and vice versa.

Called to perfection

We are created in God's image and likeness, and are called to be the best we can be; to be the best in the Son. This is God's will for us, our sanctification, according to the Scriptures (1 Thes 4:3). Jesus summarized it succinctly for us: "Be perfect as the heavenly Father is perfect" (Mt 5:48). We attain perfection by being like God in love. This is the only source of our happiness and peace in this earthly life; we are restless without it.

Scriptures and questions for self-reflection and journaling

    1) Genesis 12:1–4
2) Leviticus 19:2
3) Hebrews 5:1

✗ Do I have a plan to know the faith by praying and studying the Scripture and the Catechism?
✗ How do I live out fruitfully my baptismal identity as God's child, in daily friendship with Jesus?
✗ Am I God's instrument to touch other peoples' lives with the love I receive from Jesus?

Chapter 3

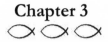

The Identity and Mission of Jesus Christ:
The Savior of the World

To do your will is my delight; my God, your law is in my heart! (Ps 40:9).

Who is Jesus Christ?

We will examine the question of Jesus' identity by drawing on three areas: Sacred Scripture, Tradition and the Magisterium, as the sure source of historical, biblical and spiritual knowledge of Jesus. As we do we will gain some understanding of God the Father, and of Jesus Christ Himself; of our Blessed Mother and Saint Joseph; the Angels, the Saints, the Church, the Apostles; and the testimony of believers since the two thousand years of Christianity.

The sources of Divine Revelation

Sacred Scripture is Divine Revelation

Sacred Scripture contains what God has revealed of Himself that is necessary for our salvation. Since the fourth century, the Church has taught the dogmatic formula that God is the author of Sacred Scriptures. "Flavius Josephus attributes to the twenty-two protocanonical books of the Old Testament Divine authority, maintaining that they had been written under Divine inspiration and that they contain God's teachings"[55] (Contra Appion., I, vi–viii).

> Since Scripture is the written word of God, its contents are Divinely guaranteed truths, revealed either in the strict or the wider sense of the word. Again, since the inspiration of a writing cannot be known without Divine testimony, God must have revealed which are the books that constitute Sacred Scripture.[56]

In His earthly ministry, Jesus upheld the authority of Sacred Scripture, that it cannot be broken (Jn 10:35). He even appeared to His disciples to remind them that everything written about Him in the Law of Moses—Genesis, Exodus, Leviticus, Numbers and Deuteronomy, and in the prophets and the psalms must come true (Lk 24:44). He maintained that not an iota of the law will pass, till all are fulfilled (Mt 5:18).

From the Scriptures then, the Father testifies to Jesus saying: "This is my beloved Son, with whom I am well pleased; listen to him" (Mt 17:5, ESV). Jesus said of Himself, "I am the way, and the truth, and the life. No one comes to the Father except through me" (Jn 14:6, ESV). He also said, "You search the scriptures, because you think you have life through them; even they testify on my behalf. But you do not want to come to me to have life" (Jn 5:39–40). Jesus declared He is the bread from heaven that gives life. This living bread from Heaven that we must eat to have life is His flesh given for the life of the world (Jn 6:51).

Tradition

"The word *tradition* (Greek *paradosis*) in the ecclesiastical sense, refers... to the thing (doctrine, account, or custom) transmitted from one generation to another."[57] "Holy Scripture is therefore not the only theological source of the Revelation made by God to His Church. Side by side with Scripture there is Sacred Tradition, side by side with the written revelation there is the oral revelation."[58] For example, the doctrines of the Immaculate Conception and the Assumption of our Lady are rooted in Sacred Tradition. Catholic theologians have proved that the Bible alone was not sufficient to resolve all dogmatic questions. To be logical and consistent then the non-Catholics must admit unwritten traditions as Divinely revealed. Otherwise, by what right did they rest on Sunday, and not on Saturday as the Lord's day? How could anyone regard infant baptism as valid or baptism by infusion? How could anyone permit the taking of an oath, since Christ had commanded that we swear not at all?[59]

Ignatius of Antioch in 110 AD described how the Christian faith was transmitted through bishops, priests and deacons. The canon of the New Testament scriptures was proposed in 180 AD and formalized in 397 AD The discovery of sacred texts on an individual in the difficult first century of Christianity in the Roman Empire, beginning with Nero's (64 AD) persecution, often meant imprisonment and death. That persecution lasted three hundred years until the Roman Emperor Constantine, the Great Beneficiary of the Christian faith, issued his Edict of Milan (313 AD) which opened the door for Christianity to become the official state religion. However, the powerful witnesses of Christian martyrdom caused the faith to spread wide.[60]

The core teaching of Christianity transmitted through Tradition was the life of Jesus Christ. This teaching was preserved in the Apostles' Creed, the fish symbol that adorned the catacombs, and the early Christian churches. The fish became, as it were, the secret code to introduce the Christian faith to others. As a sign that one was a believer, or intending believer, a Christian would draw one half of the curve representing the fish, and the other would complete the cryptic symbol by drawing the other half of the curve as shown in the illustration below.

The fish symbol captures the central meaning and the essential creed of the Christian faith; the Greek word for fish is ιχθυς or ichthus, an acronym for Jesus Christ, Son of God, Savior.[61]

Jesus Christ, Son of God, Savior

I   X   Υ   Θ   Σ

Ιησους	ι	Jesus
Χριστος	χ	Christ
Θεου	θ	of God
Υιος	υ	Son
Σωτηρ	ς	Savior

Figure 1[62]   *The early fish symbol of Christianity*

The statement "Jesus Christ, Son of God, Savior" expresses both the person of Christ and His mission. It says who Christ is—the Son of God—, and it reveals His mission—to save us. Both truths are contained in this ancient fish symbol.

The fish symbol gained wide usage for two main reasons. Firstly, most of the first-century Christians were illiterates, and secondly, the production of written Scripture was a laborious and monumental task, because every single page had to be hand-written on papyrus! Hence, only a few elites had the written Scripture in their hands. Due to these limitations, the oral tradition of the Church and the Apostles' Creed were a vital resource to teach and guide the early Christian community in their faith.

The Magisterium

The Magisterium is the living teaching authority of the Church founded by Jesus Christ. It is grounded in the divine commission Jesus gave His Apostles before His Ascension. He instructed them to teach believers all He had commanded them, to go and make disciples, and to baptize converts using the Trinitarian formula He gave them: "In the name of the Father and of the Son and of the Holy Spirit" (Mt 28:18-20, RSV). To these three vital and immutable commands, the Son of God, in whom all authority in Heaven and on earth resides, added and guaranteed the promise of divine presence and assistance to the Apostles until the end of time: "I will be with you always" (Mt 28:20, RSV). This makes it clear that Christianity is not a religion of the book. Jesus did not give His followers a text of His teachings, nor did He point them to a book as their rule and guide for interpreting the faith He handed to them. Rather, He left them with the Church of the living God, that is, the body of believers, those who have expressed their faith (implicitly or explicitly) through baptism into Christ. To this Church, the Catholic Church, the "pillar and bulwark of the truth" (1 Tim 3:15, RSV), He appointed Peter as head: "I say to you, you are Peter, and upon this rock I will build my church" (Mt 16:18). Jesus of Nazareth invested Peter with the authority of the keys to bind and loose (Mt 16:19, see Is 22:15-25). Jesus preached, taught and healed; He did not write nor dictate. He freely used and appealed to the Hebrew Scriptures in the exercise of His Divine ministry. He explained and interpreted it for His hearers that they may understand and believe in Him (Lk 4:21). Christ by no means intended to replace His preaching and teaching authority with the Bible. In addition to giving us the Church, He also gave us the formulae and rituals of the Sacraments: "Do this in memory of me" (Lk 22:19; Mt 28:19, 6:9-13). As He went about preaching God's Kingdom, He commanded His Apostles to do the same, to go everywhere and proclaim that God's kingdom is at hand (Mt 10:7). The Gospel of Mark also records Jesus' final commission to His Apostles before ascending into Heaven: "Go into all the world and proclaim the Gospel to all creatures" (Mk 16:15).

Jesus did not command His Apostles to write, but to preach and teach all nations what He taught them. He sent them to call sinners to repentance and to saving faith. Under Divine inspiration, some of the Apostles wrote to supplement oral tradition, and as a way to formalize and standardize their teachings. Saint Paul's writings were never intended to replace his teachings. The very texts that show us Christ instituting His Church and the Apostles founding the churches and spreading Christ's teachings throughout the world are the same texts that show us the Church instituted as a teaching authority. The Apostles claimed for themselves this authority in their ministry. They sent out believers, even as they had been sent by Christ, and Christ had been sent by the Father. They were sent out with the power to teach and explain doctrine, to govern the Church and to baptize.[63] It is the living Church and not the Scripture that Saint Paul refers to as the pillar and the unshakable ground of truth[64] (see 1 Tim 3:15). What then is the truth that the Church proclaims of Christ's identity and mission?

The Church through the centuries had furthered the mission of Jesus; announcing and witnessing in the power of the Holy Spirit, the truth of the

Gospel as commanded by our Lord. This universal mission of the Church is fulfilled in the "proclamation of the mystery of God, Father, Son, and Holy Spirit, and the mystery of the incarnation of the Son, as [the] saving event for all humanity" and is captured in the Apostles' Creed.[65] The Church proclaims the truth of Jesus' identity as: "Son of God, Lord and only Savior."[66]

The mission of Jesus Christ

To know one's identity is to know one's mission, because mission issues from identity. Jesus knew His identity and mission. He declared His identity and mission to His Apostles, the Church, and the world: "I am the living bread that came down from heaven" (Jn 6:51). Jesus came to carry out the Father's will, not His own. And the Father's will is this: "That I shall lose none of all those he has given me, but raise them up at the last day. For my Father's will is that everyone who looks to the Son and believes in him shall have eternal life..." (Jn 6:39–40, NIV). The clearest statement in Scripture that spelt out Jesus' mission is John 3:16: "For God so loved the world that he gave his one and only Son, that whoever believes in him shall not perish but have eternal life" (NIV). Jesus reaffirmed His mission in these words: "I came that they may have life and have it more abundantly" (Jn 10:10).

In the Annunciation narrative, an Angel of the Lord revealed to Joseph in a dream that the Child to be born of his Virgin spouse, Mary, will be named Jesus; through Him will people be saved from their sins (see Mt 1:20–21).

As Jesus began His public ministry He declared that He came to serve and not to be served, "and to give His life as a ransom for many" (Mk 10:45). Upon entering the synagogue on the Sabbath in Nazareth, as was His practice, Jesus was handed a scroll of the prophet Isaiah. He unrolled it and found His mission there, and read it to the congregation: "The Spirit of the Lord is upon me, because he has anointed me to proclaim good news to the poor. He has sent me to proclaim liberty to the captives and recovering of sight to the blind, to set at liberty those who are oppressed, to proclaim the year of the Lord's favor" (Lk 4:18–19, ESV).

At the Family Healing Retreats, I emphasize the Divine Personhood and mission of Jesus Christ. He is the only Healer; without Him we can do nothing. Getting to know Jesus personally will help build our faith and sustain us in the pursuit of healing for ourselves and our families. The contemplative approach emphasized in this book, calls us to slow down and pay attention to Jesus' actions in our souls. It calls for purity of intention, that is, intention whose sole object is to please God alone. Unless we pay attention and begin to notice and remove the clutter that create duplicity in our hearts, and block us from hearing and seeing His beautiful works in us, we may remain distant and even be disconnected from our true identity, and so unable to fulfill our mission. Our true identity aligns with holy simplicity to bring about the fulfillment of our mission in God's will through union with Him. Without self-knowledge, this union with Christ, which is the goal of the Christian life, will remain elusive if not impossible to attain.

Jesus fulfilled His earthly mission successfully. One day He saw a man blind from birth. He smeared his eyes with clay mixed with His saliva, and told him: "Go and wash in the Pool of Siloam" (Jn 9:1–7). The man washed and could see. Jesus healed the lepers and the crippled. He cast out demons from persons held in bondage, and He raised the dead. The crowds testified, saying: "He has done all things well. He makes the deaf hear and (the) mute speak" (Mk 7:37).

When the gentile, Cornelius, and his family were converted to the faith, Peter spoke saying, "In truth, I see that God shows no partiality" (Acts 10:34) whether one is a Gentile or Jew. He told them how God anointed Jesus of Nazareth with the Holy Spirit and power, and how His goodness knew no limits as He went to all the towns and villages healing all those under demonic bondage; they witnessed all His mighty works (Acts 10:38–39).

Jesus did not keep His mission to Himself. He gave His disciples the power and authority to heal and set the captives free; to give new life to the people through the Good News. He said to them, "See, I have given you authority to tread on snakes and scorpions, and over all the power of the enemy; and nothing will hurt you." (Lk 10:19, NRSV). Jesus further empowered them saying, "Truly, truly, I say to you, whoever believes in me will also do the works that I do; and greater works than these will he do, because I am going to the Father. Whatever you ask in my name, this I will do, that the Father may be glorified in the Son. If you ask me anything in my name, I will do it" (Jn 14:12–14, ESV). In the name of Jesus Christ, the disciples brought hope and healing to people everywhere as they raised the dead, healed diseases, and called sinners to repentance, giving them the experience of salvation in Christ Jesus.

Every encounter with the risen Christ since the two thousand years of Christianity has always borne tremendous fruit. The resurrected Jesus appeared to the Eleven who were gathered in the Upper Room for fear of the Jews. He greeted them, saying, "Peace be with you... [and] He showed them his hands and his side. The disciples rejoiced when they saw the Lord" (Jn 20:19–20). The presence of Jesus always produces consolation, peace and healing. Our God is the God of consolation. He is God of the living not of the dead (Mt 22:32). The ministry of Jesus brought hope and healing to those in despair and bondage. The Holy Spirit, who is the Lord and Giver of life, continues this mission of Jesus in the Church today through us. He is the guide of the interior life and the source of true healing and freedom in the inner self.

Soon after Pentecost, Peter boldly proclaimed to the Sanhedrin the identity and mission of Jesus:

> If we are questioned today because of a good deed done to someone who was sick and are asked how this man has been healed, let it be known to all of you, and to all the people of Israel, that this man is standing before you in good health by the name of Jesus Christ of Nazareth, whom you crucified, whom God raised from the dead. This Jesus is 'the stone that was rejected by you, the builders; it has become the cornerstone.' There is salvation in no one else, for there is no other name under heaven given among mortals by which we must be saved (Acts 4:9–14, NRSV).

Peter's testimony was direct: only at the name of Jesus can we be saved! This mission of Jesus entrusted to the Apostles continues through their successors—the Bishops of the Catholic Church, the Priests who collaborate with them, and all the faithful. We need to re-discover the power in the name of Jesus as our only hope of success in the New Evangelization efforts. On this depends the survival of the Church, and the world. There is need in our time for the renewal of the priesthood from within, priesthood that is grounded in its true identity as sheep in relation to the Good Shepherd who calls and knows His sheep by name.

Jesus' revealed mission can be summarized as follows:

- To reveal the Father's love (Jn 14:31; 1 Jn 3:1–3).
- To give us life in abundance (Jn 10:10).
- To show us that He loves the Father and obeys Him (Jn 14:31).
- To teach us how to pray and be reverent (Mt 6:6; Lk 11:1; Heb 5:7).
- To teach us how to suffer joyfully (Heb 12:2).
- To seek and save the lost (Lk 19:10; Jn 3:17).
- To baptize us with the Holy Spirit and fire to free us from the slavery of sin (Lk 3:16).
- To give us eternal life (Jn 11:26; 3:16).
- To conquer the darkness of our lives (Jn 12:3; 1:5).
- To take away the sin of the world (Jn 1:29; 1 Jn 3:5).
- To show us the way to the Father (Jn 14:6).
- To make us His friends (Jn 15:15).
- To show us how to love the Father (Jn 14:31).
- To teach us humility and patience (Mt 11:29).

▸ To restore our sonship and daughtership with the Father (Jn 1:12).

▸ To save us from our sins (Mt 1:21).

▸ To set captives and oppressed free, give sight to the blind, and cast out demons (Lk 4:18).

▸ To give us faith (Lk 17:6).

▸ To destroy the devil's works (1 Jn 3:8).

▸ To call sinners to repentance (Lk 5:32; Mk 1:15).

▸ To give us His Body and Blood to eat and drink (Jn 6:51).

▸ "To reclaim the royal image [in us], which had become coated with the filth of sin."[67]

▸ To teach us how to love and serve one another as He loves and serves us (Jn 13:34; 14–15).

▸ To commission us to continue His work of building God's Kingdom by baptizing all nations (Mk 16:15–16).

▸ To save the world (Jn 3:17).

The testimony of Jesus

The words and actions of Jesus reveal and testify to His own identity. Jesus has intimate and complete knowledge of Himself. Because of His Divine self-knowledge, He freely offered His life for the sheep without reservation in the sacrifice of the Cross. "I am the good shepherd, [who] …lays down his life for the sheep" (Jn 10:11). On other occasions, He would say: "I am the light of the world" (Jn 8:12); "I am the way and the truth and the life. No one comes to the Father except through me" (Jn 14:6). He further said, "As the Father knows me and I know the Father; and I will lay down my life for the sheep" (Jn 10:15). By far, the most striking and convincing sacred text that reveals Jesus' knowledge of His Divine identity is found in His encounter with the Samaritan woman, who said to Him: "I know that the Messiah is coming (he who is called Christ); when he comes, he will show us all things." Jesus answered her, "I who speak to you am he" (Jn 4:25-26).

These Scriptures and others attest to Jesus' deep self-knowledge. Because of this, Jesus commanded so much authority that the prideful scribes and Pharisees would question Him: "By what authority are you doing these things? And who gave you authority to do this?" (Mk 11:28, NIV). The crowds on the other hand, marveled at Jesus' power and authority, and they glorified God who gave such authority to human beings (Mt 9:8).

Every baptized person needs to discover this identity and mission of Jesus in order to love and imitate Him, so as to live a bold, active and uncompromising Christian discipleship. As we grow in the likeness of Jesus, we discover and mature in our own identity and mission as His disciples.

Then we become His worthy ambassador to the nations. The interiority of Christ's life, identity, and mission is to be reflected in each man and woman and in the character of each family. That is why Jesus calls us to imitate His humble and meek Sacred Heart. This imitation and likeness to Jesus is the source of true authority and freedom for persons and families.

Prayer in the name of Jesus

The invocation of the holy name of Jesus makes present His Person—the God-Man. God first revealed His holy name to Moses in the burning bush: "I am who am" (Ex 3:11). Under this name, God was to lead the Israelites out of slavery in Egypt to a land flowing with milk and honey (Ex 3:16–17). Under this name, Moses was to experience the Divine presence in the mission to lead God's people out of slavery. God answered him, "I will be with you" (Ex 3:12).

Before His Ascension, Jesus assured His disciples: "All power in heaven and on earth has been given to me" (Mt 28:18). He then commissioned and empowered them to convert all nations by preaching and teaching, so that they too may live His commandments. He assured them, "And behold, I am with you always, until the end of the age" (Mt 28:18–20).

The holy name of Jesus is for believers what "I-am-who-am" is for Moses. It is power and authority. The God who revealed Himself to Moses in the burning bush, is the God who revealed Himself in the living flames of love on the cross. Jesus promised believers that in His name they would perform wonders (Mk 16:17). Those who believe in Him, and who live in total obedience to His command, experience the power of His name. As they preached God's word, they were encouraged by the fruit that accompanied them (Mk 16:20).

Peter and John experienced the healing power of the name of Jesus when they met the crippled beggar. Peter looked at him and said, "I have no silver and gold, but what I do have I give to you. In the name of Jesus Christ of Nazareth, rise up and walk!" (Acts 3:6, ESV). Peter took him by the right hand and raised him up. The man's legs were made strong, and he leaped and stood up immediately, and began to walk. He went into the temple with them walking and leaping and praising God (Acts 3:7–8, ESV).

But the Sanhedrin were angry and questioned them, "By what power or by what name did you do this?" (Acts 4:7, ESV). Peter fearlessly responded that the crippled man was saved in the name of Jesus the Nazorean whom they crucified. This Jesus whom the Father raised up from the dead, it is by His name that the crippled man was made well (Acts 4:9–10, ESV). He boldly stated that there is no other name, except that of Jesus, by which humanity is saved (Acts 4:12).

Saint Paul likewise makes a similar bold claim: "That at the name of Jesus every knee should bend, in heaven and on earth and under the earth, and every tongue should confess that Jesus Christ is Lord, to the glory of God the Father" (Phil 2:10–11, NRSV).

The name of Jesus uttered in faith is always able to destroy all evil and bondage, and set the captives free. The power in the name of Jesus Christ is the power present in His Divinity and Sacred Humanity. It is the power of God in Him, because in Him the fullness of the Divinity resides. He is the image of the invisible God (Col 1). This power is always available to save people who go to God in the name of Jesus, because He sits now at the right hand of the Father making intercession for us (Heb 7:25).

The Church always intercedes in the name of Jesus. This means that effective and life-giving intercession is always prayer to the Father, in the name of Jesus Christ, and offered in the power of the Holy Spirit. Such intercession breaks barriers and knocks down walls, and it destroys the kingdom of darkness in the human hearts, and in the world.

Prayer in the name of Jesus should be offered in faith without doubting. "For the one who doubts is like a wave of the sea that is driven and tossed about by the wind" (Jam 1:6). James also says that the prayer of faith has the power to heal and save the sick person (James 5:15). To pray in the name of Jesus is to pray, not with our lips, but with our hearts and our whole life. It is the whole life of a person that prays. To pray in the name of Jesus is to cultivate an intimate relationship with Jesus as Lord. It is to trust that whatever we ask for will be granted (Jn 14:13). But we cannot trust God if we do not know Him. John says that to know God is to keep His commandments. When we keep God's commandments, we act in truth and show that His love has been made perfect in us. This obedience to God's word shows we are in union with Him (1 Jn 2:3–5). In this union, we imitate Jesus' humble lifestyle and conform ourselves to His death.

This book emphasizes and prepares us to deepen our relationship with the Lord Jesus as the necessary condition for experiencing the healing and liberating power of His name. Jesus desires a heart-to-heart connection with us that invigorates and vivifies our spiritual lives, and releases the power of the Holy Spirit in our families and in the Church. To foster this heart-to-heart communication, Jesus assures us that as long as His word dwells in us, and we are in Him, our prayers will be granted. By the fruit we bear we glorify the Father and show that we are disciples of Jesus (Jn 15:7–8).

Getting to know Jesus Christ

The Christian perfection that Jesus calls for (Mt 5:44), which this book helps to stir up in us, and which the Holy Spirit brings about in us, is only possible in and through Jesus Christ. Paul says that it is Christ who holds all things together. Things visible and invisible and, things in heaven and on earth have meaning only in Christ, since all are created through Him and for Him (Col 1). How do we know this Christ—the Anointed Son of God, who will baptize with the Holy Spirit and fire? This is the Christ who comes to cast fire on the earth, and who desires that the fire were already ablaze in our hearts.

Pope Francis says there are three open doors through which we know Jesus Christ. In his homily at the Friday Mass on May 16, 2014 in the Santa Marta residence, he described knowing Jesus as the most important work in our lives. Studying Jesus is not enough to know Him, he said, because it ends up in ideas about Him and leads us nowhere.[68] Rather, every effort that leads to and engages our minds and hearts to effect our interior transformation will open us to know Jesus, so that we can love Him with our whole mind and heart and soul and strength.

The first open door to knowing Jesus is praying to Him. Merely studying about Him without praying is useless.[69] Jesus is a trusted friend we need to know at a personal level. This means we have to dialogue with Him daily. The two disciples of John who followed Jesus came to know Him personally. They said to Him, "where are you staying?" (Jn 1:38). He invited them to come and see; when they saw where He was staying, they stayed with Him (Jn 1:39). To help us grow in knowing Jesus, our Blessed Mother Mary invites us to Pray! Pray! Pray!

The second open door is to celebrate Jesus through His Sacraments. They "give us life, they give us strength, they nourish us, they comfort us, they forge an alliance with us, they give us a mission."[70] The Pope said the Church is all about celebrating the Sacraments as a way to foster knowledge and an encounter with Jesus. Jesus promised to be with us until the end of time. To fulfill this promise, He commanded us to celebrate His memory: He took bread, blessed and broke it, and gave it to them saying, "Do this in remembrance of me." Then He took the cup of the new covenant in His Blood, and gave it to them, saying, "Do this, as often as you drink it, in remembrance of me." As often as we celebrate Holy Mass, we proclaim the death of the Lord until He comes again (1 Cor 11:24–26). The two disciples on the road to Emmaus came to know Jesus in the breaking of bread (Lk 24:35). Jesus has continued to touch many hearts through the redemptive Sacrifice of the Cross.

The third open door to knowing Jesus is to imitate Him. For this purpose, the Pope said we should dust off our Bibles and reflect on the Gospels often to learn what Jesus did, what He taught us; and then try to imitate Him.[71] By reflecting on the Gospels, we learn to imitate Jesus' obedience and humble submission to the Father's will. We learn of His life of sacrifice, and His rejection of worldly honor and desires. We learn of His perseverance and faithfulness to prayer in silence and solitude. We learn of His love for the poor and the sinner. We learn how to ask from God and of His power and authority over the forces of nature. We learn how to avoid falling into temptations, and to live a life totally pleasing to God.

We also grow and mature in our knowledge of Jesus through the study of Sacred Tradition, that is, the beliefs, teachings and practices of the Apostles and their successors and the Church Fathers that were handed down to us from the early centuries of that one Church founded by Christ, which subsists today in the Catholic Church. Sacred Tradition helps us to know the culture in which the early Christians lived the faith and celebrated the Sacraments and the liturgy. It situates for us the contexts in which the Bible was written and preached to Jews and Gentiles, so that we dispel the illusion and don't assume for one moment that the Bible fell down from the sky like a meteor in the Tunguska wilderness in Siberia. We learn about the lives of the Saints and Martyrs and the heroic sacrifices they made on account of their knowledge and love of Jesus, for the sake of gaining eternal life.

We know Jesus through the operations of the Magisterium of the Church to whom Jesus gave the mandate: "Teach them all I have commanded you," and to whom He attached a promise of divine presence and assistance: "I am with you always, until the end of the age." "As the Father has sent me so I send you." "He who hears you hears me, and he who rejects you rejects me." Since then, many have come to repent and believe through the preaching of the Word of truth (Acts 2:32–40). Many today from all religions are hearing the Word preached and becoming part of the one Church that Jesus founded, the holy Catholic Church. The Magisterium has exercised this mandate of Christ continuously and unbroken for two thousand years of the Church's history since the event of Pentecost in Jerusalem through the various Church and Ecumenical Councils, Synods and Encyclicals, as well as the definitive and non-definitive declarations through her ordinary and extraordinary organs. Jesus said those who love Him obey His word, and His word includes all the truths of Divine Revelation given to us in Sacred Scripture, Sacred Tradition and the living Magisterium.

The identity and mission of the Christian

I touched on the subject of Christian identity earlier in chapter 2. It is important to address the subject further in relation to mission, since both are related and are intimately and inseparably associated with the identity of the Messiah, our Lord Jesus Christ.

The term Christian (*christianos in Greek),* or little christs, was used to refer to the followers of Christ Crucified, those baptized into His death and raised to new life in the resurrection (Rom 2:12; Col 6:4), who knew themselves as "disciples" or "believers" in the Divine Person and ministry of Jesus of Nazareth. It was a derogatory term which possibly originated and was used by non-believers.[72] It is used in the Bible for the first time in the city of Antioch in Acts 11:26 and then in Acts 26:28, and 1 Peter 4:16.

The identity of the Christian

Paul says that the Holy Spirit gives testimony that all who believe in Christ are children of God, sons and daughters of the Father (Rom 8:15–16; Jn 1:12; 1 Jn 3:1–2; Eph 1:5; Is 43:4). This identity as sons and daughters by adoption in the Holy Spirit is the cause of the rejoicing for which Jesus says, our names are written in Heaven (Lk 10:20). To be Christian is a supernatural identity by which we are gifted and marked as belonging to God in Christ Jesus. This identity orients and destines us beyond this passing world. Our destiny is Heaven where Jesus, seated at God's right hand (Jn 14:3) forever intercedes for us (Heb 7:25). A Christian then should easily be identified by the evidence of this divine fire of love and truth in him or her. This is why Saint Catherine of Siena famously said of the Christian, "If you are what you should be, you will set the whole world on fire." Christians should be fire and light in the darkness.

We are living temples of the Holy Spirit, whose anointing we received at Baptism and Confirmation (1 Cor 3:16). By this, we have been called into the service of the Savior. Jesus descended from Heaven and calls all who do the Heavenly Father's will into a new identity as His brothers and sisters and mother (Mt 12:5). He shared with us the words He heard from the Father. In doing so, He gives us another identity as His friends (Jn 15:15).

With our baptismal identity as Christians also comes a great responsibility. Jesus did not come to do His own will, but that of the Father (Jn 6:36) to whom He was totally conformed, so that all might be saved through His name. Christians are likewise called to perfect conformity to Christ as their true identity, so that they may fulfill the mission entrusted to them by the Savior.

The mission of the Christian

The mission of the Christian is defined by Christ who sent him. He sends us, just as He was sent by the Father (Jn 20:21). A servant at best strives to be like his master. The Christian is sent to preach the Gospel of God's Kingdom, to drive out demons and to heal the sick in the name of Jesus (Mk 16:17–18). In doing so, he or she is charged with calling sinners to repentance through words and actions as qualified ministers of God's covenant love in Christ (2 Cor 3:6).

The Christian is on the mission to follow Christ wherever He goes, to be with Him, listening to the words which the Father gave Him for us (Mk 9:7; Jn 14:10), and to obey His commandments.

The foremost mission of the Christian is to attain a supernatural life, which consists, first, "in being in the state of grace, in being a friend of God, and in living in the state of active faith which works through charity." If we did only one thing in this life, which is to maintain ourselves in the state of grace, "it would mean perfection, for it would suppose extreme care in not offending God."[73] We were created for this divine purpose, and the earth is only a preparation to attain it.[74] We have received the power to live and act in a supernatural state, to think and love, and to live the life of God and of Heaven even on this earth. The Sacraments exist…to augment and renew this desire in us always.[75]

To fulfill our identity and mission as Christians, Jesus chose us. "You did not choose me, but I chose you and appointed you so that you might go and bear fruit—fruit that will last—and so that whatever you ask in my name the Father will give you" (Jn 15:16, NIV). Our baptismal vocation which inserts us into the identity and mission of the Christ, as little christs, demands sanctity from us. Clearly, since an authentic vocation must be a call from above and not a self-willed act, it requires that we surrender. For this reason, the Christian's mission and identity have a strong Eucharistic origin and dimension. There is no mission without an identity. A Eucharistic identity leads to a Eucharistic mission.

This mission is the most important of all, for its aim "is the service of our Lord Jesus Christ, in His most glorious condition on earth, in the solemn and perpetual exposition of the Blessed Sacrament."[76] In the Eucharist, as the source of our identity and mission, we become one with the Church in her four distinguishing marks:

1)   *One* – as Jesus is one with the Father and the Holy Spirit, so the Christian becomes one with the Blessed Trinity and the entire Heavenly Hosts in the Holy Eucharist.

2)   *Holy* – we become united with the Holy One of Israel, the Child that will be born of the Virgin who is called holy, the Son of God (Lk 1:35), and with His Holy Spirit in the communion of saints.

3)   *Catholic* – prayer is the universal language that binds Catholics to God and to other believers in the Mystical Body in the one act of adoration of God in the Holy Eucharist, with the angels adoring: "Holy, holy, holy is the Lord God Almighty" (Rev 4:8).

4)   *Apostolic* – as baptized, we are also sent as the Apostles were. In the Holy Eucharist, we share in the apostolic response to Jesus' call and invitation, "follow Me," and are faithful to His command to go and make disciples of all nations, and giving them life and the experience of salvation in intercessory adoration until He comes again. Like the Apostle Paul, we rejoice to bear the marks of Jesus in our body through a life of sacrifice making up whatever is lacking in the suffering of Christ for the sake of His body, the Church (Gal 6:17; Col 1:24).

The Christian called by Jesus to the mission to love as He loves (Jn 15:17), is to be the salt of the earth, and the light of the world (Mt 5:13–14). We have been raised up as lights to conquer the darkness of this world by our faith (1 Jn 5:4–5; Jn 1:5), and to make the difference through an irreproachable life of holiness. In this mission to be perfect, "we ought to have the holiness of Mary, of the angels, and of the saints, since we have the same occupation here on earth that they have in Heaven around the throne of God…"[77] For this reason, we are to honor our identity and mission by growing in the virtues.

In our mission to serve the Lord as He served us (Jn 13:14–15; Mk 10:45), we adore Him. For adoration is an expression of the virtue of religion. It is therefore the most excellent virtue. "It is also the exercise of the theological virtues of faith, hope and charity," because God is their immediate object.[78] Therefore, they "hold the first rank amongst all the virtues and communicate their eminent dignity to the virtue of adoration."[79]

The Christian, anointed and strengthened in Christ's mission by the Sacrament of Confirmation, enlists in the spiritual combat for souls. It is to this Christian soldier that Paul invites to put on the armor of God, while holding his ground and resisting in faith, knowing that our battle, which is not with flesh and blood, but with the evil spirits that roam the earth seeking those to devour (Eph 6:10–18), always belongs to the Lord. And when our mission is accomplished, we will say confidently with Paul: "thanks be to God! He gives us the victory through our Lord Jesus Christ" (1 Cor 15:57; 2 Cor 8:16, ESV).

Scriptures and questions for self-reflection and journaling
1)   Matthew 16:13–16
    2)   Luke 7:17–23
3)   John 15

✘ Do I truly believe that I am God's child and He is my Father?
✘ Do I listen to Jesus as the Father has commanded in Luke 9:35 and Mark 9:7?
✘ How do I desire and labor to be more and more like Jesus?

Chapter 4
✂ ✂ ✂

Understanding Prayer and Discernment of Spirits in Personal and Generational Healing

Whoever is wise, let him understand these things; whoever is discerning, let him know them; for the ways of the Lord are right, and the upright walk in them, but transgressors stumble in them (Hos 14:9, ESV).

The way of prayer is the way of life

Saint Alphonsus Liguori once said that those who pray will be saved, and those who do not pray will not be saved. A discussion on prayer is necessary in dealing with personal and intergenerational healing. Jesus' healing ministry made present to our human experience the Kingdom of God that is promised to the elect. Without prayer, the graces of healing may not flow. Besides, prayer provides the necessary firepower to conduct the spiritual warfare that lie beneath bondage issues. Prayer is cultivating a relationship with God, and remaining true to that relationship. It disposes us to receive all that God desires to give. "How much more will your heavenly Father give good things to those who ask him" (Mt 7:11).

Prayer is primarily a gift of God. It is also an art to be learned, practiced and perfected. We need to learn how to pray from the Teacher of prayer, the Holy Spirit. Prayer is listening. Prayer is receiving. Prayer is a journey of allowing God to fulfill our deepest desires. If in prayer we are able to notice interior movements in us and pay attention to them, we are on our way to being '*pray-ers*.'

We learn to pray by watching how Jesus prays. If we truly desire to pray well, we must study and imitate Jesus Christ. Nothing else can replace this practical truth. Every prayer of Jesus was answered by the Father, because He had an intimate indwelling relationship with His Father.

To understand the prayer power of Jesus, let us examine the unique relationship Jesus has with His Father. Our human relationships are external, though a spiritual bond connects friends, spouses and relatives, and all the faithful in the body of Christ. But Divine relationships are different. They are internal; *indwelling* would be the right word. Jesus said: "I and the Father are one" (Jn 10:30). Jesus used the occasion of Philip's question in John 14:8: "Master, show us the Father" to teach us the indwelling nature of Trinitarian relationship. He said, "Whoever has seen me has seen the Father. How can you say, 'Show us the Father'?" (Jn 14:9). Jesus further states: "Believe me that I am in the Father and the Father is in me, or else, believe because of the works themselves" (Jn 14:11). "The words that I speak to you I do not speak on my own. The Father who dwells in me is doing his works" (Jn 14:10).

Jesus desires that we have the same kind of relationship He has with the Father, and to enjoy the same love the Father has for Him. He invokes the image of a branch on the vine, "Remain in me, as I also remain in you. No branch can bear fruit by itself; it must remain in the vine. Neither can you bear fruit unless you remain in me" (Jn 15:4, NIV). The condition for our remaining in Him is that we keep His commandments (Jn 15:10; 1 Jn 3:24). If we remain in Jesus and allow His word to remain in us, then whatever we ask for will be granted (Jn 15:7; 1 Jn 3:22).

Jesus is a prayer warrior. The Letter to the Hebrews tells us that Jesus, when He lived in the flesh, "Offered prayers and supplications with loud cries and tears to the one who was able to save him from death, and he was heard because of his reverence." Jesus, though He was God's Son learned obedience through His suffered and was made perfect. Now, He has "become the source of eternal salvation for all who obey him" (Heb 5:7–9).

A spiritual mentor and inspiration, Father Emmanuel Edeh used to say, "If you take God seriously, God will take you seriously." If we take God seriously we must find time daily to pray as Jesus did. We will do so with dedication and reverence and obedience to Jesus Christ, no matter the situation we may find ourselves. A prayerful Christian is a powerful Christian; a prayerless Christian is a powerless Christian. Prayer is life itself. Prayer is to a Christian what water is to fish. The life of fish is water. If you want to kill a fish take it out of the water. If you want to kill a Christian, stop that Christian from praying. Our true enemy then is that one which does not want us to pray, or prevents us from praying by its many tactics— the evil one.

Jesus demands that we make His Father's house a house of prayer for all people (Mk 11:17), because we are the temples of the living God (1 Cor 3:16). The Apostles implored our Lord: "Teach us to pray" (Lk 11:1). He said to them, "But when you pray, go into your [inner] room and shut the door and pray to your Father who is in secret. And your Father who sees in secret will reward you" (Mt 6:6, ESV). To attain this prayer of secret that catches God's attention; Jesus invited His Apostles to go by themselves to a quiet place to rest and contemplate the mystery of God's love for them (Mk 6:31–32). Jesus was often seen alone praying in silence and solitude to the Father. We learn to pray by praying as Jesus prays.

Satan's goal for us is to make prayer difficult and boring, if not impossible. He wants to make it what it is not, namely, an assignment to be finished, a project to be accomplished, and an action with a moral right or wrong. It is always good to remember when we pray, that God is love! There is no right or wrong way to love. Simply love! Simply pray! God loves us the way we are. So, love the way you are, and pray the way you are. And remember to love the way you pray, and pray the way you love. Prayer invites us to taste and see that the Lord is good. Satan's goal, motivated by envy, is to deny us the joy and intimacy with Christ that prayer brings. It would stop at nothing to distract and derail us from loving and praying, and experiencing the intimacy of divine love.

Jesus said that Satan's mission is to steal, kill and destroy (Jn 10:10, ESV). He comes to steal our identity and dignity in Christ by blocking our communication with God. In this way he leaves us empty and confused, feeling like nobodies. He comes to steal the word of God sown in our hearts, so that we don't understand it, and it dies; so that it grows no root and lasts only for a time when faced with the trials of life; so that worldly anxieties and the lure of riches choke God's word in us to death, and it bears no fruit (Mt 13:19–22). When we allow the evil one to succeed in his plans, fear and discouragement may set in. Then negative thoughts and despair may follow. Sooner or later, thoughts of hopelessness may set in, and the feeling that there is no way out for us. Some may even entertain thoughts of death (death-wish). If these remain unchecked, a person may even think of harming himself/herself, or taking one's life. All these signs point to a ruptured relationship with God that prayer guides against.

In order to reverse this process, it is necessary that we begin to cultivate a healthy prayer life rooted in God's word. We must bear in mind that God is not a medication, neither is prayer a medication. God desires a relationship with us, because He is love. "They shall be my people, and I will be their God" (Jer 32:38; Eze 11:20) is the promise of our Good God that litters the pages of the Bible. God is love. Love is about relationship. Love is about communication. "For God so loved the world that he gave [communicated] his one and only Son..." (Jn 3:16, NIV). The unique quality of our communication with God, which we call prayer, is marked by receptivity. God's unique and generous communication with us is marked by His self-emptying love—*kenosis*.

God's generosity gives all we need to be saved; our generosity is to receive all that God gives for our salvation. If we do not receive from God above, we cannot bear fruit for the Kingdom of God here on earth. The most fruitful and life-giving activity of the human person is to receive what God gives. "For God so loved the world, that he gave his only Son, that whoever believes in him should not perish but have eternal life" (Jn 3:16, ESV). Conversely, we can say, we so loved God that we received His only Son and so have eternal life. To believe in God is to receive what God has given, His Son, Jesus Christ. John the Evangelist makes this point clear for us. He says when we accept this gift of God's Son, when we believe in His name—Jesus, we receive power to become children of God (Jn 1:12). As we believe in Him, so we must belong to Him.

Listening is a unique character of the prayer of receptivity. It is important that we learn how to listen. Listening is receiving. Listening is contemplation. Listening is life. An attitude of listening is a sign of humble disposition toward God, as 1 Samuel 3:10 teaches us: "Speak, Lord, your servant is listening." God says: "Come to me heedfully, listen, that you may have life" (Is 55:3).

How do we listen, dear readers? When we listen, we pray with the heart. To listen we need to pay attention to the movements of our hearts, what Saint Ignatius of Loyola calls *affective movements*. In this listening mode, we become aware of *thoughts, feelings and desires* that arise in our hearts in prayer. Growth in prayer requires that we become self-aware; meaning, that we become conscious of what is stirring inside of us. This awareness fosters self-knowledge. If we lack self-knowledge we will not progress in prayer, and we will not grow in holiness. Lack of self-knowledge means lack of God-knowledge. To know ourselves is to know God, and to know God is to know ourselves.

Man, know thyself

The Christian life is a supernatural life, and its ultimate goal is Heaven. Jesus' call to us to "be perfect as the heavenly Father is perfect" (Mt 5:48), is a call to divinization realized through intimate knowledge, love and union with God. Because we cannot unite with or love what we do not know, it is important that we seek to know who God is and listen to Him, and to know who we are. Knowledge of God will lead us to love of God. "May I know Thee that I may love Thee," a saint once said. Knowledge of God will help us to realize how much God has blessed us, so that we can thank Him. This knowledge will give us the light to see ourselves, our miseries and faults, so we can have a healthy and just contempt of ourselves and grow in true humility. May I know myself in order that I may despise myself. The fruit of self-abasement is growth in divine love.

God is everything and we are nothing. We know God through the light of reason, through creation, and through revelation. In these ways we learn all that He has revealed of Himself: His existence, His nature and attributes, as well as His inner life and relationship with us. Holy souls take delight in contemplating the mysteries of God, for example, Saints John of the Cross, Teresa of Jesus, and the wonderworker Charbel Makhouf, OLM, the Maronite monk and priest from Lebanon.

The Blessed Trinity is the source of divine life. We know God through the Church built on the Rock of Peter's faith, for the Church is the pillar and bulwark of the truth (1 Tim 3:15). We encounter God in the Sacraments which Christ gave to the Church. Knowledge of God leading to love of God helps us to practice the presence of God—awareness of God. We learn to see God in others and respect and honor them; we avoid sin and seek to grow in perfection.

Importance of self-knowledge

Self-knowledge is the state of a soul and the awareness of it in this life, which a person has through the grace of God. It takes into account our human nature as both spiritual and physical being—embodiment. Through our bodies, we come to know and are known by the reality around us. But also through our bodies, we are hidden from ourselves and the reality around us. Through our bodies, we know ourselves and yet remain hidden from ourselves and the world around us. Self-knowledge is distinguished from full knowledge which is only possible beyond this earthly life, in that it is partial. Here, we see dimly as in a mirror; but in the Beatific vision, we shall see and possess complete knowledge of ourselves even as we are fully known by God (1 Cor 13:12). The consciousness of self-knowledge is the port of agreement, or the point of encounter and union between the soul and God, which becomes the synergy that propels the soul into even deeper love, union and revelation of God. We see this dynamic in the encounter when Nathanael asked Jesus how He knew him. Jesus had said of him, "Here is a true child of Israel. There is no duplicity in him" (Jn 1:47). In these words of Jesus, Nathanael's knowledge of himself and Jesus' knowledge of him reveal an agreement in Nathanael that ignite in him the fire of discipleship that glorified God and endured even to his martyrdom.

Jesus recognizes and knows every pure soul. That is, one who has true self-knowledge, a soul without duplicity or hypocrisy or double standards. Such a person also knows, loves and believes God, wholeheartedly, as Nathanael's confession of faith shows: "You are the Son of God; you are the King of Israel" (Jn 1:49).

Jesus' promise to Nathanael is also offered to every soul that strives perseveringly and single-mindedly to gain authentic self-knowledge: "You will see greater things than this…Amen, amen, I say to you, you will see heaven opened and the angels of God ascending and descending on the Son of Man" (Jn 1: 51). Could this promise be the reward of the beatific vision, and of salvation for Nathanael for living the mystery of self-knowledge? Jesus rewards those who labor to gain self-knowledge, those who live lives of prayer and contemplation to attain it. A pure and single-minded soul like Nathanael's, one rich in self-knowledge, dwells in a state of nakedness and nothingness before God, and of dependence on God for something more. Here, there is selfless contentment with the true self and true humility. To possess true self-knowledge is to arrive at the point of total acceptance of one's own nature and state in God's scheme of things. Such a person is potentially innately equipped to overcome the stresses of life with greater facility. Of this state Saint Paul would say: "Then the peace of God that surpasses all understanding will guard your hearts and minds in Christ Jesus" (Phil 4:7). To live and operate outside of self-knowledge is, simply and frankly put, prideful, fearful, and unfulfilled living.

To follow Jesus then means to commit to discover one's self-identity in truth. The rich young man in Matthew's Gospel chapter 19, was offered this grace of true interior peace that is the heaven within he seeks (Lk 17:21, KJV), but he turned it down, and went away sad and a slave of his passions. When Jesus invites us to "Follow me," He invites us to a journey of self-discovery. To willingly accept His Divine call, is to set out on the path of true discipleship. God is His own existence; He has full and perfect knowledge of Himself; He is all-knowing. A disciple of Jesus is one who has this hunger within to know and possess the "I" of ones being. Only by following Jesus can He satisfy this hunger in us for true self-integration and freedom.

Saint Paul emphasized the importance of self-knowledge when he advised Timothy, his spiritual son, to be self-possessed in all circumstances, if he were to compete well, and finish the race and keep the faith, as he did (2 Tim 4:5). With self-knowledge come the spiritual blessings in the heavens that uplift us as God's friends, and we rejoice because what pleases God is known to us. A healthy and true self-knowledge is God's gift; it does not come from us. It is a revealed knowledge which we can grow in. We are created by God, not out of necessity, but out of His overflowing love and mercy, and for God. The objective reality of who we are is not subject to our personal interpretations, modifications, or feelings, nor those of others. Our identity is defined by God alone, we came from Him and we belong to Him. We cannot change our identity. True self-knowledge means to see and know ourselves as God sees and knows us, and to act in conformity with God's Divine foreknowledge of us. True self-knowledge brings freedom which unleashes in us the fruit of the Holy Spirit (Gal 5). True self-knowledge is salvation.

Self-knowledge will lead to self-control, which in turn leads to perseverance, perseverance to piety, piety to care for others, and care for others to genuine love of our brothers and sisters as commanded by Jesus. Transforming self-knowledge when fully attained, means there is a harmony in the three powers of the soul: intellect, memory, and will. There ceases to be any inordinate desire in the soul, but only a longing to be filled with

God, as in Psalm 63. Without this maturity in self-knowledge, we cannot persevere in the trials of faith, nor can we attain faith's goal, *salvation,* that is, transforming union with Jesus Christ, which is a sharing in the Divine nature. In summary, we see that self-knowledge leads to conformity to the Divine Will, and it equips us to fulfill the Divine command of love with greater facility.

Two years after joining the Intercessors of the Lamb in 1999, I realized as I reviewed my prayer journal that the Lord had been speaking with me on the theme of self-knowledge and identity. It was many years later that I began to understand why the Lord placed so much emphases on identity and self-knowledge in my relationship with Him. To be saints we must know who we are in truth. We need God, we cannot save ourselves. Our identity is a gift to be received with gratitude, since every aspect of us is God's gift; we cannot redefine ourselves, nor can anyone or institution redefine our identity in God. In Christ we are who we are.

We are created in God's image and likeness as male and female (Gen 1:26, 27). The divine image in us is male and female. The only relationship that can authentically be called spousal is that between a man and a woman who vow themselves to each other for life. Only such a relationship truly reflects the divine image. God the Creator gave His blessing to male and female: "Be fertile and multiply; fill the earth and subdue it. Have dominion..." (Gen 1:28). Our identity in God and before God therefore is as male and female. This cannot be redefined. Only as male and female can we fulfill God's command to "be fertile and multiply." A second century homily says: "There is a greater spiritual dimension to the [divine] image of male and female. Male signifies Christ, and female signifies the Church, which according to both the Old Testament and the New Testament, is no recent creation, but has existed from the beginning."[80]

Saint Teresa of Avila taught in the *Interior Castle* that lack of self-knowledge constitutes a major problem in the spiritual life. Without it, she says, it is almost impossible to attain Christ-like perfection. She wants us to pay particular attention to self-knowledge as an indispensable prerequisite for advancement in the mansions of the spiritual life.

In the First Mansion, Saint Teresa invites us to enter the mansions by the room in which humility is practiced, which is 'self-knowledge.' Since the whole edifice of the spiritual life is built on humility, humility therefore must always be at work like the bee at the honey-comb.[81] All is lost if humility is lost, but we cannot advance in humility without self-knowledge. Self-knowledge helps us grow in humility.[82] "Mark well, however, that self-knowledge is indispensable, even for those whom God takes to dwell in the same mansion with Himself."[83] Therefore, our eyes must be fixed on Jesus rather than on ourselves, we are to practice self-reflection rather than self-absorption. Without self-knowledge we will not grow in holiness, because humility will be lacking; self-knowledge will inspire us to seek to reach the summit of perfection.

Our Lord said to another saint, Saint Catherine of Siena, in *The Dialogue:*

> You ask for the will to know and love me, supreme Truth. Here is the way, if you would come to perfect knowledge and enjoyment of me, eternal Life: Never leave the knowledge of yourself. Then, put down as you are in the valley of humility, you will know me in yourself, and from this knowledge you will draw all that you need.[84]

Further, the importance and necessity of self-knowledge is brought to our attention in the question Jesus posed to His disciples at Caesarea Philippi: "Who do you say that I am?" (Mt 16:15). While in addressing this question personally to His disciples, Jesus was teaching them to contemplate Divine mysteries, to listen to the inner voice of God in their hearts revealing to them His identity. On a retreat once, it was brought to my attention that also implied in this question was Jesus inviting His disciples to reflect on their own identity—"who are you?" On an annual 8-Day silent retreat, my director suggested the above Scripture text and invited me to dialogue with Jesus on the question: *"Jesus, who do You say that I am?"* It proved to be an enlightening prayer exercise.

Authentic self-knowledge will never lead to self-condemnation or acts of self-hatred or any actions that are opposed to God's definition of who we are as His precious children. Self-knowledge will cause us to look up to Jesus and imitate Him for the fulfillment of our true identity, through conformity and obedience to God's will. In this way, we experience the Divine Mercy of Jesus in forgiveness, healing and reconciliation, love and encouragement.

Lack of self-knowledge

Lack of self-knowledge will create confusion in us and make us have illusions about our true identity and mission. We may judge and attempt to redefine who we are according to our feelings, our good or bad character, or changing moods, or based on other people's opinion of us. In truth, these criteria have nothing to do with our true identity in God's eyes. In addition to depriving us of interior peace, lack of self-knowledge opens us to several possible dangers.

Thomas à Kempis said that, "A man who lives at peace suspects no one. But a man who is tense and agitated by evil is troubled with all kinds of suspicions; he is never at peace with himself, nor does he permit others to be at peace."[85] Saint Seraphim of Sarov said, "When a man lives in peace,

God reveals mysteries to him," mysteries about oneself and about God Himself.

Some of the dangers that can arise from lack of self-knowledge include:

Spiritual blindness can mislead us to practice rigid and extreme penances without regard for the virtue of moderation. We become numb and insensitive to the desires and promptings of the Holy Spirit, who alone makes us holy. Yielding to the path the Spirit chooses for us is our only route to holiness, not the path we choose. We fail to see our true potentials and greatness, as well as God's promises to us. We are blinded to life, beauty, love, and truth and to the true meaning of creation, which we are charged to subdue and have dominion over. We are blinded to God's will that is our greatness.

Presumption or false optimism creates in us blindness, giving us a false light by which we see ourselves as already perfect when in truth we are not.

False confidence will lead us along blind and empty pathways. It manifests as actions of strength, but are not. They are rather actions of pride, arrogance and lack of true humility. We overreact or underreact to situations where we should remain calm, peaceful and re-collected.

Selfishness makes us pay unhealthy attention to our thoughts, feelings, and desires; we become self-centered, and are blinded to the Lord's desires, and the needs of others.

Fear and discouragement rooted in pride will lead us to exaggerate our faults and belittle ourselves in order to appear humble and brave, but it is all false. This false humility is actually a cover up of some deep seated weakness or emptiness which is not being acknowledged. We fear and are ashamed of our weaknesses, and dismiss or neglect our strengths. True self-knowledge acknowledges weaknesses and hardships without shame, and prays with Paul, when I am weak, it is then I am strong (2 Cor 12:10).

Self-righteousness makes us stiff and rigid in spiritual and moral observances, which manifest as harshness, which is sometimes hard to detect, especially toward people we do not like. We intimidate them, more so if we are placed over them.

Honor seeking when relating with people we like. We justify, approve, allow or excuse their faults and evils in order to keep a "nice" image when we are with them. We become enablers to such persons, rather than being positive role models for holiness.

We fail in God's friendship. The goal of the Christian life is transforming union with Christ (Christ-like perfection). All the promises of God are to bring us to share in His Divine nature (2 Pet 1:4), but lack of self-knowledge makes this goal very difficult, if not impossible. We conform ourselves to worldly standards and so cannot discern God's will, and what is good, pleasing and perfect, since our minds are not yet renewed in Christ (Rom 12:1–2).

The image and likeness of God in us is lost. Without self-knowledge, we grow old in a foreign land, without peace, wisdom, and are defiled with the dead. We surrender our glory and privileges, and indeed, our rights as God's children, and we live as aliens, to our own lose. To live out the full capacity of self-knowledge, is to live constantly reclaiming in ourselves, the image and likeness of God in which we were created. It is to live the new life in Christ; the image we lost in Adam, is redeemed in Christ.

The Pharisees' treatment of Jesus best exemplifies this extreme spiritual blindness arising from intense lack of self-knowledge. They lacked authenticity in words and actions that have their fullness in the truth revealed in Jesus, whom they rejected and tried to intimidate. Spiritually blind persons do not see as God sees, though they may be morally outwardly correct. They see by their own false and erroneous light coming from their deceptive and darkened spirituality.

If one does not know he is an alcoholic or workaholic, he will not take remedial measures. If one lacks self-knowledge, how does she know that masturbation or any form of self-abuse is self-hatred? Such persons are deliberately consuming spiritual cyanide, which they would never do were they informed in real life that they were ingesting cyanide? Lack of self-knowledge will make us live in a state of fear and denial. If I don't know that I am an angry man or woman, there will be no desire to want to be loving and patient with others. The wisdom of Carl Jung says: "Everything that irritates us about others can lead us to an understanding of ourselves." When we know ourselves we act with moderation in all things created. We will not abuse ourselves or created things, but will use them to achieve the end for which we were created—Heaven.

Saint Dorotheus, an abbot and an Eastern Father (eleventh century) taught that, "If a person is engaged in prayer or contemplation, he can easily take a rebuke from his brother and be unmoved by it."[86] Strong brotherly or sisterly affection may also cause a person to be interiorly undisturbed, since "love bears all things with the utmost patience."[87] He said:

> But someone may be disturbed and troubled at another person's words, either because he is not in a good frame of mind, or because he hates his brother. There are a great number of other reasons as well. Yet the reason for all disturbance, if we look to its roots, is that no one finds fault with

himself. This is the source of all annoyance and distress. This is why we sometimes have no rest.[88]

Abbot Dorotheus continues, "It does not matter how many virtues a man may have, even if they are beyond number and limit. If he has turned from the path of self-accusation, he will never find peace. He will always be troubled himself, or else he will be a source of trouble for others and all his labors will be wasted."[89]

Saint Dorotheus assures us that:

The man who finds fault with himself accepts all things cheerfully— misfortune, loss, disgrace, dishonor and any other kind of adversity. He believes that he is deserving of all these things and nothing can disturb him. No one could be more at peace than this man... The man who thinks that he is quiet and peaceful has within him a passion that he does not see. A brother comes up, utters some unkind word and immediately all the venom and mire that lie hidden within him are spewed out. If he wishes mercy, he must do penance, purify himself and strive to become perfect. He will see that he should have returned thanks to his brother instead of returning the injury, because his brother has proven to be an occasion of profit to him. It will not be long before he will no longer be bothered by these temptations. The more perfect he grows, the less these temptations will affect him. For the more the soul advances, the stronger and more powerful it becomes in bearing the difficulties that it meets.[90]

Gaining self-knowledge

Self-knowledge is a difficult knowledge to attain for various reasons. We need a great deal of discipline on our part. It is not natural for us to pay attention and listen to our interior, such as seeing ourselves seeing, hearing ourselves hearing, and paying attention to our thoughts, feelings, words, actions and the longings of our hearts. Our embodied nature causes us to be attracted easily and readily to physical things more than spiritual things. For this reason, we hesitate and fear to enter into ourselves to attend to our inner city, as it were. To do so is to approach reality contemplatively; this is very healthy for us spiritually, physically, emotionally and mentally.

"People naturally shrink from anything that brings them face to face with themselves – which is exactly what the spiritual life does."[91] "We need courage and considerable honesty to face even the superficiality of life, but if one is obliged to take a good straight look at what lies under the surface, and particularly at what lies deep within oneself, one winces and runs a mile. Far greater honesty and courage is required to remain and face the facts."[92]

We are afraid to discover our faults, but when we do, we are challenged to change for good. And this is good in itself.

The Gospel message is about the newness that Jesus brings. In our fallen nature exists a tension between the flesh and the spirit (Gal 5:17). It is a real interior war between the old man in us, and the new man recreated in Christ Jesus.

Through baptism we are called to live a spiritual life. However, our flesh places a limitation on this call. Jesus warned His disciples, "The spirit is willing but the flesh is weak" (Mk 14:38). Saint Paul shares his experience of this complex interior struggle between the flesh and the spirit in his Letter to the Romans, chapters 7 and 8. He also taught in Galatians 5:17, that there is a war for supremacy between the higher life of the spirit and the lower life of the flesh. "It is the spirit that gives life, while the flesh is of no avail" (Jn 6:63). God's word is spirit and life. Yet many faithful Christians do not know this. They resign themselves to live in perpetual mediocrity and misery by their lack of self-knowledge. Lack of self-knowledge creates problems in our relationships with God, with ourselves, and with others. It leaves us confused and unsure of who we are in the deepest aspects of our being. We are deceived into taking our identity from our feelings, or what the world says we are. It prevents us from blossoming and attaining the goal God has set for us, to be saints. We live as mere shadows of our true-selves. We live unfulfilled lives.

To gain self-knowledge we need to invoke the light of the Holy Spirit. Saint Catherine of Siena heard God saying, "One comes to knowledge of truth through self-knowledge. But self-knowledge alone is not enough. It must be seasoned and joined with knowledge of me within you."[93] This teaching of Jesus shows that self-knowledge and God-knowledge go together; we cannot have one without the other. Self-reflection is the principal way of gaining self-knowledge. This means being consciously aware and present to our interior movements and moments of thoughts, feelings and desires.

We should fix our eyes on Jesus Christ who calls us to learn from His gentle and humble spirit, and find rest in His love (Mt 11:29, GNT). Sometimes for us, it is confusing and uncertain what flows from our human nature, and what comes from the action of grace; what is willfully done and what is not. To discern these aspects of us we need to pay a great deal of attention: we need insight, humility, honesty, courage, perseverance, and truth. We need quiet and contemplation. We need spiritual guidance from a knowledgeable spiritual person. The light of self-knowledge comes gradually; one bit of knowledge leads to more and deeper knowledge and prepares the way for a deeper insight and more knowledge. In this way we grow more and more in self-knowledge, as God knows us.

Our true identity comes from the Cross of Christ. The cross is the filter that excludes everything of this world capable of distorting and confusing this identity; this is why Paul boasts of the cross (Gal 6:14). Jesus gives us the recipe for gaining true self-knowledge: "Whoever wishes to come after me must *deny himself, take up his cross,* and *follow me.* For whoever wishes to save his life will lose it, but whoever loses his life for my sake will find it. What profit would there be for one to gain the whole world and forfeit his life? Or what can one give in exchange for his life?" (Mt 16:24-26)[94] (emphasis mine).

We need to exercise some aspects of the contemplative life to attain true self-knowledge. The regular practice of Examination of Conscience will help us grow in self-knowledge. Saint Louis Marie de Montfort devotes the First Week (Part II) of the 33-Day spiritual consecration exercises to gaining knowledge of self, if the goal of union with Jesus is to be realized. He recommends that the following exercises will help us grow in self-knowledge: "prayers, examens, reflection, acts of renouncement of our own will, of contrition for our sins, of contempt of self, all performed at the feet of Mary."[95] He says it is through her, as Mediatrix of all Graces and Seat of Wisdom that we hope for the light to know ourselves. The nature of the self is a mystery and it is a gift from the Father. So, the mystery of self-knowledge can only be resolved when, by God's grace, we are strengthened with power in the Holy Spirit in the inner self, so that rooted and grounded in love through faith in Christ dwelling in our hearts, we grasp the full measure of the truth and the knowledge of God as He is in Himself, and are "filled with all the fullness of God" (Eph 3:16–19). This resolution obviously is only possible beyond this life when God will be fully revealed and known. Then, we shall see Him as He truly is, and shall be like Him, and enter into the fulfillment of all our desires (1 Jn 3:2).

Praying effectively and fruitfully

If we pray correctly we will experience God's healing and peace. The Father desires this for us, Jesus promised it (Jn 14:13; 15:7; 15:16; 16:23), and the Holy Spirit realizes it in us (Rom 8:10–11; 1 Jn 3:24; Gal 5:22–23). The Holy Spirit is the fruitfulness of our prayer. To pray effectively and fruitfully is to pray from a place of surrender and strength, that is, from a place of the experience and intimacy of God's love. It is to pray with humility and faith (Lk 18:13–14a) in total resignation to God's will. It is to pray with our hearts immersed in the Sacred Heart of Jesus and Mary.

Jesus is perfectly disposed as God to answer our prayers. Praying according to the will of Christ makes our prayer effective and fruitful for our healing. Just as all of Jesus' prayers were heard by the Father because of His reverence (Heb 5:7), so too our prayers will be heard when we pray with the disposition of Christ. For He says, whatever we ask the Father in His name, the Father will grant us (Jn 16:23; 15:16). It is easier for God to raise Lazarus from the dead after four days in the tomb, than it is for a mother to wake her son up from sleep. Jesus died that we might live fully! It is natural for God to pour Himself out generously and unconditionally for our sake. But it is not natural for us to receive God's outpouring of love, because of our fallen nature. We do so by grace.

To pray effectively is to pray with our hearts. It is to pray with our whole being; with love and out of love for Jesus, as the Blessed Mother teaches us. It is then that prayer becomes a resting place with Jesus. Prayer of the heart always leads to spiritual healing, and may produce physical healing. Healing, it must be stressed, is always the fruit of a relationship with God; hence it begins in the Spirit and must be led by the Spirit.

Ignatius of Loyola says that fruitful prayer, one that fills and satisfies the soul, is not about too much knowledge. It is rather about grasping things more deeply and intimately with our hearts and savoring them for our nourishment and benefit. According to Ramon Maria Luza Bautista, SJ: "Our best prayers are those that come from the inner most recesses of the heart, bringing before our God what really matters to us. In this way we are able to bring to Him that part of ourselves which is most authentic and real where our deepest self is engaged, where our truest self is involved."

In *Wood for the Fire*, Bautista insists that to engage in this prayer of touch and encounter, we need "wood" or "matter" to help us focus more, to move us forward and kindle our devotion and sentiment for God. The wood may be a Scripture passage, a Gospel verse or a Psalm of Thanksgiving that speaks to our present situation. When such point for prayer stir our "inner emotions of consolation and desolation, they bring us face to face with our real selves and with God, leading us to a deeper experience of conversion and eventually drawing us closer to Him" who loves us. Our will is conformed to His, and our prayers are heard.

Jesus perfectly conformed His thoughts, words and actions to the Father's will. He taught us how to act: "Truly, truly, I say to you, the Son can do nothing of his own accord, but only what he sees the Father doing. For whatever the Father does, that the Son does likewise" (Jn 5:19; see 14:10–11, ESV). He also said, "For just as the Father raises the dead and gives life, so also does the Son give life to whomever he wishes" (Jn 5:21). The Letter to the Hebrews 7:25 assures all who seek healing from bondage, that Jesus, "is always able to save those who approach God through him, since he lives forever to make intercession for them."

To pray effectively, our prayer must conform to God's will for us. Jesus did the perfect will of the Father, and His prayers were answered (Jn 6:38, 14:10; Heb 5:7). To pray correctly, we should pray with faith; believing without doubt, that what we ask for will be given (Jam 1:6). We are to dispose ourselves interiorly so that our prayer is the prayer of Jesus to the Father.

How do we pray? How do we dispose ourselves for effective fruitful prayer? Prayer time is always God's time, not ours. It is a time to knock, ask and seek to grow in relationship with God who loves us uniquely as we are. God must be the focus of our prayer. Prayer should not be success oriented; it should be relationship and intimacy oriented. Seek to be in love with God first. Come to prayer with a love-seeking heart, not a shopping list of things we want God to do for us. God is looking for lovers, those who worship in spirit and truth (Jn 4:23). Are you love-sick? Go to God in prayer. Talk to Jesus in your heart. He invites us as He did the Apostles: "Come away by yourselves to a deserted place and rest a while" (Mk 6:31). Jesus desires intimacy with us, the same intimacy He has with the Father, "As the Father has loved me, so have I loved you. Abide in my love" (Jn 15:9, ESV). "I am ascending to my Father and your Father, to my God and your God" (Jn 20:17, ESV).

How fruitful our prayer is will depend largely on how well we prepare for prayer, how well we listen, how well we finish, and how faithful we are. We must remember that the goal of prayer is to have a heart-to-heart encounter with God, like Moses had in the burning bush (Ex 3:1–20). We follow where the Bridegroom leads. He leads us to green pastures and, to springs of living water to refresh our drooping spirit (Ps 23). When we are in a state of grace, our prayers objectively, are more powerful and fruitful. James 5:16 tells us that the prayers of a holy and righteous person is powerful indeed. Scripture also says that the prayers of the humble pierces the heavens and obtains graces, renders justice, repays vengeance, and even executes judgement, and the Lord does not delay in responding to such prayers (Sir 35:21–23). But no one knows with certainty, objectively speaking, when a person is in a state of grace; we can at best only conjecture. All we can do is, at least strive to be faithful every day to the demands of Christian perfection, knowing that all that is necessary for us to live a life of devotion and godliness have been given to us so that we may share in the divine nature and be fruitful and pleasing to God (2 Pet 1:3–11). We have access to these graces in the unchanging deposit of faith handed down to us by Jesus and the Apostles, through the Sacred Scriptures, Sacred Tradition, and the Magisterium, as well as the celebration of the liturgy and the Sacraments of the Church.

• • •

The power and effectiveness of Jesus' prayer is rooted and grounded in His self-surrendering love of the Father: "Our Father... your kingdom come, your will be done..." (Mt 6:9–10). Scripture says that Jesus withdrew a second time and prayed again, "My Father... your will be done!" (Mt 26:42). Saint Cyprian asks: "What more effective prayer could we then make in the name of Christ than in the words of his own prayer?"[96]

The dynamics of praying are similar to climbing a mountain. We need preparation before we begin climbing the mountain. If we do not prepare well, the climb may not go well. No one simply jumps to the top of the mountain. It is a gradual process filled with lots of planning, mistakes and uncertainties. But with perseverance, we get to the top. When we are done up there, we begin the descent phase. No one jumps down from the mountain top; else, he will get hurt. We plan our descent. We consider all the routes; sometimes we do not descend the way we ascended.

The following helpful hints will guide us to pray effectively and fruitfully.

Hints on how to pray
These hints will help us resolve distractions and disturbances in prayer.

- ✓ Find a suitable place that is free of distractions
- ✓ Assume a comfortable praying posture; compose yourself to enter God's presence
- ✓ Make an act of reverence as you allow your body and spirit to be still, surrender
- ✓ Leave all worries, anxieties and concerns behind as you quiet down
- ✓ You might imagine yourself in God's hand (Is 49:16)
- ✓ Ask of God the grace you desire in this prayer time
- ✓ Read slowly the pre-selected Scripture text, read it a few times

The body of the prayer
- ✓ Pause where you feel drawn, and ponder like Mary did
- ✓ Respond with your heart to what draws you to God's presence
- ✓ Converse with the Father, or the Son, or the Holy Spirit, (or with the Blessed Mother) share your heart with Him, and listen to what He says to you?
- ✓ Journal prayer experience and, your insights, feelings, thoughts, and desires.

We should be free to go back to the preparation hints should we feel unsettled or disturbed during prayer itself.

Hints on how to conclude prayer
✓ Avoid ending prayer abruptly
✓ Speak freely as a friend to a Friend, a child to a Father (Colloquy[97]). Jesus said to Peter, "Simon, son of John, do you love me?" "Lord you know I love you."
✓ This is not a time to hide. We have to be honest with ourselves. For example, Martha said to Jesus, "Lord, if you had been here, my brother would not have died."

Review of prayer time (to be done after the prayer time is ended):
✓ Was I faithful to prayer time?
✓ What grace did I pray for?
✓ Did I pray with a Scripture text?
✓ What was I doing in prayer, where did I dwell?
✓ What was enjoyable? What was distasteful?
✓ What did I hear Jesus say to me in prayer?
✓ How did I respond?

Prayer helps us to grow in interior awareness and discernment, in this way we see things from God's viewpoint and not from ours.

Interior disposition for true discernment

Spiritual discernment is seeking to know what God knows on issues affecting us. It is seeking God's light and the truth in any situation. To have a discerning heart, one must have a prayer life; meaning, we must spend time daily to be quiet and listen to God. We cannot discern if we do not pray. Those who pray must have a desire to do God's will. If we do not care what matters to God, it will be impossible to arrive at the truth in any discernment process. Such an attitude of not caring may even cast shadow on the state of our hearts with God. Scripture says: "You will know the truth, and the truth will set you free" (Jn 8:32). The truth we seek in discernment is a person—Jesus Christ. We need to remain at ground zero, i.e. neutral, as much as possible, if we are to objectively discern the truth. Bias will ruin any attempt at discerning the truth.

Discernment is not about how we feel, or what we want or think about issues. Such an approach would block authentic discernment. The right attitude in discernment is, "Lord, show us Your will in this situation." The attitude of seeking God's mind creates a life-giving openness to the Holy Spirit that makes discernment easy, accurate and fruitful for holiness. After the Ascension of the Lord, the Apostles had to discern who to choose to replace Judas to join their ranks. They prayed: "You, Lord, who know the hearts of all, show which one of these two you have chosen to take the place in this ministry and apostleship from which Judas turned aside to go to his own place" (Acts 1:24–25, ESV). In the Old Testament, Israel had to discern whether to engage her enemies in battle. The king gathered about four hundred prophets, and asked them: "Shall I go to attack Ramoth-gilead or shall I refrain?" (1 Kgs 22:6). The fruit of true discernment is always interior freedom, peace, conformity to God's will, and ultimately, union with God.

Openness to God in discernment frees us from the deceptions of personal bias. Jesus' Apostles struggled with this defect. When Jesus first announced to them His impending passion and death; they were, unfortunately, involved in a fight for who would be the greatest (Lk 9:46). Like the Apostles; our disordered attachments, affections, opinions, presumptions, and selfish desires will cloud our ability to discern God's will for our happiness.

Humility, the acknowledgment of the truth of who God is, is a pre-requisite for authentic discernment. We grow in humility as we grow in the experiential knowledge and love of God. This knowledge comes through listening and paying attention to God's presence to us in prayer, and pondering His word in Sacred Scripture. Jesus' strength in discernment is a fruit of His intimate knowledge of the Father: "As the Father knows Me, even so I know the Father..." (Jn 10:15, NKJV). "For I have come down from heaven, not to do My own will, but the will of Him who sent Me" (Jn 6:38, NKJV). Jesus' whole attention is on the Father. His spirituality can simply be summarized as—*Father*.

The deeper our experiential knowledge of God, the less we will depend on someone else to tell us what they think God is saying to us. We need patience to wait on God to gently reveal His mind as much as we are able to handle. God knows us more than we know ourselves, and we must trust that He can lead us safely to green pastures, that place of rest and peace in our hearts.

Need for spiritual direction

To develop the attitude and gift of discernment, regular Consciousness Examen and spiritual direction are important. Pope Emeritus, Benedict XVI, said, "The Church continues to recommend the practice of spiritual direction, not only to all those who wish to follow the Lord up close, but to every Christian who wishes to live responsibly his baptism, that is, the new life in Christ."[98] He continued, "Spiritual direction is a matter of establishing that same personal relationship that the Lord had with his disciples, that special bond with which he led [those who followed] him, to embrace the will of the Father (cf. Lk 22:42), that is, to embrace the cross."[99]

We are too close to ourselves that our spiritual blind spots are not readily visible to us. We need someone else to help us be objective about ourselves. We are easy prey to the evil one, if we are without guidance. Spiritual direction helps us to grow in humility; it challenges us to surrender control of our will, to bring things in our lives into the light. It helps us to break down our defenses and attachments. "A holy soul is one which, by the help of grace, has freely submitted to God's will, and all that follows this free consent is the work of God and never that of man, who blindly abandons himself and is completely indifferent about everything."[100] One who does not have a spiritual director does not know how much he has already been deceived. Purity of heart is an indispensable quality of a discerning heart. We can pray to grow in inner discernment in these words:

Oh Lord Jesus Christ, the Light of all hearts; banish the darkness in me by the light of Your truth. Enlighten my mind, my heart and my will by the radiant glow of Your Spirit. Grant me the inner peace to discern right from wrong, through the Immaculate and pure heart of my Mother Mary. Help me to listen to Your Shepherd's voice calling me by name within, that I may abandon myself to the Father's will in faith and love. Amen (repeat often)

Saint Ignatius of Loyola gives us rules to guide us in discerning spirits. These are based on the inner movements of thoughts, feelings and desires of our hearts. These rules (see Appendix IV) which are suited for the First Week (#313-327), will help us to understand and recognize to some extent the various movements caused in the soul, to accept the good ones, and reject the bad ones.[101] These rules will help us better evaluate our spiritual experiences, and dispose us to do God's will. We shall apply some of these rules in discerning personal and generational bondage situations.

The Christian Anthropology of the Heart

The discernment of the movements and voices of our hearts can be challenging. It may require some understanding of the spiritual structure of the human heart. Biblically speaking, the heart is understood "as the deepest place of relation and truth in persons. It is the seat of spiritual insight and the grounding in faith."[102]

In Scripture, heart means soul. "At the center of the human heart is spiritual being," with all the associated spiritual experiences. These include the spiritual realities of the evil one's temptations and activities that put us in bondage, as well as the stirrings and promptings of the Holy Spirit in love that are tasted here.[103] "Rightly understood Saint Ignatius of Loyola's 'Rules for the Discernment of Spirits' [see Appendix IV] are based upon and teach us that the heart's deepest affective movements are spirits."[104] These movements are made up of our intellect's thoughts, our body's emotions, the powers of our will to make choices, and the creative capacity of our imagination. These movements all merge together at the center of our heart's affectivity, at the center of our human spirits.[105]

"Our feelings in the biblical sense of wholeheartedness are not merely emotions. They connote personhood and a primal affective word (*urwort*) within that speaks; this is the fundamental meaning of *sentir* in Spanish and *sentire* in Latin."[106]

The diagram of the Christian Anthropology of the Heart (Figure 2) helps us to gain insights into the dynamics of our inner reactions to the different stimuli that affect us. Three main levels are distinguished as shown below.

Level I: The surface psychological

This outermost layer of the psychological structure of the heart is non-spiritual in nature. Here, thoughts, feelings and desires are experienced only superficially. They do not last long. "They change rapidly and are easily swayed by external stimuli such as weather and the tone of others' opinions." They are "also easily affected by the bodily senses' dependence upon the quality and quantity of sleep, food, sunlight, etc. The voice of the indwelling Holy Spirit is not heard at this level, because He does not dwell here."[107]

Level II: The deeper psychological

The affective movements: feelings, thoughts, and desires at Level II are deeper and more complex than at Level I, but they are still non-spiritual in nature. Since they do not endure, they do not directly affect our relationship with God. Some of the factors that influence our hearts movement and human development will "include family relationship, ethnic temperaments that mold and imprint deep patterns of feeling and thinking into our psyche. Our DNA or genetic makeup, the activity of sexual desires, cultural assumptions regarding beauty and economic security and deep moods..."[108]

These factors of nature and nurture dramatically influence how and what we hear, and what we carry in the interior psychological structure of our hearts. Our "feelings and thoughts, [as well as] the voices that speak in Level II, are governed by the pleasure/pain principle."[109] Based on this principle, "we make choices continually to take care of ourselves" by striving to "maintain a healthy balance of tasting the goodness of human pleasure, as we daily live with and endure existential pain."[110] We differ greatly at Level II in our ability to withstand different levels of pain and discomfort.[111] As in Level I, the indwelling Holy Spirit does not dwell at Level II.

Level III: The spiritual

This is the deepest level of our hearts' experience where the indwelling Spirit is readily and directly accessible, and where our daily living encounters with Jesus and His Cross are registered. "It is here through baptism that God's voice abides within us and is presently speaking, addressing us in love (Jn 14:18–31). God's voice is always experienced here as consolation so long as we are seeking after God so as to do the Father's will."[112]

The spiritual senses of our hearts at Level III are thoughts, feelings, the will, the imagination, and desires that we can detect and discern as either consolations or desolations that affect our souls positively, to heal and set us free to love as Jesus loves or negatively, and to keep us in bondage and darkness.[113]

Prayer is a dialogue and a heart-to-heart conversation with God. What matters in this dialogue is that we acknowledge what is happening inside our hearts and talk to God about them. This revealing of our hearts to God opens us to receive the Holy Spirit who seeks to encourage, heal, console and reveal the fullness of God to us; so that we may witness to the world Jesus' love for the Father, and to experience that love ourselves (Jn 14:18–31).[114] The key to experiencing and tasting this transforming love of the Holy Spirit amidst our daily crosses and activities is to know how to listen to God's Word in our hearts.[115]

It is worthy of note that the affective movements of the interior life: thoughts, feelings and desires, at the three levels of the heart are not at all simplistic. They are connected with one's present or remembered experiences. At any given moment there can be a whole mass of vexing jumble that requires careful discernment. This anthropology provides a tool to do this.[116]

"Consolation at Level II can easily be mistaken for authentic spiritual consolation, thus one can live his life pursuing pleasure and psychological consolation only." Consolation at Level III comes directly from God; it is not simply a remnant of God's action. Desolation at Level III has several roots, many of which have their origin in Level II.[117]

A significant desolation at Level II (psychological desolation), if not prayed with or discerned (talk to Jesus about it), will most likely lead one into desolation at Level III (spiritual desolation). Our contemplative prayer must integrate the affective movements from Level II; otherwise, our prayer can atrophy into mere routine, rubric, or mechanics, losing the intimacy we crave.[118]

The sign of a true spiritual growth and maturity is that we are becoming more sensitive and docile to the desires of the Holy Spirit within us, until we attain transforming union. Then the words of Jesus comes true that he who loves Me obeys My Words, then I and My Father will love him and make our home in him (Jn 14:23). The purpose of our lives is this communion with God; this is where joy and true happiness flow from.

The true children of God are those who are led by the Spirit of God (Rom 8:14). In this state of existence, Paul's words become reality: "It is no longer I who live, but Christ who lives in me (Gal 2:20, ESV). Here, the Holy Spirit has more room in our hearts, as the Level III layer expands and takes over control of our interior life. We become Jesus in the sense that He lives in us and that our actions by grace are penetrated with His love and holiness (see Figure 3).

CHRISTIAN ANTHROPOLOGY OF THE HEART

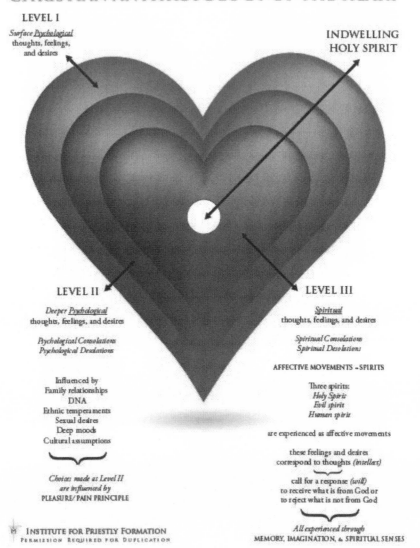

*This image is used with permission
from Institute for Priestly Formation*

Figure 2: *Christian Anthropology of the Heart*

A Heart in Transforming Union

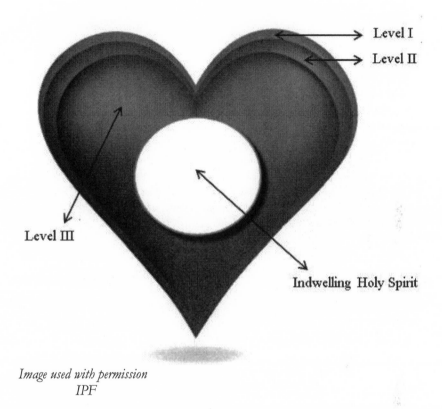

Image used with permission
IPF

Figure 3 *Christ now lives in me*

Spiritual consolation and spiritual desolation

The two basic discernible affective movements of consolation and
desolation help us to know whether our spiritual experiences are of God or
not. The presence of generational blessing or bondage can be discerned
based on signs which show consolation or desolation. This in turn can help
direct a course of action to deal with the distresses of bondage.

Spiritual consolation is an interior movement felt in the soul inflaming it
with love of God. Consequently, the soul can love no other creature on
earth for its own sake, but only in the Creator of them all. It is also
consolation when one sheds tears that move to love of God either due to
sorrow for sin or because of the sufferings of Christ or for another reason
that is immediately directed to the praise and the service of God. Finally,
consolation is every increase of faith, hope and love, and all interior joys

that orient to heavenly things and to the salvation of one's soul by filling it with peace and quiet in its Creator and Lord.[119]

"Spiritual consolation is a dimension of our being that is co-natural with God's Holy Spirit, the Comforter, the Consoler. Spiritual consolation is God's Indwelling Word, whenever we are 'seeking after him, feeling after him so as to find him' (Acts 17:27–28)."[120] In consolation, we are encouraged to stay with or remain in the consolation, and to return often to the place of consolation to receive more of the Lord's presence. Jesus went up Mount Tabor with Peter, James and John to pray. The disciples were enjoying the Lord's presence when, His face, body and clothes became dazzling white; then two men, Moses and Elijah, were seen conversing with Jesus. The disciples cherished the experience and wanted more of it: "It is good for us to be here! Let us make three tents" and remain here. They were flooded with more consolation: the cloud enveloped them, giving them a deeper prayer experience of the Trinity (Lk 9:28–36).

Spiritual desolation is all that is contrary to consolation as described above: darkness of soul, turmoil of spirit, inclination to low and earthly things, restlessness arising from many disturbances and temptations which lead to want of faith, hope, and love. The soul is slothful, tepid, sad, and separated, as it were, from its Creator and Lord. As consolation is opposed to desolation, the thoughts arising from both are opposed to each other.[121] Desolation experiences are not evils to be avoided, neither are they sins. We should seek to understand their meaning and causes and use them as stepping stones to grow closer to God.

"Spiritual desolation points to a dimension of our heart that is lovesick, sick to receive and appropriate more love from God (Mt 9:12)."[122] In desolation, we are encouraged to stay with or remain in the place of desolation; it is there Jesus will come to set us free. Before the resurrection, Jesus instructed His disciples to remain in Jerusalem—a place of death, fear and desolation. But the disciples were running away to avoid arrest and death in the hands of religious leaders who crucified Jesus. Jesus appeared to them on the way and in Jerusalem and consoled them: "He showed them his hands and his side. Then the disciples rejoiced when they saw the Lord" (Jn 20:20, NET; Lk 24:13–36). Jesus also appeared to two of His desolate disciples on the way to Emmaus, and they said: "Were not our hearts burning (within us) while he spoke to us on the way and opened the scriptures to us?" He revealed Himself to them in the breaking of bread. They were filled with joy and returned to Jerusalem (Lk 24:30–32).

Consolations and desolations can be discerned in hearts and in family situations. At one of the Family Healing Retreats, a family reported experiences of terrors, divisions, illnesses, and other symptoms of bondage. Investigation showed that their ancestral generations had practiced freemasonry. This information was helpful in directing us on how to pray specifically and effectively for them. The presence of the signs of bondage: divisions, mishaps, tragedies, illnesses and other distresses tear down and destroy families. Jesus desires that our families be healthy and faith-filled. Families should be platforms where holiness flourishes and where saints are formed.

Saint Ignatius of Loyola outlines three steps to help us discern the experiences of consolation or desolation, so that we may gain interior freedom.[123] These steps are adapted in this book to help us discern situations of personal and generational bondage, so we can pray more effectively to receive healing.

Become aware

We notice and acknowledge the stirring in our hearts, such as, thoughts, feelings and desires. These stirrings keep us in touch with our interior selves. Being able to identify and examine them will help us discern their origin and the right course of action to take.

Understand the experience (gaining knowledge)

Once the presence of these movements is acknowledged, we should seek to understand them through self-reflection and recollection to determine if they are spiritual or non-spiritual in nature. If spiritual, we further discern whether they are from God or not. Self-reflection will also help us to gain knowledge about ourselves and prepare us to take appropriate action.

Take action

If we determine that our experience is from God, then we accept it as God's will for us. But if not, we resist and reject it. We fight and dissociate ourselves from it. Scripture says: "Resist the devil and he will flee from you" (Jam 4:7).

These three steps can be used to discern whether family situations are symptomatic of bondage. We should not discern family issues alone, but in concert with other persons more knowledgeable than us. In this way discernment is more reliable, since it is a group effort, we have support and are protected within the group.

Let me illustrate the three steps in discerning interior movements using our Lord's own experience before His Passion. Some Greeks who came up to worship at the feast in Jerusalem asked Philip, "Sir, we would like to see

Jesus" (Jn 12:21). Philip and Andrew then informed Jesus. Becoming aware of the reason for the visit, Jesus was filled with emotions and said to them: "The hour has come for the Son of Man to be glorified... Now my soul is troubled. And what should I say—'Father, save me from this hour'? No, it is for this reason that I have come to this hour" (Jn 12:23, 27, NRSV).

Jesus became aware, and promptly acknowledges His distress feeling – "I am troubled now." He understood the reason for this distress feeling – the arrival of the hour of His Passion. He also understood that "it was for this purpose that I came to this hour." Finally, He understood that it was the Father's will that He arrive at this hour. This was all triggered by the arrival of some Greeks. Having understood the reason for His affective movements, Jesus freely accepts it as God's will. In doing so He glorifies God saying: "Father, glorify your name" (Jn 12:28). Jesus is a good Discerner, because He is a good Listener. We can be good discerners too if we learn to listen to our inner selves; to our thoughts, feelings and desires, imagination, senses, and our will as Jesus did.

Become aware: acknowledge and identify with the reality

When we become aware of signs of family bondage, it is important we acknowledge the bondage. Diseases have symptoms by which they are diagnosed. Similarly, bondages have symptoms that manifest them. Just as interior desolation can be detected through thoughts, feelings, and desires; personal and generational bondage can likewise be detected by noticeable signs: divisions, anger, impatience, and other negative behavioral patterns or events: lust, miscarriages, accidents, occult terror, bedwetting, nightmares, and other manifestations and diseases (which are sometimes very specific), addictions, murders, and a host of other signs, including paranormal phenomena. Sometimes, these occurrences may follow certain patterns.

We should refrain from blaming ourselves or others for these experiences. We should be objective and patient and praying, remembering that no suffering can affect us that has not been permitted by God. We must have an open mind to all that God wants to reveal to us about our situation. We should try to gather as much information about your family tree as possible. We may visit our native homes of origin and ask deep questions. We can make phone calls to relatives and friends who can provide valuable ancestral information needed for informed intercession for the healing of our family trees.

Saint Ignatius of Loyola's "Rule" for spiritual discernment can help guide us in this process. Rule 13 (#326) for example, observes that the enemy conducts himself as a false lover who seeks to remain hidden and does not want to be discovered.[124] Satan would prefer that we keep things in the dark and not tell anyone. It knows that once its evil plans are exposed to someone spiritually knowledgeable in its wicked ways, such plans will fail. Satan dwells in spiritual darkness and secrecy.

Our Lord Jesus on the other hand wants us to bring things into the light. "What I say to you in the dark, tell in the light; and what you hear whispered, proclaim from the housetops" (Mt 10:27, NRSV). "He who follows Me," Jesus says, "does not walk in the dark, but has the light of life" (Jn 8:12). Sometimes much evil may be hidden in our family trees, and Satan does not want them revealed, nor does it want us to know of its involvement in them. Satan's goal is to keep our generations in perpetual bondage. For this reason we must do everything we can to get all the information we need. We should keep talking with the Holy Spirit in prayer, as well as our spiritual director or confessor, and family members in the process. We need team work. When we have the Holy Spirit's light, evil cannot hide. We are advised to keep a journal of our findings and experiences. In the Scriptures, God often instructed prophets to write down valuable information for their remembrance as the following citations show: Exodus 17:4, 34:1, 34:27; Proverbs 7:3; Isaiah 30:8; Jeremiah 30:2, 36:2; Ezekiel 24:2; and Habakkuk 2:2.

Journaling our experiences in prayer will help us keep track of interior movements, and refresh our dialogue of prayer with God. We should take seriously our call to freedom and salvation in Christ. Satan does not take our destruction lightly. We must use every means at our disposal to investigate and gather relevant information about our families with respect to distressful situations. We do something similar when we visit the doctor's office for our health issues. We should do the same when we come to Doctor Jesus with our family distress. Jesus' mission to all generations is to proclaim liberty to captives and free the oppressed (Lk 4:18). His method of healing is different from earthly physicians. He came to save us and to lay down His life to ransom us from bondage. It is by His wounds that we receive healing (Is 53).

We should seek the light of the Holy Spirit about what He wants us to know about our family trees. We read of a powerful example of the importance of information gathering in family healing and spiritual warfare in Joshua 2:1 and 7:2. God instructs Moses to send spies to reconnoiter the land of Canaan to gather information about the land, its people and produce. With this knowledge, the Israelites were well informed and prepared to storm and take possession of the land that God had promised them. We too must be prepared to take back what the enemy has stolen from us, so that every soul in our families comes into full possession of life in Christ.

As we acknowledge the reality of generational bondage, we should distance ourselves from the evil choices of our ancestors. We should bravely identify with and share in the responsibility for their failings. In doing so, we are not claiming to have committed their sins, nor are we taking responsibility for the sins of our ancestors. *No!* We are also not asking God to punish them for their sins. *No!* Love is powerful and compassionate. Love identifies with the one who suffers—this is compassion. Because we love our ancestors, we identify with them in their weaknesses and failings; just as we take pride in their strengths and successes, and even boast of them.

Jesus, true God and true Man, identified with our fallen human nature in becoming human. He also took responsibility for our sins, and suffered the humiliating death of the Cross (Phil 2:8). Saint Paul says that Jesus, who is sinless as God, took upon Himself our sins, and became sin, so that we might become the holiness of God (2 Cor 5:21). Prophet Isaiah wrote: "It was our infirmities that he bore, our sufferings that he endured. He was pierced for our offenses, crushed for our sins, upon him was the chastisement that makes us whole, by his wounds we are healed" (Is 53:4–5).

We are ambassadors of our ancestors; we represent them now before the whole world. When people encounter us, they encounter them. We are their legacy not only in their good qualities about which we boast, but also in their negative qualities that embarrass and shame us. We carry both legacies in us. As intercessors with Christ, we stand in the gap for our ancestors, because we love them in and through Jesus, even as He first loved us and gave His life as a ransom for our sins. We all have been purchased at a great prize in the Blood of the Lamb.

Understand: relate and receive from the Lord

As we try to understand the bondage situation in our families, it is important we talk to Jesus about them. He wants to reveal to us things about our families so we can ask the Father for healing in His name, and receive every spiritual blessing. "Jesus is our only Master, Who can teach us; our only Lord on Whom we ought to depend; our only Head to Whom we must be united; our only Model to Whom we should conform ourselves; our only Physician Who can heal us; our only Shepherd Who can feed us; our only Way Who can lead us; our only Truth Whom we must believe; our only Life Who can animate us; and our only All in all things Who can satisfy us."[125]

As we relate or dialogue with the Father or Jesus or the Holy Spirit, we ask for light to understand how God wants us to cooperate with Him to restore our freedom and that of our beloved ancestors, who may still be in captivity in ways we may not know. In this relational prayer, we choose to come under the Fatherhood of God, through the Lordship of Jesus Christ.

This choice awakens our spiritual senses, and deepens our hearts' desires. We become more open to receive God's desires for us. In this openness, we exercise our faith and ask for our daily bread as Jesus taught (Mt 6:11). In asking, we may receive; in seeking, we may find; and in knocking, the door may be opened to us (Lk 11:9). But we must do these in faith, not doubting.

No doubt, we often identify confidently with the blessings and successes of our ancestors: wealth, children, position and influence; so too, we should identify confidently with their struggles, pains and failures. Job, who experienced the joys of success and the pains of suffering blesses the Lord who gives and takes away (Job 1:21). The one and the same God is present when the Sun is shining and when it is raining, in good times and in bad. The Letter to the Hebrews has these words of hope for us. Discipline, at first brings pain; but those who have been trained by it later experience the fruit of joy, peace and righteousness. The letter enjoins us: "So strengthen your drooping hands and your weak knees. Make straight paths for your feet, that what is lame may not be dislocated but healed" (Heb 12:11–13).

Take Action: repentance and confession, renunciation and deliverance

Repentance and confession

Some decisive action is needed when we have acknowledged and understood our situation. Repentance is the line drawn in the sand for a new beginning into freedom. Jesus made repentance the first, and the key invitation of His public ministry: the Kingdom of God has come, so we must repent and believe in the Good News of the Gospel (Mk 1:15, NIV). Repentance is the way forward to reconciliation with the Father. The Prophet Jonah proclaimed to the Ninevites, "Forty days more and Nineveh shall be destroyed" (Jonah 3). The king and the people repented, and Nineveh was spared from ruins.

Jesus held up for us as the model of repentance the sinful woman, who, moved by love, washed His feet with her tears and dried them with her hair. And He said to her, "Your sins are forgiven… your faith has saved you; go in peace" (Lk 7:36–50). Jesus knew her intentions and understood the depth of her sorrow for her many sins. She was healed.

It is not necessary in generational investigation for family healing to probe to know who sinned, or what precise sins were committed. We are certain Jesus knows all that. More importantly, He loves and embraces all our generations in His Divine Mercy. He has objectively pardoned all our sins. Now, He desires that we repent, change our lives and be freed.

Repentance is the open door to freedom. In repentance we exercise our free will to choose God.

The celebration of the Sacrament of Penance (Confession) is an important aspect of repentance and of family healing. It is first an act of obedience to Jesus, who personally instituted this Sacrament of healing in the Church. Through it, we acknowledge the truth of our sinfulness; express our need for God's mercy, and an inner openness to receive His love. At the Family Healing Retreats, I encourage participants to celebrate this healing Sacrament as a sign of their repentance. In addition, they can make intercessions and reparation for generational sins that may be affecting them, especially during the Eucharistic celebration, and other devotional prayers. Such prayers for forgiveness and healing from personal and generational sins are highly encouraged by the Church.

Generational intercessions and reparation should be motivated by love for our ancestors whose sins may have opened the door to our bondage. Prayers of this kind, offered within the context of the Eucharistic celebration can free us from bondage and our ancestors from purgatory. We read in 2 Maccabees 12:46, "Thus he made atonement for the dead that they might be freed from this sin." We surely want to be like Judas Maccabeus, who acted in a very excellent and noble way when he sent collections to Jerusalem to provide for an expiatory sacrifice for the sins of those who had fallen, because he had the resurrection of the dead in view? (2 Mac 12:43). In anticipation of the glory of eternal life for our ancestors, we can offer to the Father, the Sacrifice of the Cross for their freedom and redemption.

The sting of Satan is sin. Once sin has been repented of and confessed, Satan is rendered totally powerless over the sinner. For the faithful and practicing Christian, the protection against Satan is regular confession of sins, and experiencing the love of the Father. Such a Christian may still experience ancestral bondage due to the effects of the sins of his/her ancestors, or if God wills that His works be revealed through it (Jn 9:3).

As stated earlier, it is not necessary to probe for what sin allowed the evil one entry into the family tree, or who committed it. Jesus does not give us the example of such probing in His healing ministry. In dealing with those who came to Him, Jesus on a few occasions directly pointed out that people's bondage was due to their personal sin(s). He warned the man who was crippled for thirty-eight years, and whom He healed on the Sabbath, not to sin again so that "nothing worse" may befall him (Jn 5:14). He said to the woman in bondage to sexual addiction, "Go, (and) from now on do not sin any more" (Jn 8:11). It is significant and necessary that Jesus issues these warnings to challenge and deter sinners from continuing to violate God's commandments. The Church, following Jesus' example, also calls believers to repent and abstain from sinful lifestyles, since this might open them up to something worse too.

The presence of bondage on a family member who is striving for Christian perfection, may be a sign that Satan is exercising some legal claim (Col 2:14) within the family tree as a result of sins not yet absolved or forgiven, or that the work of God is being revealed through it (Jn 9:2). We do not have a way to know this for certain, unless of course, it is revealed to us by the Holy Spirit.

Satan knows what sins opened the doors to it to inflict bondage on the person or family tree. As long as the open door or predisposing factor is in place, Satan is able to initiate and perpetuate any evil of its choice until it is stopped dead on its tracks in the name of Jesus. When a mad dog is let loose, it can cause much destruction until it is restrained. Satan is a mad dog that should be retrained and rendered harmless by taking away its legal claim and power, which is sin (Col 2:14). The Blood of Jesus has destroyed sin; this Blood is our salvation and freedom.

Bondage as a desolation experience is permitted by God for three reasons: it is caused by us, because we are slothful and tepid about our spiritual lives; to test our faithfulness to Him. Do we seek the God of consolation or do we seek the consolation of God? God wants us to grow in self-knowledge, and realize that any progress in the spiritual life is always a grace and not the fruit of our personal effort[126] (see Appendix IV). When faced with the desolation of bondage, Saint Ignatius of Loyola encourages us to resist it, to be patient and persevere in prayer, knowing and hoping that it will pass. Relief comes only in God's time for our ultimate benefit. Here, we are confronted with a mystery that defies explanation. Paul says that no one knows God's mind. No one has offered Him advice or counsel in order to ask a return payment. All we have are from God, and we belong to Him (Rom 11:34–36). Let us give thanks to God for He is good. His love is everlasting.

Saint Padre Pio encourages us to accept all things that come to us in this life as if they have come directly from the hand of Almighty God. God desires and labors for our salvation. He is able to accomplish it as He chooses. Saint Pio says: "We must pray, hope and don't worry."

As part of generational healing prayers, participants are encouraged to make atonement and reparation for the sins of their ancestors that they may experience the redemption promised by Christ through our intercession.

There are biblical examples of generational intercession offered by righteous men and women in salvation history for the healing of their sinful ancestors. In Daniel 9:22–23, Daniel offers prayers of intercession to God on behalf of all Israel, who were presently in exile. God answered his prayers and sent the Archangel Gabriel, who said to Daniel: "I have now come to give you understanding. When you began your petition, an answer was given which I have come to announce, because you are beloved." In praying for the present situation of exile of his people, Daniel recognized and acknowledged the past sins of his ancestors.

When we pray out of love for our ancestors, God responds in mercy, because we are His beloved. God wants us to be intercessors for our families, so they can be released from bondage. Generational intercession is most pleasing to God, who "wills that all be saved and come to the knowledge of the truth" (1 Tim 2:4), and the experience of perfect freedom.

The effectiveness of generational intercession will depend on several factors: union with Jesus, who is our Intercessor at the right hand of the Father (Heb 8:1); acknowledging and identifying with the failures and weaknesses of our ancestors, since we their descendants may be weighed down by the effects of their sins passed down to us. Our identification with the sins and faults of our ancestors is an act of love that draws down God's mercy upon us. Paul urges us, "Bear one another's burdens, and so fulfill the law of Christ" (Gal 6:2, ESV).

Jesus commands us to repent and believe the Good News (Mk 1:15). For every sin, Jesus says, we must Repent! Jesus came to set the captives free and to give us freedom; but we must repent. God is the one who grants the graces of repentance and forgiveness of sins (Acts 5:31); we should ask for this grace perseveringly.

The road to healing begins with repentance. Repentance opens the door for renewed friendship with God. It dislodges the evil hold on us, leaving us free to choose God always, even on behalf of our families. Through repentance we receive the gift of the Holy Spirit (Acts 2:38), and are more deeply able to glorify God. The Blessed Mother, filled with the Holy Spirit glorifies God saying: "My soul proclaims the greatness of the Lord, my spirit rejoices in God my Savior" (Lk 1:46–47). The fruit of a converted and pure heart is the praise of God's goodness.

Apart from bringing us into a deeper experience of interior freedom and reconciliation with God, repentance brings with it the spiritual authority of faith, which strengthens us to stand fast against the tactics of the devil (Eph 6). By the authority of faith, we are able to claim back what Satan has stolen from us by his envy and deception, that is, our identity and freedom as God's children. Faith gives us strength never to compromise the revealed truth of Sacred Scripture, and the divinely inspired teachings of the Church handed down to us through the Apostles. We cease to be afraid of Satan and his demons, because we are filled with God's love, and armed with the Blood of His Son.

When family healing prayers are offered in faith, ancestral bondages are broken and we are released from our interior prisons, and experience family reconciliation and healing. Since we still reserve the right to exercise our free will as we wish, subsequent sins can reopen the doors to bondage, and complicate and plunge us back into bondage. Personal choices for holiness can exclude us from experiencing the consequences of the bondage effects of ancestral sins.

By our baptismal vows, belong and we are committed to God as His children, but sin harms our covenant bond with God. The more serious the sin, the more harm that is done, and the stronger is Satan's power and effects on us. We know that the consequences of mortal sins are more severe than those of venial sins.

Renunciation and deliverance

The desolation resulting from bondage is an evil that must be resisted. Scripture commands us to surrender to God, to resist the devil, and he will flee from us (Jam 4:7). The bondage of the evil one entered our lives and family through the misuse of free wills. We must renounce all evil choices, and choose God in order to receive the new and abundant life Jesus promised. Part of resisting the evil may involve deliverance.

Deliverance is spiritual warfare. Before ascending into Heaven, our Lord commissioned His disciples to preach the Gospel message to all nations (Mk 16:15). The sign of their faith will be revealed in casting out demons, handling serpents without harm. They will drink deadly poisons and no harm would befall them, and sick people will be healed by the laying on of hands (Mk 16:17–18). Earlier, Jesus gave the seventy-two disciples who rejoiced that even the demons were powerless before them, power and authority to trample upon snakes and scorpions, which symbolize demonic forces, and they have nothing to fear (Lk 10:19). He assured them that Satan has already been defeated and thrown down and out like lightning out of Heaven (Lk 10:18).

Even though Jesus had empowered us to trample underfoot the full force of Satan's kingdom, dealing with Satan and his wicked army of demons is not always easy, for the simple reason that many Christians do not know who they are and the power of the Holy Spirit invested on them at baptism. Satan's power is powerless power. Jesus' power is powerful power. Satan's power is empty power, while Jesus' power is fullness of power. There is no real comparison between these two powers. To Jesus belongs Almighty power. At the mention of His holy name, every knee must bend, in heaven, on earth and under the earth, and every tongue must confess the Lordship of Jesus Christ, to the glory of the Heavenly Father (Phil 2:10–11).

Spiritual desolation and dark night of the soul

At the Family Healing Retreats, I have been asked questions regarding desolation and "dark night." Let us briefly distinguish between the two experiences, since this book addresses only the bondage experiences of desolation. Spiritual desolation and dark night are two spiritual experiences with different origins, goals, and fruits.

Spiritual desolation

Spiritual desolation is an affective or interior movement of the heart that can adversely affects our relationship with God. It is never caused by God. However, God permits it for our ultimate good. Spiritual desolation produces effects contrary to spiritual consolation (see Chapter 4). Saint Ignatius of Loyola says that both desolation and consolation occur alternately as part of our spiritual journeys.

Simply described, spiritual desolation is a state of decreased faith, hope and love. We are made aware of spiritual desolation experiences through our thoughts, feelings, and desires. Desolation experiences fluctuate; they are not permanent. It is important we try to understand why we are in desolation. This will help us to take necessary action to resolve them in our prayer encounters with the Lord: the good to accept them for the grace God desires that we receive through them, and the bad to reject them.

Desolation experiences can manifest as sadness, anxiety, depression, abandonment feelings, lack of desire to pray, lack of interior peace, heaviness and blockage, and so on (see Appendix II). The fruit of spiritual desolation in a soul, provided there is a desire to do God's will, is repentance and conversion, and a deeper trust and surrender to God.

The "Dark Nights"

The dark night of the soul is a passive spiritual experience in which God brings a soul into union with Him through the purification of both the senses and the spirit. It is called passive because it is not what we do; it is rather God's action in our souls.[127] The person undergoing the dark night experiences a painful lack or privation which includes, "darkness in the intellect; aridity in the will regarding the exercise of love; emptiness of all possessions in the memory; and a general affliction and torment as a consequence."[128] John of the Cross says that, "Such persons receive an understanding of their own misery and think they would never escape from it."[129]

The painful experiences and the fruits of this transformation process are due to contemplation, which is an inpouring of God into the soul, giving it knowledge that both purifies it and illumines it.[130] There are no adequate human controls for a soul going through the dark night, because before God only poverty, confidence, and abandonment remain.[131] "If the night darkens, it does so only to give light; if it humiliates, it does so only to exalt; if it impoverishes, it does so only to enrich. The soul becomes as it were, 'a new creation.'"[132]

"What is essential [in the dark night] is that the sufferings and privations bring about a growing response of faith, hope and love." Without this transformation the dark night will fail to purify and produce fruit in the soul.[133] It is important to note that the dark night is not depression, nor is it evil; it is a purification that God brings about in the souls of His friends in order to unite them more intimately with Himself. Only God determines how, when and how long a soul goes through the dark night, as she is plunged into the abyss of darkness, nothingness and abandonment in the overwhelming fire of desolation. In this graced-filled process, God roots out from the soul the deepest attachments to sin, the self, the world, people, and all imperfections, so that the only attachment that remains in the soul is to God alone for His own sake. During the dark night, the soul remains strong in spirit, by the grace of God, and is able to perform charitable works. She is not wearied or handicapped by the temptations, anger and hatred toward God and self, and suicidal tendencies that are sometimes associated with individuals suffering from depression. The three stages of growth in holiness usually accompany the dark nights: the purgative way, the illuminative way, and the unitive way (see Chapter 1).

Scriptures and questions for self-reflection and journaling

(1) Mark 6:31 (2) Ephesians 3:14–19 (30) Jeremiah 29:11–14

✗ Lord Jesus, who do You say that I am?
✗ Do I take time regularly to reflect on my interior experiences of consolation/desolation; to appreciate more deeply God's love for me in all the circumstances of my life?
✗ Holy Spirit, am I truly and really convinced that the Lord is my Good Shepherd and there is nothing I shall want?
✗ Father, why am I afraid when Jesus has assured me: Even though you walk in the valley of darkness you should fear no evil?

Chapter 5
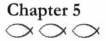

Understanding Basic Spiritual Warfare

Be brave and steadfast; do not be afraid or dismayed because of the king of Assyria and all the throng that is coming with him, for there is more with us than with him (2 Chron 32:7).

Spiritual warfare

Spiritual warfare began in the Garden of Eden when the serpent (Satan), the most cunning of all the animals God created, used lies and deception to cause Adam and Eve to disobey God. As a result, they lost the state of original innocence: that state of "'purity of heart,' which preserves an interior faithfulness"[134] to God, to truth and the correct order of creation.

God said to the serpent in Genesis 3:15: "I will put enmity between you and the woman, and between your offspring and hers; He will strike at your head, while you strike at his heel." Saint Paul tells us we do not struggle with flesh and blood, but with spiritual evils: principalities and powers, with spiritual darkness that rule the world, and with the evil spirits in the heavenly realm (Eph 6:12). Because of this spiritual war, Paul enjoins us to wear the armor of God always, and to stand firm against the devil's tactics (Eph 6:11). We are brothers and sisters in the human family, called to love as Christ loves us. We are not enemies to one another. Our real enemies are the devils.

The war of the two kingdoms

Jesus said that we cannot belong to two worlds nor serve two masters. We must choose to serve either God or mammon (Mt 6:24). To serve, love, listen and obey God is a proof of faith, which brings healing and freedom. Anything else is sin and corruption, and these lead to bondage under the devil's rule. To serve God is to reign with Christ in the Kingdom of Heaven. To serve mammon is to be a slave of the devil in the kingdom of darkness.

Saint John's Gospel speaks of the contrast between light and darkness. He says that Jesus is the light of this world. "The light came into the darkness and the darkness did not overcome it" (Jn 1:5). Paul teaches that there is no fellowship between light and darkness, nothing in common between righteousness and lawlessness, and between Christ and the devil (2 Cor 6:14).

The war of the two kingdoms is played out in our mortal combat with sin and evil in our lives. This is why Jesus Christ became flesh, suffered and died. The war between good and evil is waged in our hearts. Each moment of our lives we are faced with a choice of right or left, holiness or sinfulness, good or evil, virtue or vice, morality or immorality, heaven or hell, and obedience or disobedience. It is a choice between Jesus and Lucifer; between life and death.

Saint Ignatius of Loyola's Meditation on the Two Standards helps us to understand the nature of this war. He places Jesus, our supreme Leader and Lord, on one side; and Lucifer, the deadly enemy of our human nature, on the other side. Satan is seated on the vast plain in Babylon on a throne of fire and smoke, with terror and horror everywhere. It sends its demons to all parts of the world, and all spheres of human life, overlooking no one. The demons are to bring the men and women of the world to him by laying traps for them and binding them in chains. Their strategy is first, to tempt them to covet riches; for those who have riches, to cling to them, so that they may attain the empty honors of this world. In this way, people will become proud and have absolute security and dependence on themselves. They will be persuaded and convinced that they do not need anyone else, and that God is not really important. Satan's approach can be summarized thus: first, —riches; second, —honors; and third, —pride. These vices arise from the three steps the devil has devised.[135]

Saint Ignatius pictures Christ our Lord as the sovereign and true Commander. His appearance is beautiful and attractive. He is standing in a lonely place in the great plains of the region of Jerusalem. He chooses many disciples and sends them throughout the world to spread His Good News to men and women, no matter what their state or condition may be. He tells them to help everyone by drawing them to the highest spiritual poverty, and actual poverty, if it pleases God. God is to be our only security; not riches and status. Possessions are useful only to the extent that they bring us closer to God. The disciples are to lead the people to desire and accept the insults and contempt that the world puts on them as Christians. This will produce humility in them, because in humility, we are totally dependent and surrendered to God in all things. Humility does not resist God but acknowledges Him as the center of the universe, not us.[136]

The summary of Christ's plan is: first, —spiritual and actual poverty instead of riches; second, —accepting and desiring insults and contempt instead of worldly honors; and third, —humility instead of pride.[137] The challenge then before us is, —who do we choose: Jesus or Satan? The battleground in this decision is our human free will. The battle line is drawn.

My first combat experience

The Lord drew me into spiritual warfare in a most unusual way. I had read a lot on the subject while growing up, but never had any personal combat experience. Following my discernment struggles leading up to the priestly vocation, the Lord called me to join the Intercessors of the Lamb[138] in Omaha, Nebraska, in 1999. There, I continued to learn more about spiritual warfare, since it was the charism of the community.

On my first vacation to Virginia as a Postulant with the Intercessors, I had my first combat experience with demons. A friend of mine had invited me to come to her house so I could express my gratitude for a favor I received from a woman. While there, the woman was open to hearing God's Word. I began preaching the Gospel to her. About fifteen minutes into my evangelization, she suddenly became agitated and acted strangely the moment I repeated Jesus' words: "Man does not live by bread alone, but by every word that comes from the mouth of God" (Lk 4:4).

At those words, she jerked in terror and stared blankly at the wall in front of us. With her arms raised, she shook violently and repeatedly, saying: "Don't let them take me, please don't let them take me." Next, she slumped into her chair as if dead. I realized at that moment that she was under some diabolical attack. For me, the evil one had overstepped its bounds. I did not go there for trouble; Satan provoked trouble by attacking a child of God in my presence. I could not simply walk away from the situation; I had to deal with it, whatever it was. I was totally convinced she was not dead. It was all very strange! We took her to a couch, and for the next three hours, I battled Satan and his demons that were attacking this woman.

When the battle was over, the woman said the demons had told her to hit me in the face and run out through the door. But she was unable and afraid to hit me because a huge and powerful angel in battle gear was standing behind me. I found out later that he is Saint Raphael the Archangel (*I encourage the reader to please read the Book of Tobit and get to know Saint Raphael*). The woman would not have succeeded in escaping, because my faith instinct alerted me earlier to lock the doors in the house.

During the battle session, in which I had prayed prayers of deliverance, the evil spirits hid in the closets and rooms in the house. The woman saw the demons attempting to 'flow out' like some black liquid from under the closets. At one point, no sooner did she enter the restroom than she jumped out screaming, because the demons were there waiting for her. We sprinkled the entire house with exorcised salt, and that sent the demons fleeing. The woman was set free by the power of the Precious Blood of Jesus Christ, the King. We were very happy for that.

The devil and the demons

The identity and mission of Satan

Satan and the demons are fallen angels. By their disobedience they lost their dignity as "angelic persons;" they are now "it" (Rev 12:3–4). Satan is known by different names: the devil, the evil one, Lucifer, the Dragon, the old Serpent, Beelzebub, the prince of darkness, the deceiver, unclean spirit, the tempter, a liar, the father of lies, the accuser, and "a thief and a robber."

Jesus speaks of the identity and mission of Satan when He said: "From the very beginning he was a murderer and has never been on the side of truth, because there is no truth in him. When he tells a lie, he is only doing what is natural to him, because he is a liar and the father of all lies" (Jn 8:44, GNT). Satan does not enter the sheep barn through the main gate. He climbs over elsewhere as thieves and robbers do when they perpetrate evil (Jn 10:1). "A thief comes only to steal and slaughter and to destroy" (Jn 10:10). Satan is absolutely evil. There is no love in him whatsoever, and he is absolutely incapable of loving. He is a damned creature who is committed to our physical, moral and spiritual destruction.

Demons are disobedient creatures of God. They hate God and they hate human nature. They hate life, creation, purity, morality and holiness. They hate everything, including themselves. Demons are nasty and wicked. They are deadly to the salvation of our souls; they are very mean and do not care. Lying is their native tongue. They are legalistic and opportunistic, and they come to steal, slaughter and destroy. They are thieves and robbers. We never beg or negotiate with demons, and we should avoid speaking to them. Demons do not obey people; they obey only Jesus Christ the Lord.

Human beings cannot deal successfully with demons, except in the Holy Name of Jesus Christ. The only language demons understand is a command, given in faith, in the name of Jesus. For demons to obey us, we must speak with the authority of Jesus Christ. Demons know when we have that authority, and when we don't. We may not even need to speak a word; they know if Jesus is speaking through us or not. Demons know that we are children of God by our Baptism, but they also know that many baptized Christians do not know the power and authority of their baptismal vows. This is why Satan gains advantage over many Christians, and puts them in a hopeless bondage.

There are several open doors through which demons can gain entrance into human beings and hold them captive. Sin is the common denominator of the open doors. Sin denies us authentic human freedom. Sin dehumanizes, defaces and degrades our dignity as God's children. The open doors to spiritual contamination and bondage are treated under two categories: primary and secondary open doors. The primary open doors (chapters 7–13) are the Seven Capital Sins: anger, envy, sloth, gluttony, greed (avarice), pride, and lust. The secondary open doors (chapters 14–18) are: prenatal (in-utero) and postnatal (childhood) wounds and traumas; unholy soul-ties and affections; occult, Freemasonry and New Age involvement; denial of God and rejection of the Church; and, finally, generational transmission. The secondary open doors are complications of the primary open doors.

To talk about or focus on demons is neither pleasant nor interesting. In fact, it can be depressing. Jesus did not focus attention on them; He does not want us to focus on them.

God is love! Jesus teaches us to direct our attention on the Father and His love for us. The Father is greater than all. No one can take us out of His hands (Jn 10:29). It is extremely fulfilling, fruitful, interesting, and life-giving to talk about God; to speak to God; to listen to God; and to experience God. It is blissful and enjoyable to be with God. God is good! God is perfect Goodness. God is All in all.

Paul says that when we were God's enemies, He reconciled and saved us by the death and resurrection of His Son, Jesus. So now, through Christ Jesus, we can even make God our boast (Rom 5:10–11). All our attention must be on God. Since we have an adversary who seeks our eternal destruction—Satan and its wicked demons, it is important to have some basic and necessary knowledge of this enemy in order to do battle and overcome it as we struggle to attain salvation in Christ. James 4:7 says we should always submit to God, and resist the devil, and he will run away.

The legendary Chinese military thinker, Sun Tzu (fourth century BC), whose work, *The Art of War,* outlines bedrock principles of war strategy, once said: "Know yourself and know the enemy and you can fight a hundred battles without any danger of defeat." Jesus Christ dealt a great deal with demons in His ministry. As our Commander-in-Chief, He teaches us how to fight them. It is in the Flesh and Blood of Jesus Christ that the battle with the devil was won definitively for all time. On the Cross, Jesus defeated Satan, sin, and death. Christians are called to replicate this victory in their own spiritual battles, and in the Church.

Jesus once said to Saint Catherine of Siena that Satan has prepared a bed for her in Hell. Similarly, Satan has prepared a bed in Hell for all of us who follow Jesus. Our merciful Jesus assures us He is going to prepare a place for us in the Father's house. Then He will return to take us with Him, so that we will always be with Him and never be separated from Him (Jn 14:2). It is completely up to us to choose where we want to be: in the

Father's peaceful mansion, or in Satan's house of horror? For this reason, God gave us the gift of free will to make that choice in total freedom. Saint Catherine of Siena chose Jesus; we too should choose Jesus always.

God respects our free will. He does not impose His will on us. He desires that we be free, and He offers us His love freely. Through our free will we choose to obey God, and through it we choose to turn away from Him. Let us listen to the wisdom of Baruch 4:28: "As your hearts have been disposed to stray from God, turn now ten times the more to seek him." Jesus' encounter with the blind Bartimaeus illustrates how God always seeks our consent before He acts. Jesus asked him: "What do you want me to do for you?" (Mk 10:51). We see another example of the power of free will as Moses addressed the Israelites:

> Here, then, I have today set before you life and prosperity, death and doom. If you obey the commandments of the Lord, your God, which I enjoin on you today, the Lord, your God, will bless you in the land you are entering to occupy. If, however, you turn away your hearts and will not listen, you will certainly perish... I call heaven and earth to witness against you: I have set before you life and death, the blessing and the curse. Choose life, then, that you and your descendants may live (Deut 30:15–19).

Jesus tells us, "If you love me, keep my commandments" (Jn 14:15).

Spiritual warfare is not between God and the demons. God is the Almighty. He is the Creator of all things, visible and invisible. No creature of God can challenge Him. Spiritual warfare is not between the Holy Angels and the demons. The war of the angels has definitively been won and lost. Scripture speaks of this war:

> Now war arose in heaven, Michael and his angels fighting against the dragon. And the dragon and his angels fought back, but he was defeated, and there was no longer any place for them in heaven. And the great dragon was thrown down, that ancient serpent, who is called the devil and Satan, the deceiver of the whole world—he was thrown down to the earth, and his angels were thrown down with him (Rev 12:7–9, ESV).

Spiritual warfare is waged for the salvation of the souls of human persons created in the image and likeness of God. The arena of this warfare is the human free will. The Holy Angels and the Saints are with us to help us in this mortal combat. Jesus our Savior is with us; we should not be afraid. All we need to do is stay close to Him and be calm, follow Him, trust Him, and love and obey Him.

The tactics of the devil

Demons live in spiritual darkness. They are completely devoid of God's light. They do not have information about God's plan for us. They cannot read our hearts or minds. However, they spend a great deal of time studying, learning and mapping out strategies for our eternal destruction. They can easily pick up, and are attracted by negative emotions around us. These negative vibrations include, among others: unforgiveness, anger, fear, doubts, unbelief, impatience, lying, all forms of impurity and immorality, bad thoughts, idleness, daydreaming, and fantasies—as well as New Age and occult curiosity. These human actions emit negative signals that demons can pick up. Demons hang around persons involved in these activities that generate negative emotions or energy. This is very much like emotional vibrations that people can pick up when others are tense or angry. In short, any human actions that violate God's commandments and the official teachings of the Church make such persons beehives of evil spirit activity.

Negative energy draws evil spirits just like flies are drawn by foul or rotten smell around carcasses. Our Lord said, "Where the body is, there also the vultures will gather" (Lk 17:37). Once evil spirits pick up negative energy in human activity, they begin to study our weaknesses and strengths before launching vile attacks and temptations at our weak points. Demons are isolated, defeated creatures that prowl about looking for someone to devour; they prey on idle minds.

To resist demons, we need to be familiar with their tactics. Demons are not family oriented; the only time they congregate and work together is when they want to destroy souls. Demons are copycats, they cannot originate anything. They own nothing, not even an inch of this world that is created by God. They make bogus claims designed to confuse and deceive. They can issue threats, which are nothing more but empty threats. The devil even tried to deceive Jesus. "Then he took him up and showed him all the kingdoms of the world in a single instant. The devil said to him, I shall give to you all this power and their glory; for it has been handed over to me, and I may give it to whomever I wish" (Lk 4:5–6). Satan claims what does not belong to it in order to deceive souls. Demons watch what God is doing in His precious humans and they try to copy it. They hide and often disguise themselves so we don't suspect they are involved in the evils they mastermind in this world. They can hide and operate behind perceived charismatic leaders, who seek popularity and fame and often make unfulfillable promises. We must be vigilant and discerning.

Demons do not like us bringing things, especially negative events in our lives, into the light or sharing our hearts with God. They behave like bats that hide in the darkness; as soon as light comes in, they flee. Demons also behave like flies. They like to attach to wounded areas of our being, especially, spiritual, emotional and psychological wounds; there, they form nests or strongholds. Even though demons mask and disguise themselves, people with spiritual sight can detect and discern their activities behind the masks. The Holy Spirit's gift of Knowledge equips us to unmask demonic deceptions and lies.

When we don't resist demons, they seem not to bother us much; they feel at home inside us. But this is only a deceptive tactics. In such cases, they don't have to worry about achieving their goals, because we have made it easy for them. Sooner or later, they will begin to execute their evil plans, and the effects will show. But once their plans are brought into the light, they become vicious and fight back like wounded lions. Fear is an effective demonic weapon on believers.

When we are involved at any level of spiritual warfare, we should always be prepared for possible retaliation from demons, especially, when they lose battles. Sometimes demons win the battle over us, but they never win the war. Lack of self-knowledge on our part is a powerful weapon in the hands of demons to win spiritual battles over us and put us in bondage. This is why the Greek philosopher, Socrates,[139] as reported by Plato, said: "Man, Know Thyself."[140] Socrates also said, "An unexamined life is not worth living." (Refer to Chapter 4 on self-knowledge)

Levels of spiritual warfare

We are susceptible to six levels of spiritual contamination, namely, *temptation, infestation, depression, obsession, oppression,* and *possession.* These require three main levels of spiritual warfare to combat them, as the Holy Spirit directs:

1) *Exorcism* may be required in dealing with cases of full-blown demonic possession.

2) *Deliverance* may be required in cases of infestation, depression, obsession, and oppression.

3) *Prayerful vigilance* is necessary in cases of temptation.

These three spiritual combat levels are called for especially when persons become exposed to demonic influences through various ways of contamination.

The Archbishop of Mexico City, Norberto Rivera Carrera, in his pastoral instruction, expressed concern over the widespread increase in the different forms of occultism and New Age spirituality among adults and young people today.[141] As a case study, Father Amorth, the chief exorcist of the Diocese of Rome, observes that: "It is estimated that barely 12 percent of population of Rome attends Mass; it is well known that where religion regresses, superstition progresses."[142] Similarly, we can say that where faith is in decline, various forms of evil will be on the rise. It follows also that charity will likely be trampled underfoot. The Church is not excluded from this rising phenomenon of religious indifference. She must take care not to be part of this growing cancer of unfaithfulness to the truth. She must uphold the Gospel truth at all cost and not deny Christ in favor of public opinion.

Any level of demonic influence if left unchecked can create serious problems of health and wellbeing. Such influence can generally deaden a person's spiritual life rendering him/her numb to the need for holiness, and insensitive to the things of God.

Temptation

This is the ordinary and the most common activity of demons, and it affects all men.[143] God allows the ordinary activity of demons, but He arms us with the grace to resist. In doing so we are strengthened spiritually,[144] provided we do not give in to the temptation. All other cases of demonic influences—extraordinary activity—happen also only with God's permission. God does not desire that we be under any evil influence. Since we have the gift of free will, He allows us to experience the consequences of our choices.[145]

Everyone is subject to the devil's temptation. But temptation itself is not a sin. James 1:13 says: "God is not subject to temptation to evil, and he himself tempts no one." In this world, we cannot avoid temptation. In Job, it is said that "Man's life on earth is a warfare [temptation]" (Job 7:1).[146] Temptation is a sign of our human weakness and vulnerability resulting from the loss of original innocence by Adam. "We are tempted when we are drawn away and trapped by our own evil desires. Then our evil desires conceive and give birth to sin; and sin, when it is full-grown, gives birth to death" (Jam 1:14–15, GNT).

Human nature is created weak. God made us the way we are, and He looked at us and found us very good (Gen 1:31). Adam and Eve did not fall when they were tempted because they were weak; they fell into sin because they did not depend on God when they were tempted. When we rely on ourselves to fight temptation and evil, we fall. Our weakness is a gift so we can rely on God for everything and be strong.

Throughout our lives, one temptation succeeds another. "All the saints passed through many tribulations and temptations, and have profited by them,"[147] because they persevered and relied on God. Scripture calls blessed those who persevere in temptations, since it proves them righteousness and makes them eligible to receive the crown reserved for God's friends (Jam

1:12). We cannot overcome temptations by running away from them. By patience and true humility we become stronger than our enemies - the evil spirits.

Prayerful vigilance is the remedy for temptations. Jesus warned His Apostles, "Watch and pray that you may not undergo the test. The spirit is willing but the flesh is weak" (Mk 14:38). Jesus Himself was vigilant when He was tempted by the devil in the wilderness after He fasted forty days and forty nights (Lk 4:1–13). His three temptations cover all the possible areas of human weakness through which we are tempted. Jesus was victorious in His temptations because His eyes were fixed on the Father, and He believed every Word of the Father in the Scriptures.

Lack of self-knowledge, fear, lack of confidence in God and an attitude of duplicity or double standards, disobedience and compromises, often mark the beginning of all evil temptations. Peter learned a great deal from Jesus, and he warns us: "Be sober and vigilant. Your opponent the devil is prowling around like a roaring lion looking for (someone) to devour" (1 Pet 5:8).

Vigilance means that our eyes must always and everywhere be fixed on Jesus, then the Holy Spirit can inspire and lead us. He will arm us with the sword of the Spirit, His word of truth in the Bible. Then we can spot the enemy, and resist and overcome him by standing fast in the faith. We should develop plans for living holy lives and remaining faithful to our spiritual resolutions. We are tempted in different degrees, "according to the wisdom and equity of the ordinance of God, who weighs the state and merits of men, and pre-ordains all for the salvation of the elect."[148] We must not, therefore, despair when tempted, but pray to God with much fervor that He may… help us in all tribulation."[149] Paul says: "No trial has come to you but what is human. God is faithful and will not let you be tried beyond your strength; but with the trial he will also provide a way out, so that you may be able to bear it" (1 Cor 10:13).

We Christians, weak and sinful as we are, and always subject to temptations, must win the battle at the level of temptation when the enemy is still kept at bay; else, we will have to contend with him inside of ourselves. Should this happen, we will have to escalate warfare to the level of deliverance.

Deliverance
Deliverance is aimed at freeing from spiritual affliction those experiencing infestation, depression, obsession, and oppression.

Spiritual infestation

Demonic activity affects the exterior of persons, animals, houses, and other objects as flies would infest a rotten flesh or filthy places. The person's interior life is not affected.

Spiritual depression

This can be the result of a demonic influence and may produce all the signs of classical depression. Several effects can result, which may include lack of interest in life, feelings of emptiness, etc. These attacks are often triggered by some predisposing factors within the individual. This is often made possible by an interior disconnect with God at a deep level. Depression is a collapse from within a person resulting from lack of a healthy, life-giving relationship with God.

Spiritual oppression

This is a supernatural attack on people by demons. The afflicted persons feel weighed down by demons, as if carrying tons of weight. There is feeling of being confined or closed in within oneself, and a general lack of inner freedom. Diabolical oppression may be experienced as a dark cloud over an individual with the feeling of life being sucked out of him, or heaviness within.

I was involved in a heavy-duty deliverance session on a certain young man for about four days when I was a member of the Intercessors of the Lamb (read account below). Three days after this ministry, I began to feel a dark evil cloud enveloping me gradually; it increased in intensity as the days went by. On the third day, I became really uncomfortable as if getting sick. It dawned on me that I was under a serious retaliatory demonic oppression (I was taught as an Intercessor of the Lamb to expect such retaliation). I was spiritually suffocating, I felt weighed down and locked in, and I had fear. I immediately alerted some Brother Lambs (as we called ourselves) in the community and they prayed deliverance over me; the situation lifted instantly and I felt completely free. For us God anointed Jesus of Nazareth with the Holy Spirit and power at His Baptism; He went about healing those oppressed by demons, and He did much good in people's lives (Acts 10: 38).

Oppression can manifest as awareness of lack of freedom in one's inner self, spiritual suffocation, health problems that often have no known cause, and a general lack of wellbeing. Other symptoms may include nightmares, bedwetting, bondage to and bouts of anger, cursing and blasphemy, vulgarity, addictions, spiritual blindness, paralyzing fear, panic attacks, division in families and so on. External situations and events affecting relationships, finances, etc. may sometimes accompany these attacks.

Spiritual obsession

This is a demonic attack, harassment or torment which may involve illnesses inflicted on persons from outside. The illnesses may manifest symptoms inconsistent with known illnesses, which point to the certainty of their evil origin. The afflicted persons are aware of abnormal phenomena around them, some of which have physical evidence. "Almost always obsession influences dreams."[150] They can affect persons in sinful situations (need deliverance), as well as virtuous and holy persons, but for different reasons. Father John Hardon, SJ referred to the diabolical experiences of the Curé of Ars, Saint John Vianney, as obsession. Saint Padre Pio and Saint Paul of the Cross experienced demonic obsession, though all three men lived holy lives. Father Amorth refers to the affliction of these saints as *"External physical pain caused by Satan."* No exorcism or deliverance is needed in these cases, only prayers.[151]

Deliverance is also called minor exorcism. Priests, by their ordination as co-workers with the bishops, exercise this charism as an integral part of their sacerdotal (priestly) office. No permission of the local ordinary is required for priests to perform deliverance. It is important, however, that priests receive training and be knowledgeable in such matters before engaging in deliverance ministry. Experience and effectiveness come with time and practice. It is not enough simply to know how to recite a set of prayers, or to do so in any particular language. Deliverance authority comes through faith in Jesus Christ. Demons respect and obey the language of faith-authority. Demons, or any enemies for that matter, do not like to lose battles. They often retaliate against the priest or those involved in deliverance ministry. Those engaged in spiritual warfare should be well prepared so they are not surprised by demonic retaliation.

Deliverance may involve spontaneous or set prayers, or simply a person's presence. It may also comprise actions or a combination of actions; or it may be a direct or indirect challenge of demonic activity in a person. Sacred Scripture relates that as Peter passed by, his shadow cured all the sick, and delivered those under demonic captivity (Acts 5:15–16). Of Paul, Scripture says: "So extraordinary were the mighty deeds God accomplished at the hands of Paul that when face cloths or aprons that touched his skin were applied to the sick, their diseases left them and the evil spirits came out of them" (Acts 19:11–12).

A man with a demon

A certain man came to me at one of our Intercessor of the Lamb Conferences. He claimed demonic presence and disturbances inside of him. He said he had had a 'spirit friend' from his childhood; this man was addicted to weight-lifting. I was alerted to the demonic presence in him when, as I facilitated one of the group sessions, I would raise my right hand over the group and prayed, this fellow would start bending over toward the ground. This happened several times that it caught my attention. I spoke with him privately outside the group. I asked why he reacted that way to my prayer. He said he did not know; only that some force was pushing him to the ground. I invited an Intercessor Lay Companion to join me to pray with him; I was a religious Brother at the time.

During the prayer session, I requested he look directly into my eyes and not take his eyes off of me. To my surprise, after a few minutes of locking his gaze on mine, he began to violently and in a bizarre manner swing his head left to right and right to left to avoid making eye contact with me. I asked him why he was doing that, he said he did not know. My judgment was this: the unclean spirits in him could not bear to look into my eyes, to see the Jesus who dwells in me by baptism, since I was not yet ordained a priest.

Demons fear Jesus Christ, the Anointed Son of God. They fear and are threatened to encounter Him. A certain man with an unclean spirit confessed saying: "What do you want with us, Jesus of Nazareth? Have you come to destroy us? I know who you are—the Holy One of God!" (Mk 1:24, NIV). A priest who was a spiritual mentor to me effects deliverance when he sprinkles holy water on the congregation.

These examples are given to teach us that persons can be delivered from demonic influence through deliverance prayers prayed by the baptized in the Name of Jesus. While a lay person cannot pray in the imperative and command demons to leave another person (i.e., directly give orders such as "Satan, I command you to leave" or "Evil spirit, I cast you out"), they can pray to Christ and ask that by His Holy Name, His Precious Blood, or some other way by some other attributes of Christ that a person be delivered from demonic activity. Of course, it is never within the competency of lay persons to make a judgment that someone is possessed or not because only priests who are trained in exorcism ministry can do this. With humility we need to recognize that great prudence must be used: it will not always be simple to figure out what is happening nor always easy to categorize what is or is not of the demonic and how it can be resolved. We must love and obey Jesus Christ and His Church. We must be taught by God as well as follow the directives of the Church and cooperatively work with her pastors in order to be effective in spiritual warfare.

Human training alone will not suffice to prepare us to wage war on demons, however skilled and knowledgeable a person may be. Spiritual warfare is the domain of the Holy Spirit. Paul says: "For though we walk in the flesh, we are not waging war according to the flesh. For the weapons of our warfare are not of the flesh but have divine power to destroy strongholds. We destroy arguments and every lofty opinion raised against the knowledge of God, and take every thought captive to obey Christ..." (2 Cor 10:3–5, ESV).

Pope Leo XIII composed a deliverance prayer which priests are encouraged to pray when the activity of evil spirits is suspected. According to the Pope's instruction, the laity may also recite this prayer in their own name for themselves, but not allowed to pray this over others. The Church recognizes the need for the people of God to be freed from evil spirits. Therefore she follows in the footsteps of Jesus by inserting deliverance prayers in her prayers and liturgies.

Our Lord Jesus taught us to pray, "Our Father... Deliver us from evil" (Mt 6:9, 13). Jesus prayed to the Father before His Passion saying, "I do not ask you to take them out of the world, but I do ask you to keep them safe from the Evil One" (Jn 17:15, GNT). In the Liturgy of the Eucharist, the Church prays for deliverance from evil, "Deliver us Lord we pray from every evil..." There is a deliverance/exorcism prayer in the Rite of Baptism. This rite should never be omitted by the ordinary ministers of this Sacrament, as sometimes happens.

It is important, in dealing with persons who may be contaminated, that their dignity as God's children be honored in such ministries. In this regard, the confidentiality of these persons should be protected with utmost sensitivity.

The virtue of humility disarms and crushes the pride of demons at all levels of spiritual warfare. Humility is pure truth and it does not fail. Because demons are natural liars, they are easily vanquished by humility and truth. God is quick to respond to the prayer of humble people. Scripture says, "The prayer of a humble person goes past the clouds and keeps on going until it reaches the Lord Most High, where it stays until he answers by seeing that justice is done and that the guilty are punished" (Sir 35:17, GNT).

**Jesus, meek and humble of Heart;
make our hearts like unto Thine (pray three times)**

Exorcism (major)

Spiritual possession

Diabolical possession occurs when a person's body has come under the control of demons, such that they speak and act through the victim's body (not the soul) without the victim's consent. The person in this case is not morally culpable. Possession is the most extreme form of demonic affliction. Signs of possession include: speaking foreign languages or in tongues, extraordinary strength, revealing the unknown, and a variety of other symptoms of varying severity,[152] such as strange and unnatural behaviors, sudden and extreme temperature variations, etc. "God at times also allows extraordinary satanic activity—possession, evil influences—to increase our humility, patience, and mortification."[153]

"Exorcism is directed at the expulsion of demons or the liberation from demonic possession through the spiritual authority which Jesus entrusted to his Church."[154] The Catechism treats the subject of exorcism under "Various forms of sacramental," indicating that exorcisms are not sacraments but sacramentals; meaning, "sacred signs which bear a resemblance to the sacraments."[155] Through them we experience sanctification in the Christian life.[156]

A major exorcism, simply called *Exorcism,* can be performed only by an ordained priest with the permission of the bishop.[157] An in-depth treatment of the topic of exorcism is beyond the scope of this book. Suffice it to say that exorcism is spiritual warfare at its highest. It is the Church's direct confrontation against the highest powers of darkness that wage mortal combat for the damnation of souls.

In this confrontation, the Church is mindful of our Lord's promise: "And I tell you, you are Peter, and on this rock I will build my church, and the gates of hell shall not prevail against it" (Mt 16:18, ESV). Jesus Christ is with His Church at all levels of spiritual warfare; hell has no chance, because we are, "...a chosen people, a royal priesthood, a holy nation, God's special possession, that you may declare the praises of him who called you out of darkness into his wonderful light" (1 Pet 2:9–11, NIV). We are now God's people, washed in His Divine Mercy, and called to "keep away from worldly desires that wage war against the soul" (1 Pet 2:10–11). We are not strangers any more, but citizens with all the saints and God's holy family, "built on the foundation of the apostles and prophets, with Christ Jesus himself as the chief cornerstone" (Eph 2:19–20, NIV). We claim this as our destiny, in the name of Jesus.

Power and authority in spiritual warfare

Those who execute wars must have authority to do so. The first war was the war of the angels. It was a war between obedience and disobedience, truth and lie, and between light and darkness. Michael had the authority of the Blessed Trinity to execute this war. He did and won. God declared war between the woman and the serpent and, between her offspring and the serpent's offspring. God also made it very clear where the victory belongs; He will crush the serpent's head (Gen 3:15).

The Holy Name of Jesus: – The authority of spiritual warfare

All authority in spiritual warfare comes from Jesus, the Second Person of the Most Blessed Trinity. He is God, and the Son of God. He is one with His Father, the Creator of all things. Jesus has power to forgive sins. He is the Lamb who was slain to receive power and riches, wisdom and strength, honor and glory and blessing (Rev 5:12). Jesus has a name above all other names. At the name of Jesus, every knee must bow, and every tongue must confess that He is *Lord*.

The leaders of the people asked Jesus, "By what authority are you doing these things? And who gave you this authority?" (Mt 21:23). Jesus demonstrated great power and authority by casting out demons; raising the dead; curing the lepers, the crippled, the blind, the deaf and the lame; and forgiving sinners; above all, He preached the Kingdom of God.

In posing these questions to Jesus, the chief priests and the elders recognized that people do not exercise authority on their own. Those who speak and act do so in the power and authority of another.

In His public ministry, Jesus acknowledged that He was sent by the Father. He is therefore invested with the Father's authority. "The words that I speak to you I do not speak on my own. The Father who dwells in me is doing his works" (Jn 14:10). Early in John's Gospel, Jesus said: "… a son cannot do anything on his own, but only what he sees his father doing; for what he does, his son will do also" (Jn 5:19).

The authority of Jesus comes from His intimate relationship with His Father. He took that relationship seriously, and so He could say with confidence that the ruler of this world has no power over Him (Jn 14:30). After His resurrection, He declared, "All power in heaven and on earth has been given to me" (Mt 28:18). Saint Paul would say: "Therefore God has highly exalted him and bestowed on him the name that is above every name, so that at the name of Jesus every knee should bow, in heaven and on earth and under the earth, and every tongue confess that Jesus Christ is Lord, to the glory of God the Father" (Phil 2:9–11, ESV).

Jesus conferred this authority on His disciples, and commanded them: "As the Father has sent me, so I send you" (Jn 20:21) to make disciples of all nations by calling sinners to repentance; baptizing them in the name of the Father, and of the Son, and of the Holy Spirit, and teaching them to observe all the commandments (Mt 28:19–20).

The highest authority that can ever be exercised on earth is the authority to save a soul by setting it free from sin. Only the authority of love which lays down its life for another can achieve this. "As the Father knows Me, even so I know the Father; and I lay down My life for the sheep" (Jn 10:15, NKJV; 15:13; see Rev 5:12). This authority was exercised humanly, eternally, exhaustively and definitively by Jesus when He died on the cross, and rose from the dead.

When Jesus healed the paralytic whose sins He forgave, He said to him, "Rise, pick up your stretcher, and go home" (Mt 9:6). The crowds were struck with awe and they praised and glorified God who gave such authority to human beings (Mt 9:8).

Jesus shared this authority from His Father with His disciples in many ways and at different levels. He breathed on the Apostles: "Receive the holy Spirit. Whose sins you forgive are forgiven them, and whose sins you retain are retained" (Jn 20:22–23). To them also He "gave... power and authority over all demons and to cure diseases" (Lk 9:1). To the seventy-two disciples who rejoiced at their successful first evangelization mission, Jesus said: "Behold, I have given you authority to tread on serpents and scorpions, and over all the power of the enemy, and nothing shall hurt you" (Lk 10:19, ESV). Finally, before ascending to His Father and our Father, Jesus said, "And these signs will accompany those who believe: In my name they will drive out demons; they will speak in new tongues" (Mk 16:17, NIV). This is a clear reference to all Christians. All are included in Jesus' final prayer before the Passion; all those who profess faith in Him through their message (Jn 17:20).

The authority of Christians

The authority of Christians comes from Christ, as long as they remain obedient and faithful to His commandments (Jn 14:15). Jesus tells us that apart from Him, we can do nothing (Jn 15:5). To engage in successful spiritual warfare, we must possess and exercise authority greater than our own over the demons. Since no servant is greater than his master, a servant is content with exercising his master's authority. Believers in Christ share in and exercise the authority He bestowed on the Church through the Apostles (Mt 16:18–20; Jn 14:12). This authority essentially is to bring souls out of darkness into the wonderful light of conversion, reconciliation, friendship and salvation in Christ (1 Thes 5:5). Jesus promised, "You will receive power when the Holy Spirit comes upon you" (Acts 1:8).

Peter and John were arraigned before the Sanhedrin, because at the "Beautiful Gate" in Jerusalem, they had healed the man crippled from birth by invoking the name of Jesus. They boldly answered, "Salvation is found in no one else, for there is no other name under heaven given to mankind by which we must be saved" (Acts 4:12, NIV).

Our authority over demons at the six levels of spiritual warfare is always exercised in the name of Jesus, the Lord. Demons cannot deny the identity of Jesus, nor can they challenge His authority. We see Jesus' power and authority in action when He met the man with an unclean spirit; the spirit said: "What do you want with us, Jesus of Nazareth? Have you come to destroy us? I know who you are—the Holy One of God!" (Mk 1:24, NIV).

Fear degrades the authority of God's love in Christians. A Christian who is afraid should never engage in spiritual warfare. Judas Maccabeus, renowned for his many victories, was "panic-stricken" and "discouraged" as he readied to engage Bacchides in battle. Besides, his army, out of fear, melted away. Against all advice from his own comrades, he proceeded into battle. He not only lost the battle, he was killed (1 Mac 9:7–18).

The authority of Christians in spiritual warfare comes from their intimate relationship with Jesus Christ. This authority grows as we immerse ourselves in serious daily prayer, living an authentic spiritual life rooted in the truth revealed by God in Sacred Scripture, taught and handed down to us by the Apostles in the Church; not "truth" according to our thoughts and feelings, nor according to the laws made by political establishments: supreme courts, presidents, federal and state legislators, and so on. Their laws and policies are oftentimes pagan, promulgated without any regard to natural and divine law. They are designed to convert their citizens into pagans and enemies of God at the expense of the salvation of their souls. But we are citizens of Heaven and members of His family "built on the foundation of the apostles and prophets, with Christ Jesus himself as the chief cornerstone (Eph 2:19–20, NIV). Faithful Christians, even in their weaknesses, are warriors with the authority of the Spirit (Joel 4:6). As they pray in the power of the Holy Spirit, they call upon Christ to set persons free from bondage. It is Christ who sets persons free in response to the prayers of Christians.

Demons recognize and know Jesus as, "Jesus of Nazareth," and also as, "the Holy One of God" (Mk 1:24). However, demons cannot accept or proclaim that "Jesus Christ is Lord" (Phil 2:11). This statement of faith and allegiance, the most powerful statement in all of Sacred Scripture, is an acceptance of the total submission to the authority and the lordship of the Son of God. Demons, because of their immense pride, cannot willingly surrender to Jesus. They will not do it! The authority believers have over demons is rooted in this proclamation of faith, that Jesus is Lord. Paul says that, "… no one can say, 'Jesus is Lord,' except by the Holy Spirit" (1 Cor 12:3). Our power over demons derives from the fact that we have surrendered to Jesus Christ as our Lord and God, and as our Savior.

Saving faith for Paul means to confess the lordship of Jesus Christ through our words, and to believe in our heart that He has been raised from the dead by the Father (Rom 10:9). The evidence of our belief is that our actions conform to those of Christ. Anyone, therefore, who does not accept the Lordship of Jesus Christ, has no power over demons. This acceptance of faith when operational in a person can be manifested in different ways, essentially through hearing and obeying the voice of the Good Shepherd (Jn 10:27) and renouncing sin. Jesus also said He will lead other sheep who are outside the fold, so that they too will hear His voice and be under one shepherd (Jn 10:16).

The authority of Satan

Does Satan have authority? If so, where does his authority come from? Jesus said He saw Satan fall from heaven like lightning (Lk 10:18), meaning, Satan lost all connection with Heaven by his disobedience. Revelation 12:7 tells us that the angels fought a war in heaven. Michael and the holy Angels fought against the dragon and its angels and drove them out of heaven. Satan and its demons are cut off eternally from God, who has supreme power and authority over all creation. Satan does not have any authority whatsoever from God, except of course the permission to tempt us, and no more. Where then does Satan get its power to torment and hold God's children in bondage?

The power and sting of Satan is sin. It wields this power over those who choose to disobey God through sin and live in sin. Sin dehumanizes us, and makes us subjects of Satan and its demons. As a general rule, the power Satan has over a person is the power that person has given over to it through sin. God and Satan are not equals by any means; God is, **God the Almighty**; but Satan is a creature. God's power is powerful power; Satan's power is powerless power. It can only act within the limits of God's permission and ordinance, for the fulfillment of His eternal purpose for man. Satan cannot kill us, but it can make our earthly life as miserable as possible. Repentance frees us from Satan's power, and restores us to grace in Christ. Repentance is not an option; it cannot be avoided without grave harm to the soul.

There are cases, however, and by the permission of God alone, where some holy persons have suffered much in the hands of demons: Saint Padre Pio, Saint John Mary Vianney, and many others serve as examples. This is a mystery; may God be glorified in His mysteries.

The role of faith in spiritual warfare

Faith in Jesus Christ heals and delivers us from all evil; it eliminates fear. The Apostles realized their great deficiency in faith, so they prayed and implored our Lord to increase their faith. In Matthew 17:17–20, a man came and knelt down before Jesus imploring Him to cure his son, who was a lunatic and suffers severely; His disciples had earlier failed to cure the boy. At that, Jesus said: "O faithless and perverse generation, how long will I be with you? How long will I endure you? Bring him here to me." After Jesus had driven out the demon and cured the boy, His disciples asked Him: "Why could we not drive it out?" Jesus replied: "Because of your little faith. Amen, I say to you, if you have faith the size of a mustard seed... Nothing will be impossible for you." All the baptized, and all called by Confirmation into the mission of Christ, should pray daily for an increase in faith. We cannot make excuses or devise clever arguments to explain our lack of faith.

Jesus often acknowledged the role of faith in the recipients of His healing. He acknowledged the faith of the Centurion, whose servant He healed: "I tell you, not even in Israel have I found such faith" (Lk 7:9). To the Canaanite woman whose daughter was healed, Jesus said: "O woman, great is your faith! Let it be done for you as you wish" (Mt 15:28). To the woman afflicted with hemorrhages for twelve years, who believed in her heart: "If I but touch his clothes, I shall be cured" (Mk 5:28). To her, Jesus said, "Daughter, your faith has saved you. Go in peace and be cured of your affliction" (Mk 5:34). But in His home town of Nazareth, Jesus could not work mighty deeds; their lack of faith amazed Him (Mk 6:3–6).

Some signs of lack of faith in a person are fear and worry. When in fear, we should not engage in spiritual warfare. We should manifest our fears to Jesus in prayer, and try to understand why we are afraid. We should consult with our spiritual directors to help guide us in discerning the underlying issues. The presence of fear means we are lacking in love. Jesus says over and over again, "Do not be afraid... little flock" (Lk 12:32). As we reflect and examine ourselves and our fears, we should ask, are we allowing God to love us? It is God's perfect love that dispels all our fears (1 Jn 4:18).

Let us pray:

God, all-powerful Father,
Fill your people with the light of your Holy Spirit,
That, safe from every enemy,
We may rejoice in singing your praises.
Grant this through Christ our Lord. Amen.[158]

Onward into battle, Christian soldier

Saint John Paul II gave a prophetic speech that should cause every Christian to wake up to the reality of the challenge that faces us today. He said:

> We are now standing in the face of the greatest historical confrontation humanity has ever experienced. I do not think the wide circle of the American society, or the wide circle of the Christian community realizes this fully. We are now facing the final confrontation between the Church and the anti-church, between the Gospel and the anti-gospel, between Christ and the antichrist. This confrontation lies within the plans of Divine Providence. It is therefore, in God's Plan, and it must be a trial which the Church must take up, and face courageously.[159]

He also said:

> We must prepare ourselves to suffer great trials before long, such as will demand of us a disposition to give up even life, and a total dedication to Christ and for Christ... With your and my prayer it is possible to mitigate this tribulation, but it is no longer possible to avert it, because only thus can the Church be effectively renewed. How many times has the renewal of the Church sprung from blood! This time, too, it will not be otherwise. We must be strong and prepared, and trust in Christ and His Mother, and be very, very assiduous in praying the Rosary.[160]

Saint John Paul II's prophetic statement to the Bishops of the United States and to the world speaks directly to the Christian soldier. Chosen and marked by Baptism to belong to God, and drawn by Confirmation into the saving mission of Jesus Christ, the Christian is called to reflect and respond. John Paul's words were followed by those of his predecessor, Pope Emeritus, Benedict XVI, who said in his opening homily at the 2005 papal conclave: "We are building a dictatorship of relativism that does not recognize anything as definitive and whose ultimate standard consists solely of one's own ego and desires."[161]

The increasing secularization and "the dictatorship of relativism," the dethronement of God and His laws in every facet of society, the vicious and diabolical attacks on human life and dignity, the acceptance and promotion of immoral lifestyles, and the hypocrisy and double standards in religion, are becoming normative experiences of daily life. Faced with these massive onslaughts of new paganism and evils, Saint Paul says to the Christian soldier, "The hour has already come for you to wake up from your slumber... The night is nearly over; the day is almost here. So let us put aside the deeds of darkness and put on the armor of light" (Rom 13:11–12, NIV).

We must put on the armor that is the Lord Jesus Christ, and make no provision for fleshly desires if we are to survive this imminent confrontation (Rom 13:14), and march onward into battle successfully. It is indeed the confrontation between the Gospel and the anti-gospel, between Christ and the antichrist, between good and evil, and between truth and falsehood. We must choose to be holy, as we have been chosen by God in Christ to be holy and sinless before Him (Eph 1:4). We cannot serve God and the world at the same time.

Many Christians seem to be totally oblivious of this mortal combat; they allow themselves to be carried away by all kinds of false teachings and lifestyles contrary to revealed truth in Sacred Scripture. Jesus hinted at this development when He said: "You are misled because you do not know the scriptures or the power of God" (Mt 22:29). One reason for this state of affairs is that many have lost touch with their true dignity as sons and daughters in Christ. This problem evokes the subject of self-knowledge, so indispensable in acquiring humility, and waging successful spiritual warfare.

Without self-knowledge, we will lack humility. And without humility we cannot lay down our lives for Christ, should it be required of us. Our identity as sons and daughters of the Father in Christ comes from our relationship with God. The real questions confronting us as we undertake the mission to re-evangelize the world are these: Do we know who we are as sons and daughters of the Father? Do we act out of this identity? Do our actions, words and thoughts reflect this knowledge? If our answers to these questions are positively *yes,* we will have the confidence and holy boldness to challenge evil in defense of Gospel truth, no matter the consequences. But if we are disconnected from the knowledge of our true selves; we will be in spiritual darkness, and fear will rule our lives. We will lack confidence and will be discouraged in following Christ, even to Calvary.

The faith-filled Christian, one who has made the resolve to follow Christ, must strive to avoid sin at all cost. Sin is a personal act; it cannot be identified with Satan.[162] Though Satan's activities certainly lead to sin, he cannot be held responsible for men's sins. "He is distinct from the evil which he causes to be committed."[163] For this reason, John the Evangelist says, "Everyone who commits sin is a child of the devil; for the devil has been sinning from the beginning. The Son of God was revealed for this purpose, to destroy the works of the devil. Those who have been born of God do not sin…" (1 Jn 3:8–9, NRSV).

Sin, always an act of disobedience to God, breeds fear. Fear is never of God; it is a powerful tool of the evil one to derail our journey to God. John says: "There is no fear in love, but perfect love casts out fear. For fear has to do with punishment, and whoever fears has not been perfected in love" (1 Jn 4:18, ESV). When we are afraid, we should do well to investigate our fears as suggested earlier. Whatever we are afraid of has power over us. Fear will limit our openness to God and make us fear Him for the wrong reasons. We should talk to Jesus about our fears; He is the Father's love and mercy to us. He comes to love and heal us.

The Armor of God for Spiritual Combat

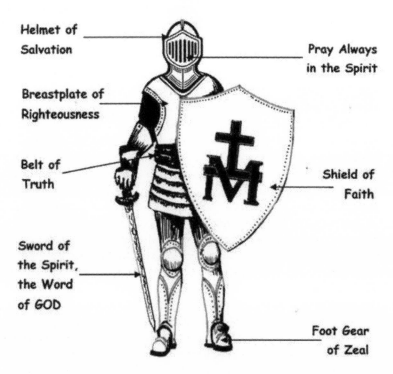

Figure 4:   *The Christian Soldier in the full Armor of God*

Prayer for Spiritual Warfare

"Blessed be the LORD, my rock,
who trains my hands for battle, my fingers for war;
My safe guard and my fortress, my stronghold, my deliverer,
My shield, in whom I trust…" (Ps 144:1–2).

The Armor of God explained

Helmet of salvation
"And take the helmet of salvation" (Eph 6:17).

Every soldier must cover his head to protect the brain and the senses, and his life. The helmet has saved, not only the lives of countless soldiers in battle, but also their ability to function as human beings. The spiritual helmet protects the mind, our ability to discern and to judge right from wrong, our ability to reflect and contemplate, and our ability to reason, hear and see. At baptism we were anointed on our forehead and ears and mouth with sacred oil with the sign of salvation, the cross. The crown of our head was anointed with Sacred Chrism, and we were conformed to Christ as priest, prophet and king. This means that our lives are now one with Christ as priests. We can now choose to offer our bodies as a living sacrifice, in union with Christ, the Priest, holy and acceptable to God, our spiritual worship. In a real and sacramental way the helmet of salvation was put on us. It protects our intellect from Satan's lies and falsehood. Our thoughts mold us, and they influence our actions. Saint Paul warns us not to conform our minds to worldly things. Rather, we are to be transformed by allowing our minds to be renewed. We should have the mind of Jesus, constantly pre-occupied with the Father's Kingdom. This is how we discern the good, holy and perfect will of God in every situation (Rom 12:1–2).

The New Age garbage, which includes *Harry Porter*, many TV shows and children's games, coupled with the immoral and bad examples in the secular media, are corrupting the true faith in the minds of young people and putting their salvation at risk. Paul expressed fear that just as the evil one "deceived Eve by his cunning, your thoughts may be corrupted from a sincere (and pure) commitment to Christ" (2 Cor 11:3). Holy vocations, especially to the priesthood and religious life fail to be realized, because the minds of young people have been corrupted with lies and falsehood regarding the teachings of Jesus Christ. The faith handed down to us by the Apostles is dangerously being corrupted when we water down the truth of God's Word, and conform our thoughts to public opinion and political correctness. To be saved, we must obey the truth as taught by God. Heavenly things must be our focus, not earthly ones (Col 3:2). Peter says we should encircle our minds and set our hopes on the grace Christ brings to us at His revelation. Attaining the holiness of the Father must be our first mission in this life (1 Pet 1:13–16).

Pray always in the Spirit
"With all prayer and supplication, pray at every opportunity in the Spirit. To that end, be watchful with all perseverance and supplication for all the holy ones" (Eph 6:18).

Prayer is the very life of the Christian soldier as water is the life of the fish. Jesus commands us to watch and pray to avoid sinning when we are tempted (Mk 14:38). In order that we might pray well in the spirit, our mouth and ears were anointed with oil at baptism. Prayer is hearing God the Father speak and talking to Him in a loving friendly way. It is in the dialogue of prayer that the Christian learns to hear God's voice, to recognize Him (Jn 10:27; 1 Sam 3:10), and experience His love. In speaking to God, we share our joys and sorrows; we ask questions and receive instructions on how to live the spiritual life. We are pilgrims on the way of faith; sometimes we stray and need to get back on track. The faith walk is not rosy; we face many challenges and dangers. The lips that pray have hearts that listen. Paul tells us not to fear and be anxious, but by prayer offered in gratitude, we talk to God. Then His peace and joy that is beyond understanding will fill our minds and hearts in Christ Jesus (Phil 4:4–9). Without this peace of mind and heart, we cannot successfully wage spiritual battles. Only peaceful hearts receive God's revelation and instructions.

Battle survival depends heavily on reliable communication with the Commander-in-Chief and with fellow believer-comrades in the body of Christ. We must communicate, i.e., be connected and be in relationship with the Commander-in-Chief through prayer. He has the battle plan and the war strategy for victory. Jesus wants us to remain in Him as He remains in us. Like a branch on the vine, so the Christian soldier must remain in Jesus. Those who listen and remain in Him will bear much fruit; they will be victorious always (Jn 15).

Breastplate of righteousness
"So stand fast… clothed with righteousness as a breastplate" (Eph 6:14).
The breastplate protects the vital organs, such as the heart, lungs, ribs, the intestines and so on. The righteousness of God in us is Jesus Christ through whom we have been reconciled with the Father. We do not have any righteousness of our own apart from Christ. His righteousness gives us confident access to God's throne. Jesus is God's power and wisdom in us. "The LORD has success in store for the upright of heart" (Prov 2:7). Jesus is the totality of our righteousness before God. He is the righteousness who intercedes for us before the Heavenly Father (1 Jn 2:1). The breastplate was placed on us sacramentally at baptism, when the priest anointed our breast with holy oil making a sign of the cross. Without Him, we are bound to fail. Our boast then must be in Christ Jesus (1 Cor 1:30–31). The psalmist says: "The upright of heart shall follow the just judgment of God" (Ps 94:15). Jesus said that those who are pure of heart shall see God (Mt 5:8). Jesus is our sanctification and redemption, He is our righteousness and victory; Paul tells us to put Him on (Rom 13:14).

Shield of faith
"In all circumstances, hold faith as a shield, to quench all (the) flaming arrows of the evil one" (Eph 6:16).

The shield stops arrows, stones, and all projectiles and missiles shot at a soldier. The devil hates Christian soldiers, so it bombards us with temptations, lies and deceptions to make us disobey God and be separated from Him. Our faith is the shield to stop all that. Faith comes through hearing God's word (Rom 10:17). God's word is spirit and life. It is food for the Christian soul, even as it was for Jesus. Saint Jerome said: "Ignorance of the Scripture is ignorance of Christ." To have God's word, understand it, and be rooted in it is to know the Lord Jesus Christ. He is our shield (Ps 3:4; 33:20). Every word spoken by God is a shield to the Christian who takes refuge in Him (Prov 30:5–6), so that we walk by faith and not by sight. Faith does not only ward off evil, it opens the door for us to be filled with the strength of the Holy Spirit.

To grow in faith like Abraham (Gen 22), we must obey God's commandments with our whole heart. Jesus said those who love Him must keep His commandments (Jn 14:15). This is how we are begotten by God as His children, as John says, "Whoever is begotten by God conquers the world. And the victory that conquers the world is our faith" (1 Jn 5:4). Faith makes us pleasing to God (Heb 11:6); it makes all things possible.

Belt of truth
"So stand fast with your loins girded in truth" (Eph 6:14).

Truths bring freedom; lies put us in bondage. A belt around our waist makes us ready for contest. It gives confidence, and helps put all our energy into our upper body. Weight lifters know the value of belts around their waist before championships.

Satan is the father of lies; he uses deception, misinformation and half-truths to create confusion. His words may sound like truths, but they are not truths. Satan's lies say that Jesus did not really multiply the loaves of bread, He simply made everyone bring their loaves and share them with others; that the miracles of Jesus were merely devices to attract people and did not really happen; that there is really no hell, and that everyone simply goes to Heaven, irrespective of the choices they make and the lifestyles they live. Satan's lies say that the Holy Eucharist is only a symbol, and it is not really the Flesh and Blood of Jesus Christ, who at the Last Supper took bread, blessed and broke it, and gave it to His disciples saying, "Take and eat; this is my body" (Mt 26:26). Then He took a chalice filled with the fruit of the vine. He gave thanks and gave it to them saying, "Drink from it, all of you. For this is My blood of the new covenant, which is shed for many for the remission of sins" (Mt 26:27–28, NKJV). Divine life is received

● ● ●

when we worthily eat and drink the Flesh and Blood of Jesus Christ in the Most Holy Eucharist (Jn 6:53). Jesus is God's word made Flesh and Blood for us.

Satan comes to steal God's word sown in our hearts, so that we die spiritually and bear no fruit for God's glory (Jn 10:10; Mt 13:19). If he fails to steal it, he then poisons God's Word in us upon which our salvation depends. He blurs the difference between truth and falsehood, and good and evil; he tells us to just be nice, rather than be holy and perfect like God; he tells us that objective truth does not exist, and that whatever we feel is the truth becomes the truth; he leads us to believe that popular culture is the new gospel, and that the Church's divinely inspired and transmitted teachings are out of touch with reality and public opinion, and should be archived in museums.

Lying is Satan's native tongue. He deceived Adam and Eve with lies, and they ate from the tree of good and evil, which they were forbidden by God to eat. So if we must eat from the tree of perfection, which is the Cross of Christ our Savior, we must wear the belt of truth always. Jesus is truth! Lies make us spiritually closed, blind and numb to sin; it wounds our humanity. Truths make us open, vigilant and sensitive to the presence of the Spirit of truth. Satan knows Scripture and can quote it easily. But the question is whose voice is speaking the Scripture? Is it the voice of the Good Shepherd who laid down His life for the sheep? Or is it the voice of the deceiver? Jesus said, "My sheep hear my voice; I know them, and they follow me" (Jn 10:27).

Paul says we must put aside falsehood and speak only the truth (Eph 4:25). Evangelization is about proclaiming the truth that Jesus died, and God raised Him from the dead. Evangelization will fail if we do not uphold and proclaim the truth revealed by Jesus Christ, and handed down to us by the Apostles. Any compromise of the truth will kill the true faith and endanger souls. Paul keeps speaking and says, stop lying and put away anger, fury, malice, slander and obscene language from your mouths, because the old self is dead and we have put on the Lord Jesus Christ through our baptism (Col 3:8–10). Jesus confronted and defeated the Deceiver with the truth of God's word which He received, and which He is.

Foot gear of zeal
"And your feet shod in readiness for the gospel of peace" (Eph 6:15).
Without boots, a soldier can easily be disabled by a stone or nail on the ground. He cannot fight without boots on. Zeal is spiritual mobility for God's works. The Christian soldier must be swift and mobile in his/her foot gear, taking up different tactical positions as is necessary. Prophet Isaiah says, "How beautiful upon the mountains are the feet of him who

brings glad tidings, Announcing peace, bearing good news, announcing salvation, and saying to Zion, 'Your God is King!'" (Is 52:7). The wisdom of Proverbs 4:26–27 says: "Survey the path for your feet, and let all your ways be sure. Turn neither to right nor to left, keep your foot far from evil." The Letter to the Hebrews 10:12–14 says that, Jesus, who sits forever at God's right hand after His victorious sacrifice that destroyed sin, now waits for His enemies to be put beneath His feet. Likewise, in union with Jesus; our feet, like those of Mother Mary in combat boots, are destined to crush the serpent's head in warfare (Gen 3:15).

Sword of the Spirit: the Word of God
"And take... the sword of the Spirit, which is the word of God" (Eph 6:17).
A soldier without offensive capability will ultimately fall and be eliminated. What soldier goes into battle without his rifle fully loaded to destroy the enemy before the enemy destroys him. When I played active soccer, my coach drummed a maxim into our heads during team's training sessions. He told us repeatedly, "The best defense is to have a strong offense." God has given us the most powerful offensive armor for spiritual warfare: the sword of the spirit, God's Word that is spirit and life. God's Word became flesh in Jesus Christ, who is the Bread of life. God's Word spoken with faith destroys demonic strongholds. Demons like to dwell in people, because they know God dwells in us. We should never give demons any chance to dwell in us for any reason. We must strive to close all the open doors to bondage mentioned in this book. We are the Father's precious sons and daughters. We must be armed for victory with the Bible, because Jesus was armed with it.

The Letter to the Hebrews 4:12 says: "The word of God is alive and active, sharper than any double-edged sword. It cuts all the way through, to where soul and spirit meet, to where joints and marrow come together. It judges the desires and thoughts of the heart" (Heb 4:12, GNT). In his vision of Christ, the Warrior in Revelation 1:16, John sees Jesus' right hand holding seven stars, and a two-edged sharp sword comes out of his mouth and his face is as brilliant as the sun at its brightest. "Out of his mouth came a sharp sword to strike the nations" (Rev 19:15). "He wore a cloak that had been dipped in blood, and his name was called the Word of God" (Rev 19:13).

The totality of the Armor of God for spiritual warfare is *holiness!* God says: "Be holy, for I, the LORD your God, am holy" (Lev 19:2, 11:45; 1 Pet 1:15). The Armor of God was placed over us in a real and sacramental way when at baptism a white garment was placed over us and the priest said, "Bring this garment unstained into the everlasting life of Heaven." We are the great multitude before God's throne and before the Lamb clothed in white. We are the ones who have survived the great testing and tribulations of this world, and through perseverance have washed our robes and made them white in the Blood of the Lamb (Rev 7).

The laity and spiritual warfare

By virtue of baptism, the laity are called in their own way to spiritual warfare in union with Jesus Christ, who is Priest, Prophet and King, for the salvation of souls. Their involvement in spiritual warfare, especially if done publicly, should adhere to diocesan guidelines and that of the Holy See. There are daily spiritual battles we all must fight, irrespective of whether we are laity or clergy, and irrespective of whether it is done privately or publicly. Jesus mentioned that the first sign believers will see as they proclaim the Gospel to all nations is that demons will be cast out in His name (Mk 16:17). He said this in the context of commissioning His disciples. This means that the laity can exercise this charism of the Holy Spirit in the Church within the guidelines permitted by the Apostles and their successors—the bishops of the Catholic Church.

Exorcism is exclusively reserved for priest(s) duly delegated by the local bishop to exercise this ministry in accord with the Code of Cannon Law #1172, and the instructions contained in *Inde Ab Aliquot Annis*.[164] This document states: "that no member of the Christian faithful can use the formula of exorcism against Satan and the fallen angels, extracted from that which was made law by Leo XIII."

Father Gabriele Amorth, the chief exorcist of the diocese of Rome and Fr. Francis Martin have clarified the third point in *Inde Ab Aliquot Annis*. They said that the laity's private use of Pope Saint Leo XIII's prayer of exorcism against demonic influence is not part of the restriction imposed by the Congregation for the Doctrine of the Faith (CDF) instruction. This means that the laity can use this prayer privately as directed by Pope Saint Leo XIII himself. Cardinal Joseph Ratzinger, then Prefect of the CDF, also stated that the restrictions in the third point of the CDF document apply to public assemblies. In any circumstances, public and private, lay persons are not permitted to pray this prayer over another.

It is not permitted for the lay faithful to seek to know the names of demons by addressing them directly, or expel them. Such actions are reserved for exorcists and priests who by priestly ordination are vested with the authority to do so, but in addition, are equipped and knowledgeable in such ministry. Albeit, seeking to know the names of demons does not necessarily guarantee their expulsion. This approach in my opinion is not necessary, and can be a fruitless exercise. Any information we seek in our combat with demons we surely can receive from the Holy Spirit, if we ask Him. Jesus said if we ask we will receive (Mt 7:7). We ask God in order to receive; we do not ask demons. God is our compassionate and generous Father, who does not ration His gifts. Information gotten from demons is potentially loaded with problems; only a priest trained in exorcism should deal with such matters.

Jesus Christ, the Eternal High Priest, is the Chief and only Exorcist. He is God and has the authority to say to a demon, "What is your name?" (Lk 8:30). We should go to Jesus if we need information about dealing with demons. He promised that the Holy Spirit will reveal to us all truth (Jn 16:13). The Holy Spirit is the revealer of mysteries (Dan 2:47). He reveals to us things that are to come, and what is necessary for our salvation. Allowing demons to speak to us directly, we who are God's precious children, is giving them honor they do not deserve. Demons are damned creatures; they cannot but obey Jesus Christ. Anyone who is harassed by evil spirits should turn to Jesus, and should take his/her relationship with Jesus seriously. Only Jesus Christ knows how to deal with demons. He created them good, but through pride they chose to be evil; they now belong eternally to hell by an act of Divine justice. Jesus has given the Church the authority to deal with them. Let us turn to the Father, as Jesus taught, and pray that He deliver us from the evil one.

The contemplative emphasis of this book invites us to cultivate a one-on-one relationship with the risen Lord. We should take seriously the celebration of the Sacraments, especially the Holy Eucharist and Penance. The divine power of Jesus Christ is active in the Sacraments. Too much emphasis on the satanic is a distraction. It is not spiritually healthy. It is important to remember that demonic infestation for which one seeks deliverance occurs through sin. The emphasis for the Christian is to live a holy life.

Holiness of life will keep the doors to the demonic permanently closed, and open them perpetually to Christ's love in our lives and our family trees. The Christian faithful is invited to pray for God's intervention by asking the intercession of the Most Blessed Virgin Mary, Saint Michael, Saint Raphael and Saint Gabriel the Archangels, the Apostles and the Saints even in spiritual battles of Christians against evil spirits.[165]

The faithful should center their lives on our Eucharistic Lord, and strive to grow in faith in the pursuit of perfection. Jesus said: "Everything is possible to one who has faith" (Mk 9:23). "Suffice it to say that the best offensive and defensive protection against demonic interference in the laity's exercise of [Christian discipleship] is to live a holy life."[166] Father Amorth cites how Saint Catherine of Siena brought about the freedom of a demoniac through her prayer of faith when an exorcist could not. Saint Catherine's prayer "was not an exorcism, [or a direct prayer of deliverance]; she was neither an exorcist nor a priest. But she was a saint"[167] The lay faithful are called to be saints.

Tactics and weapons of spiritual warfare

To wage a successful spiritual warfare, self-knowledge and God-knowledge are necessary. Self-knowledge helps us to grow in humility, the virtue and weapon demons fear the most in believers. Self-knowledge helps us know our strengths and weaknesses, and will help us guard against the pitfalls of pride. It will protect and fortify us against the devil's tricks.

Scupoli says that when the subtle serpent perceives that we are committed to a life of holiness, "and sees all our desires tending to God alone, fortified against ordinary satanic delusions, he transforms himself into an angel of light, he urges us to attain perfection, hurrying us on blindly and without the least regard for our own weakness."[168] The devil fills our minds with holy thoughts supported with Scripture passages and the examples of great saints. He does this to make us fall through an indiscreet and precipitous fervor. He inspires us with extreme fasting and mortifications, giving us a false impression that we have done well and are advancing in the likeness of Christ, only to pull us down through vanity. When we have become dispirited, we become slothful in fulfilling our spiritual exercises in the practice of virtue.[169] We become blinded by a presumptuous optimism, and "carried away by an indiscreet zeal for suffering, they fall into the snare they themselves have helped to contrive, and they become the scorn of devils."[170] One effective means against these delusions and deceptions of the devil is to have recourse to a spiritual director or a confessor. We need to exercise moderation in external and internal penances, while leaving room for necessary spiritual growth. Obedience, not self-will, is the key to victory.

The Sacraments and sacramentals

Sacraments
Jesus said He is at work, because the Father is at work (Jn 5:17). Christ's greatest work is securing our salvation. He accomplished this work by His suffering, death and resurrection. Christ gave us the Sacraments, and is always present and at work in the Church's liturgy. The holy sacrifice of the Mass is the supreme sacrament. In the Holy Eucharist, the real and substantial presence of Christ is most evident by faith. Because of the

presence and action of Christ in the sacraments, they are efficacious in bestowing freedom and healing.

The primary purpose of the Sacraments is our sanctification. They also build up the body of Christ. Through them we offer to God our worship and praise. The sacraments, because of the power of Christ in them, cause deliverance and healing in personal and generational bondage. In them, we encounter the same Christ who went about doing good deeds and healing those oppressed by demons, raising the dead and curing lepers; Jesus who says to the sick, the lame, and the lepers, "Your faith has saved you" (Lk 17:19); and who rebuked the unclean spirits saying, "Mute and deaf spirit, I command you: come out of him and never enter him again!" (Mk 9:25). We should take care to celebrate the Sacraments worthily, especially the Holy Eucharist and Penance.

Sacramentals

These are sacred signs which bear the resemblance of the sacraments. Sacramentals produce spiritual effects on us through the intercession of the Church; they dispose the faithful to receive the chief effects of the sacraments; and they make holy various human activities.[171]

Because of their spiritual effects, sacramentals are powerful weapons against demonic influences. They render holy human activities, places, and objects such as crucifixes, rosaries, the Brown Scapulars, holy Bibles, holy water, salt, blessed oils, and other religious items. Some of these—blessed salt, water and oils, etc.—, can be consumed with food and drinks. Exorcisms, prayers, novenas, and other devotionals are regarded as sacramentals.

A well-known scapular miracle story occurred in May of 1957. A Carmelite priest in Germany published the unusual story of how the Scapular saved a home from fire. An entire row of homes had caught fire in Westboden, Germany. The pious inhabitants of a two family home, seeing the fire, immediately fastened a Scapular to the main door of the house. Sparks flew over it and around it, but the house remained unharmed. Within five hours, twenty-two homes had been reduced to ashes. The one structure, which stood undamaged amidst the destruction, was that which had the Scapular attached to its door. The hundreds of people who came to see the place our Lady had saved are eye-witnesses to the power of the Scapular and the intercession of the Blessed Virgin Mary.

David's stone that brought down Goliath of Gath represents the power of a sacramental to bring down the evil that threatens God's people in our world today. It is advised that we have sacramentals blessed by a Catholic priest before they are used, to impart the grace for which we wear and use them.

The virtues as weapons of spiritual warfare

God prepared us for spiritual warfare at the start of our spiritual journey at Baptism. He gave us the gifts of faith, hope, and love in seed form. As we mature spiritually, we are to fan these gifts into flame so that they burn brightly and bear holy fruits in our lives. Virtues are weapons available to us for our daily battles with the kingdom of darkness.

Our *faith* grows as we listen to God's Word. Faith in Christ shields us from the fiery darts of doubt which the evil one shoots at us all the time, especially in moments of desolation. The enemy uses fear, discouragement and despair as effective weapons to make us lose confidence in God our Father, and in ourselves. But when Christ dwells in our hearts by faith (Eph 3:17), nothing of this world can shake our inmost calm. Faith makes us like the rock of Gibraltar. When all else fail, faith does not. Faith makes all things possible. Saint Cyril of Jerusalem said: "In learning and professing the faith, you must accept and retain only the Church's present tradition, confirmed as it is by the Scriptures." He enjoins us to keep unblemished the faith we have received, until the coming of our Lord Jesus Christ.[172] For according to Saint John Fisher, "He who disbelieves even a single article of the faith is justly held guilty of disbelief in the whole faith."

The virtue of *hope* helps us overcome dangers, by pulling us up beyond the struggles of the present moment. By hope we know that we are not alone, and that victory awaits us on the horizon. Scripture speaks of Jesus' hope in His suffering: "For the sake of the joy that lay before him he endured the cross, despising its shame, and has taken his seat at the right of the throne of God" (Heb 12:2). We are victorious when we fix our eyes on Jesus, our joy, our hope and our King. Hope never disappoint, because God's love in Christ has been lavished on us in the Holy Spirit (Rom 5:5). Our hope lies in the promises of Jesus, who said He will go to prepare a place for us, and He will return to take us to Himself (Jn 14:3). "Whatever you ask in my name, this I will do, that the Father may be glorified in the Son. If you ask me anything in my name, I will do it" (Jn 14:13–14, ESV). We should arm ourselves with all His promises. We are born for combat. We are destined for victory. Paul says that even when we were dead in our sins and fleshly desires, Jesus gave us divine life along with him. He forgave us, cancelling Satan's bondage against us, "with its legal claims, which was opposed to us, he also removed it from our midst, nailing it to the cross; despoiling the principalities and the powers, he made a public spectacle of them, leading them away in triumph by it" (Col 2:14–15). This victory is the fruit of God's love.

Love is the most perfect of the virtues, because love never fails (1 Cor 13:8). "God is love" (1 Jn 4:16). Love casts out all fear and helps us stay focused and rooted in God's word: "I am with you always" (Mt 28:20),

Jesus said. "I will not leave you orphans" (Jn 14:18); "You are precious in my eyes" (Is 43:4). "Remain in me, as I also remain in you... If you remain in me and I in you, you will bear much fruit; apart from me you can do nothing" (Jn 15:4–5, NIV). "As the Father loves me, so I also love you. Remain in my love" (Jn 15:9). Paul prays that we all be rooted and grounded in love (Eph 3:17).

We grow in the theological virtues of faith, hope and love by faithfulness to our states of life in holiness, and by the constant surrender to God's will. The virtues call us to live an intense friendship with Jesus. We are Jesus' friends if we keep His commands (Jn 15:14).

The daily spiritual exercises of prayer, personal self-reflection and recollection, meditation on God's word and His mysteries, and a life of charity towards our neighbor will foster an intense friendship with Jesus. Life of personal chastity and purity in imitation of the sinless life, and heroic virtues of our Blessed Mother Mary will draw us ever closer to the compassionate Heart of her Son, Jesus.

Commanding the high grounds

In any warfare, securing the high grounds is a guarantee for victory. This is why nations spend huge sums of money on aerial warfare. These include the development and use of stealth fighters and bombers, as well as drones and surveillance technology. Aerial warfare has expanded into the arena of space, with manned and unmanned overt and covert operations in space stations and satellites circling the globe all the time. These military activities by different nations are geared toward gaining the high ground advantage.

In Old Testament and primitive warfare, once a nation had gained the mountain heights, that nation was sure to win the battle. The Israelis seized the Golan Heights because it was a strategic high ground in their war with Syria. This was a deciding factor in the Six-Day War of 1967, between Israel and the Arabs.[173]

The contemplative faithful, like the eagle that soars high close to the sun and sees everything, also soars high in the spiritual mansions close to God and sees as God sees. As we mature in contemplative prayer, we become seasoned, skilled, sensitive and alert to situations of spiritual danger. This is because we have begun to "pray at every opportunity in the Spirit" (Eph 6:18), since the Holy Spirit, exclusively and unchallenged, commands the high grounds of spiritual warfare. In this contemplative maturity, we begin to experience the effect of Paul's words: "For, although we are in the flesh, we do not battle according to the flesh, for the weapons of our battle are not of flesh but are enormously powerful, capable of destroying fortresses" (2 Cor 10:3–4).

Contemplation is the spiritual high ground in our battle with evil spirits. It is God's high ground under the command of the Holy Spirit; the battle and the victory always belong to the Lord. Moses often entered the contemplative high ground to seek God's mind in Israel's war with her enemies. In Exodus 17:8–12, Amalek attacked Israel. As the battle raged, Moses entered the contemplative high ground, and Joshua mowed down the enemy with the sword.

Contemplatives listen and pay attention to God's presence and directives. They are responsive to what God is doing within them. They live and move and have their being in God. Jesus said He is the light of the world. "Whoever follows me will never walk in darkness, but will have the light of life" (Jn 8:12, NIV). A person in union with Christ has light within her to see the enemy who prowls in the darkness ready to devour the next prey. The contemplative high ground allows the prayer warrior to eavesdrop on the enemy, to locate its positions and movements and decode its strategies; and ultimately to defeat it in combat. It is to this contemplative soul that Prophet Isaiah refers when he said: "He made my mouth like a sharp sword; in the shadow of his hand he hid me; he made me a polished arrow; in his quiver he hid me away. And he said to me, "You are my servant, Israel, in whom I will be glorified" (Is 49:2–3, ESV).

The deliverance power of truth

Truth is a Person! Jesus said: "I am the way and the truth and the life…" (Jn 14:6). Humility goes with the truth. Humility acknowledges the truth that Jesus is the Lord. God's word guarantees and safeguards the purity of truth in hearts that welcome it. Jesus said to the Jews who were trying to kill Him, "I am telling you the truth: everyone who sins is a slave of sin. A slave does not belong to a family permanently, but a son belongs there forever. If the Son sets you free, then you will be really free" (Jn 8:34–36, GNT).

To avoid the bondage and slavery of sin and live in freedom as God's child, Jesus invites us to remain in His word, then "you will know the truth, and the truth will set you free" (Jn 8:32). Truth reveals God's face, manifests His glory in all things, and fulfills His will. Truth serves God's purpose and does not violate the law of charity.

Tactics and weapons of the enemy

Satan's main weapons of warfare are: lies, deception, intimidation, half-truths, discouragement and fear. Militant secularism and the "dictatorship of relativism" aim to blur the distinction between sin and the sinner. This attempt should be resisted. Jesus makes the distinction between the two clear when He said to the crippled man, "Child, your sins are forgiven" (Mk 2:5). We are to hate sin, but love the sinner; the two are very distinct.

Sin is Satan's power, territory and dwelling place. Holiness is incompatible with sin. Holiness is becoming sin-less, more and more. The sinner is loved and welcomed and accepted in Christ's divine mercy. Jesus came to seek and to save those who are lost. He does this by calling sinners to repentance. The Church, in her supernatural mission of evangelizing the world, must call sinners to repentance. The Church must denounce sin as an evil, just as Jesus Himself did. Jesus said to the woman caught in the act of adultery, "Neither do I condemn you. Go, (and) from now on do not sin any more" (Jn 8:11).

The attempts by our growing pagan and secular cultures to blur the difference between sin and the sinner have led many including unfortunately, even some in the Church's hierarchy to equate sin with the sinner. For these people, to denounce such sins as: abortion, euthanasia, fornication, homosexuality (sodomy), cohabitation, contraception, and other intrinsically evil acts as evil, is to hate the sinner. This dangerous trend threatens to destroy the moral fabric of human civilization founded on objective truth, rooted in natural and moral laws, and most importantly, on the revealed truth of Sacred Scripture.

Pope Emeritus Benedict XVI sounded the alarm when in his last homily before his election as Pope said, "We are building a dictatorship of relativism that does not recognize anything as definitive and whose ultimate goal consists solely of one's own ego and desires."[174] Pope Francis re-echoed this danger in his address to the Diplomatic Corps, saying that the "tyranny of relativism" makes everyone his own criterion and endangers the coexistence of peoples.[175]

Could this be what Saint Pope Paul VI meant when, on June 29, 1972, he said that the "smoke of Satan" has entered the sanctuary of the Church? There is no doubt we have entered the time of confrontation between the Gospel and the anti-gospel, between the Church and anti-church, and between good and evil. But Paul warns: "Do you not know that the unrighteous will not inherit the kingdom of God? Do not be deceived. Neither fornicators, nor idolaters, nor adulterers, nor homosexuals, nor sodomites, nor thieves, nor covetous, nor drunkards, nor revilers, nor extortioners will inherit the kingdom of God" (1 Cor 6:9–10; Gal 5:19–21, NKJV).

God never fails. Truth will never fail. We must trust the words of our Lord Jesus in the Scriptures, "And I tell you, you are Peter, and on this rock I will build my church, and the gates of hell shall not prevail against it" (Mt 16:18, ESV). The gates of Hell will surely and truly not prevail against the Church, but we must resist evil with faith rooted and grounded in love and truth. We need the courage of Saint Athanasius, who in his struggle against the heresy of Arius that the Son of God was created and did not always exist, declared: "If the world goes against the truth, then let it be Athanasius against the world."

What about manifestations and retaliations in spiritual warfare?

Manifestations may occur in spiritual warfare associated with family healing. I have not personally experienced any during the Family Healing Retreats. When they occur, they reveal demonic resistance. Mark's Gospel details a case of manifestation in the public ministry of Jesus. A boy with an unclean spirit was brought to Him because the Apostles could not cast out the spirit. Mark says that when the evil spirit saw Jesus, it "immediately threw the boy into convulsions. As he fell to the ground, he began to roll around and foam at the mouth" (Mk 9:20).

Demons like the spectacular. They like to put on a show in order to draw attention. We should not be scared when they do this; it is only a show and nothing but a show designed to instill fear. Demonic manifestations may occur during deliverance because demons hate themselves. They are creatures of hate, and their governing rules are jungle justice and survival of the strongest. More powerful demons beat up and torture weaker ones. During a deliverance, they may fight for which of them stays or gets kicked out first; they resist being cast out. One way to avoid this as much as possible is to keep binding them in the name of Jesus. The binding inactivates and weakens them. In doing so, we are restraining them, so they can be expelled.

No enemy likes to lose battles. Demons do not like to lose battles either. Anytime we engage demons to curb their evil activities, such as praying to the Lord that those under demonic influence be freed; they often retaliate, more so if we are dealing with heavy-duty warfare, as in the cases of occult involvement.

Everyone needs training before waging spiritual warfare. Humanly speaking, we all need some training before going to war. Spiritual warfare is not different, since we are dealing with demons we do not see, but are present. Part of the training in spiritual warfare is to be familiar with how demons retaliate so that we can guard against them.

Training can be acquired through experience; or by working with someone who is familiar with spiritual warfare. It is said that experience is the best teacher; and again, practice makes perfect. The training by the Holy Spirit is absolutely indispensable if we are to succeed in spiritual warfare. "They shall all be taught by God" (Jn 6:45). Without the Holy Spirit, we are simply no match for demons, no matter our depth of knowledge and the human training we may have received.

Demons can retaliate in a whole number of ways depending on the preparedness of those involved in the ministry, and the circumstances of the situation. They can retaliate against us directly or indirectly by attacking relatives and loved ones. They can retaliate with fear, anger, discouragement, hopelessness, fatigue, depression, oppression, and temptations. They can attack our bodies, or they can jam, block and disrupt electronic equipment, cause vehicle failure and plumbing difficulties in homes, and so on. They can attack relationships and create division, or inflict sudden illnesses and other inconveniences. This is how they show they are mad at us and hate us. But that is all they can do. A seasoned Christian soldier should not be afraid of these harassment, they are nothing but scare tactics.

Just recently, a prayer partner and I had prayed with someone who meddled with the occult many years ago. The goal of the prayer was not deliverance. During the prayer session the Holy Spirit began to reveal to us some evil spirit activity, as the spirits tried to obstruct our prayer. I had to bind and cast out the evil spirits. Three days later, my lay prayer partner reported being attacked in her dream. She also complained of a crooked spine and needed chiropractic attention. The health problem befell her overnight; she had no prior vertebral discomfort. As I listened, I began to suspect demonic retaliation. I told her she may not need chiropractic care, and proceeded to pray with her on the phone; I specifically came against curses and spells, etc. placed on her. No sooner had I finished praying than she said her pain and discomfort were gone. This confirmed my earlier suspicion of demonic retaliation. She did not go to see a chiropractor and she is okay.

Once after a deliverance ministry I tried to fax a document to a priest. I made several attempts at sending this fax, all to no avail. This caught my attention. So I would pray each time before attempting to fax the pages. But nothing changed; the fax would not go through. I realized I was being blocked; I suspected retaliation. As I thought of what else to do, suddenly an idea came to mind. I proceeded to place the pages I wanted to fax on the altar used for the celebration of Holy Mass, while I prayed. Next, I went to the fax machine, and the document faxed smoothly.

Retaliation can be this simple and subtle. The evil spirits wanted to get me upset, but I kept calm; I understood clearly in my mind the evil intentions of the evil spirits. The evil one is happy when he succeeds in making us angry over the little things of every day that God allows for our growth in holiness. If we don't want to fall into his traps, we must stay close to Jesus, our Light, through prayer.

Whenever we suspect retaliation, we should remain calm; the evil one likes to provoke. Do not fall for the temptation to easily get angry. It is a trap, and an open door to lose interior peace. We should converse with the Holy Spirit in our hearts, and ask the intercession of our Blessed Virgin Mary, the Queen of Peace. We should call upon the Archangels Saints Michael, Raphael, and Gabriel, and our Holy Guardian Angels to assist and defend us. We should not be shy to call a prayer partner to say a short prayer with or over us. We should call a priest familiar with this kind of ministry to pray over us and bless us. These are ways we can fight demonic forces. Do not take anything for granted; we are in a spiritual combat. So, be combat ready! Be vigilant! Fight!

A life of holiness can make us immune to any harm from enemy retaliation. We are to remain in constant union with Jesus Christ through our prayer life, while rooted in the truth. Should Jesus permit Satan's attacks to affect or harm us, it is only so that good may come out of it. Such suffering will glorify God and save souls, and ultimately bear good fruit in our lives. Such suffering must be accepted for love of Jesus, whose permissive-will allows it to happen. The case of Saint Padre Pio of Pietrelcina (feast day September 23) serves to illustrate this point. He was constantly beaten and bruised by demons, but his holiness was profound and preserved.

Satan is extremely limited in what it can do. Satan is a defeated, condemned and damned creature. It cannot be in more than one place at the same time. Only God is omnipresent, He can be in many places at the same time. He is everywhere. He gives this grace to whomever He chooses, hence the reason for the phenomenon of bilocation in the life of some saints like Saint Padre Pio.

We should always expect retaliation from the demons whenever we wage battles with them and win. Whether demons succeed or fail depend on our vigilance and preparedness. If we let our guards down and allow pride and sin to creep into our lives, the enemy, who is an opportunist, may succeed in harming us and create unnecessary hardships and suffering for us. We must maintain fervor and vigilance in prayer always, and we must keep our armor of God on for battle all the time. This is to say, we must remain humble and faithful to our relationship with Jesus Christ by observing His commandments as He requests, out of love for Him. This is holiness.

The role of our Blessed Mother in spiritual warfare

Our Blessed Mother's involvement in spiritual warfare goes back to the very beginning of creation in the Book of Genesis. After the devil had deceived Adam and Eve to disobey God, God declared war: "I will put enmity between you and the woman, and between your offspring and her offspring; he shall bruise your head, and you shall bruise his heel" (Gen 3:15, ESV).

As Jesus began His public ministry, He refers to His Mother as, "woman." Scripture does not record Jesus referring to His Mother as "mother," but always as "woman." Through a woman—Eve, the devil deceived and gained control over humanity. Also through a woman—Mary of Nazareth, humanity gained victory over Satan, and tramples it underfoot through the Cross of Christ.

The intercessor at Cana

At the wedding feast of Cana, Jesus called His Mother, "woman," to denote her mission in salvation history as conceived in God's will. As woman, Eve, denotes "mother of all the living" (Gen 3:20). Also as the woman, Mary, denotes Mother of all the redeemed, because she is *Redemptoris Mater,* Mother of the Redeemer. Her mission was revealed at the foot of the cross when Jesus, before His death, said to His Mother, "Woman, behold, your son." Then He said to the disciple, "Behold, your mother" (Jn 19:26–27).

We do not see the Blessed Virgin Mary involved in spiritual warfare in the Gospels. The Gospels deal with the birth and mission of the Savior. The Blessed Mother's mission in the Gospels comprises: first, to bring forth Jesus and give Him to the world, to protect, teach and nurture Him as His Mother; secondly, to teach us how to imitate Jesus as His disciples by an obedient-contemplative openness to His word; and thirdly, by her active support and participation in His mission as she accompanied Him to Calvary. It was at the cross—where Jesus defeated Satan, sin and death, as He completed His mission from the Father—that the Blessed Mary received her mandate for spiritual warfare as the New Eve. She is the first of all the redeemed of her Son. By her Immaculate Conception, God's word in Genesis 3:15 declaring war between the woman and Satan and between their offsprings, begins to take effect. For the first time since the creation of the world, a human creature is born who is without sin, and who reflects the image of the All Holy God. This is a terror to the devil and its demons.

**O Mary, conceived without sin,
Pray for us who have recourse to thee[176] (pray three times)**

"Full of Grace"

The woman greeted as, "Full of grace," is the sign of a total and perpetual openness to God. At the Foot of the Cross, Mary of Nazareth receives as children, all the redeemed of her Son. As Jesus hung on the Cross dying, He said: "Woman, behold your son" (Jn 19:26). The Blessed Mary was first revealed by God as "woman" in Genesis 3:15, in a prophetic missionary way, because, even though she did not yet exist, she was very much in God's plan of salvation. At the cross, she is again revealed by God as "woman," in a vocational missionary way, because, since she now exists, God inserts her in His plan of salvation. Mary's womanhood (her perpetual virginity) reveals her inner identity and innate openness to receive God: "Behold, I am the handmaid of the Lord. May it be done to me according to your word" (Lk 1:38). At the cross, she receives her mission, which was earlier prophesied, as mother of all the redeemed through her spousal union with the Holy Spirit: "The Holy Spirit will come upon you, and the power of the Most High will overshadow you" (Lk 1:36). Mary's missionary "motherhood of the redeemed" therefore, is present and effective in the Church in a real spiritual way. She is the prototype of the Church.

We are the spiritual children of Mary of Nazareth. This is the mission we too received at the Foot of the Cross. As Jesus hung up there dying, He said to us through John: "Behold, your mother" (Jn 19:27). At the cross, we received our mission to be her children. As Mary received us as her children at the cross, so we are to receive her as our mother at the cross, by the authority of Jesus Christ, the Savior of the human race. We enter into this mission in real time through our baptism. Mary received her mission and fulfilled it through her spousal union with the Holy Spirit at the Annunciation. In the same way, we received our mission at the cross through baptism—the Sacrament of our identification with the suffering, death and resurrection, and glorification of Jesus; we are to fulfill our mission through our spousal union with the Holy Spirit whom we received at baptism.

The Woman in combat boots

In Revelation, we see the Blessed Virgin, as the image of the Church, involved in spiritual warfare. It says: "And a great sign appeared in heaven: a woman clothed with the sun, with the moon under her feet, and on her head a crown of twelve stars. She was pregnant and was crying out in birth pains and the agony of giving birth" (Rev 12:1–2, ESV).

In times of danger and distress, God normally gives us signs to encourage and inspire hope in us. When Israel was embattled and threatened with extermination, God sent Esther to the rescue. Our human nature is designed to connect with and understand signs as evidence of God's presence. In the Book of Isaiah, the Lord sent Prophet Isaiah to reassure and encourage Ahaz, king of Judah, as Jerusalem was about to be besieged by enemies. As a sign of His presence, the Lord requested of

Ahaz: "Ask for a sign from the LORD, your God; let it be deep as the netherworld, or high as the sky!" (Is 7:11). But Ahaz, in his false humility, refused to ask for a sign. Then God said through Isaiah, "The LORD himself will give you this sign: the virgin shall be with child, and bear a son, and shall name him Immanuel" (Is 7:14). The sign given is that of the *virgin with child*. This virgin is the sign of hope and victory in warfare; she is Our Lady of Victory, Our Lady of Hope, who was revealed to us in the apparition of Our Lady of Pontmain in France (1871).

Her four powers

In Revelation 12, the first of the two signs given shows the four powers of the "woman" for spiritual warfare. These powers are integral to her identity, vocation and mission as Mother of God, Christ's disciple and Co-Redemptrix:

(a) *"A woman."* This is the prophetic victorious "woman" of Genesis. It is in the womanhood or virginity of Mary of Nazareth that she is always and totally open to God in a humble contemplative receptivity. By this power she bore the fruit of the Incarnate Word, as Mother. This contemplative openness is necessary for waging a successful spiritual warfare. It is an openness that first receives before it bears witness. In receiving, she magnifies and glorifies God as demonstrated by the woman of the Magnificat, Mary: "The Almighty has done great things for me, holy is His and name" (Lk 1:49).

As "woman," Mary showed a profound depth of obedient-faith. She not only believed that what God spoke to her would be fulfilled (Lk 1:45), she became the first disciple of her Son, in that she heard God's word and observed it, and she did the will of the Heavenly Father (Mt 12:48). "Indeed the blessed Mary certainly did the Father's will, and so it was for her a greater thing to have been Christ's disciple than to have been his mother, and she was more blessed in her discipleship than in her motherhood."[177]

(b) *"Clothed with the sun."* Light is a synonym for God (1 Jn 1:5; Jn 8:12). To be clothed in light is to be clothed in the fullness of God's holiness and power. It is to be full of light. Our Blessed Mother is Our Lady of Light. She is full of grace (Lk 1:28). Here, she is already clothed in the full armor of light (Rom 13:12). It is of the highest privilege granted to the woman to enter and share in the victory that belongs to God alone. "At his second coming, Jesus will be clothed in light as in a garment."[178] He is King of the Universe. In like manner,

For Mary, present in the Church as the Mother of the Redeemer, takes part, as a mother, in that monumental struggle; against the powers of darkness which continues throughout human history. And by her ecclesial identification as the 'woman clothed with the sun' (Rev 12:1), it can be said that 'in the Most Holy Virgin the Church has already reached that perfection whereby she exists without spot or wrinkle.'[179]

(c) *"On her head [is] a crown of twelve stars."* This refers to the Queenship of Mary by which she receives and participates in the victory, glory, and governance of Her Son Jesus, King of the Universe, and the Lord of Heaven and Earth. The Blessed Mary is the Queen Mother, in the like of the "Hebrew title *Gebirah* for the Queen mother of a Judahite king of the House of David."[180] She, who is full of grace, assumed into heaven and crowned Queen over all things, reigns with her Son, the Lord of lords, the Victor Ever-Glorious, and the Conqueror of Satan, sin and death.[181] The victorious Queenship of Mary is the triumphant realization of the enmity between her and the serpent. In the third Fatima apparitions on July 13, 1917, Mary Our Queen, the only "12-Star General" in God's army, would prophetically state, "In the end, My Immaculate Heart will triumph."[182]

(d) *"She was with child and wailed aloud in pain as she labored to give birth."* This represents the Motherhood of Mary by which she is Mother of the Church. The Church is the offspring of Mary, even as she is also her prototype. The experience of her being in pain as she labored to give birth speaks of her spiritual Motherhood of all the redeemed, as Jesus the Savior willed it for her at the Cross, "Woman, behold your son." Biological birthing is laden with labor pains. Spiritual birthing comes with greater labor pains as souls are born into eternal life through the Church. Paul says: "My children, I am suffering birth pains for you again until Christ is formed in you" (Gal 4:19, GW).

The Immaculate Conception

The foundation of all the powers bestowed on our Blessed Mary is her Immaculate Conception, by which, through the singular favor of God, she was kept unstained from original sin. In the holy name of Mary therefore is contained all the graces and power of God for spiritual warfare, which are available to us, her children.

Two Church-approved apparitions of our Blessed Mother reveal her victory over the poisonous serpent. The first is that of Saint Catherine Labouré, virgin. Catherine was born on May 2, 1806 in France. On November 27, 1830, our Lady showed her a vision of the medal of the Immaculate Conception, universally known as the Miraculous Medal. The medal was created in response to the request of our Blessed Mother. On its front side, the Blessed Virgin is standing on a globe crushing the serpent beneath her feet. Saint Catherine's description of her original vision says that our Lady appeared radiant as a sunrise, "in all her perfect beauty." In Saint Catherine's vision, the following words form an oval frame around Mary: "O Mary, conceived without sin, pray for us who have recourse to thee."

The power of God working through the Immaculate Conception is seen in the conversion of a Jewish agnostic, Alphonse Ratisbonne.[183]

This rabidly anti-Catholic Jew, from a prominent banking family in France, had been heaping ridicule and blasphemy on the Church. When a Catholic acquaintance dared him to wear the Miraculous Medal and recite a *Memorare*, Alphonse accepted. Our Blessed Mother appeared to him in a blinding light in the church of Sant'Andrea delle Fratte and he was instantly converted.[184]

Alphonse, who one moment had been attacking the Church, could not wait to be baptized, went on to be ordained a priest. He worked for the conversion of his fellow Jews. This miraculous conversion through the wearing of the Miraculous Medal honoring Mary's Immaculate Conception caused Saint Maximilian Kolbe to use this medal as an ideal means for winning other souls for Christ through his *Militia Immaculatae*.[185]

The second apparition that reveals the victorious Queenship of Mary is that of Guadalupe. The first apparition of the Virgin of Guadalupe was on the Feast of the Immaculate Conception (celebrated at that time on December 9, 1531) to the humble Aztec Indian, Juan Diego on Tepeyac Hill, Mexico.[186] The image depicts the Virgin standing on a crescent moon. The Aztec word for Mexico, "Metz-xic-co," means "in the center of the moon." The moon also symbolizes the Aztec moon god, fertility, birth, and life.[187]

The significance of the Virgin of Guadalupe apparitions in the spiritual war between light and darkness is told by Warren Carroll, when he wrote: "Careful records were maintained by Father Toribio Motolinia… who… in 1536… reports that he and one other priest had baptized 14,200 Indians in five days. In Mexico as a whole, he declared that there had been no less than five million baptisms since the arrival of the twelve friars under Fray Martin in 1532."[188] Carroll said that the flood of baptisms of the Indians in Mexico, which continued during the remaining years of the life of Juan Diego and of Bishop Zumárraga, who died within a few days of each other in the spring of 1548, reached approximately nine million.[189] This demonstrates the power of the Blessed Virgin to win souls for Christ by crushing the head of the serpent, a victory that is available to those who invoke her holy name in intercession, and in spiritual warfare.

Our Blessed Mother's holiness is attested to by the woman who shouted out from the crowd as Jesus preached. She said: "Blessed is the womb that carried you and the breasts at which you nursed" (Lk 11:27). Jesus replied, "Rather, blessed are those who hear the word of God and observe it" (Lk 11:28). The Mother of Jesus, more than anyone who ever lived, heard God's words and pondered them. She lived God's word to the full. She is Mother of the Incarnate Word of God; the Word that was made flesh and dwelt in our midst. It is in this quality of receiving God's Word and observing it that we, Christians, are called to imitate our Blessed Mother's exemplary discipleship. This is the contemplative approach that I emphasize in this book. It requires that we slow down and pay attention to God's Word, so that as we are nourished by it, and transformed by it, God becomes our strength as we become more and more like Christ.

Saint Louis Marie de Montfort spoke of the woman who heard and kept God's Word and pondered them in her heart (Lk 2:19, 51; 1:29). He calls us to imitate the ten principal virtues of the Blessed Virgin: her profound humility, lively faith, blind obedience, continual mental prayer, mortification in all things, surpassing purity, ardent charity, heroic patience, angelic sweetness, and divine wisdom.[190]

The Legion of Mary, a pious Marian society in the Church founded by Frank Duff on September 7, 1921, strongly promotes devotion to the Blessed Virgin Mary. Her role in spiritual warfare is reflected in the Legion's prayer Antiphon to the Magnificat called, *The Catena Legionis:* Who is she that comes forth as the morning rising, fair as the moon, bright as the sun, terrible as an army set in battle array?[191]

**O Mary, conceived without sin,
Pray for us who have recourse to thee (pray three times)**

Pitfalls in spiritual warfare

The Christian soldier must guide against certain pitfalls. Nothing should be taken for granted in our daily experiences of spiritual warfare. The enemy is serious and resolute in its determination to secure our eternal destruction and damnation. Our primary duty is to stay close to Jesus. We need to be awake to the realities of our situation. We should not allow bondage to distract us from following Jesus. We are not victims because we may be experiencing personal or ancestral bondage. We are victors with and in the Cross of Christ, and with Paul we can boast: "I can do everything through Christ who strengthens me" (Phil 4:13, GW). We must fight the good fight like soldiers of Christ. I call these pitfalls: Victim Mentality Syndrome (Chapter 6). Jesus did not have a victim mentality approach in His suffering to save the world. The intimate knowledge between Him and the Father caused Him to lay down His life for the sheep (Jn 15:15). Jesus was grateful to the Father for the opportunity to suffer and die for us. "For this reason the Father loves me, because I lay down my life that I may take it up again" (Jn 15:17, ESV).

Be near, O Lord, to those who plead before you,
and look kindly on those who place their hope in your mercy,
that, cleansed from the stain of their sins,
they may persevere in holy living
and be made full heirs of your promise.
Through our Lord Jesus Christ, your Son,
who lives and reigns with you in the unity of the Holy Spirit,
one God, for ever and ever.[192] *Amen.*

Scriptures and questions for self-reflection and journaling

1) Luke 4:1–13
2) Revelation 17:14
3) Ephesians 5:8–11
4) Revelation 3:7–12

✗ How am I protecting my mind and senses, my flesh and my heart from the poison of evil?
✗ How am I allowing the Holy Spirit to lead me to accomplish the Father's mission for me?
✗ What is keeping me from seeking and experiencing union with the Lamb?
✗ What are my strengths as children of God by baptism?

Chapter 6

⊂✕⊃ ⊂✕⊃ ⊂✕⊃

Understanding Suffering and Bondage

But he was wounded for our transgressions, crushed for our iniquities; upon him was the punishment that made us whole, and by his bruises we are healed (Is 53:5, NRSV).

Suffering and bondage in the economy of salvation

Bondage is suffering; suffering came upon us as a result of the sin of Adam and Eve, and our personal sins and the sins of others. The issues of suffering are related to the issues of evil, which raise age-old questions: Why is there evil in the world? Why do we suffer? Is there a meaning for human suffering? We know that suffering was not part of God's original plan for humanity. It is the result of sin.

In the Paschal Mystery of Jesus Christ—true God and true Man, suffering has a new meaning; it has assumed a salvific (saving) character. Paul's ministry of proclaiming the Cross and the Gospel to all nations brought him much suffering. Because he was focused on God, he experienced joy in his suffering. Once he said: "Now I rejoice in my sufferings for your sake, and in my flesh I am filling up what is lacking in Christ's afflictions for the sake of his body, that is, the church…" (Col 1:24, ESV). Paul's discovery of joy in the midst of suffering was a process. It brought him in touch with his weakness—the weakness of Christ in him, and he gloried in the cross of Christ.

Disciples of Jesus share willingly and lovingly in His suffering and death. Jesus tells His followers to deny themselves, pick up their crosses, and follow in His footstep (Mt 16:24). Dietrich Bonhoeffer[193] said: "When Christ calls a man, He bids him come and die." Jesus is the Suffering Servant of God (Is 53), who came to suffer and die to redeem humanity. Jesus calls us to imitate His meek and humble Heart. His compassionate Heart identifies with our sufferings; He suffers with us. Jesus' Heart suffers when we suffer, because He loves. In our sufferings, let us make reparation to His Sacred Heart for all the abuses and indifference committed against Him.

Personal and generational bondage is a suffering that calls for prayer. The poor and the suffering need a savior; suffering begs for redemption and salvation. Naturally, human nature in itself has no remedy for suffering. This human need for redemption in the face of suffering awaits the fulfillment of the hope when all our tears will be wiped away in the new creation (Rev 21:4). Suffering creates desolation experiences for us. We know that God does not cause desolation. Suffering, though necessary for our salvation, occurs only within the permissive will of God.

We can distinguish necessary suffering from unnecessary suffering. Jesus said to His two disciples on the road to Emmaus: "Was it not necessary that the Messiah should suffer these things and then enter into his glory?" (Lk 24:26, NRSV). The Messiah's necessary suffering expiated the death penalty incurred by the disobedience of Adam and Eve (Gen 2:16–17), and our own disobedience also. The suffering and death of Jesus alone reconciled us to the Father and repaired the damage in our relationship with Him.

Suffering that is necessary for salvation may not go away until the purpose for which it is allowed is accomplished. The necessity of Christ's suffering reveals God's inner response to the problem of sin and death. Hence, Jesus invites His friends to take up their crosses daily and follow Him. He rebuked Peter for attempting to persuade Him to abandon the Cross by which He was to fulfill the Father's will and save the world. "You are an obstacle to me. You are thinking not as God does, but as human beings do" (Mt 16:23). The Apostle Paul boasts: "We proclaim Christ crucified" (1 Cor 1:23), and he called the Crucified Lord the True Wisdom of God (1 Cor 1:24). Paul recounts His experience of necessary suffering when, because of the many divine favors granted him, a thorn in the flesh was given to him in the form of an angel of Satan, who beat him, to keep him from being proud. Three times he begged God to remove the cross, but God said: "My grace is sufficient for you, for my power is made perfect in weakness" (2 Cor 12:9, NIV). With that, Paul resigned himself to God's will.

In the history of the Church, God has often chosen certain souls to be His instrument of purification for the world. These souls include among others, Saints Peter and Paul; Saint Agatha; Saint Padre Pio of Pietrelcina, who bore the stigmata (wounds of Jesus) on his body for fifty years, which disappeared before his death; Saint Rita of Cascia; Saint Maximilian Kolbe; and the entire compliments of the Church's martyrology; Christians who freely gave their lives, out of love for, and in union with Christ for the faith. These victim souls are precious in God's eyes. They accepted their suffering for the sake of Christ and in union with Him. Through the cross of suffering, God's children enter into true glory (Heb 2:10). The joy of the Psalmist rings out: "O taste and see that the Lord is good" (Ps 34:8, NRSV).

There are also unnecessary sufferings. These kinds are not from God, and they create bondage and prevent our growth in perfection. Those under the yoke of unnecessary suffering are the captives and the oppressed that Jesus came to set free in the power of the anointing of the Holy Spirit (Lk 4:18). Sin burdens the soul and imposes bondage on us. Jesus spoke of this kind of bondage when he said to the paralytic, "Son, your sins are forgiven" (Mk 2:5). The man's bondage of paralysis prevented him from relating with God as a son. Sin had robbed him of his freedom and held him bound.

Bondage can also be transmitted through the generational line as in the case of the woman who was bent over for eighteen years, incapable of standing erect, because she was crippled by a spirit (Lk 13:11–16). A closer look at the case of this crippled woman is examined in Chapter 18. A detailed treatment of bondage issues is contained in Parts II and III of this book.

Suffering that is not necessary for our salvation will lift if we pray correctly, and with faith, in accordance with God's will. It is not God's desire that we be burdened, suffer unnecessarily and die in this world. Jesus denounced the scribes and the Pharisees for making people suffer unnecessarily, "They tie up heavy burdens, hard to bear, and lay them on the shoulders of others; but they themselves are unwilling to lift a finger to move them" (Mt 23:4, NRSV). Jesus never places burdens on us; He came to set us free, and to invite those in unnecessary suffering to come to Him and find rest and peace (Mt 11:28). The Family Healing Retreats address these kinds of sufferings. It is a ministry of setting the captives free in the name of Jesus.

Below are some points to help us discern necessary suffering (*true crosses*), and unnecessary suffering (*false crosses*).

Guidelines for discerning true and false crosses
True cross: – permitted by God (necessary suffering)

These sufferings or crosses are permitted by God; when and how we will be delivered from them depends only on God in conformity to His will for the good of souls.

- It does not lead us to sin, we stay away from sin.
- It motivates us to live holy lives.
- We are drawn to prayer.
- We persevere in the suffering and do not give up our friendship with God.
- It brings us joy of heart (Jam 1:2).
- It generates confidence and conviction (Rom 8:38).
- We grow in humility and obedience.
- We have respect and love for God's creation.

- We grow in self-knowledge and healthy love of self.
- We love the Church and her teachings and doctrines.
- God reveals Himself in the suffering—He gives consolation (Ps 34:8).
- We will endure until its purpose is accomplished.
- It will lead us to bear witness to the truth.
- Signs and wonders will accompany it.
- We would not complain (Mt 6).
- The soul is flooded with grace.
- We are filled with hope in Christ's promises.
- It causes us to give thanks for sharing in Christ's saving and victorious mission.
- It will not go away, grace will be given to bear the cross (2 Cor 12:9)
- God gives consolation in the trial (2 Cor 1:3–4).

False cross: – they are caused by our sins and failings (unnecessary suffering)
These sufferings are caused by our sins and failings, and are generally our fault. However, they serve to purify us. We must repent and ask God's mercy, and offer reparation. They will go away when our relationship with God is restored.
o   It leads to sin (an evil).
o   It pulls us away from living holy lives.
o   The soul is slothful in prayer.
o   It causes sadness in our soul and lack of peace.
o   We use the suffering as an excuse not to pray.
o   We make excuses for not being faithful.
o   We use our weak humanity to rationalize and justify sinful actions.
o   Our human weakness becomes an excuse for failure.
o   We are disconnected from ourselves; we are in the dark.
o   We try to cover up faults with faults.
o   It makes us pitiful and shameful victims.
o   We are hopeless and depressed.
o   We do not have true repentance of heart, no desire to change.
o   We are weary, anxious and burdened.
o   We get mad at God, at others and at ourselves.
o   We complain about everything and blame others.
o   It causes us to be easily angry and frustrated.
o   We manifest low self-esteem, poor self-image, and lack of confidence in ourselves.
o   We try to intimidate others to cover up our weakness.
o   We are fearful of many things.

The mystery of human suffering

Saint John Paul II's Apostolic Letter *Salvifici Doloris* details the mystery of human suffering. This section will draw on the rich teachings in the Pope's letter.

The subject of human suffering is complex and varied. According to Saint John Paul II, human suffering is mysterious and multidimensional all at once. We suffer in different ways, in ways not always considered by medicine. Suffering is deeper than sickness and is deeply rooted in humanity itself.[194] The two components of human suffering, physical and moral, are distinguishable because the human person is both body and spirit—the immediate or direct subject of suffering. While the words "suffering" and "pain" can to a certain degree be used synonymously, physical suffering is present when "the body is hurting" in some way, whereas moral suffering is "pain of the soul."[195]

Pain of the soul is spiritual pain. It cuts deeper than the "psychological" dimension of pain that accompanies both moral and physical suffering. As there are vast forms of physical suffering, there are similarly vast forms of moral suffering. But moral suffering seems, as it were, less identified and more difficult to deal with in therapy.[196] When faced with moral suffering we are invited to turn to God who sent His Son Jesus Christ to suffer and die for us.

One time in my private prayer, our Lord Jesus gave me some insight into the mystery of human suffering. I understood that, ontologically speaking, i.e., in the true nature of what a human being should be. Jesus is the first to suffer, and He suffers with us when we suffer, because of His union with us. He is true God and true Man. Jesus is holy and innocent. He is the only begotten Son of God who became flesh to save us from our sins. In the Eucharistic Prayer IV, we pray: "He is like us in all things, but sin." Sin kills. The Bible says that "the wages of sin is death" (Rom 6:23).

Saint Augustine's insight makes this point clearer. He said that humanity as one, through Adam and Eve, in committing original sin, stabbed itself in the heart to death with a dagger. In this dead state, humanity was totally helpless. It required Another to bring it back to life again. Jesus—the life of the world—, came and resuscitated humanity back to life. He declared: "I am the resurrection and the life" (Jn 11:25). By Jesus' suffering, death and resurrection, He has given humanity new life. Prophet Isaiah refers to Jesus as the 'Suffering Servant' (Is 53), and he prophesied: "Through his suffering, my servant shall justify many, and their guilt he shall bear" (Is 53:11). Jesus Christ came into this world to give His life as a ransom for us. All our sufferings have their ultimate meaning in the context of Christ's suffering. Through our sufferings, we participate in the sufferings of Christ for the redemption of the world. It follows then that for us to suffer is a special privilege granted to us by the Father, who alone calls us into fellowship with His Son, both in His death and resurrection, because Christ is the One who truly suffers when we suffers. Jesus said to Paul, "Saul, Saul, why are you persecuting me?" (Acts 9:4). Peter says: "Christ suffered for you, and left you an example to have you follow in His footsteps" (1 Pet 2:21).

Does suffering have value?

Suffering brings conversion of heart, and purification from sin to those who endure it. When we freely accept suffering for the sake of Christ, we express our love for Him. This gift of love fully revealed in the Cross of Jesus brings men and women to share in the divinity of Christ who humbled Himself for us. This kind of suffering carries no shame with it, because it is from God. It brings delight and healing to the soul and to human relationships. Suffering freely accepted proves our righteousness in Christ before the world. Saint Stephen exemplified this by forgiving his executioners, and Saul their leader (Acts 7:58), who later became Paul. Such suffering glorifies God and bears holy fruits in the Holy Spirit: love, joy, peace, patience, kindness, generosity (goodness), faithfulness, gentleness, and self-control (Gal 5:22–23, NIV).

Suffering and intercession

Human suffering calls for intercession to the Father, in and through Jesus Christ, and in the power of the Holy Spirit, asking for those who suffer special graces of perseverance and healing. In our intercession for those who suffer, we follow the example of the Holy Spirit, who intercedes for the weak and the distressed according to God's will in groanings beyond words (Rom 8:26–27). Generationally transmitted suffering likewise calls for generational intercession for the graces of healing and perseverance for those under the yoke of generational suffering. Saint Paul encourages us in our suffering to "Bear your share of hardship along with me like a good soldier of Christ Jesus" (2 Tim 2:3). Prayers of intercession offered to the Father, in the name of Jesus, and by the power of the Holy Spirit, open doors to God's healing graces to flow down on us. In response to personal sins and suffering, we can make personal Confession of sins, and receive absolution from the priest for them. Outside of Confession, it is possible and encouraged to pray for freedom from the effects of ancestral sins. We can do this through our prayers as we assist at Mass; and by offering Masses for our ancestors, we can make reparation for their spiritual good.

Examples of generational confessions abound in the Old Testament. Daniel prayed and confessed the sins of his people Israel, saying: "O Lord, the great and awesome God, who keeps covenant and steadfast love with those who love him and keep his commandments, we have sinned and done wrong and acted wickedly and rebelled, turning aside from your commandments and rules" (Dan 9:4–5, ESV).

Likewise, we can make generational confession and intercession in our private prayers, begging God's mercy for the sins committed by our ancestors, the effects of which could well be the cause of our bondage. It is common practice for Catholics to offer the sacrifice of the Holy Mass for deceased relatives, that their sins may be expiated.

Sacred Scripture contains deep lessons on human suffering. Saint Pope John Paul II taught that the Old Testament (OT) provides some examples of situations which bear the signs of suffering, especially moral suffering:

> The danger of death, the death of one's own children and, especially, the death of the firstborn and the only son, the lack of offspring, nostalgia for the homeland, persecution and hostility of the environment, mockery and scorn of the one who suffers, loneliness and abandonment, the difficulty of understanding why the wicked prosper and the just suffer, and the unfaithfulness and ingratitude of friends and neighbors.[197]

In the OT, moral suffering is often linked to the pain of specific parts of the body: the bones, kidneys, liver, viscera, and heart. Moral suffering has a "physical" element, which affects the whole person.[198] Saint John Paul II further explains:

> Man suffers whenever he experiences any kind of evil. The OT identifies suffering with evil, because it did not have a specific word in its vocabulary for suffering. So every suffering is an evil. With the Greek translation of the Bible from Hebrew, we have a verb which means "I suffer." So suffering is no longer directly identifiable with (objective) evil, but expresses a situation in which man experiences evil and in doing so becomes the subject of suffering.[199]

The reality of human suffering raises the question about the essence of evil: what is evil?[200] Christianity attempts to answer this question by proclaiming the essential good of existence and all that exists. Christianity acknowledges the goodness of the Creator and proclaims the good of creatures. Man suffers (experiences bondage) because of evil, which is a certain lack, limitation or distortion of the good. Man suffers because of a good from which he is cut off or deprived. People who suffer become similar to one another through the analogy of their situation, the trial of destiny… and through the persistent question of the meaning of suffering. Suffering poses a challenge to communion and solidarity.[201]

The existence of personal and collective (generational/family) suffering raises the question—why? What are its purpose and meaning? Physical pain is a common experience in the animal world, "but only the suffering human being knows that he is suffering and wonders why; he suffers, humanly speaking, in a still deeper way if he does not find a satisfactory answer."[202]

Similar to the question of suffering is the question of evil. Why is there evil in the world? This question in some way is related to the question about suffering. According to Saint John Paul II, individuals put this question to one another, people to people, and man addresses them to God, as the Creator and Lord of the world. Man does not put this question to the world from where his suffering comes from. Human questions about evil and suffering cause frustrations and conflicts in the relationship of man with God and some people have reached the point of denying God because of them. We know that all of creation opens the eyes of our soul to the existence of God: His wisdom, power, and greatness; evil and suffering on the other hand seem to obscure this image, sometimes in radical ways, especially in the daily drama of so many cases of undeserved suffering and of so many faults without proper punishment.[203]

Suffering as punishment for sin

Saint John Paul II attempts to answer the question of the existence of evil by reflecting on the story of the just man, Job. Without any fault of his, Job is tried by innumerable sufferings: he lost his possessions and his sons and daughters, and he himself is afflicted with a grave sickness. Three old acquaintances visit him and individually try to convince him that the reason for his sufferings was that he must have done something seriously wrong. Suffering, they say is always punishment for one's crimes. It is sent by the absolutely just God and finds its reason in the order of justice. For Job's friends, suffering has meaning only as a punishment for sin. It is limited only to the level of the justice of God, who repays good with good and evil with evil.[204]

The point of reference in their argument is the doctrine found in the OT writings which show suffering as punishment inflicted by God for human sins. It is important to note that the God of Revelation—the Lawgiver and Judge—, is first of all the Creator. He gave together with existence the good of creation. When man consciously and freely violates this good, he offends the Creator and transgresses the law. This transgression biblically and theologically speaking is sin.[205] The idea of punishment for moral sin safeguards moral order in the same transcendent sense in which the order is laid down by the will of the Creator and Supreme Lawgiver. From this we derive one of the fundamental truths of religious faith, based on Revelation, namely, that God is a just Judge who rewards good and punishes evil.[206] The opinion of Job's friends shows a conviction that is part of the moral conscience of humanity: "the objective moral order demands punishment for transgressions, sin and crime."[207] From this opinion we can conclude that suffering appears as a "justified evil."[208]

Job in his response to his friends challenges the truth of the principal that identifies suffering with punishment for sin. He is aware of the good he had done and knows that he does not deserve suffering as punishment. God vindicates Job by acknowledging that he is not guilty; he reproves Job's friends for their accusation. Job's suffering is that of an innocent man; "such a suffering must be accepted as a mystery which the individual is unable to penetrate completely by his own intelligence."[209]

"While it is true that suffering has a meaning as punishment, when it is connected with a fault, *it is not true* that *all suffering is a consequence of a fault and has the nature of a punishment*."[210] This thesis is proved in the OT in the case of Job. His is the suffering of an innocent man: suffering without guilt. Job's suffering was not a punishment. God permitted his suffering as a test because of Satan's provocation.[211] But why?

Suffering as test of righteousness

In the Book of Job 1:9–11, God consented to test Job with suffering to demonstrate his righteousness. Job's suffering was a test of his righteousness and not a punishment for his sins. In this test, Job proved righteous before God. His suffering was the foreshadowing of the Passion of Christ. The attempt in the Book of Job to resolve the "why" of suffering based on punishment for sin fails, because the Book shows that suffering afflicts the innocent, but it does not yet give the answer to the problem. The Book of Job does not explain the suffering of the just man Job. In fact it seems to trivialize and impoverish the concept of justice which we encounter in Revelation.[212]

Suffering as correction and means to conversion and holiness

In the account of the just man Job there is a movement pointing beyond the idea that suffering exists as punishment for sin. There is an educational value attached to suffering as punishment—that of correction. "In the sufferings which God inflicted on the Chosen People is included an invitation to His mercy, which corrects in order to lead to conversion as we read in 2 Maccabees 6:12: "Now I beg those who read this book not to be disheartened by these misfortunes, but to consider that these chastisements were meant not for the ruin but for the correction of our nation."[213]

The Scripture text above affirms the personal dimension of punishment, where the objective evil of an offense is repaid with another evil (i.e. the punishment). It opens the possibility of rebuilding goodness in the one who suffers. Suffering must serve for the conversion of heart, that is, the rebuilding of goodness in the one who suffers, who can recognize the merciful hand of God calling him to repentance. Penance serves to overcome evil which is present in man in different forms. It also serves to strengthen goodness in man and his relationship with others and with God especially.[214]

Suffering as means of redemption (perfection in love)

In Jesus Christ, suffering has been conquered by love. At the heart of God's salvific work and the Christian theology of salvation are Jesus' words to Nicodemus: "For God so loved the world that He gave His only begotten Son, that whoever believes in Him should not perish but have everlasting life" (Jn 3:16, NKJV). "Salvation means liberation from evil, and for this reason it is closely bound up with the problem of suffering."[215] The reason God gave His Son to "the world" is to free it from evil, which brings with it suffering. Jesus was to accomplish this liberation from evil through His own suffering, and in this supreme act, love is fully revealed, the infinite love of the Eternal Father and the Only Begotten Son toward humanity and the world.

Here, we consider a new dimension of the meaning of the "why" of suffering, namely, the dimension of Redemption. The Old Testament already gives a hint of this dimension in the words of the just man Job: "For I know that my Redeemer lives, and at the last he will stand upon the earth. And after my skin has been thus destroyed, yet in my flesh I shall see God, whom I shall see for myself, and my eyes shall behold, and not another" (Job 19:25–27, ESV).[216]

The dimension of suffering as punishment that was discussed earlier focused on suffering in its multiple temporal meaning. But now, in this redemptive dimension, Jesus' words to Nicodemus refer to suffering in its fundamental and definitive meaning. Salvation in its fullest sense means experiencing eternal life through faith in the Son of God. The opposite of salvation is not only temporal suffering, or any kind of suffering, but the definitive suffering: the loss of eternal life or, being rejected by God – damnation. "The only-begotten Son was given to humanity primarily to protect man against this definitive evil and against definitive suffering."[217] In His salvific mission, the Son must therefore strike evil right at its transcendental roots from which it develops in human history. These roots of evil are grounded in sin and death, which cause the loss of eternal life. Jesus' mission is to conquer sin and death. "He conquers sin by His obedience unto death; He overcomes death by his resurrection."[218] He conquers the evil one by the Blood of His cross.

● ● ●

Christ's mission to crush evil at its roots refers to two types of evil: firstly, evil as well as definitive and eternal suffering (so that man "should not perish, but have eternal life"); and secondly, evil and suffering in the here and now. Human suffering is tied to the sin of the beginnings, what Saint John calls the 'sin of the world.' These are the sinful personal actions and the social processes in human history. The "sin of the world" also refers to the sin of disobedience of our first parents which plunged humanity into darkness. It is this sin that the Lamb of God came to take away by His obedient suffering and death on the Cross. So "at the basis of [all] human suffering [and bondage], there is the complex involvement of sin."[219]

Christ's victory over Satan, sin and death, which He accomplished by His Cross and Resurrection, did not abolish suffering in this life, nor did it free humanity from sickness. Rather, it shed a new light upon all suffering; this light is the Gospel—the Good News. At the heart of this light is the truth that Jesus reveals to Nicodemus: "For God so loved the world that he gave his only son." "This truth radically changes the picture of man's history and his earthly situation, in spite of the sin that took root in this history both as an original inheritance and as the 'sin of the world' and as the sum of personal sins."[220]

In His saving mission, Christ identifies increasingly with human suffering. He was anointed with the Holy Spirit, and "went about doing good," He set the captives free and liberated the oppressed; He came to seek and save the lost; and His actions addressed primarily those who were suffering and seeking help.

> He healed the sick; consoled the afflicted; fed the hungry; freed people from deafness, blindness, leprosy, the devil and various physical disabilities; three times He restored the dead to life. He was sensitive to every human suffering, whether of the body or of the soul. Christ also taught the people. At the heart of his teaching are the eight beatitudes, which are addressed to people tried by various sufferings in this temporal life: the poor in spirit, 'the afflicted,' those who hunger and thirst for justice.[221]

Jesus identified most intimately with human suffering when He freely accepted to suffer in His humanity. He reminded His disciples that in Jerusalem He will be handed over to the religious leaders, and custodians of the law, who will condemn, mock, and spit on Him and torture Him, and kill Him. He also said that after three days, He will be raised up (Mk 10:33–34). In His human nature, Christ experienced fatigue, homelessness, and misunderstanding, even on the part of His close friends. More than that, He became increasingly more isolated and encircled by hostility and the preparation for putting Him to death. He spoke to His disciple about His impending agony: "I am troubled now. Yet what should I say? 'Father, save me from this hour'? But it was for this purpose that I came to this hour" (Jn 12:27). Christ's suffering in the plan of eternal love has a redemptive character.[222]

Our free entrance by Baptism into the sufferings of Christ should reflect in our openness and free acceptance of the trials of this life. This acceptance gives clarity to Jesus' words about John the Baptist: "I tell you, among those born of women there is no one greater than John; yet the one who is least in the kingdom of God is greater than he" (Lk 7:28, NIV). Our free participation in the redemptive sacrifice of Christ makes us co-redemptors, since by our adoption as God's children in the Holy Spirit, and our sharing in Christ's sufferings, we have become "heirs of God and joint heirs with Christ" (Rom 8:16–17).

Our sufferings as Christians by which we identify with Christ are also our weapon against evil and a source of healing. "By His wounds we have been healed" (1 Pet 2:24, NRSV). The mighty deeds of the OT prophets: Moses, Elijah, Elisha, Joshua, Isaiah, and so on, cannot compare with the actions of the Christian who is in union with the Crucified and Risen Christ. Though powerful in the wonders they performed, the action of the prophets did not save a single soul. Our sufferings and actions as Christians, however, flowing from our union with Christ save souls.

Christ suffers voluntarily and innocently, and in doing so He gives the answer to the "why" and the meaning of suffering, both by His teaching, that is, the Good News, and by His own suffering, which is inseparable from His teaching.[223]

Suffering as an act of reparation for sin

Suffering opens the door to spiritual renewal from within. As we have said, suffering has meaning as punishment for sin. The Blessed Virgin Mary spoke of this dimension of human suffering in her first apparition to Lucia, Jacinta, and Francisco at Fatima on May 13, 1917. She spoke to the children about the seriousness of sin which merits temporal punishment. She also spoke of the reparatory dimension of suffering in her words to the children: "Do you want to offer yourselves to God and endure all the sufferings that He may choose to send you, as an act of reparation for the sins by which He is offended and as a supplication for the conversion of sinners?"[224]

To this question Lucia promptly responded on behalf of the three, "Yes, we want to." "Then you are to suffer a great deal," the Lady promised, "but the grace of God will be your comfort."[225]

"Victim Mentality Syndrome" (VMS)[226]

Sometimes in the course of carrying our crosses, we develop a victim mentality attitude that prevents our sacrifices from being meritorious. We must do our best to guide against this attitude of the heart. Scripture reminds us, "It was fitting that God, for whom and through whom everything exists, should, in bringing many sons to glory, make perfect through suffering the leader of their salvation" (Heb 2:10, NJB). Suffering should not make us victims; it should rather train us to be victors with Christ, the Victorious Lamb. The following guidelines may serve to help us identify and combat VMS in our lives.

Recognizing VMS

- We pity ourselves and want everybody to pity us.
- We tell everyone our problems in order to draw attention .
- We are not faithful to prayer.
- We constantly complain and blame others.
- We do not listen to or accept advice.
- We are not obedient.
- We seek salvation but refuse to embrace the cross of Jesus.
- Our focus is not on Jesus.
- We rely too much and give undue attention to our feelings.
- We have a rebellious spirit.
- We are afraid to suffer.
- We easily compromise so we can be thought well of by others.
- We blame others for what they are not responsible for.
- We blame ourselves for what we are not responsible for.
- We blame and get mad at God for our problems.
- We lack interior confidence and conviction.
- We are easily defeated by events and circumstances around us.
- We are negative and pessimistic about life.
- We blame ourselves for the tragedies and mishaps that happen in our lives.
- We resort easily to anger, or are easily frustrated.
- We are fearful of everything and every decision.
- We find it difficult to make up our minds on important issues.
- We take things too personal even when it is not intended.
- We are easily offended by others remarks and actions when these are not intended.
- We have poor self-image and lack self-confidence.
- We dwell too much on our faults.
- We hold onto our sins even when God has forgiven them.

* * *

- We refuse to forgive others and harbor grudges.
- We are self-absorbed and selfish.
- We carry a guilty conscience and low self-esteem.

The reason for VMS, which is essentially a problem of worldly thought process arising from past woundedness within, is lack of self-knowledge, which makes us unaware of interior problems causing us lack of peace in ourselves. It may also be a sign of some psychological problem that may require the attention of a qualified professional, provided such a person has first made a correct and prior diagnosis of the problem. What are presented in this book are not criteria for determining psychological or any human illness. Rather, they are exclusively for personal self-examination and prayer as we seek deeper interior freedom and peace in the Holy Spirit.

How to combat VMS

- ✘ We acknowledge the reality of VMS. If we deny it's presence, we deny ourselves.
- ✘ We are practice self-reflection (not self-absorption), and self-recollection.
- ✘ We pray for the grace of desire to receive God's love.
- ✘ We seek spiritual direction.
- ✘ Regular celebration of the Sacrament of Penance.
- ✘ We pray the 'Litany of humility' daily or often.
- ✘ We should pray with John the Baptist: Lord Jesus, You must increase, and I must decrease (Jn 3:30).
- ✘ We pray for faith in Jesus Christ.
- ✘ We should pray often for a new outpouring of the Holy Spirit into our hearts.
- ✘ Join a prayer group and share you experience of faith with others.
- ✘ Renewal of our minds.

We should pray to grow in faith in Jesus Christ, and to seek total transformation by renewing and purifying our minds. This way we can discern God's perfect will (Rom 12:2). Paul claims, "we have the mind of Christ" (1 Cor 2:16), and that he serves God's law with his mind (Rom 7:25). Peter says that holiness requires that our minds be healed and alert and fully sober, so we can set our hopes on the grace to be received at the revelation of Jesus Christ (1 Pet 1:13). We renew our minds by meditating on the Passion of our Lord, and pondering His Word day and night.

Faith is a shield against all satanic attacks (Eph 6:16). On the strength of Jesus' words, we should ask the Eternal Father for the gift of the Holy

Spirit. He does not ration this Gift, but gives Him generously to those who ask Him (see Lk 11:13). When the Holy Spirit is active in us, we do not blame others or ourselves for the distresses in our lives. Rather, we bring these emotional problems to God in the intimate dialogue of prayer. But when the Holy Spirit is not active in us, we do the contrary; we blame ourselves and others, and God for problems for which we should take responsibility, as matured Christians. We make our problems and ourselves the focus of our prayer. We do not keep our eyes on Jesus Christ, because we lack a healthy interior life.

Scriptures and questions for reflection

1) Colossians 1:24
2) Revelation 3:7–12
3) 1 Peter 4:13–19

- ✗ Father, what is keeping me from not letting go of myself and surrender to You?
- ✗ Lord Jesus, what are my fears about denying myself, taking up my cross and follow You?
- ✗ Holy Spirit what prevents me from accepting my daily trials and challenges as a sharing in Jesus' cross?

Part II

Chapters 7—13

The Seven Primary Open Doors to Bondage

———————————

Glory be to Jesus; honor to Mary and Joseph!

Understanding the Open Doors and Bondage

Open doors

Let us look at scenarios of open doors. If you are visiting a friend, you can enter her home only when she opens the door for you. There may be several doors, but you enter only through the door she opens for you. I went to a restaurant, and there on the door was a sign with an arrow which read: "Enter through the west door."

Open doors allow us access into a space. Jesus said: "Behold, I stand at the door and knock. If anyone hears My voice and opens the door, I will come in to him and dine with him, and he with Me" (Rev 3:20, NKJV). We have power to open doors or close them. God placed the keys of the house of David on Eliakim's shoulder with the promise, "When he opens, no one shall shut, when he shuts, no one shall open" (Is 22:22). Our free will is decisive in opening doors either to Jesus or to the devil. First we have to hear, and then we have to open. The evil one cannot open the door in us. It has no rightful access unless there is an open door through which it enters.

I will discuss two sets of open doors: the primary open doors, which are the Seven Capital Sins (chapters 7–13), and the secondary open doors, which are complications of the primary open doors (chapters 14–18).

Bondage

A priest once asked me to explain the term bondage. Bondage describes a state in which freedom is compromised, either physically, morally or spiritually. Whatever limits the full exercise of our God-given freedom or the freedom God desires we have, puts us in bondage. "A person may be bound up with his or her own ailment (physical or moral defect)."[227] For example, a man with a withered hand, or another with leprosy, or the woman bent over and incapable of standing erect; all these speak of limitations in their physical (and spiritual) abilities. They are handicapped, not free, and are said to be in bondage. "Bondage [here] is primarily the restriction occasioned by the defect itself."[228]

The limitation imposed by the condition may be total or partial; it may be physical and/or moral and/or spiritual. Sin limits our true freedom in Christ. As such, sin is bondage. Because sin attracts and promotes demonic activity, bondage can become complicated due to evil spirit activity. Sin is a spiritual malady that limits or disrupts our communion with God; it is defiance, opposition and disobedience to God's commands. Original sin imposed a limitation on our freedom as God's children. From Scripture, we learn that original sin brought both physical and spiritual death to human life (Gen 2:17; Wis 2:24; Rom 5:12–14).

A convicted criminal is normally confined to prison to limit his freedom. Similarly, when a person commits sin, a spiritual crime resulting from the conscious misuse of free will in violation of God's commandments, that person experiences a limitation of freedom in one's self in his relationship with God and in his full rights as God's child. This limitation of freedom imposed by sin can render the person vulnerable to spiritual contamination and captivity. Just as when our immune system is weak or compromised, we are vulnerable to infection, leading to illness, and even death.

Demons can gain access to a person's interior life through the weakness or opening created by sin; the person becomes bound or blocked or chained by demons inside of them. Bondage can affect one or more family members, and can in turn be transmitted through the generational lines, leading to generational bondage. Symptoms of generational bondage are discernible in persons from an ancestry where bondage is present. Bondage can manifest in a person as sinful acts, addictions and behaviors. It can also manifest in non-sinful ways, but always with some suffering or inconvenience.

Someone in a state of grace can experience bondage arising from his or her ancestral lineage. In dealing with personal or generational bondage, it is important to investigate and understand the root causes. This will help us take appropriate response measures. As we struggle with bondage, Paul assures us that God's grace at work in us is stronger than the power of sin and bondage (Rom 5:20). Where bondage exists, Christ's grace abounds in abundance to help us overcome. Jesus our Savior is full of grace and truth. The Blood of Jesus Christ is always able to break all bondage, and that is why we conduct inter-generational healing sessions.

The seven primary open doors to bondage: the Seven Capital Sins [229] *(vices)*

Saint Thomas Aquinas says that, "a capital sin is that which has an exceedingly desirable end so that in his desire for it a man goes on to the commission of many sins all of which are said to originate in that vice as their chief source."[230] What makes a sin capital is not its gravity or seriousness, but the fact that it leads to the commission of many other sins. The Seven Capital Sins are: anger, avarice, gluttony, lust, envy, sloth and vainglory (pride).[231] These can be experienced emotionally.

Revelation 12:3 tells of another sign that appeared in the sky. It was a huge red dragon, having seven heads and ten horns. The seven heads of the dragon speak very much of the Seven Capital Sins. Every sin falls into one or the other of these seven sins. Satan uses its seven heads to strike at us, as it attempts to separate us from the love of our Heavenly Father. Divine

Revelation tells us that we belong to God (1 Jn 3:2; 1 Cor 6:19; Lev 20:26; Eze 36:28), but also that the evil one rules the whole world (1 Jn 5:19). The Seven Capital Sins comprise the spirit of the world, which constitute the portals of Satan's hold on us. At the start of the 33-Day preparation for total consecration to Jesus Christ through Mary, Saint Louis Marie de Montfort wants us to get rid of the spirit of the world in us by intensified prayer, knowledge through study, and the spiritual exercises of self-denial, penance, the practice of the virtues through strict adherence to Gospel moral codes and, devotion to the Blessed Mother, and the imitation of Christ.

We are at war! God declared this war in Genesis 3:15, and ever since, we have been at war, whether we know it or not. Jesus Christ is our Commander-in-Chief in this spiritual war. Revelation 12:7 tells us that in heaven war broke out; Saint Michael and the Angels battled the red dragon and its demons and drove them out. The dragon in anger pursued the woman who gave birth to the male child, who will rule the nations, and waged war against her and rest of her offspring, those faithful to God commandments, and who witness to the death and resurrection of Jesus— members of the Church (Rev 12:5–18; Mt 16:18).

In our struggle with the capital sins, we see that the law of our fallen nature is at war with the law reason. As a result, reason becomes subjected to the law of error, causing death to reign in our body. The remedy for this disorder is the grace of God in Christ Jesus, which enables us to acquire the discipline of daily detachment and dying to the flesh. This is Saint Paul's principle of Christian living: "For me life is Christ, and death is gain" (Phil 1:21). This principle should inspire in us a desire to die to self, which, because it is ruled by feelings, craves pleasure in the capital sins, so putting our souls in bondage as a result. The grace of God in Christ is offered to us in the whole sacramental economy of the Church, as well as in her penitential disciplines, which are the fruit of the Paschal Mystery. This precisely means that, not only are our sins forgiven in the gift of God's mercy through the Sacraments, we are also radically transformed morally in our interior life in charity in the gift of the Holy Spirit poured out into our hearts (Rom 5:5), making us participants in the divine nature (2 Pet 1:4), and able to love as God loves (Jn 13:34), in the gift of spiritual regeneration as sons and daughters of God (Jn 1:13). This is how we escape the corruption of the evil desires of the flesh that the capital sins inflict on us. Having been so favored in Christ, Saint Peter demands that we supplement our "faith with virtue, virtue with knowledge, knowledge with self-control, self-control with endurance, endurance with devotion, devotion with mutual affection, mutual affection with love" (2 Pet 1:5–7). This he says would ensure our remaining in God's grace so that we do not return to worldly defilement through sin, which would make our last condition worse than the first. "For it would have been better for them never to have known the way of righteousness than after knowing it to turn back from the holy commandment delivered to them" (2 Pet 2:21, RSV).

The warnings of Peter, Paul and the Apostles, appear to be characteristic of the leaders of the early Church, and the Church Fathers. They should make us take seriously the radical moralism of the New Covenant. Jesus, in calling us to the perfection of God's standard of morality and charity, prescribes for believers the way of perfection. We must deny ourselves, and make a convinced commitment to follow Him. He said if any members of our bodies cause us to sin, we should cut it off or pluck it out; it is better for us to enter God's Kingdom maimed, crippled, and without an eye, than to be thrown into Gehenna with our whole body intact, where the worms don't die and the fire burns eternally (Mk 9:43–50). Jesus also warns those who cause the "little ones who believe in me to sin, it would be better for him to have a great millstone hung around his neck and to be drowned in the depths of the sea" (Mt 18:6). The rigorous and uncompromising high moral standards prescribed in the New Covenant are aimed at, and have the sole goal and purpose of the total renovation of our hearts and minds—interior man—in charity. Thus interiorly reformed in the core of our nature in God's image in the grace of the Incarnation and the Blood of Christ, in the words of Saint Irenaeus, "We regain in Christ, what we lost in Adam," and we attain the cleanliness hands and purity of heart necessary to ascend the mountain and see God (Ps 24:3–4; Mt 5:8). We become in Christ, truly a new creation (2 Cor 5:17), and are able to meritoriously do good works by loving God and neighbor and, are made coheirs of Christ's glory in Heaven. As Jesus put it, we have passed from death to life (Jn 5:24). For this to happen, Jesus says, "Be on your guard!" (Lk 17:3).

Some Biblical events teach us about the Seven Capital Sins. In the Old Testament, the army commander of the king of Aram, Naaman, was a leper. Prophet Elisha directed him to go and wash seven times in the River Jordan. He became angry and refused to obey the prophet. Reluctantly, he obeyed when his servant begged him to give it a try. He went down and washed seven times and was healed. We are told his flesh become like that of a little child; he was cleansed (2 Kgs 5:14). In the New Testament, we read that Jesus had cast out seven demons from Mary Magdalene (Mk 16:9). Naaman was in the bondage of leprosy, while Mary Magdalene was in the bondage of sexual addiction. Both were set free from their bondage.

We need the power of Jesus Christ present in the Seven Sacraments of the Church to free us from the bondage of the evil one through sin. Demons can gain access into our lives when we give in to any of the Seven

Capital Sins. At Baptism we receive the Seven Gifts of the Holy Spirit: Piety, Fortitude, Counsel, Understanding, Knowledge, Fear of the Lord, and Wisdom. These *Isaiah gifts* are necessary for our personal sanctification. When these gifts are enflamed and active in us, we are not ravaged or held captive by the capital sins, since the commission of any of the capital sins is always a free act of the will.

Jesus warns us to watch and pray constantly, and to be vigilant so that we may not fall into temptation (Mt 26:41). To help us in our trials, Jesus gives us His Mother, Mary, to teach us and intercede for us. She interceded for, and with the Apostles, in the Upper Room for the outpouring of Holy Ghost Fire on Pentecost day. We need this Pentecost Fire today in our battles with the evils of this world.

When I was a member of the Intercessors of the Lamb, we had formation on the capital sins. I understood from our formation that for effective intercession, and to help others grow in faith in Christ, we first have to face the reality of these sins in ourselves. When we have reclaimed territories of sin in ourselves, then we are ready to be God's instruments to reclaim them with and for others. This contemplative formation in the capital sins in the community lasted few months. We examined how the capital sins were present in us individually and as a community. As part of that process, we prayed for the seven-fold bathing of the Holy Spirit fire upon ourselves. We explored the power of Jesus' Seven Last Words from the Cross as antidotes against the Seven Capital Sins. Luke the Evangelists tells us that those who were present when Jesus cried His last Words from the Cross and surrendered His spirit to the Father, went home beating their breasts (Lk 23:44–48); an outward sign of deep repentance of the heart. Jesus' last Words cause us to repent and be healed of the encroachment of the capital sins in our lives. Moderation must be at work in the heart and soul of anyone combating the capital sins. It is "… moderation, not a fierce defense that beats back a fierce attack."[232]

As we examine the Seven Capital Sins with the goal of recognizing their presence in us, we shall walk with the Blessed Mary, ever-Virgin. We shall invoke the unfailing intercession of her Seven Sorrows, as we seek freedom from the bondage of the capital sins. Through her sorrows by which she participated in the redemptive suffering of her Son, we receive graces from Almighty God to be faithful to the call to holiness. The Blessed Mary is truly "Full of grace." Through her openness to God in her Seven Sorrows, the Blessed Virgin Mary enters the pain and suffering of every human person that she might intercede with Jesus for our salvation. Simeon prophesied that a sword would pierce her soul to reveal the thoughts of many hearts (Lk 2:35).

John the Evangelist reminds us: "For all that is in the world—the lust of the flesh, the lust of the eyes, and the pride of life—is not of the Father but is of the world. And the world is passing away, and the lust of it; but he who does the will of God abides forever" (1 Jn 2:16-17, NKJV). In considering each of the Seven Capital Sins, we will also provide the corresponding virtues, namely, the Seven Capital Virtues to counter and defeat the temptation to fall captive to each of the seven vices. These virtues are: Humility, Liberality, Chastity, Meekness, Temperance, Kindness and Diligence. But recognizing the capital sins in us can pose a special challenge, as the Psalmist acknowledges: "Who can discern his errors? Forgive my hidden faults. Keep your servant also from willful sins; may they not rule over me. Then will I be blameless, innocent of great transgression" (Ps 19:12–14, NIV). When our hearts are blameless and we are innocent and live free from sin, the words of our prayer and the meditations of our hearts become a living sacrifice and praise pleasing and acceptable to God.

The relationship between the primary and the secondary open doors to bondage

Our fallen nature, the result of original sin committed by Adam and Eve, makes us susceptible to the primary open doors, which in turn make us vulnerable to the secondary open doors. The interactions of the primary open doors that lead to the complications of the secondary open doors can be illustrated with a few examples.

The emotional wounds and traumas of preborn infants and children are due to hurts they experienced and their not receiving God's love for which they exist. When a pregnant mother is abused and battered, the child in her womb is traumatized by the experience. This can predispose the child to emotional wounds, which open doors to bondage. This is so because the capital sins of anger, pride, envy, sloth, etc. are already at work in the batterer; the defenseless child is hurt, wounded, and dented in his/her emotional well-being. On the other hand, if a child receives the love for which he/she exists, the child grows and matures well and is nourished spiritually into a healthy, happy, holy child.

In another example, when the gift of relationship, by which we are to love one another as Jesus loves us, is abused, unholy soul-ties can develop. This happens because persons who are in unholy ties are vulnerable, and have predisposing factors present: lust, gluttony, envy, greed, pride, and a complex interior mix of these weaknesses, which are opposed to virtue, morality and the truth of Christ. The natural result is the bondage of unholy soul-ties

In generationally transmitted bondage, the dynamics are similar. For an evil effect to be passed down the generational line, i.e., to one's offspring, the ancestors themselves must have been in the grip of sinful bondage through involvement in some evil, for example, occult activities like freemasonry or witchcraft, which in turn is a consequence of pride, greed, sloth, anger, envy, etc.; all these working together to draw individuals away from a faithful, loving, obedient, and morally sound life, which places persons in opposition to God. The effects of occult involvement may then be transmitted inter-generationally to descendants with their attendant desolating consequences. In many cases, the persons suffering from bondage are completely unaware of the origin of their felt misery.

Finally, any number of combinations of the seven capital sins can interact in a person to create a variety of secondary open doors to bondage which have discernible manifestations.

Man destined to be coheir with Christ in Heaven

Man is the only creature God created for Himself. God created man in His own image as male and female. He formed him from the clay of the ground and breathed His life-giving spirit (*Ruah*) into him. So, Man became a living being (Gen 2:7).

Only God has the right to be in us because He created us. He dwells in our innermost self. He is closer to us than we are to ourselves. Saint Paul reminds us that our body is a temple where God's Spirit dwells, and that we do not belong to ourselves (1 Cor 6:19). We are precious gifts to ourselves. We have dignity. In Christ, we are made worthy and called to live in freedom. The Holy Spirit's presence in us guarantees our freedom (2 Cor 3:17). So, Jesus invites us to remain in Him as He is in us (Jn 15:4).

In chapter 3, I discussed the identity and mission of Jesus. We understood that Jesus came to set us free to live life to the fullest. Bondage compromises the freedom we have in Christ; it is an evil that must be resisted both in persons and families. While Satan is not responsible for the evils we commit, he is certainly involved in their commission. It brings with it death, as Scripture says; by the devil's envy, death entered our world, and those who are in its grip experience death (Wis 2:24). Sin empowers Satan to hold us in its grip, but sin itself is not identified with Satan. Sin is "a personal act of men, and also the state of guilt and blindness which Satan seeks effectively to cast [persons] into and keep them in."[233]

In the next several chapters, I shall discuss the open doors to bondage. These "open doors" are entry ways through which the evil one cunningly and unlawfully enters our individual and family lives to influence, control, and hold us captive. To be freed from these bondages, it is important that we understand the operations and tactics of the devil so that we can close the doors to its entry, and open the doors to life and freedom in the Holy Spirit.

Disobedience to God's Commandments, which occur by the free act of the will, is the root cause of all open doors leading to spiritual bondage. Adam and Eve were blessed with the authority of God to be fertile and multiply and to fill the earth and have dominion over all of material creation. By their disobedience, the whole world came under the power of the devil (1 Jn 5:19), instead of being under the dominion of Adam and Eve and their descendants, as God desired. Satan was even so bold as to similarly tempt the Son of God, Jesus Christ, as we read in Matthew 4:1–11.

Scripture says that the devil led Jesus up to a very high mountain, and showed Him the beauty and magnificence of the kingdoms of the world, and said to Him, "All these I shall give to you, if you will prostrate yourself and worship me" (Mt 4:8–9). Jesus replied, "Get away, Satan! It is written: 'The Lord, your God, shall you worship and him alone shall you serve'" (Mt 4:10). By this victory over Satan, its lies and deceptions, Jesus our Lord obtained for us the power to reject Satan's temptations and be faithful to God's commands. He wants us to be victorious over Satan and the full force of its kingdom (Lk 10:19). Through obedience and faithfulness to all that Jesus commands, we become coheirs with Christ of eternal life. This divine promise awaits fulfillment in us.

We are called to holiness

In 2 Peter 1:3-4, the first Pope, Peter, tells us that God's Divine power has graced us with all that is necessary to live genuine lives of devotion and holiness through the knowledge of Jesus, who by His own power and glory has called and chosen us, and has bestowed on us precious gifts and promises through which we may share in His Divine nature, "after escaping from the corruption that is in the world because of evil desire." We encounter the word "inordinate" in the description of each of the Seven Capital Sins. It speaks of an interior disorder in our nature that needs to be re-ordered and healed. This disorder, arising from the effect of original sin committed by our first parents by the free act of the will has left humanity in a wounded state where we lack sanctifying grace. As a result of this disorder, we resist Jesus' call to be perfect as the Father is perfect. This disorder or woundedness in our nature leads to the abuse of reason which we call sin. Sin resists a life of holiness which God's grace has bestowed on us through Baptism.

The Archbishop of Omaha, George J. Lucas, in his Chrism Mass homily at Saint Cecilia Cathedral, Omaha, Nebraska on April 14, 2014, posed a question to the congregation, and by extension, to the whole Church that drew my attention. He said, "We are God's holy people –

anointed—chosen in Christ to be saints. This is why we have been created; for this we are redeemed in the blood of Christ." Then he asked twice, "Why do we fight it? Why do we fight it?" Finally, he added, "Perhaps we have been able to explore that a little bit during Lent."

It is important that we explore the reasons we fight holiness. Our joy is in being holy. The fulfillment of all our desires is in being holy. The freedom that we seek as Christians is possible only in being holy. As we grow in self-knowledge, let us contemplatively examine our hearts using the self-examination questions following each of the Seven Capital Sins; they are our recipe for interior freedom and peace. When we have recognized and identified these sins in us, we should take appropriate steps to combat them and close the doors to bondage completely in our lives and protect our generations. Sins have consequences beyond the sinner. Its line of effects includes our families and generational lines, and the whole Body of Christ to which we are connected by a spiritual bond. Sin can potentially keep us in bondage as is evident in the capital sins and their complications which are detailed below.

The capital sins work against the call to holiness for which reason Jesus established the Catholic Church, and instituted the Seven Sacraments. The Church has as one of its unique characteristics—*holiness*. The Church enlightened by the Holy Spirit, taught a key doctrine in the Second Vatican Council document *Lumen Gentium,* Chapter V: *The Universal Call to Holiness in the Church.* In it, the Council Fathers said, "that all the faithful of Christ of whatever rank or status, are called to the fullness of the Christian life and to the perfection of charity; by this holiness as such a more human manner of living is promoted in this earthly society."[234]

Pope Saint John Paul II in his Apostolic Letter *Novo Millennio Ineunte,* which laid down his vision for the Third Millennium and beyond, placed the highest priority on holiness or sanctity of life. He said, "First of all, I have no hesitation in saying that all [personal and] pastoral initiatives must be set in relation to holiness."[235] The saintly Pope said this was the ultimate meaning of the Jubilee indulgence. He pointed out that the Council Fathers stressed "holiness as an intrinsic and essential aspect of their teaching on the Church. The rediscovery of the Church as 'mystery', or as a people 'gathered together by the unity of the Father, the Son and the Holy Spirit', was bound to bring with it a rediscovery of the Church's 'holiness', understood in the basic sense of belonging to him who is in essence the Holy One, the 'thrice Holy' (cf. Is 6:3)."[236] Baptism is our "true entry into the holiness of God through incorporation into Christ and the indwelling of the Spirit." Therefore, the Pope said, "It would be a contradiction to settle for a life of mediocrity, marked by a minimalist ethic and a shallow religiosity." Life in the seven capital sins contradicts the supernatural life we have by baptism.

The common remedy for the capital sins is a program of disciplined interior prayer to establish an intense and living relationship with Jesus Christ. In this regard, John Paul II placed as a priority a plan to arrive at this holiness. He said, "The time has come to re-propose wholeheartedly to everyone this *high standard of ordinary Christian living*: the whole life of the Christian community and of Christian families must lead in this direction." For the Pope, "the paths to holiness are personal and call for a genuine 'training in holiness', adapted to people's needs. This training in holiness calls for a Christian life distinguished above all in the art of prayer."[237]

For John Paul II, "prayer cannot be taken for granted. We have to learn how to pray, as it were learning this art ever anew from the lips of the Divine Master himself," who responded to the disciples request: "Lord teach us to pray!" (Lk 11:1).[238] "Prayer develops that conversation with Christ which makes us his intimate friends." The Pope concluded, "Our Christian communities must become genuine 'schools' of prayer, where the meeting with Christ is expressed not just in imploring help but also in thanksgiving, praise, adoration, contemplation, listening and ardent devotion, until the heart truly 'falls in love.'"[239] Only when we have fallen in love with Jesus, do we begin to live a mature and abundant life in the Spirit.

In emphasizing the role of prayer to combat the capital sins in our lives and foster a deeper relationship with God, Saint John Paul does not in any way minimize the priority the Church attaches to the celebration of the Sacraments, the primary means of growing in holiness and sharing in the divine nature in a created manner. The Sacraments convey grace to us, especially, sanctifying grace, which in us is a supernatural quality, an active and lively principle drawing us to imitate God in our desires and appetites. Sanctifying grace enables us to overcome the weaknesses of our flesh that make us vulnerable to the capital sins; they perfect our nature so that our natural abilities and gifts are elevated and receive a supernatural character. Coupled with the infused Theological and moral virtues we receive at Baptism, God equips us with all the spiritual blessings we need for a genuine life of godliness. We are encouraged then to celebrate Penance and receive the Holy Eucharist in a state of grace to help us defeat sin and overcome bondage in our lives and families.

Freedom and free will in relation to the bondage of sin

In the quest for freedom in our rational nature, success or failure lies in the proper exercise of free will. It is important to understand freedom and its violation by sin, as we begin to discuss sin and bondage. Jesus said that those who believed in Him, by remaining in His word, will truly be His disciples, they will know the truth, and the truth will make them free. But the Jews protested claiming they had never been in bondage because they are children of Abraham by descent. Jesus makes them understand that it is sin that limits people's freedom and puts them in bondage: "Everyone who commits sin is a slave of sin" (Jn 8:34). A slave remains a slave until he is set free by another. Jesus then claims for Himself as God's Son, the right and the power to free those in bondage to sin (Jn 8:36). It is Christ's Sacrifice of Atonement that frees us from the capital sins and all sins, and from the bondage of demonic powers over us due to sin. This reality is made available to us during the Eucharistic Prayer at Mass when the Priest prays: "This is the chalice of my Blood, the Blood of the new and eternal covenant, which will be poured out for you and for many for the forgiveness of sins" (CCC 601, 613).

We learn that freedom is the ability to deliberate between varieties of goods. All of our choices are to satisfy some good purpose, and to fulfill some inward desire for our well-being. Our will is always attracted or drawn toward the good. Sin, a disorder of our appetite, essentially results when we choose goods of lesser value over goods of greater value. This choice naturally debases and dehumanizes us, and so is always unjust. It is immoral. The greater good, that is, one of higher value, may not necessarily gratify our fleshly appetite like the lesser goods would, but they help align our will to God's will, and make us pleasing to Him. The reason we choose less valuable goods over more valuable ones, though they may be harmful to us, is because we have a fallen nature; our human nature is wounded due to Original Sin. This sin weakened our nature, and corrupts and distorts our value system, and we suffer morally from concupiscence. Our desires and attachments are disordered: we love wrongly by loving things we should not love, and shun things we should love; we are prideful, lustful, slothful, impatient, resentful, uncharitable, and egoistic. We make decisions based on our feelings, because we are burdened by immoderate attachments to sensual pleasures and worldly goods. These defects make us not desire readily the good and pure and holy things of God. We prefer physical and transient goods over spiritual and transcendent ones; God being the most transcendent and ultimate Good we ought to desire and possess for our ultimate and perfect happiness and freedom.

Through the reception of Sacraments of the Church, which are the fruits of the saving death and resurrection of Jesus Christ, we receive sanctifying grace that objectively heals our disordered appetites. The Sacraments primarily heal our will and emotions, enlighten our intellect which often tends to be darkened by sin, and strengthen our spirit. In the state of grace then, the gifts of the Holy Spirit become active and operational in our will and faculties, so that we begin to see beyond the physical, to see and choose the more valuable spiritual goods, which conform us to God's will, so that we become the saints we are called to be. The state of grace empowers us to live morally sound lives, in accord with the spirit of Christ, making us able to resist all cravings of the flesh. The flesh wage war against the spirit and vice versa, because they are diametrically opposed (Gal 5:16-17). When we are in a state of grace, sin becomes less appealing and attractive to us; we see clearly to choose goods that accord with our redeemed nature in Christ. Salvation indeed means to walk solidly the path of the moral life. Since our will has been illumined by the light of the Holy Spirit in this state of grace, our hearts begin to gaze, as Saint Paul says, on things above where Christ is seated at God's right hand interceding for us, rather than on earthly and fleshly things that satisfy only our feelings and passions, and do not help us experience the new life in Christ (see Col 3:2; Heb 8:6). This is what the Apostle means when he taught: "Therefore, if anyone is in Christ, he is a new creation; the old has passed away, behold, the new has come" (2 Cor 5:17, RSV). The new life in Christ is a victorious life of grace, one of total freedom, purity and wholeness, because grace makes us immaculate and incapable to sinning or offending God's holiness in which we share through Baptism. God's grace makes us perfect like Jesus. It makes us happy. After all, grace, like the moral life, is the science of human happiness, flourishing, fruitfulness, and freedom. It makes us like Mother Mary, who shares most fully and most eminently, and to the utmost plenitude, in the perfection of Christ, her Son, because she is "Full of grace," as she is incapable of sinning. In this state of freedom, we choose God and all that is for His glory and honor. This is the honor and dignity of the sinless Virgin Mary whom we venerate as the Immaculate Conception. Sins, especially the capital sins, which are committed through our free choice, deprive us of grace, and all its attendant fruits, and make us slaves and enemies of God, ourselves and others.

We ask the intercession of the Mother of God, the Angels and the Saints in combating sin. After the spiritual exercises that accompany each of the Seven Capital Sins, we may pray with King David, the prayer of cleansing and pardon—Psalm 51, especially verse 10: "Create in me a clean heart, O God, and put a new and right spirit within me" (RSV). And this prayer inscribed on the Miraculous Medal, in a vision the Blessed Virgin Mary, the Immaculate Conception, gave to Saint Catherine Labouré in 1830, for the world:

"O Mary, conceived without sin,
pray for us who have recourse to thee." (pray three times)

Spiritual exercises in preparation to review the self-reflection questions for the Seven Capital Sins

◗ Pray and invoke the grace and light of the Holy Spirit to bless and make your efforts fruitful (note: *God must be the focus and the center of this interior examination, not ourselves*).

◗ Lay aside distractions that may cling to you; take a few minutes to quiet down. Fix your eyes—thoughts and attention—on Jesus. "Be still and know that I am God" (Ps 46:10).

◗ Consider who God is. He is *Primo Principio* (First Principle), Almighty, All Powerful, All Holy; think of His unique love for you, and how precious you are in His eyes; seek Him alone (note: *extremely important step, return to it often*).

◗ Place yourself in God's loving presence. Consider how He loves you in creating you, in forgiving your sins, and in saving you in Christ Jesus. Consider a promise of Jesus in the Scriptures, and apply it to yourself. For example, "I will not leave you orphan." "I will be with you always." "I have redeemed you." "Even should a mother forget her child, I will not forget you." He knit you together in your mother's womb, "Whatever you ask of the Father in My name, I will give you." "You are Mine." "I will be your God." Do not worry. Be not afraid.

◗ Rest like a child in "Daddy's" lap (surrender); let Him simply hold you. Think of God's goodness with gratitude. Tell Jesus what is in your heart. Do not be in a hurry; simply **be;** and rest in God's love.

Then pray meditatively and repeatedly:

Holy Spirit, open my heart to the Light. Fill me with repentance and Your merciful love. Help me to see myself as You see me. Help me to see what in me needs to change and what needs to stay. In the name of Jesus, my Light and my Truth.

Practice these suggested steps before beginning the review of the "Self-Reflection Questions" for each of the capital sins. Remember to draw your strength from the Lord and from His mighty power. Ask for the grace to hunger and thirst for holiness and for friendship with the Lord Jesus. Ask Jesus to make you a saint, from the conviction and confidence that you recognize that His grace is enough, and it can heal and transform you into a saint. Ponder Paul's words to us not to conform ourselves to this world's standards, but to be transformed in our whole being by renewing our minds, so we may discern what is God's will and "what is good and pleasing and perfect" before God (Rom 12:2).

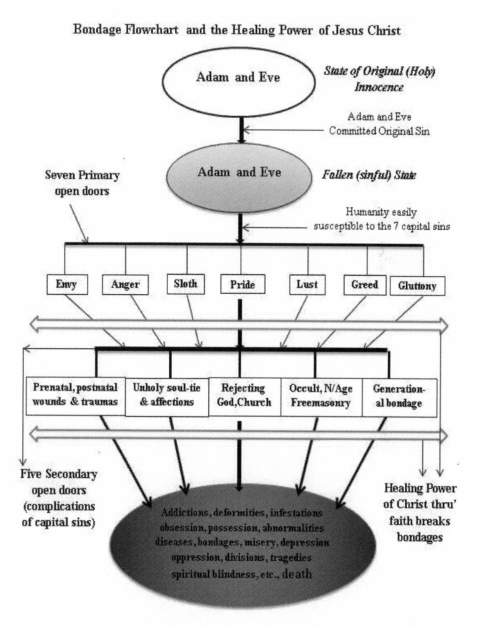

Chart 1: *Bondage flowchart*

Chapter 7

⊂✕⊃ ⊂✕⊃ ⊂✕⊃

Primary Open Door 1: Envy

A sound heart is life to the body, but envy is rottenness to the bones (Prov 14:30, NKJV).

Envy can be felt as an emotion. Saint Thomas Aquinas says envy is sorrow or grief we have for desiring another's good.[240] The good that is desired is regarded by the envious person as being withheld from him, leaving him impoverished. The goods desired may be status, reputation, abilities, honor, personal traits, and material or spiritual things or situations. Envy is a common temptation. The envious person thinks others are smarter, luckier, richer, more respected, holier, more attractive, and better and more gifted in all respects—mind, body and spirit, than himself. This assumed deprivation arising from envy causes grumbling, complaining, ingratitude, sadness, and heaviness, and ultimately isolates the person and bears the fruit of death.

Envy limits and blocks our interior freedom as sons and daughters of our Heavenly Father. A child for example, has a right to be loved. But if that child is deprived of love for which he has a right to receive, the seed of envy may be sown, then develops and festers, and manifests later as the child matures. In dealing with the sin of envy, a human distortion of reality, there is also an evil spirit of envy which can attach to wounded areas within us and complicate issues.

In the Scriptures, envy shows up strongly in the parable of the prodigal son (Lk 15:11–32). The elder son became envious of his younger brother who received from their father, forgiveness and a hero's welcome after squandering his father's estate. Because of envy, the elder brother got angry at his father and refused to enter the house (the kingdom), even when his father begged him. Because of envy McElhone says, "It is hard for us to rejoice whole-heartedly at the success of others; it is easy for us to feel glad at their failures."[241]

Someone may be envious at another, who soon after a short period of coming to faith in Christ, begins to experience signal graces through the generosity and providence of God. Such is the case in Jesus' parable of the Laborers in the Vineyard (Mt 20). The landowner said to the laborers who complained that equal favors were granted to their fellow laborers who arrived later than them: "Are you envious because I am generous?" (Mt

20:15). They felt cheated and deprived, even though they were paid the agreed wage; they hoped to get what did not belong to them, the wages of others; they were ungrateful and disrespectful of the householder (Mt 20:12–14). Envy wages war against the generosity of God. Jesus warned His followers not to be envious of wealth (Mt 6:19–21).

Our secular and materialistic society has become a huge trap to keep people in the bondage of envy. It keeps us focused on satisfying our pleasures, passions and feelings. Human life is easily and callously disposed of because wealth concerns have become the primary determinant of people's motivations, identity and worth. But envy makes the envious wither quickly like the grass and soon die away like the green plants (Ps 37:1–2).

In the Gospels, the scribes, the Pharisees and the chief priests were envious of Jesus' wisdom and authority, as well as His influence (Mt 26:57–58). The chief priests handed Jesus over to Pilate for crucifixion out of envy (Mk 15:10). Pontius Pilate envied Jesus' popularity, influence and authority (Jn 19:8–11).

Scripture says: "But by the envy of the devil, death entered the world, and they who are in his possession experience it" (Wis 2:24). The first murder in human history, the killing of Abel by his brother Cain, was fueled by envy: Abel's offering was accepted by God, while Cain's offering was rejected (Gen 4:1–11). Joseph was sold into slavery to Egypt by his brothers because of envy, for Joseph was their father's favorite son (Gen 36:1–28).

The evil one lost its place in Heaven; through envy it wants us to rebel against God, and lose our inheritance in Heaven. Jesus has gone to prepare a place for us in Heaven (Jn 14). The devil envies our relationship with God, and the peace and joy of the Holy Spirit that are ours as children of God. The devil wants to destroy our relationship with God with sadness, disquiet and turbulence in our hearts, by keeping our attention fixed on the passing things of this world. Self-denial will strengthen us to combat envy, because it will conform us to the heroic poverty of Jesus.

Envy disrupts our interior peace by keeping our attention fixed on others and what they are doing, instead of keeping our eyes fixed on Jesus and His love and Divine will for us. Jesus cautions us: "For what does it profit a man to gain the whole world and forfeit his soul? For what can a man give in return for his soul?" (Mk 8:36–37, ESV).

Envy self-reflection questions:
* Do I rejoice when others fail?
* Who do I hate or dislike?
* Do I accuse others?
* Where do I tend to rebel in my life and why?

- Does envy cloud my judgment or opinion of others and their dignity?
- Do I envy the rich?
- Am I sad about others' abilities, learning, or spirituality?
- Am I sad that others are more humble than I am, or more obedient than I am?
- Do I detract, calumniate, or find fault with others?
- Am I competitive?
- Am I envious when others are praised?
- Do I envy power, honor, or reputation?
- Do I feel that God loves others more than me?
- Am I bothered at others' gifts of imagination, memory, understanding, wisdom, or insight?
- Does it bother me that someone is holier or more virtuous than I?
- Am I sad that others are more gifted than I am?
- Am I caught up in other people's business and affairs?
- Do I accept help when it is offered?
- Am I a possessive or a controlling person?

The weapons against envy

Weapons of the Spirit

When the Spirit of the Lord came upon us at Baptism, He gave us His First Gift of **Wisdom.** Wisdom is the most perfect gift of the Spirit; it is the spotless mirror of God's power (Wis 7:23–30). It equips us to fight the capital vice of envy. *The Spirit of Wisdom* (Is 11:2) enlightens our souls to see reality from God's viewpoint. Wisdom directs us to fix our eyes on Heaven; to discern and relish divine things; to embrace eternity; and to see the nothingness of everything worldly.[242] The gift of wisdom moves us to embrace the Cross of Jesus every moment of our lives as the means of entering into divine life. The Cross is the tree of life (Gen 2:9). This knowledge makes Paul say, "May I never boast of anything except the cross of our Lord Jesus Christ, by which the world has been crucified to me, and I to the world" (Gal 6:14, NRSV). Envy attacks our relationship with God by keeping us focused away from Him; but wisdom directs our gaze on Heaven.

The Armor of God to wage war against the sin of envy is the *Sword of the Spirit, the Word of God* (Eph 6:17). The Bible says: "In the beginning was the Word, and the Word was with God, and the Word was God (Jn 1:1, NKJV). God's Word became flesh; He is Incarnate Wisdom. This Word of God, Jesus, is the wisdom and the power of God (1 Cor 1:24). He is the fullness of the Divinity; to possess Him is to possess the victory over envy.

Word from the Cross

Our Lord Jesus Christ dying on the Cross spoke the *Second Word* that destroys the sin of envy in our hearts: ***"Amen, I say to you, today you will be with me in Paradise"*** (Lk 23:43). All our words and actions, like the thief's, should reflect our hunger for Heaven: "Jesus, remember me when you come into your kingdom" (Lk 23:42). The choice for heaven must be today, not tomorrow. "Oh, that today you would hear his voice: 'Harden not your hearts…" (Heb 3:15). Jesus showed that He came for sinners and the sick, not the righteous and healthy (Mt 9:13). The envious person rejoices in sin; Jesus hates sin, but loves the sinner.

May we pray for wisdom to see and embrace Jesus daily in our crosses and trials. "Blessed is the man who knows what it is to love Jesus, and to despise himself for the sake of Jesus." Christ's love will not admit of a rival.[243] Jesus commands us to love one another as He loves us. Kindliness or love for one's neighbor is the virtue that counters envy, because it directly attacks the distress and sorrow that arises within the envious person over the good fortunes and blessings of others.

In our dialogue of prayer, let us share with Jesus our struggles with envy. Journaling will help us get things out into the light, as we share with Him our feelings, thoughts and desires, and then listen to His instructions on how to fight this sin. Our prayer and journaling should be concrete and real in asking our Lord to reveal to us His strategy for this warfare. We can reflect on the following questions in our prayer: What are my deepest desires in life? What occupies most of my time? Where is my attention directed in prayer—on myself, others, or God? These self-examination questions and those listed above can provide us with early warning signs that envy is creeping into our lives. We must be courageous in seeking help, including regular spiritual direction.

Envy as a capital vice can lead us down the dirty and crooked path of gossip, lies, and cheating. It will cause us to conceal, disobey and criticize, because we feel deprived and cheated.

Prayer exercises that teach us to surrender will be effective in transforming our hearts. Meditation on Isaiah 53 will teach us Jesus' life of total surrender to the Father as the Suffering Servant. In the Sermon on the Mount, Jesus taught: "Blessed are the poor in spirit, for theirs is the kingdom of heaven" (Mt 5:3). To possess God's Kingdom, we must be emptied of the earthly kingdom. We need God's grace to detach from worldly things, so that together and in union with the Blessed Mother we may give our unconditional fiat to the Father: "Behold, I am the handmaid of the Lord. May it be done to me according to your word" (Lk 1:38).

When the Holy Spirit moves us to pray the Lord's Prayer, the "Our Father…" we invoke the Kingdom of God to come fully into our hearts, as we hallow His name and seek His will to be accomplished in our lives.

• • •

Satan has no place in God's Kingdom, because it is the Kingdom of God, the Kingdom of life, light, love and mercy. It is the Kingdom that only the child-like and the humble are capable of receiving. God's Kingdom is within us (Lk 17:21; Jn 17:3, 14:23, 6:53; 1 Cor 6:19). It is there that the fruit of God's Spirit is tangible, visible and overflowing. This is what Saint Irenaeus of Lyon, a Bishop and an early Church Father meant when he said, "the glory of God is man fully alive." The *Shekinah* glory is upon us. We must be filled with God, because God desires we be like Him, to be holy and perfect like Him (Lev 19:2, 1 Pet 1:15, Mt 5:48).

Closing the open door of envy

The first step toward healing is to acknowledge the sickness. It is necessary we acknowledge envy when it rears up its ugly head inside us. Time of prayer in self-reflection to examine its occurrences, and how we opened the door to envy is necessary. Then we can start closing the open door. We need the light and strength of the Holy Spirit to take radical steps to combat it. Time spent in dialogue with the Divine Physician in prayer, and listening for His instruction is indispensable in this effort. Else, envy will take root quickly and isolate us from God.

The habit of praise and thanks to God for any good done, no matter the good and who does it, will help eradicate envy from our hearts. Paul says that "whatever you do, whether in word or deed, do it all in the name of the Lord Jesus, giving thanks to God the Father through him" (Col 3:17, NRSV; Eph 5:20). Praising and blessing God in every situation and for all things will open our hearts to His generosity and healing love. We begin to pay less attention to what others are doing, and what they have. We stop comparing ourselves with others, and how God is blessing them and not us. In this way we close the door to envy and to spiritual bondage.

God gave us various physical and spiritual gifts for our good and the good of others, and for the building up of God's Kingdom on earth. We have a responsibility to use and grow these gifts, so that they bear fruit worthy of God's Kingdom (Jn 15:8). Paul reminds us that the Spirit's gift to each person is for some benefit (1 Cor 12:1–11), and ultimately to glorify of God. If we focus on God and the gifts He has given us, and on improving our gifts and using them to build up God's Kingdom, we would not be distracted and burdened with envy by focusing on others and what God is doing in their lives.

Even for those who strive for holiness, Peter's experience shows how easily we can fall prey to the sin of envy. Peter saw John and said to Jesus, "Lord, what about him?" Jesus replied, "What if I want him to remain until I come? What concern is it of yours? You follow me" (Jn 21:21–22). This may surely have been embarrassing for the first Pope, who now holds the keys to the Kingdom of Heaven (Mt 16:19). It is sinful to want to be like others or want what they have. We should be content to want to be like Jesus; to be the best God has created us to be. As the saying goes, "if you cannot be a tree, be a shrub and be the best." We should not perceive the prosperity, gifts and abundance of others as our loss and deprivation. God alone satisfies; His will for us is the best. Saint Teresa of Avila gives us words of encouragement: "Let nothing disturb you, let nothing frighten you, all things are passing away: God never changes. Patience obtains all things. Whoever has God lacks nothing; God alone suffices." Saint Peter, pray for us who suffer from envy. Amen.

At the root of this attitude is a spiritual blindness about our identity. Deep rooted envy reveals a lack of self-knowledge. We should use every means at our disposal to gain self-knowledge. This will help us to accept and love ourselves the way we are, and to accept and love others the way they are; then the wall of envy will start tumbling down.

In the fight to overcome envy, the intercession of the Mother of Sorrows is necessary. By her faith and union with the Passion of her Son to save the world, she entered into the pain of all humanity. She is the Mediatrix of all Graces; Mother of the Cross. Through her, let us pray for the grace of generosity, which is revealed in the Cross.

We invoke the graces of the pain our Blessed Mother suffered at the *Sixth Sorrow*: Jesus' Body is Taken Down from the Cross (Lk 23:52–53), to heal the wound of envy in our hearts. These graces will help us to be content with God's personal and unique love for us. May the gaze of Mother Mary as she held the lifeless body of her Divine Son in her arms, inspire us to go to Jesus, who gives us hope and life by His resurrection. We pray for the renewal of faith, hope and love in our hearts: First, to experience God's love, and second, to love Him and all creatures for His sake. In this regard, we should strive to imitate the virtues of our Blessed Mother, especially, her ardent charity, profound humility and blind obedience.

Spiritual warfare against envy

There are evil spirits that associate with the sin of envy, *viz*, envy, resentment, low-self-esteem, hatred, anger, fear of failure, fear of rejection, fear, self-condemnation, self-pity, hostility, unforgiveness, etc. These spirits aim to disrupt our relationship with God, by having us focus on worldly things. We must be vigilant and use the means prescribed above to close the doors to envy. Refer to chapter 5: "Understanding Basic Spiritual Warfare."

Chapter 8

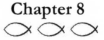

Primary Open Door 2: Avarice (Greed) or Covetousness

Where there are great riches, there are also many to devour them. Of what use are they to the owner except to feast his eyes upon? (Ecc 5:10).

Avarice, Saint Thomas Aquinas says, is the inordinate desire and love of riches and worldly goods.[244] Our corrupt nature craves corrupt goods in an inordinate way. This sin is said to be the root of all sins. Scripture says, "The desire for money is the root of all evil" (1 Tim 6:10). There is a tendency in us, because of our wounded human nature, to want to attach to things. God created us with the capacity to desire, hunger and thirst in order to be satisfied. This is a most beautiful gift of our humanity given to us to desire to be like God. We are created in His divine image and likeness. Our deepest hunger is for God. Only God can fill the deepest longing of the human heart. Saint Augustine's personal search for meaning in life brought him to the conclusion that, "our hearts are restless until they rest in God."

Our only healthy and life giving attachment should be God. For this reason God said, "I, the Lord, am your God... You shall not have other gods besides me" (Ex 20:2–3). God also said, "You shall not covet your neighbor's goods" (Ex 20:17). Avarice comes against these commandments, because "strange gods" and "neighbor's goods" take the place of God in our hearts, and these do not satisfy and never can satisfy.

If we are greedy, we are out of balance within ourselves and with God. Things are no longer properly ordered, and we know it and feel it. When there is avarice we do not love ourselves and our neighbor, and we do not love God. We love the things we desire more than God. We are willing to sacrifice everything and anything for that which we desire. In fact, we will sacrifice time, family, resources, relationships, talents, and ultimately eternity for that which we are greedy of.

Jesus said, "Where your treasure is, there your heart will be" (Mt 6:21). Greed is its own treasure. It loves itself, consumes itself, serves itself, and destroys itself. Greed is its own master; there is no love of God, because the greedy person has a divided heart. No one can at one and the same time love two masters, "You cannot serve God and Mammon" (Mt 6:24), Jesus said. The greedy person is god unto himself/herself. The predicament of the greedy person is that his heart is not rules by charity, but by attachment to possessions. As such, he is not, and cannot be a servant, since the logo of a servant's heart is the cross of Christ. The cross is the logo of *agape* love, and suffering its motto; and the greedy person lacks both.

Jesus knows well our capacity to desire things. So, He placed a blessing upon it, "Blessed are those who hunger and thirst for righteousness, they will be satisfied" (Mt 5:6). Saint Augustine taught that desire is all it takes to possess. If you want to possess God, desire God. If you want to possess a car, desire a car. If you want to possess chocolate ice-cream, desire it. You will possess what you desire, because you desire.

The rich young man in the Gospels came to Jesus and expressed his desire for eternal life. But he went away sad because he had another master—his possessions. His goods possessed him because he had bonded himself so strongly to them. He did not have control over his possessions, his possessions controlled him. What a lamentable predicament. Greed functions like an octopus or a squid. It will not let go of whatever it latches itself onto. This grabbing onto is characteristic of greed. It is a driving appetite in us, and we find every possible excuse to possess that which our hearts desire.

Jesus strongly cautions that we guard against greed, because our lives do not depend on possessions. He illustrates this teaching in the parable of the rich fool, who did not care about the wellbeing of the poor around him. In his greed, he tore down his barn, built a larger one to store his plentiful harvest, and said to himself, "You have so many good things stored up for many years, rest, eat, drink, be merry!" But God calls him a 'fool,' and that same night his life was demanded of him. "Thus will it be for the one who stores up treasure for himself but is not rich in what matters to God" (Lk 12:15-21).

A greedy person is like cancer in the body. Cancer is notorious and deadly, because it grows out of control only benefiting itself. As cancer does not exist for the good of other cells in the body, so is the greedy person in the Mystical Body of Christ. Ann Voskamp said that, "Cancer is what refuses to die to self," and so cannot benefit others. Such is the life of the greedy; it is not rich in what matters to God. Charity alone matters to God. A greedy person lives a life opposed to the cross of Christ, and so is cancer in the Body of Christ. He accumulates wealth only for himself, while others languish and die in abject poverty. Cancer is not, and cannot be a servant of others, because a servant must have Christ-like virtues. Christ came not to be served but to serve and to offer His life in atonement for our sins, and as an oblation to ransom many (Mk 10:45).

I visited a friend not long ago, and we went out in the evening to eat in a restaurant located in a huge casino. This was my first time being in this kind of place. I saw men and women seated upright, looking onto screens in front of them. They had strings that hooked them to colorful machines. I watched them closely, but did not understand what they were doing. They appeared to me to be in a different world. I asked my priest friend why these people had strings hooking them to those machines, and what they were doing. He had a very good and loud laugh at my question and explained that these men and women were gambling on slot machines because we were in a casino. It blew me away. These people are driven by a deep desire for instant wealth. What drew my attention was their utter concentration on the slot machines. I was told that some of them spend the whole day there. They come prepared with lots of hard earned money. They go home empty-handed, but they return and keep coming back.

The Pharaohs of Egypt were so greedy that they kept the Israelites in bondage under hard labor, and milking them for 430 years. God said to Pharaoh through Moses, "Let my people go to worship me in the desert" (Ex 7:16). Pharaoh would not let God's people go, because greed had latched itself onto him. He fed off from the Israelites' slave labor and enriched his kingdom. He was greedy of the forced labor of the Israelites. This is how powerful and deadly greed can be. It took the death of all the first-born of the Egyptians and their livestock to force Pharaoh to let the Israelites go. Greed can make us hold onto the passing things of this world, even to the death, and sadly, even to the loss of eternity.

Jesus poses a question to anyone with a tendency toward greed: "For what will it profit a man if he gains the whole world and forfeits his soul? Or what shall a man give in return for his soul?" (Mt 16:26, ESV). He gives us hope and encouragement when He tells us not to worry about our life, what we will eat and drink; or what clothes we are to wear. Our life, Jesus says, is worth more than food and our body more precious than clothing. We are to "Seek first the kingdom of God and His righteousness, and all these things will be given you besides" (Mt 6:25, 33).

Spiritual greed

We can be attached to spiritual goods just as we can be attached to material goods. For religious persons and those aspiring to high spiritual standards, greed is a potential threat. The vow or practice of poverty helps to regulate greed in exterior and interior renunciation.[245] Greed will tend to keep the letter of the vow, but not the spirit of the vow. This will ultimately bring the greedy person to a dead end. Greed of this kind can lead to attachment to religious practices and devotions without any interior conversion, commitment and conviction. There is no authentic relationship with God. Jesus says of these people that their worship and honor is only lip service, their hearts are not with God (Mk 7:6).

Greed self-examination questions:
- Do I desire to hoard things?
- Do I have an excessive love of money?
- What is my source of security?
- Am I materialistic?
- Do I crave things I do not have?
- Am I jealous?
- Am I possessive of knowledge, devotions, books, precious items, things, or friends?
- Am I selfish or self-centered?
- Do I practice mortification (with permission)?
- Do I let things go?
- Do I complain or blame or nag?
- Is Jesus my only treasure?
- What do I value most in life?
- Do I find it difficult to give things up?
- Am I greedy?
- Do I tend to control everything around me?
- Do I get angry and lose my peace when I cannot get my way?
- Do I micro-manage?
- Do I show or feel discomfort that someone may be holier than I am?
- What is my attitude toward the Cross of Jesus?
- Is my attitude toward money causing me to lie, defraud, or fear?
- How do I feel about poverty? Am I scared of being poor?
- How is Jesus calling me to be poor today?
- Do I worry about tomorrow?
- Am I afraid of commitment?
- How do I become more detached from worldly things, and grow in interior freedom?
- Am I divided within myself? Do I have peace?
- Do I practice daily dying and surrender?
- Am I miserly?
- Am I poor in spirit?
- Am I generous?
- In what do I boast: money, wealth, position, job, power, or God?
- What gives me the most confidence in life?
- Am I afraid of dying?
- Do I have a messiah complex?
- What is my attitude to devotions?
- What are my attachments?

- Am I uncomfortable when someone is helping me?
- Do I allow people to help me, even with things I can do?

The weapons against greed

Weapons of the Spirit

When the Spirit of the Lord came upon us at Baptism, He gave us His Second Gift of **Understanding.** Paul says that we have not received the spirit of the world, but God's Spirit to help us understand the things God has freely given us (1 Cor 2:10–13). *The Spirit of Understanding* (Is 11:2) gives us the inner strength rooted in a life of faith in the truth of the mysteries of salvation to combat greed. It enlightens our minds to grasp the inner meaning of the revealed truth of our Christian faith:[246] the Incarnation, the death of Jesus on the Cross, the Resurrection, the dogma of the Immaculate Conception, etc. We grow in a deeper appreciation of them, and experience new life in Christ. Our faith ceases to be sterile and inactive, and we boldly witness the Good News without fear or favor. We become the branch on the vine that is pruned to bear more fruit for the Kingdom of God. Jesus gave His disciples the gift of Understanding as He opened their minds to understand the Scriptures and to know the signs of the times.

The Word of God, the weapon of truth, is what we need against the lie beneath the greed-drive in us. It is when we pray and ponder God's word that we come to understand God's will for us. This means we are to slow down and pay attention to God's words and actions. The greedy person lacks self-knowledge; she does not understand herself and her struggles.

The healing of greed comes through an intense prayer life, the embrace of the contemplative approach. We need the *Shield of Faith* as our armor to fight greed. Faith wards off the fiery darts of the evil one. We also need the *Sword of the Spirit: the Word of God* as a weapon of offense against greed. We must put on the *Helmet of Salvation* and the *Breastplate of Righteousness.*

God does not force healing on us; that would violate the law of love. He wants us to be part of the process of our own healing and salvation. Saint Augustine said: "God, who created us without our consent, cannot save us without our consent." Paul would say, "Therefore, my beloved, just as you have always obeyed me, not only in my presence, but much more now in my absence, work out your own salvation with fear and trembling" (Phil 2:12, NRSV).

The *Breastplate of Righteousness* (Eph 6:14) is the Armor of God the Spirit gives us to wage war on greed. Righteousness is God's cleanliness and purity and holiness; it is God's weapon. It comes against the devil's weapon of unbelief, which prevents us from understanding and practicing our faith more intensely, because we are too immersed in the things of this world and its value system.

Word from the Cross

As Jesus was dying on the Cross, He spoke the *Seventh Word* that frees our hearts from the possessive love of worldly goods: ***"Father, into your hands I commend my spirit"*** (Lk 23:46). Jesus, the Suffering Servant, willingly surrenders all to the Father. He gives Himself away for the good of others; He became a ransom for many. No one can equal the obedient poverty and surrender of Jesus revealed in these precious words spoken to the Father in His total self-sacrifice. To give away one's spirit to God is true humility. It is true poverty. It is to depend on God for security, for life, and for everything. Jesus' definitive self-surrender teaches us the power of poverty freely chosen. "I lay down my life on my own," Jesus said, "no one takes it away from me;" "I have power to lay it down and power to take it up again" (Jn 10:18, NKJV). This final self-emptying action of Jesus (*kenosis*) shows that there is no poverty greater than surrendering one's own spirit and placing it in God's hands. The struggle against greed calls us to entrust all that we are and have into God's caring hands like obedient sheep, and cease worrying (Mt 6; 1 Pet 5:7).

Saint Francis of Assisi prayed: "For it is in giving that we receive... And it is in dying that we are born to eternal life." The more perfectly we renounce and detach from worldly things, the more peaceful and happy our lives will be in this life.[247] God gives true happiness to the poor in spirit. Because of His poverty, God highly exalted Jesus, and gave Him a name above every other name, and seating Him at His right hand in glory. At the name of the Poor Man, Jesus, everyone is saved who believes and obeys Him as the Lord, the Son of God (Phil 2:9–11).

To be poor in spirit is a quality of the heart attainable by both the materially poor and rich. Poverty of spirit is incompatible with a miserly life, which is selfishness. A miser seeks to acquire and hoard things. Here, "Possession becomes a passion spreading to things that are not worth keeping or which will be wasted when kept."[248] To be stingy violates the law of poverty and offends charity. Poverty is "the means to keep regulated and normal the tendency to want to own things and to have a personal use of things."[249] The practice of poverty trains us to be generous in giving up worldly things. There is a satisfaction, a joy, and a happiness that comes by detaching from earthly things. Jesus said, "Whoever wishes to come after me must deny himself" (Mt 10:24). We must choose to die to the false self in us that seeks to attach to things. The false self is cancer to itself and in the Body of Christ.

People who are too attached to worldly things easily worry and are afraid at the slightest trial or danger. But detachment brings interior peace and stability and calm to those trained by it. Even when things are falling apart, they know and are convinced that God is always in control, and His words do not pass away.

Generosity or liberality is the virtue we need against spiritual and material greed. Jesus invited the rich young man to follow Him, if he wants to be perfect. But first he must demonstrate generosity of heart and self-emptying virtue by selling all his possessions and give the proceeds to the poor. In this way he stores up treasure in heaven, becomes free from attachment to earthly possessions (Mt 19:21), grows in conformity to Christ in discipleship, and can now practice *agape* love onto perfection. God cannot be outdone in generosity. All God's commandments are designed to help us become charitable and poor in spirit. Jesus promised, "Blessed are the poor in spirit, for theirs is the kingdom of heaven" (Mt 5:3). There is no generosity greater than giving one's life, heart, soul, body, and blood; one's all, even one's own spirit away to God. Jesus did this perfectly and without hesitation on the cross. He did it to save us. Only Jesus, by His own power, and in His nature as God, is able to give Himself away as He did. We can do the same only by His grace. Jesus will grant us this grace if we desire it; He says ask, and we shall receive. He wanted to bestow this grace on the rich young man, by inviting him to come and follow Him. It is in following, believing, and obeying Jesus' commands that we receive the grace to die to false self, and become generous in giving of ourselves. We become true servants in the Church. A true servant gives himself away for the good of others. The logo of a true servant's heart is the cross. Greedy persons do not have servant hearts, because they are opposed to the cross. They are cancer in the body of Christ, since they benefit no one but only themselves.

Our tendency to control under the guise of goodness should be examined carefully. To micro manage others is not healthy, it is greed. The false idea that 'without me, nothing will be accomplished,' is greed. It is also greed to think and act as if to indicate: "I have to do everything myself." Or, "I don't want anybody to help me." We should imitate Jesus' example of receptivity: He depended on others for food; everything He had He received—His name, His clothes, His humanity, His Apostles, the Spirit, His parents, His Baptism, His Cross, His death, and all sinners. He allowed other people to help Him: John baptized Him, Simon carried His Cross, Veronica wiped His face, He was homeless, He begged the Samaritan woman at the well for a drink of water. What great humility Jesus shows us? What great generosity of heart in poverty? What great radical receptivity? Jesus, who is God, wants to receive from us. Do we want to receive from Him?

Closing the open door of greed

The first step in healing greed is to recognize and acknowledge its presence; honesty is required. If we deny it, we deny ourselves. We need time for personal self-reflection and recollection to identify its manifestations in our hearts. One-on-one time with Jesus is necessary so He can teach us, love us, and show us the root of greed in us. The capital sins in us have roots. To eradicate them, we need to study and recognize these roots—the belief systems that drive and influence us to greed. The healing of greed brings freedom and bears the fruit of joy and happiness in our hearts. Detachment and dying to the false self should define our efforts. The prayer of John the Baptist would be apt: "He must increase; I must decrease" (Jn 3:30).

The practice of daily poverty of spirit in concrete ways will speed our recovery from greed. Jesus is our only example in this regard. Meditation on His poverty and suffering, His hidden life in Nazareth, His occupation as a Carpenter, His obedience to His parents, His life with His Apostles, His patience, abandonment and total detachment from worldly things, "I do not belong to this world" (Jn 8:23); His commitment to the mission He received from the Father, are opportunities for us to grow in intimacy and configuration to Jesus. Meditation on His Passion, His life of service, His crucifixion, and His wounds by which we are healed, will be fruitful spiritual exercises.

The deliberate and persistent practice of generosity will heal the greedy heart. Generosity expands our hearts to receive more of God, and unite us with the Poor Man, Jesus, so that we trust Him especially in trials. Dependence on the Father must be our strength and hope; this we pledged to do at our baptism, and each time we say: "Our Father... give us this day, our daily bread." This is the prayer of a child who has leaned to trust that *Abba*, Father, will provide. A greedy person does not rely on *Abba,* but steals from Him through greed, since everything belongs to the Father.

We pray that the graces of the pain our Blessed Mother suffered at the *First Sorrow*: the Prophecy of Simeon that a sword would pierce her Immaculate Heart (Lk 2:34–35), would uproot greed in our hearts. At the piercing of the Immaculate Heart, which happened at the piercing of Jesus' Heart for our sins, the secret thoughts of our hearts are revealed, and the darkness of greed exposed. Christ's light from on high dispels the darkness and falsehood, bringing us peace and healing, so that the pure of heart sees God. We also strive to imitate the Blessed Virgin's principal virtues, especially, her blind obedience, mortification in all things, continual mental prayer, profound humility and a lively faith.

Spiritual warfare against greed

Scripture says that "the whole world is under the power of the evil one" (1 Jn 5:19). The "world" here means the "value system," or the "belief system" that are opposed to God and His rule, not the world as God created it. The spirit of the world is Satan. It is the spirit of disobedience. Satan uses greed to keep us attached to this world so we do not focus and rise up to God. God is Spirit and those who worship Him must worship Him in Spirit and truth. The spirit of the world wants Catholics to believe that the Holy Eucharist is only a symbol and that it is not really, truly and substantially the Body, Blood, Soul and Divinity of Jesus Christ.

The spirits of greed collaborate destructively with other evil spirits of unbelief, lies, and deception to create confusion in the mind and heart of believers, causing deadness of faith. There are also the evil spirits of idolatry and addictions, fears, division, indecision, sloth, desolation, and a host of others at work in the greedy soul. It is not important to know all the evil spirits involved. Our attention should always focus on growing in intimacy and faith in our Lord Jesus Christ. When we have the shield of faith on, we are protected against Satan's fiery darts. We grow in faith by daily prayer, as we listen attentively and reflectively to God's word.

Chapter 9

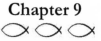

Primary Open Door 3: Pride

The sinful words of their mouths and lips let them be caught in their pride (Ps 59:13).

Pride, Thomas Aquinas says, is man aiming higher than he is. A proud man "wishes to appear above what he really is."[250] Pride is opposed to reason, and "reason requires that every man's will should tend to that which is proportionate to him."[251] "Pride is opposed to humility."[252] Humility brings man into subjection to God and His rule.[253] "Pride is love of one's own excellence," and it competes with God in excellence.[254] It strives to rise above that which is appointed to him by Divine rule and is contrary to Paul's inspired words: "But we will not boast beyond measure but will keep to the limits God has apportioned for us..." (2 Cor 10:13).[255] Saint Augustine believes that, "According to God's law, pride is a very different sin from other vices." He insists: "You will find no sin that is not labeled pride."[256] "Without pride no sin is, or was, or will ever be possible."[257]

God resists the sin of pride. As Scripture says, "God resists the proud, but gives grace to the humble" (Jam 4:6). Jesus personifies humility, and He invites us to "Learn from me, I am meek and humble of heart" (Mt 11:29). Paul speaks of Jesus' practical humility: "He emptied himself, taking the form of a slave, coming in human likeness; and found human in appearance, he humbled himself, becoming obedient to death, even death on a cross" (Phil 2:7–8).

Satan embodies pride, and Scripture says of the evil one:

How you are fallen from heaven, O Lucifer, son of the morning! How you are cut down to the ground, you who weakened the nations! For you have said in your heart: 'I will ascend into heaven, I will exalt my throne above the stars of God; I will also sit on the mount of the congregation. On the farthest sides of the north; I will ascend above the heights of the clouds, I will be like the Most High.' Yet you shall be brought down to Sheol, To the lowest depths of the Pit (Is 14:12–15, NKJV).

Jesus alerts us: "I have observed Satan fall like lightning from the sky" (Lk 10:18). The wisdom of the Scriptures teach that, "Pride goes before disaster, and a haughty spirit before a fall" (Prov 16:18). Pride rebels against God and His reign in us. The Blessed Virgin's song of praise tells us the

● ● ●

fate of the proud: "He has scattered the proud in the thoughts of their hearts; he has brought down the mighty from their thrones" (Lk 1:51–52, ESV). We can easily detect pride in our thought process if we examine our minds carefully. It all begins in the mind. The healing of pride must also begin in the mind (Rom 12:2).

The Book of Sirach 35:17 teaches that the prayers of humble people pierce the heavens, but the prayers of the proud go nowhere, because such prayers are resisted by God. The parable of the Pharisee and the tax collector shows how God highly regards the humble, but resists the proud. The tax collector is justified in his prayer, because humility makes him acknowledge his nothingness and dependence on God. He expressed his need for a savior. The Pharisee on the other hand, demonstrates his self-righteousness and self-reliance before God, and was not justified (Lk 18:10–14).

The capital sin of pride elevates self above God and others. It places self at the center of the universe, so that all else revolves around him and has reference to him. The proud man thinks that without him the world will come to a stop. He believes that if he does not perform the task, no one else can. So, he never allows anyone to help; he does it all alone. Pride is the summit of self-love. Calvary is the summit of God's love and humility. Pride manifests through disobedience and rebellion. Adam and Eve fell through pride.

Sirach 10:15 says, "Pride is the beginning of all sin." It is also the first sin committed according to Paul: "By one man sin entered into the world" (Rom 5:12). Saint Gregory considers pride to be the Queen of all the vices.[258]

The shades of pride

Pride of authority or superiority

This is excessive self-love. It tries to control everything. It manifests in words, thoughts and deeds by being angry and critical, bossy, argumentative, domineering and arrogant; and it exaggerates reality. This kind of pride causes people to be totally independent of anyone. They don't need anybody's help. They don't want anybody or God to tell them what to do. This kind of pride does not admit of weakness. It never apologizes, because that would belittle him. It is rigid and unyielding in dealing with others. It is deceptive, contemptuous and filled with contradictions. It refuses to accept advice or counsel, even from God. It ultimately leads to disobedience because it is unreasonable.

Pride of timidity

This is unfounded fear rooted in self-love by which we try to hide our weaknesses and faults to avoid being ridiculed. It is a fear that arises from others' opinion of us, whether we are liked or disliked. Pride of timidity can easily lead one to compromise principles and standards, because the only valid standards are the self; but these standards are constantly changing to accommodate what others think or say about us. There is a deep lack of self-confidence which seeks to protect or hide weaknesses.

Timid persons make resolutions, but lack the courage to keep them. They easily give up at the slightest excuse, because they lack the spiritual strength to fight daily and completely subdue timidity. Pride of timidity is afraid of failing, and so will hide that which it thinks will make it fail.

The humble person on the other hand, is not too afraid of failing or being weighed down by faults. Humble persons are calm in the struggle. They realize that God is always in control in spite of their weaknesses. Humble people forget themselves and depend on God. They live in the truth that they are weak and God is strong. This teaching we draw from the life of Saint Paul, "Therefore I am content with weaknesses, with insults, with troubles, with persecutions and difficulties for the sake of Christ, for whenever I am weak, then I am strong" (2 Cor 12:10, NET). The humble person realizes that human weakness is actually a gift by which we are to depend on God in order to be like God. Saint Augustine says, "God became man so that man might become God." It is humility that makes this possible. God's humility made Him Man; man's humility will make him God.

Pride of sensitivity

This pride results from a wounded self-love. The sensitive person is touchy and hurts easily.[259] These persons are stubbornly unforgiving, because they have spent much time searching for reasons to justify their behavior. There is a false satisfaction in not speaking to others, and they manifest false joy in ill feelings. The heart harbors grudges, anger and hostilities. There is a woundedness that comes from not being recognized, and there is a lot of brooding going on within based on the person's false view of reality. There are lots of mental rehearsals, imaginings, misjudging, planning and battles within the individual. This person is always coming up with reasons for the way things are, and the way things should be. The sensitive person is the cause of his own unhappiness and that of others. He has a wild imagination and creates improbable and almost impossible conditions[260] for a meaningful relationship. He imagines what may happen, and is always wounded by others' comments and actions, because he assumes they are directed at him. There is an unhealthy, false self-awareness that reveals an interior blindness.

Pride of complacency or vanity

Here, there is a craving to be well thought of or esteemed by others. This person is anxious to be well thought of regarding spiritual, mental and physical abilities.[261] There is a craving to want to be in the spotlight and to have everything figured out. Perfectionism, which is a state of bondage, is mistaken for perfection, which is a state of freedom, due to false assumptions.

The core problem with the pride of complacency is in the thought process. The manifestations of this pride may not be obvious, as the persons tend to deny or trivialize them, thereby making them worse. The Pharisees and scribes suffered from this kind of pride. They gloried in their own self-righteousness and looked down on others. Jesus pronounced woes on the scribes and Pharisees; He calls them – hypocrites, who are like decorated tombs, beautiful and swept clean on the outside, but inside it is all rotten and filled with dead people's bones and smells so bad (Mt 23:27).

This kind of pride is boastful, critical and legalistic. It often resorts to lies in order to appear good and perfect before others. There is an inordinate attachment to rules that compromises charity toward the neighbor. One "who is truly spiritual, or intellectual, or who lives up to a fine standard in general, or who is close to perfection, striving earnestly for it, could still be subject to vanity. He may fail to recognize what God has given him or he could use his gifts in the wrong way."[262] There is always a false motive behind the actions of the vain person. The motive is the esteem of others and self while forgetting God.[263] "They place goodness, not in faithful service to God through daily affairs, but in exceptional things, particularly devotions that attract the attention of others."[264] Their piety is offensive and their holiness suffers; people who cannot discern true and false piety see this false type, and decide they do not want to be good.[265] It is not necessarily true that such persons are vain; however, they are apt to insist on all the virtues except that which they lack—humility.[266]

Vain persons compare themselves with others, but our only standard must be Jesus Christ. Our eyes must be fixed on Jesus alone as the standard for humility and holiness. To focus on others is to reveal a deep lack of self-knowledge. This would give us a false assessment of our spiritual state and cause distractions. We then fall short of the high standards Jesus places before us—to become perfect the way our Heavenly Father is perfect (Mt 5:48). We fall short of the standard to love others as Jesus loves us (Jn 15:12).

Vanity makes a show of its gifts. It basks in vainglory and draws unnecessary attention to outward appearance while lacking any meaningful interior commitment or quality. Jesus said this of the vain Pharisees, "Woe to you, teachers of the law and Pharisees, you hypocrites! You clean the outside of the cup and dish, but inside they are full of greed and self-indulgence. Blind Pharisee! First clean the inside of the cup and dish, and then the outside also will be clean" (Mt 23:25–26, NIV). Saint Augustine wants us to understand that the sanctity of the body is not lost, as long as the sanctity of the soul remains.[267]

Christians live by the law of God written in their hearts, as the Prophet Jeremiah tells us, "I will place my law within them and write it upon their hearts" (Jer 31:33). The contemplative life pays attention to this law written in the human heart. It is a life essentially opposed to a pharisaic life. It is opposed to the vain lifestyle of mere outward appearance, a mechanical spirituality. The life of grace calls us to constant change from within, a true conversion of the heart.

When we are dealing with Jesus, He will challenge us as He challenged the rich young man when He said, "You lack one thing. Go, sell whatever you have and give the money to the poor, and you will have treasure in heaven. Then come, follow me" (Mk 10:21, NET). We all are always lacking in one thing. We are not perfect yet. The work of sanctification is never finished, until it is finished in Christ Jesus. It is a life of constantly becoming, as Paul testifies, "Not that I have already obtained this or have already reached the goal; but I press on to make it my own, because Christ Jesus has made me his own" (Phil 3:12, NRSV).

Pride of complacency can threaten and derail persons who are not yet matured in the spiritual life. Beginners in the spiritual life are quick to recognize their increased effort and progress in zeal. Beneath this progress, pride may begin to develop, and the beginners become complacent in their efforts and vain in their accomplishments. They can easily spot the faults of others and criticize them. There is a temptation to speak often of spiritual things, and even provide ready-made answers to others spiritual difficulties. This is often due to lack of prudence. The activity of the evil one becomes heightened, but since it is below their spiritual radar, it may go undetected. The vain person, in order to appear good, may even withhold faults from confessors or spiritual directors, if they have spiritual directors at all. For such persons generally direct themselves, because they cannot submit to another.

Pride of the intellect

This kind of pride claims to know it all. It tends to resist help from others, or receive advice. Like pride in general, there is excessive self-love involved. It is characterized by excessive attachment to one's ideas and opinions that lead to arguments and conflicts. Operating beneath this pride is a fear of failure that masks itself in wanting to win. In the pride of the intellect, the mind dominates and rules the heart, but in a healthy and sound situation, the mind works in harmony with the heart aided by the light of faith and reason and the grace of the Holy Spirit. Pride of the intellect easily leads to the sin of presumption. Prideful persons think that because they are practicing Christians, they can do and say whatever they like.

There was this case of a Nigerian evangelical pastor who told his church members that he was going into the lion's den in a zoo with his Bible. He boasted he would go in there and stroke the lions like Daniel did and no harm would befall him. Without the knowledge of the zoo attendants, he climbed into the zoo with his Bible in hand. When the lions were released from their cages, the beasts spotted him, went for him, and devoured him. His boastings of "Holy Ghost power" came to nothing. He did not live to tell the story of his experience.

We cannot presume that because we are children of God by baptism, that we can simply manipulate God and put Him to the test. We cannot deliberately walk into harm's way and expect God to rescue us anyway. Jesus answered the devil, "It is written, you shall not put the Lord, your God, to the test" (Mt 4:7).

Satan tempted Jesus, and said to Him: "'If you are the Son of God...' 'throw yourself down. For it is written: He will command his angels concerning you, and they will lift you up in their hands, so that you will not strike your foot against a stone'" (Mt 4:6, NIV). Jesus did not presume the Father's love for Him; to do so would mean to walk ahead of the Father instead of following Him. He taught His followers the value of obedience as a *sine qua non* for authentic discipleship. And so He says to them and to us, "Follow me."

Jesus desires to conform our hearts to His by filling them with His divine love. He wants to transform our minds to His so that we can do the Father's will. A prideful person avoids these things and so sins against faith. Jesus revealed His Sacred Heart to Saint Margaret Mary Alacoque and calls us to imitate His humble heart. God is love. It is the heart that receives God's revelations. Discernment is a gift of the heart. It is the peaceful heart that knows and understands the things of God. Jesus' Heart is a childlike Heart. Saint Seraphim of Sarov said, "All our thoughts, all our desires, all our efforts, and all our actions should make us say constantly with the Church: "O Lord, give us peace!" When a man lives in peace, God reveals mysteries to him."

Persons with intellectual pride want to reach the heights of perfection without going through the purgation process. The rich young man desired

Heaven, but refused to associate and follow the Way to Heaven—the Crucified Lord. He wanted to enter eternal life, but was not prepared to leave earthly life behind. Sometimes, we want to be free like the butterfly without first becoming like the vulnerable caterpillar that can lose its life any time. To these souls, the Holy Spirit says: "Trust in the LORD with all your heart, on your own intelligence rely not" (Prov 3:5).

Pride of ambition

This kind of pride focuses attention and energy on achievements. Here, life is all about achieving even if it means stepping on another person's life, honor, interest, and property. It is driven by the unethical philosophy that the end justifies the means. Pride of ambition has a deep, blinding effect on one's conscience. We prefer ourselves to others, and we place ourselves before and above others. There is excessive desire for praise and recognition. There is excessive confidence in the self and in one's abilities. These manifestations of excessive self-love are rooted in a deep emptiness of the heart and a profound lack of self-knowledge, as well as a deep fear of God as our most loving Father. It manifests lack of trust in God.

Pride of scrupulosity

This pride attaches excessive importance to the wrong things, things that should not merit the excessive attention that is given to them. There is misplacement of priority and the neglect of important things. It is a frequent cause of worry, frustration and unhappiness, and can lead to addictions to work and substances. Jesus said to Martha who was burdened and complaining, "Martha, Martha, you are worried and troubled about many things. But one thing is needed, and Mary has chosen that good part, which will not be taken away from her" (Lk 10:41–42, NKJV). Martha paid attention to Jesus' concern for her welfare and overcame her pride. She later lived as a contemplative and became a Saint like her sister Mary Magdalene.

Pride self-reflection questions
- Do I acknowledge the Lordship of Jesus Christ?
- Do I give credit to what belongs to God?
- Am I grateful for the gifts I have received?
- Do I recognize that I am a gift?
- Do I think of myself as above others?
- Do I readily accept advice?
- Do I tend to be bossy?
- Do I put myself first?

- Am I a perfectionist?
- Have I talked to Jesus about my pride?
- Am I critical or do I belittle others?
- Do I find myself always wanting to control?
- Do I speak ill or lie about others?
- Am I fond of blaming or accusing others?
- Am I comfortable surrendering to others?
- Do I refuse to speak to anyone or avoid others?
- Do I always have to win an argument?
- Do I ever admit being wrong? Do I apologize when I am wrong?
- Is it my habit to provide answers to other people's problems?
- Do I tend to correct people and prove them wrong?
- Do I easily get angry or irritated?
- Do I get angry when opposed?
- Do I take quiet time for self-reflection?
- Do I get angry or frustrated at my mistakes?
- Do I have a timid disposition?
- Do I willingly welcome advice and correction?
- Do I take counsel with God before I act?
- Do I seek to do God's will?
- Do I seek praise and recognition? Am I competitive?
- Does a timid behavior keep me from doing what is right?
- Have I allowed other's words or actions to prevent me from obeying God?
- Does my pride force others to walk on egg shells?
- Am I vain in my lifestyle?
- Am I too self-conscious?
- Are my weaknesses and faults leading me to fear being ridiculed?
- Do I hide my physical, mental, and spiritual abilities?
- Do I shy away from engaging in public activities?
- Am I faithful to all the Church teaches?
- Do I tend to interrupt others?
- Am I overly sensitive or wounded?
- Do I treat others as I would like to be treated?
- Do I carry unforgiveness or grudges in my heart?
- Do I talk to Jesus about prideful tendencies?
- Do I practice spiritual childhood?
- Am I thankful for the gifts others have?
- Is my piety offensive to others?
- Do I envy what other people have?

- Do I compare myself with others and what they have?
- Do I hide spiritual information from my spiritual director or confessor or superior?
- Do I criticize Bishops or Priests? Do I criticize the Vicar of Christ?
- Do I tend to complain always?
- Do I easily notice the faults of others and speak about them?
- Do I judge others or speak ill of them?
- Am I comfortable sharing and talking about my relationship with Jesus?
- Am I gentle in correcting others?
- Do I tend to defend myself or my opinion at all cost?
- Do I easily want to tell others what I know?
- Am I comfortable mentioning the name of Jesus Christ?
- Am I proud in my way of life?
- Do I feel the priest is wasting my time at Mass?
- Do I challenge legitimate authority?
- Am I worried that I am not holy?
- Am I striving to be humble?
- Am I vain in the way I comport myself?
- Am I easily attracted to vanity?
- Do I look at my wrist-watch at Mass (impatience)?
- Do I boast or exaggerate things?
- Do I celebrate the Sacrament of Penance regularly for my sins?
- Do I allow others to take the first place?
- Do I practice obedience even when it is difficult?
- Do I practice mortification or penance for others to notice?
- What is my motive for the things I do?
- Do I seek to please God alone?

The weapons against pride

Weapons of the Spirit

When the Spirit of the Lord came upon us at Baptism, He gave us His Third Gift of **Counsel.** The *Spirit of Counsel* (Is 11:2) is God's weapon against pride. Counsel is supernatural common-sense which enables us to judge promptly and rightly what we must do, especially in difficult and challenging situations so as to please God in our daily duties and trials, and by so doing gain eternal life.[268] To have the mind of Christ and the disposition of Christ is to be open to God's wise and unfailing counsel (1 Cor 2:16).

Jesus desires that we possess this gift as a safeguard against the constant menace of the devil, which sneaks about looking for someone to devour through pride. Adam and Eve did not fall into the sin of pride when they were tempted; they fell because they did not seek Counsel with God when they were tempted.

The prideful person refuses to seek Counsel with God or take advice even when it matters most. Pride would prefer to move forward blindfolded, and does not care or is *careless* of the consequences of its actions. [Wisdom] says the Lord "stores up sound wisdom for the upright; he is a shield to those who walk blamelessly, guarding the paths of justice and preserving the way of his faithful ones" (Prov 2:7–8, NRSV).

Humility is the principal virtue that destroys pride. Humility is the acknowledgment of the truth of who God is and who we are. Humility means to live under the Lordship of Jesus Christ. A humble person seeks counsel and does not move forward in the dark. Jesus teaches us to relate with the Father as He did: "I cannot do anything on my own; I judge as I hear... because I do not seek my own will but the will of the one who sent me" (Jn 5:30, 19; 8:28). Jesus wants us to learn from His meek and humble Heart. To attain this humility, Jesus draws our attention to the qualities of a child. We should become like little children, if we would enter the Kingdom of God (Mt 18:3).

The attitude of pride is total independence from God, which says "my will be done, my kingdom come." But humility says: "Thy will be done." "Thy Kingdom come." Pride darkens our intellect and weakens our faculties. It deprives us of knowledge of God and self, and we fail to understand what God is doing in our hearts. Humility allows God's light to penetrate us so that we see as Jesus sees, and accept to live in the Divine Will. Saint Gregory tells us why we should combat pride: "Pride is by no means content with the destruction of one virtue; it raises itself up against all the powers of the soul, and like an all-pervading and poisonous disease corrupts the whole body."[269]

Humility takes seriously Jesus' words: "Without me you can do nothing" (Jn 15:5). As long as we are armed with Jesus and His word, we will be victorious in all our battles. The battle between humility and pride played itself out in the encounter between David and Goliath of Gath.

The prideful boastful Goliath challenged the little shepherd boy, David, who, armed with a little slingshot and five smooth stones and the power of God behind him, goes against the giant Goliath clothed in the armor of pride. This was the battle of the two kingdoms: the kingdom of God and the kingdom of the devil. David said to Goliath, "You come against me with sword and spear and scimitar, but I come against you in the name of the LORD of hosts, the God of the armies of Israel that you have insulted" (1 Sam 17:45). In the presence of humility, pride has no chance. Saint Paul teaches us to trust God in our battles: "I can do all things in him who strengthens me" (Phil 4:13).

The Armor of God to wage a victorious war against pride is *the Helmet of Salvation* (Eph 6:17). We must put on the mind of Christ in His obedient surrender. Pride refuses to surrender and depend on God. We can only receive the gift of salvation if we are humble and obedient to all that God asks. Our prayer should be: "Father, Your will be done."

Word from the Cross

Our Lord Jesus Christ dying on the Cross spoke the *Fourth Word* that crushes pride in our hearts: ***"My God, my God, why have you forsaken me"*** (Mt 15:34). This is a cry of total dependence on God and of abandonment to the Divine Will. His was a cry of humility; a weak Man dying for others. Jesus takes on the mystery of sin in His weak Humanity by His Passion. Abused and taunted to forsake His mission by the onlookers: come down from the Cross if you are God's Son, "He saved others, he cannot save himself" (Mt 4:6; 27:42–43), Jesus knew that evil has no power over Him (Jn 14:30). In His anguish, He cried out to God in total surrender, as the Psalmist taught Him to pray: "In my distress I called on the LORD, He answered me and set me free" (Ps 118:5; 34:5). Jesus, always a child, chose to depend totally on His Daddy, Abba, as He loved His own to the very end. By this faithfulness, Jesus won for us the strength of obedient surrender to God when pride strikes us with discouragement and the temptation to quit our struggle for Heaven.

The meek and humble Jesus came to seek and to save the lost (Lk 19:10). He identified with the poor and the lowly. He went in search of the lost sheep. He performed the humble act of washing the Apostles' feet. He said to them, I did not come to be served; I came to serve you, and to give My life to ransom many (Mk 10:45). He invites us to imitate His humility, "I have given you a model to follow, so that as I have done for you, you should also do" (Jn 13:15).

Jesus showed a great act of humility, when in His innocence; He identifies with sinners, and chose to suffer for them. Paul says that Jesus committed no sin, but He became sin itself, so that in us the righteousness of God might be revealed (2 Cor 5:21). It is a great act of humility that Jesus—"in whom we have redemption, the forgiveness of sins." "the image of the invisible God;" "the firstborn of all creation;" "in him all things in heaven and on earth were created things visible and invisible whether thrones or dominions or rulers or powers—all things have been created through him and for him;" "He himself is before all things;" "in him all things hold together;" "He is the head of the body, the church;" "he is the beginning, the firstborn from the dead, so that he might come to have first place in everything." "For in him all the fullness of God was pleased to dwell" (Col 1:14–19, NRSV)—allowed Himself to be baptized by John the Baptist in the River Jordan. Jesus, the King of kings and the Lord of lords, allowed Himself to be tempted by the devil, and to be judged by Pontius Pilate. He allowed Himself to be humiliated, and die the shameful death of the cross. When we choose to suffer for what we are not responsible for, that indeed is true humility. When we serve others or perform acts of charity without asking anything in return, that is true humility. When we can turn the other cheek and not strike back, that is true humility. It is the virtue we need to defeat pride in all its forms.

Closing the open door of pride

The first step to healing pride is to recognize and acknowledge we are prideful; we seek to identify and pinpoint the symptoms of pride in ourselves. We need self-knowledge which comes through personal self-reflection, in the silence and solitude of the inner room. We also need spiritual direction to help us be objective, and deepen our relationship with God. Most importantly, we need regular time to talk with Jesus in prayer and listen to Him (see chapter 4).

We must be willing and determined to get rid of pride with the help of God's grace. The biggest problem in dealing with pride and the other capital sins is recognizing and acknowledging their presence in us. We must declare an all-out war on the 'old man.' Often, we will discover that we are not serious in our commitment to this battle. Dealing with pride calls for commitment, and dying to our false-self. Half-measures will not be enough, and nothing should be taken for granted. We must remain strongly focused on Jesus, who said that heaven is for the strong: "Strive to enter through the narrow gate, for many, I tell you, will attempt to enter but will not be strong enough" (Lk 13:24).

Oftentimes we prefer pleasure to Paradise; we want to be saved, but avoid Calvary at all cost. Jesus takes our healing most seriously. He pledged to give us life in the fullest possible way (Jn 10:10). He questioned and then healed the man who was ill for thirty-eight years: "Do you want to be well?" "Rise, take up your mat, and walk" (Jn 5:6, 8). Jesus later found him in the temple area and said to him, "do not sin anymore, so that nothing worse may happen to you" (Jn 5:5–6, 14). Jesus desires to give us life more than we desire life.

The celebration of the Sacraments of Penance and Holy Eucharist are the most powerful healing remedies for pride. Praying with the Scriptures and talking to Jesus in prayer, as well as journaling out our experiences while working closely with our spiritual directors or confessors, are important steps to getting rid of pride. We must constantly check our thoughts, as pride reveals itself mostly in our thoughts.

We must pray for humility and strive to imitate Jesus. By praying the Litany of Humility (by Raphael Cardinal Merry del Val) often and practicing humility, we grow in humility. Humility, like all virtues must be exercised in order to bear the desired fruit. Practicing silence out of principle, i.e. being quiet when it is not necessary to speak, can help us grow in self-restraint and self-control. Oftentimes we speak because we want to be well thought of by others, or out of anger. It is both penitential and sacrificial to be silent and to listen. In discussions, we are often tempted to jump in and say something. We must choose to die to our preferences and opinions, and attach little or no value to our actions. We should prefer to be taught and instructed rather than to teach and instruct. We should not be carried away by others' praise of us, rather, we should acknowledge the truth about us when it is spoken, but not dwell on it. We should avoid retaliation in thought, word, and action; and learn to let things go and move on. Hold not to the past; live in the present moment must be a rule of life.

Spiritual warfare against pride

Satan personifies the spirit of pride. Other spirits associated with pride include: lies and deceptions, which are at the service of pride; rebellion, disobedience, and idolatry, antichrist, mockery and religiosity. The jezebel spirit deserves mention; it challenges the legitimate authority of God in the Church, families, societies and cultures. The spirit of pride can use other demons to execute their evil plans, e.g., repressed spirits can be used to distract our attention with the aim of destroying our relationship with God.

In spiritual warfare, we do not rely on the weapons of this world to fight, since our battle is not with flesh and blood (2 Cor 10:4; Eph 6:12). We submit and rely on God as the Psalmist prays: I raise my eyes toward the mountains. From where will my help come? My help comes from the LORD, the maker of heaven and earth (Ps 121:1–2). He continues:

> Look to God that you may be radiant with joy and your faces may not blush for shame. In my misfortune I called, the LORD heard and saved me from all distress (Ps 34:6–7). The angel of the LORD, who encamps with them, delivers all who fear God. Learn to savor how good the LORD is; happy are those who take refuge in him. Fear the LORD, you holy ones; nothing is lacking to those who fear him. The powerful grow poor and hungry, but those who seek the LORD lack no good thing (Ps 34:8–11).

> All the nations surrounded me; in the LORD'S name I crushed them. They surrounded me on every side; in the LORD'S name I crushed them. They

surrounded me like bees; they blazed like fire among thorns; in the LORD'S name I crushed them. I was hard pressed and falling, but the LORD came to my help. The LORD, my strength and might, came to me as savior (Ps 118:10–14).

David could not fight Goliath with Saul's armor, because he could not walk in it, let alone fight with it; he needed the Armor of God as he prayed: "The Lord is my strength and my shield; my heart trusts in him, and he helps me. My heart leaps for joy, and with my song I praise him" (Ps 28:7, NIV). Clothed in God as his shield, David brought down Goliath with one stone, the Corner Stone and the Rock of Ages—Jesus Christ, our Lord.

David mortally struck Goliath on the forehead. He struck at pride, the head and the mind of the giant, and his whole frame came crashing down. He used the enemy's own sword to cut off his head. Goliath, the personification of the power and the prince and the ruler of this world (Jn 14:30, 1 Jn 5:19) was defeated. Against this ruler Saint Paul calls us to battle: "… draw your strength from the Lord and from his mighty power. Put on the armor of God so that you may be able to stand firm against the tactics of the devil" (Eph 6:10–11).

In fighting pride, we must aim at cutting off its head completely. No half measures will secure our path to holiness. Humility should be our weapon of choice in this mortal combat in which the Holy Spirit assures us, "no weapon forged against you will prevail, and you will refute every tongue that accuses you. This is the heritage of the servants of the Lord, and this is their vindication from me," declares the Lord (Is 54:17, NIV).

Jesus Christ is our ultimate weapon against pride. Satan, the spirit of pride, is always opposed to Jesus; it is the spirit of lies. Jesus is Truth. Saint John gives us a simple formula for discerning the spirit of pride from the spirit of humility: "This is how you can recognize the Spirit of God: Every spirit that acknowledges that Jesus Christ has come in the flesh is from God, but every spirit that does not acknowledge Jesus is not from God. This is the spirit of the antichrist, which you have heard is coming and even now is already in the world" (1 Jn 4:2–3, NIV). This discernment is important especially for priests and laity who engage in evangelization, and the ministry of witnessing to the Lordship of Christ. Saint Paul learned that Satan's evil design is to take our attention off of God and place it elsewhere.

Simon, the magician astounded the people of Samaria with his magic and tricks and they said of him, "This man is the power of God that is called Great" (Acts 8:10, ESV). But it took the Spirit of God in Peter to spot the spirit of deception and the fake power at work in Simon, who was not upright with God (Acts 8:18–22). This spirit of pride working through deception is strong and subtle. It can bring down families, parishes, dioceses, religious communities, prayer groups, and ministries in the Church if the symptoms of pride are not spotted and addressed early. In dealing with the spirit of pride in a person, deliverance may be necessary, especially when pride manifests as addictions.

My former community the Intercessors of the Lamb was canonically suppressed in October 2010, precisely because of pride manifested through disobedience to legitimate Church authority. It was a community that was in grave need of reform to correct abuses. It needed to be pruned, so that it would flourish and bear more fruit to the glory of God. But pride stood in the way. The founding member of the community and her collaborators opposed the legitimate authority of the local bishop. They rejected the Spirit of Counsel and in their disobedience put themselves above the Church and the authority of the Head and Bridegroom of the Church— Jesus Christ. And down like lightning the community fell, to the recesses of oblivion.

In our determination to fight pride, we must resolve to practice the virtues, which are the means to grow in the likeness of Christ, and the effective weapons against pride. Humility is the principal virtue and weapon to fight pride. Saint Augustine said that three virtues are necessary, if we are to attain holiness. The first is humility. The second is humility. And the third is humility. We acquire humility by accepting daily humiliations thankfully and without complaints. Because it is difficult to measure how humble we are, the true and sure measure of humility is obedience.

We need our Blessed Mother's intercession in our fight to overcome pride and become humble. We pray through her intercession, and by imitating her principal virtues of profound humility and lively faith. By faith she believed that all that God promised would be fulfilled. By her ardent charity, she was always surrendered and grateful for all God's actions in her life. She received herself as a gift, and all that came with her person, expressing it humbly and simply: "… He Who is almighty has done great things for me—and holy is His name" (Lk 1:49, AMP). Her heroic patience as a witness and partaker in the suffering and Crucifixion of Jesus is exemplary. The graces of the pain she suffered at the *Fifth Sorrow*: the Crucifixion of Jesus (Lk 23:46), gives us strength to accept humiliations and become humble. Our desire for humility and perfection should draw us closer to her Immaculate Heart, where we listen to her motherly plea: "Do whatever he tells you" (Jn 2:5).

**Jesus meek and humble of Heart;
make our hearts like unto Thine (pray three times)**

Chapter 10
◇ ◇ ◇

Primary Open Door 4: Gluttony

Don't feel that you just have to have all sorts of fancy food, and don't be a glutton over any food. If you eat too much, you'll get sick; if you do it all the time, you'll always have stomach trouble (Sir 37:29–30, GNT).

Gluttony is the "inordinate love of eating and drinking;"[270] which can easily lead to addictions to food, drinks and drugs. The excessive indulgence in consumables is the principal problem with gluttony. The advertisement industry has made this problem worse in their quest for profit and more profit. As a result, we are faced with the problems of obesity and other eating disorders. But we cannot blame the advertisement industry or the manufacturers of foods and drinks. We take personal responsibility for what, when, where and how much we choose to eat and drink. Jesus taught by His life that we cannot depend on earthly food and drink alone; we are body and spirit beings.

Jesus fasted for forty days and forty nights in the wilderness as He began His public ministry. Satan took its chance on Jesus, as it often does with us, and said to the Lord, "If you are the Son of God, command these stones to become loaves of bread." Jesus answered, "It is written, 'Man shall not live by bread alone, but by every word that comes from the mouth of God'" (Mt 4:3–4, ESV).

The emphasis of our earthly life cannot be on the physical alone; our spiritual self must be cared for as well. We are created in God's image and likeness. The truth is that we are most like God in our spiritual nature. "God is Spirit, and those who worship him must worship in Spirit and truth" (Jn 4:24). The temptation we face these days is to eat and drink all we want.

Gluttony seeks to please the self for the sake of the self. The glutton's goal is the self, and here lies the disorder, the preoccupation with the self. To the glutton applies the words of Saint Paul, who said, "Their God is their stomach. Their glory is their 'shame.' Their minds are occupied with earthly things." "Their end is destruction" (Phil 3:19). God is, and should be the goal of our human existence. As Paul says: "Whether you eat or drink, or whatever you do, do everything for the glory of God" (1 Cor 10:31).

We glorify God when we use the gifts of food and drink properly, that is, for nourishment. God takes our eating and drinking seriously. Jesus joined in the eating and drinking at the wedding feast of Cana. He made more wine when the wine ran short, because His Mother interceded with Him on behalf of the wedding party, "They have no wine" (Jn 2:3-11). Through eating and drinking He brought Zacchaeus the chief tax collector and his household to salvation (Lk 19:9).

In Revelation 19, the wedding feast of the Lamb is the ultimate eating and drinking banquet for all the elect, that is, those who have persevered and survived the time of great trial, and who "have washed their robes and made them white in the blood of the Lamb" (Rev 7:14). In the parable of the prodigal son (Lk 15), the father welcomes his wayward son with a feast. He ordered his servants to dress him in the finest robe, to adorn his finger and feet with ring and sandals. And he said, "Take the fattened calf and slaughter it. Then let us celebrate with a feast" (Lk 15:22–23). Jesus gives us eternal life through eating and drinking. "Whoever eats my flesh and drinks my blood has eternal life, and I will raise them up at the last day. For my flesh is real food and my blood is real drink" (Jn 6:54–55, NIV).

The sin of gluttony is not limited to excessive eating and drinking. The food the glutton seeks is "sumptuous," meaning, it is costly food.[271] The glutton exceeds in "what" he eats, or in "how much," "how" or "when he eats."[272] Too much emphasis is placed on the physical rather than the spiritual.

There are fitness centers everywhere and more are being built. Huge amounts of money are spent yearly by registered members to stay fit, but hardly do we have retreat centers for spiritual formation and exercises to nourish our souls. The result is that we are entering the so called post Christian era. The Christian faith, by every measurable statistics is in decline. More and more professed Christians no longer practice the faith; parishes are closing by the hundreds; the crises of vocations to the priesthood, religious life, married life, and single life are accelerating; secularism and relativism are on the rise; and the Church's divine teachings are being opposed more and more. Thomas Aquinas mentions some harmful effects of the sin of gluttony: "Inability to pray or follow a true spiritual standard, foolish joy, frivolity, talkativeness, [and] temptations against holy virtue."[273] These spiritual dangers should wake us up and motivate us to practice self-denial[274] and seriously pursue the call to holiness.

Spiritual gluttony is a danger we cannot overlook. It is seeking "spiritual highs" as the goal of religion without interior conversion. To worship God in spirit and truth requires that our hearts be converted. For the glutton, God is not the center of worship, but feelings. This can be an open door for Satan to derail our faith journey. The evil one would do anything to poison our relationship with God. Spiritual gluttony can be found in those who are just discovering the beauty of the spiritual life, and also on those who focus too much on the spectacular. We must realize that an authentic mystical experience is God's gift; it cannot be earned. It is grace.

A friend of mine was beginning to taste the sweetness of God, but she took it too far. Every little thing for her was magnified out of proportion and given a mystical meaning. She told me one time that she has invisible stigmata, because she had serious continuous pains on her palms. It became her focus of attention as she tried to prove it was really stigmata. The glutton hijacks God's work and makes it her own. This is the deception that spiritual gluttony can lead to. It can also lead to self-absorption and a false spirituality that worships the self as god. This is nothing else but pride. Spiritual gluttony seeks what it can get out of God, but is not interested in a relationship with God who is love.

Saint Teresa of Avila said that as we mature in the spiritual life, we become less interested in the spectacular. Spiritual gluttony will deprive us of enduring interior peace and calm that are fruits of the Holy Spirit. It will drain us of zeal for prayer. Spiritual gluttony can manifest in extreme penances such as fasting and mortification, especially when they are practiced without the permission of a spiritual director or confessor.

Gluttony can lead to failure in charity toward our neighbor because of the undue and excessive attention given to self. We can neglect the care of others, especially the poor in our midst, because we spend more than is necessary to please and satisfy ourselves. A glutton has no desire for the cross of Jesus; he flees from it. He cannot tolerate daily martyrdom, and the idea of sacrifice and suffering are shunned. Saint Paul says, "But we proclaim Christ Crucified" (1 Cor 1:23), and we carry in our body the dying of Jesus (2 Cor 4:10). He enjoins us to offer our bodies as living sacrifices, holy and pleasing to God (Rom 12:1). Christians proclaim Christ crucified more by their lifestyles, rather than by words. Paul also says that the message of the cross for those being saved, is the power of God (1 Cor 1:18).

The glutton is hidden from herself, because she pays no attention to her thoughts, feelings and desires in prayer, she allows gluttony and the other capital sins to gradually ravage her soul. The glutton is not a spiritual person, as Paul teaches us, the children of God are those who are led by the Spirit of God (Rom 8:14). A glutton is a child of this world concerned only with the things of this world.

Gluttony self-reflection questions:
- Do I like excessive eating and drinking?

- Is my eating and drinking causing me health problems?
- Do I get intoxicated?
- Do I feel discomfort from overeating?
- What is my attitude to eating and drinking?
- Is my body size from eating and drinking embarrassing me?
- Are my discussions centered on good food and drinks?
- Do I waste food and drink?
- Do I criticize or complain about food?
- Do I deny myself a little every day? If possible, at every meal?
- Do I get permission before fasting or doing penance?
- Do I live to eat, or eat to live?
- Am I easily attracted to food and drink?
- Do I binge on food and drink?
- Do I think a lot about food and drinks?
- Do I practice mortification?
- Do I love excessive food?
- Do I hide or hoard food?
- Do I pray?
- What do I seek in prayer—God or consolation?
- Do I easily give up praying?
- Do I ask Jesus daily for the gift of living water?
- Do I ask Jesus for my daily bread or for my yearly bread?
- What are my attachments?
- Do I ask God for eternal life or for earthly life?
- Do I hunger to be a saint?
- What are my desires?
- Do I depend on God to satisfy my desires?
- Is the Lord truly and really my Shepherd?
- What are my fears?
- Do I talk to Jesus about my struggles with food and drink?
- Do I have a spiritual director?

The weapons against gluttony

Weapons of the Spirit

When the Spirit of the Lord came upon us at Baptism, He gave us His Fourth Gift of **Fortitude**. Fortitude is our fighting power and firepower against the sin of gluttony. The *Spirit of Fortitude* (Is 11:2) fortifies our souls against natural fear and strengthens us to persevere in our vocation to holiness, and the joyful performance of our duties in life. Fortitude strengthens the will to undertake without hesitation the most arduous tasks; to face dangers; to trample under foot human respect; and to endure without complaint the slow martyrdom of life long tribulation.[275] Jesus said, "… the one who perseveres to the end will be saved" (Mk 13:13).

Prophet Isaiah offers the glutton a prayer of hope:

> Do you not know or have you not heard? The LORD is the eternal God, creator of the ends of the earth. He does not faint nor grow weary, and his knowledge is beyond scrutiny. He gives strength to the fainting; for the weak he makes vigor abound. Though young men faint and grow weary, and youths stagger and fall, They that hope in the LORD will renew their strength, they will soar as with eagles' wings; They will run and not grow weary, walk and not grow faint (Is 40:28–31).

The prophets of the Old Testament were men trained in the desert; their lifestyle was prayer and fasting. Abraham, Moses, Elijah, Elisha, Jeremiah, Ezekiel and Isaiah, to mention a few, were men of the desert who lived and practiced desert spirituality. In the New Testament, John the Baptist was a man of the desert. He fed on locusts and wild honey and was fearless in confronting the moral laxities of his time.

These prophets' lives tell us that without Fortitude we cannot evangelize. Fortitude does not lighten our struggles, but empowers us to embrace the struggle joyfully no matter the cost. This is zeal. Zeal consumed Jesus to act to stop the abuse of His Father's Temple (Jn 2:13-25). It is zeal for the Father that led Jesus to lay down His life for the sheep (Jn 14:31; 10:18). We are cautioned not to work for perishable food, but for the Bread and Drink of eternal life (Jn 6:27).

Jesus is our model in true fasting and prayer. He said, "Foxes have dens and birds of the sky have nests, but the Son of Man has nowhere to rest his head" (Lk 9:58). In His priestly prayer to the Father, Jesus said, "They do not belong to this world any more than I belong to this world" (Jn 17:16). Speaking to Pilate at His trial, Jesus said, "My kingdom does not belong to this world" (Jn 18:36).

We are called to fast not only from food and drink, but also from the things of this world. We should fast from unnecessary things that can harm us. Fasting and penance should always be performed with permission from our confessors or spiritual directors if they are to have merit. Otherwise, they can be self-serving and be turned into an expression of self-love and self-will. Thomas à Kempis, CRSA (ca. 1380–1471), a German canon regular and the author of *Imitation of Christ* said, "When we withdraw ourselves from obedience, we withdraw from grace." Scripture confirms that, "Obedience is better than sacrifice, and submission than the fat of rams" (1 Sam 15:22).

The Armor of God for warfare against the capital vice of gluttony is the *Footgear of Zeal* for the Gospel of Peace. Only a peaceful heart can preach the Gospel of Peace. Jesus gives us His peace and prays that our hearts not be troubled (Jn 14:27). "Above all things, keep peace within yourself, then you will be able to create peace among others. It is better to be peaceful than to be learned."[276] The spirit of indifference, relativism, compromise, ignorance, apathy, deception are Satan's tool to deny us peace of soul with God, to weaken our zeal and openness to God's Word, which must be our only nourishment and sustenance (Mt 4:4), and the foundation of our faith and of Christian perfection.

Word from the Cross

Our Lord Jesus Christ dying on the Cross spoke the *Fifth Word* that releases our hearts from the bondage of gluttony: *"I thirst"* (Jn 19:28). Jesus spent His whole life thirsting for our salvation; we in turn should spend our whole lives thirsting for Heaven, the love of God and of our neighbor. "I have a baptism with which to be baptized, and what stress I am under until it is completed!" (Lk 12:50, NRSV). Through the Samaritan woman, Jesus reaches out to all humanity, saying, "Give me a drink" (Jn 4:7). Jesus is love. He is the giver of live-giving water, as He said to the woman: "If you knew the gift of God, and who it is that is saying to you, 'Give me a drink,' you would have asked him, and he would have given you living water" (Jn 4:10, NKJV). Jesus cried out: "Let anyone who thirsts come to me and drink." Rivers of living water will gush from those who believe in me (Jn 7:37-38). Jesus came and has given us abundant life in the gift of the Holy Spirit, so that we can thirst for Heaven and the Bread of eternal life; and not for food and drink that causes us to perish, and which does not satisfy (Jn 6:27).

Lack of self-knowledge is at the heart of the problem of gluttony. There is an interior blindness that does not permit us to see the gift and the beauty of food and drink, and so we use them to destroy ourselves. The liturgical seasons of Advent and Lent are times the Church reminds us that we need to trim down our lifestyles, and live simpler, freer, healthier and more peaceful human and spiritual lives. Advent, but especially Lent, are times to be spiritual. A time of grace that allows us to attend to what matters the most, the salvation of our immortal souls. Our whole earthly life should be Lent if we want heaven to be our eternal Easter.

Gluttony can adversely affect our spiritual lives. It makes us seek consolation for its own sake, and when we fail, we become discouraged and quit praying altogether. In prayer, we are to seek the friendship of God and experience His love. Seeking consolation as the goal of prayer can lead to false mysticism, which seeks the consolation of God, and not the God of consolation. It is God we seek; not His gifts. Authentic mysticism leads to transforming union with God. We become like Jesus. Spiritual gluttony will ruin our spiritual lives; its motivation is self-centered, and its goal is the self. It darkens our senses, dulls our faculties, and numbs our appetite for heavenly things; it eventually kills our desire for holiness. Gluttony deprives us of the zeal needed to be the heralds of the Good News of Jesus Christ to the world.

Closing the open door of gluttony

Daily prayer time is the most effective means to fight the sin of gluttony. At prayer we practice personal self-reflection (not self-absorption), as we learn to notice, recognize and acknowledge the symptoms of gluttony. This recognition and acknowledgment is important in combating the sin of gluttony. God does not impose healing on us. He always seeks our consent and cooperation. Jesus asked the blind Bartimaeus, "What do you want me to do for you" (Mk 10:51)? Jesus does not assume that we want to be healed. It is very possible that we might choose not to be healed. This may sound surprising. It is even possible that we might choose to have nothing to do with Jesus, and still claim we want to be healed.

Sometimes we want quick fixes to problems for which there are no quick fixes. There are no quick fixes for the salvation of the human person. Spiritual gluttony is about quick-fixing the problem of salvation. Our deepest desire must be to seek God's Kingdom first, and then all other things will be given to us (Mt 6:33). Our salvation was purchased at the great price of the Blood of the Son of God (1 Cor 6:20). It was not easy for Jesus to give up His life, but He did it willingly, obediently, totally and unconditionally because of His infinite love for us. Jesus said, "No one has greater love than this, to lay down one's life for one's friends. You are my friends if you do what I command you" (Jn 15:13-14, NRSV).

If we truly love Jesus, we will not seek to bypass the cross through gluttony to reach salvation. Jesus is the only Way to salvation. There is no short cut through the cross. But we must pray for patience. God is patient with us. All we need is to seek Him daily. "When you search for me, you will find me; if you seek me with all your heart, I will let you find me, says the Lord, and I will restore your fortunes and gather you from all the nations and all the places where I have driven you, says the Lord…" (Jer 29:13–14, NRSV). We take up our cross daily and obediently and follow Jesus. When He says, "Stop," we stop. When He says, "Rest," we rest.

When He says, "Go," we go. Jesus says, "... without me you can do nothing" (Jn 15:5).

Martha learned from Jesus what mattered most, to sit at His feet and listen to His voice. This is the Father's commands, that we listen to His beloved Son (Lk 9:35). Jesus said, "My sheep hear my voice; I know them, and they follow me" (Jn 10:27). Mother Mary teaches us to do the same, "Do whatever He tells you" (Jn 2:5).

In the spiritual life, obedience is always the litmus test of any authentic mystical experience. Fasting and mortification practiced in obedience to our confessors or spiritual directors will help us remain in God's will. Spiritual exercises that are not regulated by obedience can potentially derail our quest for perfection. Obedience, indeed, is at once both penitential and sacrificial. Only the humble obey. Jesus said to Sister Faustina, "Only the humble soul is capable of receiving My grace. I favor humble souls with My confidence."[277] Obedience is the effective fool-proof measure of humility. Only those who obey God receive the gift of the Holy Spirit (Acts 5:32). It is the Spirit that makes us humble like Jesus—the Anointed One of God.

We need the virtue of prudence to guide us in making decisions in matters of food and drink. Faith in Jesus Christ gives us self-control and directs us to make prudent choices. The Holy Scriptures and the teachings of the Church are our compasses for making informed moral judgments on issues affecting our salvation. Listening to the voice of the Good Shepherd will keep us within bounds of reason in the use of food and drinks.

Honesty and frequent spiritual direction will help challenge us to come out of the darkness of the hidden vice of gluttony. Paul says, "Everything exposed by the light becomes visible" (Eph 5:13). Our body is not ours; it is not an object to be used and abused. We should treat it with utmost care and respect. Our body was anointed at Baptism, and our body is the temple of the Holy Spirit from God. We are not to satisfy every appetite we feel. In moments of temptation to food and drinks, we should talk to God in prayer. Moderation should be a governing principle in all matters of food and drink; excesses must be avoided.

The intercession of the Blessed Mother is powerful in dealing with gluttony and all the capital sins. Pious affection for her will inspire us to imitate her virtues of mortification in all things, blind obedience, profound humility, and her continual mental prayer.[278] I read somewhere in the writing of a mystic, that our Blessed Mother ate and drank only what was necessary to keep her body and soul together. We can practice this in smaller ways.

The graces of the pain of her *Seventh Sorrow*: the Burial of Jesus; liberates us from the grip of gluttony. This station – Jesus' burial in the tomb (Lk 23:53), was the last time Mother Mary held the body of her Beloved Son.

But the Resurrection event was to transform humanity in a whole new way. We must choose to bury gluttony, so we can rise to new life in the resurrection.

The virtue of temperance helps us to realize that our progress is not only natural but also spiritual. Temperance helps make the right motive our guiding principle, so that we may serve God better and help others do the same.[279] An inordinate desire for anything is usually accompanied by the neglect of other things. Temperance helps us moderate our lives so that we are not slaves to created things. Self-control and a well-regulated lifestyle is a powerful advantage, and "promptness and faithfulness to a daily schedule must have fruitful results…"[280]

Spiritual warfare against gluttony

The evil one hates human nature. God became man and dwelt among us to redeem us. The mystery of the Incarnation is a big blow to Satan and the demons. They cannot understand why God loves human nature so much. Christianity is an incarnational religion. Christian spirituality places emphasis on love of neighbor. Love, Paul says, is the fulfillment of the whole law, since love does not wrong the neighbor (Rom 13:10). Saint John taught, "Those who say, "I love God," and hate their brothers or sisters, are liars; for those who do not love a brother or sister whom they have seen, cannot love God whom they have not seen" (1 Jn 4:20, NRSV). John also shows us how to recognize God's spirit. The spirit that acknowledges Jesus Christ come in the flesh (the Incarnation) belongs to God (1 Jn 4:2).

Our flesh and blood is important to God. He created it, and He assumed it so that He can share His love with us, and that we might receive it and share in His divine nature (2 Pet 1:4). We have the ability to love and to receive love. God's love is our strength in spiritual warfare. And so Paul invites us to, "Draw your strength from the Lord and from his mighty power. Put on the armor of God so that you may be able to stand firm against the tactics of the devil" (Eph 6:10–11).

There are evil spirits that associate with the sin of gluttony: addictions, infirmity, fear, greed, pride, division, games, desolation, low self-esteem, self-destruction, and a host of others. We must put on the armor of vigilance and holiness at all times so we are not caught off guard. Be prepared!

Chapter 11

Primary Open Door 5: Sloth

Do not be slothful about beginning your expedition to possess the land (Jdg 18:9).

Sloth is the inordinate love of rest which leads us to neglect our daily physical, mental, and spiritual duties.[281] It is a silent and slow killer of the Christian life—life in the Holy Spirit. A slothful person is one who is drowning in an ocean of busy-ness; a life devoid of spiritual substance; an empty and hollow spiritual life. Busy-ness about many things, except that which is most important for our eternal salvation, is the easiest way to detect sloth in a person.

Sloth is present when we do not take important things seriously. The most important thing is God. Those who are casual about their relationship with God and the things of God are not only slothful, but are careless and taking a costly and unnecessary risk.

Slothful people are lukewarm; they aim in every situation or task to fulfill the minimum requirement just to get by. Slothful persons lack any meaningful prayer life. For them, God is a boring Person to be with. They attend Holy Mass but claim they "get nothing out of it," because they have put nothing into it; they have made no investments, but expect a rich reward, not planted, but expect a bountiful harvest; they profess a love without the cross, life without death. The Mass for them is a time-wasting empty show. For some, time spent at Mass is used for texting or phone calls, napping, chatting and sightseeing.

Slothful people approach spirituality, chores and studies casually and ordinarily. Yet Paul tells us to work out our salvation with fear and trembling (Phil 2:12). They procrastinate in many things and find it difficult to begin a task; when they do, they never finish. Saint Augustine was initially a slothful man; he began the spiritual life late, but ended very well as a Saint and Doctor of the Church. He writes in his Confessions: "Late have I loved you, O Beauty ever ancient, ever new, late have I loved you."

God is constantly calling us to perfection. The drive to be perfect must challenge slothful tendencies in our souls. God has given us all the means we need to be perfect. He gave us Jesus Christ (Jn 3:16); through Him He chose us before the world began, and bestowed on us every spiritual blessing at our Baptism; so that we may be holy (Eph 1:3–6). Through Him, the Holy Spirit has been lavished upon us; so that zeal for the Father's house will consume us as it consumed Jesus.

We have received the Sacraments to make us grow in fervor. God's word must dwell in our hearts since by baptism, we are *in persona Christi,* and exist for the praise of God's glory (Eph 1:12), and for the sake of His Kingdom. If we are truly living *in persona Christi* as our identity, we will not be cold and slothful, and we will exercise our Sabbath obligations with zeal, and bear much fruit. Sloth deadens our spiritual life and kills our hunger for God, so that the soul becomes weighed down by sadness, because it is not receiving divine life. For a slothful person, prayer gets more difficult and discouraging. The slothful person needs this Psalmist prayer which says: "A clean heart create for me, God; renew in me a steadfast spirit" (Ps 51:12).

Jesus calls us to be perfect as the Father is perfect (Mt 5:48). This requires that we enter through the narrow gate; the constricted and difficult road that leads to life. Mark's Gospel 10:16–27 details the story of the rich young man who, desirous of Heaven asked our Blessed Lord what he must do to inherit it. This story illustrates the serious threat sloth poses to our eternal salvation.

The rich young man claimed he had been observing the commandments from his youth. But in reality, he had allowed the weed of sloth to take over control of his heart. His religion had become mere superficial observance. He found it difficult to obey Jesus and went away sad and hopeless from the very Man who had the power to give him Heaven—Jesus Christ, the Son of God. We must do everything in our power to fight sloth in our own lives. Jesus emphasized more than once to the crowds how hard it is for worldly people to enter the kingdom of God (Mk 10:23–24).

Sloth self-reflection questions
- Am I faithful to my resolutions?
- Do I pray, and do I quit prayer at the slightest opportunity?
- Am I reverent in Church, especially, before and after receiving the Holy Eucharist?
- Am I respectful of sacred places, persons and objects?
- Do I hurry through prayer?
- Do I labor to grow in my prayer life?
- Do I practice mortification?
- Do spiritual things excite me?
- Do I practice self-reflection and recollection?
- Is my worship of God lip service or a show? Do I live an interior life?
- Do I hurry through the liturgy to get it done with?

- Do I have the maximum reverence for Jesus Christ in the Holy Eucharist?
- Am I lukewarm, not interested or indifferent?
- Do I have a desire to want to pray?
- Do I indulge in self-abuse?
- Do I skip prayer time or cut it short?
- Do I read away my prayer time?
- Do I have a habit of lateness to appointments, including Mass?
- Do I care? Do I daydream?
- Do I study the Church's teachings on faith and morals?
- Am I grounded and rooted in my faith?
- Do I view problems as too difficult to solve?
- Do I easily get discouraged or easily upset?
- Am I ruled by my feelings?
- Is my goal in life Heaven?
- Am I afraid to make a commitment?
- Do I witness or talk to someone about Jesus Christ?
- How do I feel when the name of Jesus is mentioned? Excited, uneasy, elated, or indifferent?
- Do I compromise?
- Do I identify easily with Jesus, His truth, His values, or His Church?
- Do I love being idle?
- Where do I tend to take the easy way out?
- Am I fatigued all the time? Without energy, weary, moody, or discouraged?
- Do I love inordinate rest? Inactivity?
- Do I tend to be too busy that I don't pray?
- Is my work my prayer? Am I fervent in prayer?
- Do I want to be a saint?

The weapons against sloth

Weapons of the Spirit

When the Spirit of the Lord came upon us at Baptism, He gave us His Fifth Gift of **Knowledge.** Knowledge empowers our souls to evaluate the true worth of created things. By the *Spirit of Knowledge* (Is 11:2), we see beneath the masks and pretenses of creatures. It reveals to spiritual persons the emptiness of created things, teaching us that created things serve only as means in God's plan to bring us eternal life.[282] Only those in loving relationship of faith with God receive His revelation, and please Him (Heb 11:6). The truth of this is seen in the relationship between the vine and the branches (Jn 15). For this reason, Jesus said: "Now this is eternal life: that they know you, the only true God, and Jesus Christ, whom you have sent" (Jn 17:3, NIV).

The gift of Knowledge unveils for us the truth about God and His love, and it perfects the supernatural virtues of faith, hope and love. Knowledge protects us from being slaves to the things we own. The rich young man was possessed by his possessions; he was a slave to things. Knowledge assures us that God is with us even in difficult times. It spurs us to seek the friendship of God more than everything else. Our highest achievement on this earthly life is to be known as friends of God. Knowledge equips us to gain self-knowledge, which is so valuable in combating sloth; and to grow in the knowledge of God and attain His perfection.

When we contemplate spiritual goods, they become more desirable and appealing to us. Let us meditate on the truths of our faith, while keeping our eyes fixed on Jesus. Like Mary, let us sit at His feet and listen to Truth. No aspect of our spiritual life should be taken for granted. Trusting God happens in staying with, getting to know Him in the aloneness of prayer, and loving Him. It is in this aloneness that God shares His love with us. Everything we do is important to God; they all work toward our salvation. A meditation on the Four Last Things: Death, Last Judgment, Hell, and Heaven, can help us to live a more realistic spiritual life (see chapter 2).

Our Blessed Mother at Fatima showed the three children: Lucia, Jacinta and Francesco the vision of Hell and the reality of the damned. This vision made a tremendous impact on the children for the rest of their lives. It helped them to focus on prayer, and on heavenly things which were shown to them during the apparitions.

It is good practice to try to identify our faults and work hard to overcome them. We should avoid being too comfortable in this life, and choose to live once in a while with some inconvenience. We should ask for the grace of perseverance in our prayer. Only those who persevere to the end will be saved (Mt 24:13). A life of obedience will train us in living a sacrificial life and renew our spiritual vigor. As intercessors and prayer warriors we should unite ourselves with Jesus by carrying our crosses and following in His footstep. Our sacrificial love united with the suffering of the Savior, can remit sins and bring healing to our world.

Daily prayer should be a priority; here, we express our desire to be saints. Prayer is important to overcome the sin of sloth. As Jesus sweated blood in the Garden of Olives, He said to His sleepy Apostles: "Watch and pray so that you will not fall into temptation. The spirit is willing, but the flesh is weak" (Mk 14:38, NIV). Slothful people allow their feelings to dictate the choices they make and how they act. The choice for God should be the drive for our lives. Sloth can make us procrastinate Heaven.

The *Shield of Faith* (Eph 6:16) is the Armor of God to stop the destructive slow-killing vice of sloth. Faith is both light and strength that fills the heart of a disciple with commitment and purpose in the mission to save souls. Jesus assures us that if we have faith the size of a mustard seed, nothing will be impossible for us. At His disciples' inability to free a possessed boy, He rebuked them: "O faithless and perverse generation..." (Mt 17:14–20). Faith helps us to persevere, even as it also protects. The Word of God must be aflame in our hearts like the vigil lamp in the sanctuary burning always as a sign of the Lord's Real Presence.

Word from the Cross

Our Lord Jesus Christ dying on the Cross spoke the *Sixth Word* that awakens our hearts to the subtle danger of sloth: ***"It is finished"*** (Jn 19:30). He finished God's work, not His own (Jn 6:38). Only the one who perseveres to the end in doing God's work and not his own says, "it is finished." Let us pray for the grace to persevere to the end that we might be saved (Mt 10:22). We must persevere in carrying our crosses and follow Jesus to the very end. The virtue of perseverance or diligence comes against the tepidity and sloth that kill our prayer life and deadens our zeal for the Kingdom of God. Jesus was zealous for the Father's works (Jn 2:17), and Elijah was zealous for the LORD (1 Kgs 19:10). Sloth will discourage us and leave us without the hope of resurrection through loss of faith. Sloth makes us lose everything, but zeal makes us lose nothing and gain everything (Jn 18:9). Saint Paul warns the Christian soldier: "With all prayer and supplication, pray at every opportunity in the Spirit. To that end, be watchful with all perseverance..." (Eph 6:18).

Remaining firm in our resolutions and reviewing them frequently in a spirit of commitment, is a safeguard against sloth. Holding ourselves accountable to a spiritual director will help challenge us to overcome sloth. Christ's standards in words, thoughts, and actions should be our standards as well, as we allow the Holy Spirit to form, transform and conform our minds, hearts, and will to those of Christ. Every possible means must be used to fight imperfections and faults as we strive to rid ourselves of venial sins. God's grace will always accompany us in our fight against sloth. The armor of unceasing, persistent and relentless prayer offered in the Spirit will guarantee our success to the finish line of our faith journey.

Closing the open door of sloth

Paying attention to our thoughts, words, feelings, desires and actions will help us detect sloth early. With the help of the sloth reflection questions above, we can detect the symptoms of sloth, and develop warfare strategies to combat it. The primary strategy of prayer is to journal and dialogue with Jesus about our struggles with sloth. We are too close to ourselves that we do not see our blind spots. We are not objective in dealing with interior matters about ourselves. It is wise counsel to seek spiritual direction. We should with conviction seek the things of Heaven and leave no stone unturned in growing in intimate friendship with Jesus Christ.

Love for God should motivate our actions, and influence how we speak, eat, drink, sleep, and wake; what we wear and where we go; and the friends we make and the things we watch and touch. In short, it will affect everything. Prompt obedience to all God's commands will help us fight the delay tactics of the evil of sloth.

We are to strive to imitate the Blessed Virgin in her principal virtues: her blind obedience and ardent charity, continual mental prayer, and mortification in all things. Her sensitivity to the things of God quickly moved her and Saint Joseph to run to protect the life of the infant Child Jesus. Delay would have been costly for them. They were prompt in obeying God. We too must be prompt in running away from sin. Any delay might put at risk the light of faith we received at Baptism and even eternity itself. Mother Mary and Saint Joseph did not lose the light of Christ they received. They protected it.

Through the graces of her *Second Sorrow,* the Flight into Egypt (Mt 2:13–14), the Blessed Mother, Mediatrix of All Graces, obtained for us the grace to overcome sloth in our lives so that we might become the light of the world and the salt of the earth.

Spiritual warfare against sloth

Evil spirits of sloth work in league with the demons of fatigue, lies, fear, oppression, and others, to discourage and disrupt our relationship with God. The spirit of sloth wants to delay and isolate us and cause us to fail. By isolation, it divides and conquers. By delay, heaven gradually slips away from our reach. We must be vigilant. When we recognize sloth, laziness, tepidity and idleness; we need to investigate it and resist it immediately. To look elsewhere will be a distraction and a ploy of the evil one to bring us into bondage. Sloth will blind us to the truth, and the teachings of the Church. It will numb our appetite for the truth, especially in the areas of faith and morals. We should study the faith, and be armed with the sword of the Spirit—the word of God. Jesus was armed with God's word; He was well versed in the Hebrew Scriptures.

Jesus entered the synagogue on the Sabbath, as was His habit, and was handed the scroll of Prophet Isaiah. He read it, handed it back to the attendant, and sat down and said: "Today this scripture passage is fulfilled in your hearing" (Lk 4:16–21). The risen Jesus encountered two of His disciples running away from Jerusalem. He rebuked them for their unbelief. "And beginning with Moses and all the Prophets, he explained to them what was said in all the Scriptures concerning himself" (Lk 24:27, NIV).

With His deep knowledge of the Scriptures, Jesus was able to discern God's will in His life and overcome the temptations of the devil in the wilderness. To each of the three temptations, Jesus replied: "It is written…" (Mt 4:1–11). When the devil's attacks get more fierce and difficult, seek strength and refuge in God's word.

Chapter 12

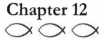

Primary Open Door 6: Anger

*It is good sense in a man to be slow to anger, and it is his glory to overlook an offense
(Prov 19:11).*

Anger is sometimes said to be an emotion which in itself is neither good nor bad. Our emotions can help keep us aware of our interior atmosphere. Aquinas says anger is a passion of the sensitive appetite—a drive or inclination to satisfy a conscious need, e.g., hunger, thirst, or need for air or sleep.[283] It is an inordinate desire in the soul to take revenge. If the desire for revenge is regulated by reason, the anger is good. Just anger is caused by "zeal for the honor of God," and it is said to be virtuous (see 1 Mac 2:24–26). But anger arising from passion which is not regulated by reason is evil, and so is sinful.[284] Scripture says that wrath and anger we must hate, but sinners cling to them (Sir 27:30). The vengeful will suffer the Lord's vengeance, but those who forgive their neighbor's offenses will experience the Lord's mercy for their sins when they pray (Sir 28:1–2).

Anger can be generated as a response to a hurt inflicted. A child in the womb, for example, may be hurt or traumatized when the mother is abused. The child's sensory bank stores the memory of the hurtful events in the subconscious mind. The memory can be re-enforced as the hurt continues to be experienced. Later in life, the hurtful memory may be triggered by outside events. Anger can become for the child a defense mechanism, a way to fight back and take revenge for the hurt inflicted so as to prevent being hurt again. Generally speaking, we do not have control over the emotions that rise up within us at any one moment, so we are not morally culpable. But we have control over what we do with the anger that wells up in us. In this case, we are morally responsible. If the anger response due to a previous hurt is not dealt with or resolved, it may fester and mature into hate. Anger and its advanced stage, hate, create problems in relationships. Anger destroys relationships.

Anger is sinful when it is not regulated by reason, and then directed at another person, or at oneself, or at God. Jesus gave us a new law to guide our spiritual life. He reminded His hearers that their ancestors were told that whoever kills will be liable to judgment. But now He says if we get angry at another, we are liable to judgment (Mt 5:21–22). This is so because anger that is sinful is willfully and freely chosen. When the will has been misused and battered by the waves of anger, it comes under the rule of anger. If we allow anger to dominate our will, we become slaves of anger feelings and actions. This situation can potentially open the door to demonic contamination and subsequent bondage. We become strongholds of anger, as anger blinds our ability to reason. The *will* is our ruling faculty; it is always attracted to the good. There is a spirit of anger which can invade wounded areas within us and form a stronghold, leading to compulsive and uncontrollable anger bouts in a person. In such a case, deliverance may be needed to free the person from such contamination.

Anger self-reflection questions:
* Am I impatient or do I easily tend toward impatience?
* Do I harbor angry or revengeful thoughts?
* Do I have outbursts of anger? What triggers my anger?
* Do anger feelings rise up in me in dreams?
* Do I yell or shout at people?
* Am I violent? Do I tend toward violence?
* Do I indulge in acts of self-hatred: addictions, masturbation, sexual misbehavior, pornography, or any form of self-abuse?
* Do I hold grudges in my heart?
* Have I forgiven anyone who hurt me?
* Do I feel let down or disappointed by God?
* Do I have anger in my heart toward God for any negative events in my life, especially childhood hurts or fearful events?
* Do I avoid or refuse to speak to someone because I am angry?
* Am I sarcastic?
* Am I stubborn and unyielding?
* Am I harsh to anyone?
* Am I easily wounded or my feelings easily hurt?
* Am I unhappy inside of me?
* Am I frustrated at myself for my sins, weaknesses, or faults?
* Do I complain?
* Am I discouraged or tend to despair?
* Do I repress signs of anger?
* Am I hard to get along with?
* Do I tend to take over control or be in control?
* Do I easily forgive others?
* Do I break things?
* Do I curse, sometimes without reason?
* Am I bitter?
* Do I love myself?

* Do I rejoice in the misfortunes of other people?
* Am I prone to revenge or try to get even with others?
* Do I indulge in self-abuse of any kind?
* Do I give the silent treatment?
* Do I ignore others as an expression of anger?
* Am I critical? Do I waste time trying to find fault in someone?
* Do I sneak around on the lookout for others' wrongs and mistakes?
* Am I restless and fail to pay attention to my feelings?
* Do I accuse, condemn or belittle others?
* Do I love as Jesus loves?

The weapons against anger

Weapons of the Spirit

When the Spirit of the Lord came upon us at Baptism, He gave us His Sixth Gift of **Piety.** Piety stabilizes us in God's peace which sinful anger takes away. The *Spirit of Piety* (Ps 143:10)[285] moves our hearts and fills them with a filial affection for God as our most loving Father. It fills us with a deep love and respect for our Most Blessed Mother and the Saints, the Church, and her visible leaders who exercise the authority of Jesus Christ.[286] Filled with Piety, we respect and honor our parents and guardians, and persons of authority in our lives and in our country, and all those we are obliged to respect. It moves us to respect and honor the humanity of all persons, including the unborn children, the aged, and infirm, because they are created in the image and likeness of God, and to treasure all of God's creation. Piety inspires us to serve God lovingly without complaints, and to value the good actions of others and forgive their faults. When the gift of Piety is active in us, we say with Jesus to the Father, "They are your gift to me. I wish that where I am they also may be with me" (Jn 17:24). We wish the best for all men and women.

The spiritual Armor of God for warfare against anger is *praying always in the Spirit* (Eph 6:18). Scripture said that Jesus rejoiced in the Holy Spirit and prayed: "I praise you, Father, Lord of heaven and earth, because you have hidden these things from the wise and learned, and revealed them to little children. Yes, Father, for this is what you were pleased to do" (Lk 10:21, NIV). Empowered by this prayer of filial intimacy, Jesus calmed the storms and tempests of anger in the hearts of His disciples (Mk 4:39–40).

Word from the Cross

Our Lord Jesus Christ dying on the Cross spoke the *First Word* that unbinds our hearts from anger: **"Father, forgive them for they do not know what they are doing"** (Lk 23:34). Forgiveness is a sign of love and obedience to Jesus' command to "love one another as I love you" (Jn 15:12). Jesus gave us the standard by which to love, that we forgive unconditionally and without limit. His words, if believed and practiced, give us the power to forgive ourselves and others. Anger in our hearts toward others will block our healing and keep us restless within, but forgiveness brings pardon and healing into our lives (Sir 28:3–4). We find it difficult to forgive because we are afraid we might be hurt again. God is not afraid to be hurt again. He calls us to practice forgiveness by teaching us to forgive, not simply seven times, but seventy-seven times (Mt 18:22). When we forgive this way, we receive God's love and become His children, because our righteousness has surpassed that of the scribes and Pharisees (Mt 5:41, 20). The love of God casts out all fear in us; it will break all bondage and bring us freedom and healing. Forgiveness brings peace and reconciliation, and opens Heaven to us.

Fear will always discourage and prevent us from taking up our cross and follow Jesus to Calvary. Fear is a powerful weapon of the devil to discourage us from obeying Jesus. We might fear that we are not worthy; we might fear we will fail or be disgraced. God knows all of that already, but when we trust in His power and promises, and surrender, His Divine power accomplishes all things in us beyond our expectations. So when we are afraid and find it difficult to love and forgive, we should ask for the grace from God who does not ration His gifts. Then we can say with Paul: "I can do all things in [Christ] who strengthens me" (Phil 4:13).

Anger may have deep roots within us. When we feel anger, we should take it to prayer and ask for the light of the Holy Spirit to understand its source within us and to pray for God's healing. We are encouraged to renew our baptismal consecration each time we receive Holy Communion at Mass, to experience a deeper conversion of heart, as we wait for the Lord in patience.

To deal successfully with anger, we need to acknowledge we are angry. To deny our emotions is to deny ourselves. We gain self-knowledge by trying to understand the root of our sinful emotions. To heal anger within us, we need to freely choose to be faithful patient disciples of Jesus who heed His word: "Whoever wishes to come after me must deny himself, take up his cross, and follow me" (Mt 16:24). Jesus' invitation must call into action within us the virtue of meekness or patience, so that we can be calm in times of conflicts and their resolution, instead of resorting to quick temper and hasty and unnecessary vengeance when situations don't go our way. Jesus gives us the recipe for dealing with our emotions. We must deny ourselves (die to the false self); we do not hang onto our anger or try to justify it by any means, or act out our anger. The false self in us wants to hang onto the anger for security. The false self believes that anger is the savior. We must be ready to die to the false self within us, because we cannot have it both ways. It is either we have Jesus or we have nothing at all. We are to freely choose chaos or peace in our hearts. Let us make the prayer of John the Baptist our own – Jesus must increase; we must decrease (Jn 3:30).

Closing the open door of anger

It is important that we acknowledge the presence of anger when it rears up its ugly head from within us. If we deny that we are angry, we harm ourselves. To deny anger when it is present shows we are hiding and not living in truth; this is pride. The important thing is to acknowledge it to ourselves, and to God. It is not fair that we lie to ourselves or be in self-denial; that is a self-imposed dark prison. God does not operate in the darkness. God is light; no darkness can be found in Him. To acknowledge anger is a sign of openness to receive healing. It is also an expression of obedient faith and trust in God, who commands us: "Refrain from anger and turn from wrath; do not fret—it leads only to evil. For those who are evil will be destroyed, but those who hope in the Lord will inherit the land" (Ps 37:8–9, NIV). We should do well to end all criticism, fault-finding and anything that destroys and lessens charity.[287]

We should seek to understand as much as we can about our anger by staying with the emotion in prayer, and letting it come to the surface in all its intensity. It is like waiting to see the full extent of the problem before solving the problem. If we start solving the problem prematurely, it will give us a false impression that it has been dealt with completely, while in reality the problem is still there waiting to erupt again like a volcano at the slightest trigger. We may journal with the Lord what is happening within us. We should address it in spiritual direction as well.

As we dialogue with Jesus the interior movements of anger—thoughts, feelings and desires, we listen to what Jesus has to say to us. It is important that we be quiet and listen to Jesus. Do not be shy to reveal your innermost self to Him. Jesus is and has the answer to all our anger problems. He is patient, meek and humble. It would be wonderful if we can go before Him in the Blessed Sacrament and be like Jacob in Genesis 32:27, who said to God, "I will not let you go until you bless me." We must let go, and let God be God. We must surrender the control of our lives to God. In surrender and total obedience to God, we can pray:

Jesus, out of love for You, I forgive … (*mention the names of people you are angry at*). Father, forgive me and grant me the grace to forgive unconditionally and completely as You have forgiven me in Christ. I forgive myself, and I thank You for loving me. In Your Spirit, renew me to live out my true identity as Your child, praising and magnifying You in and through the Immaculate Heart of Mother Mary. Amen.

May we pray this prayer often so it permeates deep into our spirit to bring release and freedom. The more we pray this way and mean it, i.e., from our hearts, the more the Holy Spirit comes to dwell in our hearts as He once dwelt fully there at our baptism. Saint Paul says that when the Lord's Spirit is present, He brings true freedom, and we experience transformation from glory to glory into His very image (2 Cor 3:17–18).

We invoke the intercession of the Sorrowful and Immaculate Heart of the Blessed Virgin that the graces of her *Third Sorrow*, the Loss of the Child Jesus in the Temple (Lk 3:43–45), would heal our anger and impatience and teach us to forgive and be patient with our weaknesses and bear others burdens calmly. In this way, we grow in patience with ourselves, with others, and with God. We pray to be renewed in faith, hope, and love and to accept and love ourselves as God accepts and loves us. We should imitate Mother Mary's principal virtues: her angelic sweetness, heroic patience, and meekness. We should also call upon the Nine choirs of Angels to help us (Chaplet of Saint Michael, Appendix V).

Spiritual warfare against anger

There are evil spirits of anger, rage and hate that operate in wounded areas of anger. If we choose not to forgive and hold unto anger, it can attract spiritual hostility from demons. When this happens, the anger may become complicated and more difficult to deal with. Other unclean spirits that can complicate anger problems may include: unforgiveness, violence, retaliation, impatience, blasphemy, self-hatred, denial, false self-esteem, and so on. These demons deprive us of interior peace, and can ruin our spiritual lives. When we have allowed spirits to gain a stronghold in us, deliverance ministry may be needed to dislodge them. After this is done, the person may then be free to deal with the underlying issues causing the anger problem.

Chapter 13
✐ ✐ ✐

Primary Open Door 7: Lust

Lust indulged starves the soul, but fools hate to turn from evil (Prov 13:19).

Lust is "the inordinate craving for, or indulgence of, the carnal pleasures which is experienced in the human organs of generation."[288] This inordinate craving involves our five senses: *touch, smell, taste, sight* and *hearing.* Lust is like a locomotive that drives sin in the soul; its ultimate desire in man is for supremacy and dominance. It aims to ravish and conquer.

Touch is particularly significant. Thomas Aquinas says, "It is the foundation of all the other senses."[289] According to McElhone, this sense should be strictly regulated because "what may seem light and even innocent, sooner or later tend to sin and serious sin."[290] The Saints were very strict in regulating this sense by their self-denial, mortification, and the wearing of hair shirts or chains that symbolized interior penance and dying to the false self.

Lust worms its way into our hearts through our senses. There it puts out the light of Christ we received at baptism, and plunges us into spiritual darkness. Paul says of lust:

> The acts of the flesh are obvious: sexual immorality, impurity and debauchery; idolatry and witchcraft; hatred, discord, jealousy, fits of rage, selfish ambition, dissensions, factions and envy; drunkenness, orgies, and the like. I warn you, as I did before, that those who live like this will not inherit the kingdom of God (Gal 5:19–21, NIV).

Lust confuses our discernment by deadening our hearts' sensitivity, making them incapable of distinguishing good from evil. We become perverted and hardhearted. We become stiff-necked and insensitive to the dictates of the light of our conscience. We fail to see the danger and seriousness of sin; we may even rationalize sin, and live it as a lifestyle. Daniel said to one of the two elder judges who falsely accused Susanna, "Beauty has seduced you, lust has subverted your conscience… Your fine lie has cost you your head…" (Dan 13:56, 59).

Our senses are great gifts from God to help us live freely and happily and enjoy being human. To be human is the most beautiful gift. Our physical senses remind us of the greater spiritual senses of our hearts. They are given to us for our awareness and happiness, to help us make right choices and good judgments, and to cooperate with God in assuring our eternal salvation. By our free choice, we make a decision for good or evil. As a sign of our gratitude, we can form the habit of consecrating our senses to God daily. Much prayer and practice are needed to acquire the virtue to maintain control of our senses so that they do not lead us astray. Physical means alone are not sufficient to keep our senses under control. We need the prayer power of the Holy Spirit.

Evil spirits can prey on us through our senses. We must exercise caution; for all that glitter is not gold. The devil deceived Adam and Eve to disobey God by proposing to their senses. It told Eve she would not die, and tricked her into believing her eyes would be enlightened, and that she would be like gods if she ate the fruit that God warned them not to eat. She allowed her senses and feelings to rule her decision-making (reason): "The tree was good for food, pleasing to the eyes, and desirable for gaining wisdom, so she ate it" (Gen 3:6–7). If we do not guard our senses, sooner or later we will begin to compromise our beliefs and the Gospel truths. We may even lose the grace of supernatural faith, and be separated from God.

A beautiful prayer to help us grow strong in our senses is:

"Create in me a clean heart, O God, and put a new and right spirit within me. Do not cast me away from your presence,
and do not take your holy spirit from me. Restore to me the joy of your salvation,
and sustain in me a willing spirit"
(Ps 51:10–11, NRSV)

Before the proclamation of the Gospel at the Eucharistic sacrifice, the priest or deacon prays, "Cleanse my heart and my lips that I may worthily proclaim your holy Gospel." Prayer awakens our senses to the things we take for granted. We are created to love and to receive love. Love is the most powerful thing in the universe. God is love. Love is nurtured by intimacy, and intimacy is nurtured by friendship. We cannot deal with lust by avoiding being in relationship. This may do harm to our spiritual growth, and we risk falling into Satan's trap. Rather, it is by being in relationship that lust is healed. We can use our reason aided by God's grace, to control sexual desires and passions. It is healthy, normal and encouraged for us to grow in intimacy, first with God and then with others while avoiding sin. Fear of the intimacy of love can drive a wedge between us and God. Love engages all the powers of our senses and soul. Love is communication, and through our senses, we communicate and relate in love.

Lust kills our fervor for prayer. The flames of lust are fanned by idleness and excessively indulging in pleasure. Too much leisure, ease and comfort, excessive eating and drinking, and curiosity about many things, can harden our hearts, pervert our will, deaden our senses, block our faculties, blind our minds, numb our feelings, corrupt our conscience and ultimately lead to loss of faith and the rejection of God. In these ways, the evil one uses lust to achieve his goals in our lives when we fail to take God seriously.

Our sense of *taste* helps us to exercise modesty and moderation in eating and drinking. Scripture says, "Taste and see that the Lord is good" (Ps 34:9, NIV). Jesus said, "It is written, 'Man shall not live by bread alone, but by every word that proceeds from the mouth of God.'" (Mt 4:4, NKJV). We eat and drink to live; we do not live to eat and drink. Excessive eating and drinking should be avoided. Fasting, abstinence, and self-denial can help us combat lust; these means should be used with the permission of a spiritual director or superior, or a person of spiritual authority in our lives. We prepare for the eschatological banquet of heaven by moderating our eating and drinking now. The evil one can use earthly eating and drinking to deny us of the banquet of the Lamb (Rev 19).

The *tongue,* our organ of speech, should reflect Christ's presence any time it is used. Vulgar words, curse words, insulting and demeaning words, false humor, lies and gossips should have no place in our speech. For Paul, these words "must not even be mentioned among you, as is fitting among holy ones" (Eph 5:3). Just as a huge forest can be set ablaze by a tiny fire, "The tongue is also a fire. It exists among our members as a world of malice, defiling the whole body and setting the entire course of our lives on fire, itself set on fire by Gehenna" (Jam 3:5–6). So, Jesus says, "Let your 'Yes' mean 'Yes,' and your 'No' mean 'No.' Anything more is from the evil one" (Mt 5:37). Our body, the temple of the Holy Spirit, is destined for the resurrection onto life.

Our *ears* can be a source of burden for our spirit. "To allow the ear undue liberty is to be careless about the spirit of the holy virtue, for things heard can and do leave strong impressions"[291] in us. Everything we hear must be pure and heavenly if we want our spirit and body to be holy as God is holy. Faith comes through hearing, and salvation is experienced through hearing: "Come to me heedfully, listen, that you may have life" (Is 55:3). The rich soil that bore fruit, is the soul that hears God's Word and understands it, and it took root (Mt 13:23).

Our *eyes* need to be guarded from the pollutions of the advertisement industries, the news, and entertainment media which deliberately target our eyes more than the other senses. The evil one has ceased control of these visual outlets to invade and hold souls captive. We are inundated with profane and obscene images everywhere and every moment. "The eyes love to wander; they want to see; they are attracted by the good and the not good; they delight in the unusual, the startling, the alluring, for they want to be entertained and amused. And, willing or unwilling, they print pictures on the imagination that memory easily brings back."[292]

Our eyes reflect the beauty of God who is light, but can turn easily into deadly enemies. Since our eyes are the window to our soul, to keep them pure, we should rest them on holy things. We can challenge ourselves by watching only the movies, shows, and Internet sites that Jesus is pleased to watch with us. Jesus said: "The eye is the lamp of the body. If your eyes are healthy, your whole body will be full of light. But if your eyes are unhealthy, your whole body will be full of darkness. If then the light within you is darkness, how great is that darkness!" (Mt 6:22–23, NIV). Saint Leo the Great says that the eye that is unclean will not see the brightness of the true light. What would be happiness for clear minds would be torment for those that are defiled. So we are to dispel the mist of worldly vanities and cleanse the inner eye of all filth of wickedness, "so that the soul's gaze may feast serenely upon the great vision of God."

Lust self-reflection questions

- Are my decisions based on my feelings or what reason tells me?
- Am I modest in clothes, speech, and thoughts?
- Do I pray perseveringly?
- Do I engage in impure conversations?
- Do I engage in immoral behavior?
- Do I violate the Sixth Commandment: fornication, masturbation, homosexuality, nudity, incest, birth control, abortion, sterilization, or pornography?
- Am I in bondage to sexual sin?
- Is my love exclusive?
- Do I read or watch things suggestive or immoral?
- Do I allow my mind to wander, to be distracted?
- What are my attachments?
- Do I visit inappropriate Internet sites or TV channels?
- Do I tend to overstep appropriate boundaries in my thoughts, words and actions in sexual matters?
- Do I pray deeply and converse with God (Mt 6:6)?
- Where do I store my treasure (Mt 6:21)?
- What thoughts do I entertain in my mind frequently?

- Which of my senses cause me the most problem? What am I doing about it?
- Do I misuse my tongue? Do I say inappropriate things? Do I curse?
- Do I over eat and overdrink? Am I sad or burdened?
- Am I controlling?
- Do I lust after power, honor, position, or material things?
- Do I crave spiritual goods and favors such as ecstasies and spiritual highs in prayer and seek the extraordinary in prayer?
- What takes my attention away from Jesus?
- Am I chaste in my marriage?
- Do my sexual beliefs and practices agree with Church's teachings?
- Do I use contraceptives?
- Is marital love bringing me closer to Jesus and my spouse?
- Are my friendships occasion for sexual temptations and sins?
- Am I compulsive in acquiring pleasure?
- Is the gift of my sexuality leading me into bondage and depriving me of life in Christ?

The weapons against lust

Weapons of the Spirit

When the Spirit of the Lord came upon us at Baptism, He gave us His Seventh Gift of **Fear of the Lord.** The *Spirit of Fear of the LORD* (Is 11:2) fills us with a sovereign respect for God as our most loving Father. By it, we detest and avoid occasions and actions that would cause us to offend God. The Spirit of holy Fear makes us have a deep hatred for the sin of lust and all mortal sins; it leads us to choose God with conviction and in truth, and even to boast in Him (2 Cor 10:17). Fear of the Lord is not associated with thoughts of hell; rather, it comes from a deep sentiment of reverence and total submission to God in all things.[293]

It is the fear that drives us to seek first the Kingdom of God; the Universal Kingship of Jesus Christ and the Queenship of His Mother, Mary; His love and holiness; His humility and obedience; and His total surrender to the Father, so that all other things will be given to us besides (Mt 6:33). In this way, we are moved to submit to the Lordship of Jesus without fear. Fear is opposed to and incompatible with love. Anyone who is afraid lacks the fullness of God's love (1 Jn 4:18). The Spirit of adoption does not enslave us to fear, but gives us power to call God "Abba, Father," when we are fearful (Rom 8:15). "The fear of the LORD is the beginning of wisdom; all those who practice it have a good understanding" (Ps 111:10, NRSV). Fear of the Lord helps us to detach from worldly pleasures capable of separating us from God. The rich young man was filled with lust for worldly goods and so could not follow Jesus, because his heart was ravaged by his possessions.

The *Belt of Truth* is the Armor of God to fight the capital vice of Lust. Lust is a deception and a distortion of the truth about our bodies and its meaning. Our body is the temple of the Holy Spirit, and is destined for sanctification. Our body belongs to God (Heb 10:5). Jesus gave us the Spirit of truth to guide us to all truth about ourselves and God (Jn 16:13), and as a weapon against the lies of lust. Jesus Himself is Truth Incarnate. As His disciples, the Spirit keeps us rooted in His word to know the truth, and be set free by it (Jn 8:31–32).

Word from the Cross

Our Lord Jesus Christ dying on the Cross spoke the *Third Word* that breaks the bondage of lust and purifies our hearts from the grip of lust: **"Behold, your Mother"** (Jn 19:27). Our Blessed Mother is the Immaculate Conception, the Mediatrix of all Graces and the Mother of Perpetual Help. God preserved her from the stain of original sin so that through her we might triumph over lust and sin. She is the purest of God's creatures. John the Beloved took these words of Jesus seriously; he took her into his home (Jn 19:27). She is the Refuge of Sinners, the Help of Christians, and the Health of the Sick, who prays for us always before her Son. Devotion to our Blessed Mother is a sure guarantee of victory in our battle against lust and the demons associated with it.

The Saints and Fathers of the Church teach us that devotion to our Blessed Mother is necessary to attain salvation.[294] This devotion "is even more necessary for those who are called to a special perfection."[295]

Closing the open door of lust

Prayer is the powerful healing remedy for lust, because it fosters an intimate relationship with Jesus. Interior prayer will help us discern the faces of lust in us. We do this by paying attention to the activities of our senses, the movements of our hearts, and the thoughts of our minds. This attitude will help us plan a strategy for winning the war on lust. We must be willing to make the necessary sacrifices to rid ourselves of lustful tendencies.

Journaling with Jesus about our struggles with lust will open our hearts to experience His love and healing. It is in the experience of Jesus' love that we are healed and transformed. In this way, we can witness with the Apostles to what we have seen and heard and touched. John witnessed to what already existed—the risen Jesus Christ. The Apostles proclaimed Jesus as the eternal life that was with the Father; He was made visible to heal us, and is the fulfillment of all our desires (see 1 Jn 1:1–2). The Apostles lived in total conformity to Jesus Christ. Jesus taught that nothing should stand on our way to Heaven. We must be prepared to get rid of any part of us that would prevent us from attaining heaven, even if it would mean cutting off our hand, or plucking out an eye, so that we are not thrown into Gehenna with our whole body. Jesus wants us to save our heads no matter the cost (Mt 5:30).

Saint John Chrysostom explains why the snake is such a wise animal. When you try to strike a snake, it will normally pull out to protect its head. In that way, it survives to bite again. Jesus gives us the principle for right disposition for healing and fruitful living: "For what does it profit a man to gain the whole world and forfeit his soul?" (Mk 8:36, ESV). God's Kingdom must be our first priority, then all else will follow. The problem of lust is that the Kingdom of God is not the priority, but satisfaction from the pleasures of the flesh. Paul wants us to live honorably, not in sexual excess and lust but in friendship with God by putting on the Lord Jesus Christ (Rom 13:13–14). He warns us not to conform to this age, but to be transformed in Christ by renewing our minds so we can discern God's will, the things that are good, pleasing and perfect for our eternal salvation (Rom 12:2).

Chastity is the principal virtue to overcome the sin of lust. Chastity is about moral integrity and wholesomeness and purity in thought, word and deed, as well as motivations. We are taught that salvation is a gift given only for those on the path of the moral life (Gal 5:19–21). Various states of life come with expectations of chastity. Those called to celibacy should strive for celibate chastity. Men and women called to marriage must strive for conjugal chastity, and those in single life should observe the chaste demands of their vocation. Saint Paul reminds us of who we are, the temple of the Holy Spirit (1 Cor 3:17).

The call to perfection is a call to holiness. To live a holy life, a sinless life, we must live intensely the Gospel message. Jesus taught in the Beatitudes that the clean of heart are "Blessed;" they will see God (Mt 5:8). When we have pure hearts by living chaste lives, we see God in others and honor and love them as His children; we do not treat them as objects. We see and treat others and the gift of our sexuality with reverence and respect. When we have pure hearts, we see the divine image of God in ourselves, and we acknowledge ourselves as beloved, and would never violate our bodies.

The motivations and intentions of our hearts are positively affected by chaste living. We need the armor of the *helmet of salvation* and the *breastplate of righteousness* to fight lust. Praying the holy Rosary daily, and with fervor will ensure our minds and hearts are focused on Jesus Christ.

The very thought of the 'Immaculate' Heart tends to make us detest impure thoughts and actions, and if we use Our Lady's devotions (i.e., Scapular, Rosary, First Saturdays) with goodwill, the light from her Immaculate Heart will drive back the darkness of evil and fill us with the joy of the triumph She has promised for us and for the world.[296]

As we strive to imitate the virtues of our Blessed Mother, especially her surpassing purity and mortification in all things, we become modest in our actions and mature in temperance. To heal the damage caused by the sin of lust, we invoke the graces of the pains our Blessed Mother suffered in her *Fourth Sorrow*: the meeting of Jesus and His Mother on the Way of the Cross (Lk 23:27). The pains that pierced her Heart will heal the disorder of our minds and hearts to serve and worship God alone in spirit and truth. She is Mediatrix of all Graces.

The guidance of a spiritual director is priceless in combating lust. Such a director should challenge us, and encourage us on the path of holiness.

Spiritual warfare against lust

The pleasure factor makes the war on lust difficult. Because of it, lust can quickly overwhelm and ravage the victim. The feelings gain control over the will and subordinate it to its powers. Our identity is intimately tied to our sexuality as males and females, because that is how we are created: "male and female He created them" (Gen 1:27). Lust can easily lead to sexual addictions that lead to spiritual blindness. The victim becomes numb to the voice of the Good Shepherd and the Spirit of truth speaking within his or her heart. This is why most victims of lust do not know why they repeatedly commit this sin. They are disconnected from their true selves, and are blind to their own destructive behavior.

This situation creates the condition for spiritual contamination and bondage to occur. If not dealt with, the contamination may worsen, and a deliverance ministry may be needed to set the captive free. In most cases of addiction to lust, there is an underlying predisposing factor, usually a woundedness created by an event in the womb or childhood. In order to resolve the problem of lust, it is important to investigate the root cause, through prayer and self-reflection, while surrendering oneself to a spiritual director. The following case illustrates this reality.

A Protestant speaker, Bob Larson, worked with a fourteen-year-old Brenda who was addicted to pornography. When he prayed with her, he experienced two separate unexpected interruptions from demons. First, he heard the word: "No-o-o-o-o!" from inside of Brenda, which interrupted his prayer. As he prayed further saying – "Lord, I know You love Brenda...

You are the Son of God and rose victoriously from the dead—" He was interrupted a second time: "No, He didn't!"

The minister realized that Brenda was in bondage to the demon of lust. He proceeded to ask: "What is your name?" The response came: "Lust. You can't make me leave. I have a legal right to be in this body!" Larson noted that "Brenda's mannerisms were gone and a male personality came over her." According to him, this demon "said he had entered through Brenda's reading of pornography." Larson demanded to know the legal right that allowed the demon to stay in her. It replied, "Her father." He gave "her the pornography. He left it lying around the house when she was a little girl. She tried to imitate what she saw in those pictures." Larson then called in Brenda's father, a deacon in a Baptist church and explained everything; he wept bitterly over his sin as Larson ministered to him. He led him in a prayer to cast out the demon of lust from his daughter. They were successful; the demon was cast out, and Brenda was freed.[297]

Other evil spirits involved in the sin of lust may include: fear, self-hatred, anger, low self-esteem, self-destruction, discouragement, despair, blockage, addiction and so on. Repressed spirits may likely be present as well. All these spirits must be expelled for persons in bondage to lust to regain their freedom.

The struggle with the Seven Capital Sins can seem like a battle for life itself. God's grace is always available to help us conquer where we must. Jesus has conquered the powers of darkness and has obtained for us the grace to do the same. We must be determined if we must win. An old *Cherokee legend* of the two wolves reminds us that it is all a matter of choice. "A fight is going on inside of me," a grandfather said to his boy. "It is a terrible fight between two wolves. One wants me to feel anger, envy, sorrow, regret, greed, lust, guilt and self-pity. The other wants me to feel hope, peace, kindness, humility, empathy and compassion." The grandson was disturbed by these words and thought about it for a while. He then asked, "Grandfather which wolf will win this fight?" The grandfather replied, "The wolf that I feed."

Be the Best in the Son

The Mystery of the Flower in the Sun
shows
The Mystery of the Christian in the Son

The joy of the flower is to show its colors to the world.
The flower cannot do this and be fulfilled unless in the Sun.
Without the Sun the flower folds its petals
and does not shine for the world to see.

The flower remains hidden and unfulfilled.
It remains hidden and does not amaze the world.
The flower remains hidden and does not bring out the best
in men, because its own best is hidden

The flower is created to amaze us with its colors.
The flower is fulfilled in itself only when it shines in the Sun,
Then it adds beauty to the world.
The flower does not exist for itself,
since it did not create itself.

For the flower to fulfill its mission from the Creator;
It must respond to the presence of the Sun.
In the presence of the Sun,
the flower becomes the best it is created to be.

The joy of the flower is the Sun.
Without the Sun the joy of the flower is not complete.
Every flower begs for the Sun to shine,
so that its joy might be complete.
The flower adds nothing to the radiance of the Sun.

In its weakness and mortality,
the flower must hurry to be its best,
before it dies to be no more.

When the flower has brightened our faces
and our world with its beauty,
Then it can rest in peace because its mission is complete.

The flower has no regrets,
since its mission is to obey its Creator.
It now returns to where it came.

From its Creator it came.
To its Creator it returns as has been willed for it:
Be it eternity or nothingness.

As the Flower in the Sun, so must the Christian be in the Son.

Part III

Chapters 14–18

The Five Secondary Open Doors to Bondage

Glory be to Jesus; honor to Mary and Joseph!

Chapter 14

ⵝ ⵝ ⵝ

Secondary Open Door I:
Prenatal and Postnatal Emotional Wounds and Traumas

You formed my inmost being; you knit me in my mother's womb. I praise you, so wonderfully you made me; wonderful are your works! My very self you knew (Ps 139:13–14).

Created for love

The Visitation narrative in Luke's Gospel helps us to understand that a pre-born child can be affected by spoken words. The Evangelist recounts that after the Annunciation of the Archangel Gabriel to Mary, she hurried to Zachariah's house and greeted Elizabeth. On hearing the greeting, the infant John leaped for joy in the womb. The Holy Spirit filled Elizabeth and she said: "Most blessed are you among women, and blessed is the fruit of your womb" (Lk 1:39–42).

John leaped for joy in his mother's womb at Mary's greeting. Mary herself was with Child by the Holy Spirit. John's joyful leaping in the womb was a baby language of praise and adoration in the presence of the God-Child in Mary's womb. Holy Mary's greeting was Spirit-filled and life giving, since she was overshadowed by the Holy Spirit, and is *Full of Grace.*

John the Baptist grew up a healthy God-fearing man of God. He was fearless in calling sinners to repentance, because he was filled in the womb with the Holy Spirit and zeal for the Kingdom of God. His identity and mission, and his approach to life were influenced largely by this experience in the womb. Saint John was born healed of original sin, according to a Church tradition. He was filled with the joy of the Holy Spirit from the womb.

The sensitivity of children

Children in the womb or in early childhood are sensitive emotionally, spiritually, and physically to their environment. They can 'hear' and perceive information and interpret them. They can sense fear and danger or joy and peace. They know when they are loved and when they are not. A woman shared with me that during her pregnancy, whenever she entered the Church for Sunday Liturgy, and there was singing, her son would leap and kick happily in the womb.

I have learnt through working with people that a preborn child can be violent as an adult, if he/she was exposed to violence while in the womb. If an expectant mother experiences abuse and violence, the child in the womb is affected by that experience and may become abusive and violent in his/her relationships as an adult.

When children in the womb or in early childhood hear words of love, comfort and grace, they feel safe, secure, loved, accepted and good about themselves, because of the positive signals associated with love. In this case, children 'believe' emotional truths about themselves and feel joyful and happy. This is why God willed us into existence—to experience His love through our parents. When children experience love this way, they are able to relate with God as a loving Father. Jesus and John the Baptist had this experience in their mothers' wombs. They felt loved and desired; they grew in their true identity to be the best they were conceived and born into the world to be. They both lived and fulfilled God's will.

From the moment of conception, children share in a human way, through the complimentary love of mother and father, in the one perfect love of God the Father. A child exists to receive love. Fathers and mothers through the bond of marriage share in this life giving love of God. Their vocation is to love their child from the moment of conception with the same love they received from God, and in which they share in their intimacy. If the preborn child, rather than receiving God's love through mother and father, receives threats in any way, either verbal or physical abuse or distress situations, the child reacts negatively. The child cringes in fear and feels unsafe. Threat signals coming through words and actions do not convey the experience of God's love to the child, but rather create emotional hurts and fears.

I worked with a woman who was plagued by panic attacks. She did not know why she suffers these attacks. Elevators and constricted spaces trigger her attacks (claustrophobia). Investigation showed that she experienced a serious traumatic birthing. Her mother had a difficult labor. Now as an adult, she has no conscious memory of that traumatic experience. However, her deep memory held the record of her trauma experience. So when she finds herself in an enclosed space, the wounded traumatic memories get triggered unconsciously, and panic attacks result.

How fear and insecurity develop in prenatal and postnatal children

Preborn infants and children are vulnerable. Like sponges, they have no resistance to the signals coming at them. These signals may be good or bad, corresponding to truth and lies, respectively. When the signals received are good, corresponding to truth, they believe truth about themselves. If the signals received are bad, corresponding to lies, they believe lies about themselves. These beliefs are coded in their memories, and can be triggered later in life. These deep held beliefs can be experienced as consolation or desolation, based on the following three markers: *thoughts*, *feelings* and *desires*. Consolation movements of the heart are: joy, peace, courage, confidence, good self-image, good thoughts about self, feeling secure, etc. Desolation movements of the heart are: fear, sadness, shame, feeling insecure, anxiety, guilt, abandonment, denial, etc.

Negative or hurtful words and actions are perceived negatively. In this case, we believe emotional lies about ourselves, creating emotional wounds in the child. These lies in turn can distort the child's perception of his/her true self and identity. They can orient the child toward negative behavior patterns later in life. Whatever belief systems are rooted or coded in the child at this stage will be felt, acted out and lived out later in life. If the child believed lies about the self, the child will feel and act out lies; if truth, the child will feel and act out truths.

Preborn infants and children, who live in war zones such as the Middle East, are constantly exposed to the danger of survival. They face the daily threats of loud noises of exploding bombs and fighter aircrafts, fear of being killed, sights of bloodshed and wounded and dead bodies, hatred, tensions, anger and despair all the time. These experiences become imprinted in the memories of these children, who are adversely affected by them. Fears, nightmares and insecurity develop and become a way of life. Hatred toward others becomes rooted in their persons, because that is what the children experienced in the womb and early years.

In his Angelus reflection on August 7, 2014, Pope Francis said that children in conflict areas are being denied their childhood.[298] "I think above all of the children, whose hope and future are wrenched away from them; dead children, wounded children, orphaned children, children who play with the remnants of war and are not able to smile."[299] When these fearful memories are reinforced in a child over a period of time, they seem to be part of the personality of the individual; they reflect it in their lived experiences and relationships.

Children are emotionally sensitive to words and actions. Their memories have the facility to store information about events and experiences right from the moment of conception. If these words and actions are incompatible with the experience of love, wounds occur which are held in the child's memory. These wounds become sources of pain, anger, hatred, sadness, violence, etc., when they are triggered. If the words and actions are of love, health and wellbeing result and are retained in the memory. These become sources of joy, peace, calm, smiles, etc., when they are triggered.

Love is the most powerful life giving experience of a child. We are created to be loved and to love. Jesus was a Man of peace; He taught and reflected peace. Peter testified to Jesus' interior calm when he wrote: "When he was insulted, he returned no insult; when he suffered, he did not threaten; instead, he handed himself over to the one who judges justly" (1 Pet 2:23). This peaceful non-threatening attitude was very profound in Jesus that a woman in the crowd hearing Him speak, cried out: "Blessed is the womb that carried you and the breasts at which you nursed" (Lk 11:27). Her words show powerfully that Jesus reflected the good and loving qualities of His Blessed Mother Mary.

The effect of mothers

There are overwhelming documented evidence that mothers and fathers have effects on their prenatal and postnatal children. "*Ideal* mothers have a high ratio of physically and mentally healthy children." "A study by Dr. Gerhard Rottmann of the University of Salzburg, Austria, found that women with negative attitudes during pregnancy had the most devastating medical problems during pregnancy and the highest rate of premature low-weight, emotionally disturbed babies."[300]

Research findings also show that "'ambivalent mothers'—those who are outwardly happy but had inner fears or regrets about pregnancy—subconsciously rejected the children, whose spiritual sensor picked up this unconscious ambivalence. The result was a large number of behavioral and gastrointestinal problems in babies."[301]

The fourth survey group, the "'confused mothers' were those who had careers or other seemingly legitimate reasons for not wanting to be pregnant but outwardly really desired a baby. At birth the children of these mothers had an unusually high degree of apathy, and were physically and emotionally lethargic, with bland personalities."[302]

The effect of fathers

Fathers also have influence on their unborn children. Dr. Thomas Verny of Toronto, Canada showed that the quality of a woman's relationship with her husband had a decisive effect on the unborn child.[303] According to Hampsch, Dr. Monika Lukesche of Constantine University in Frankfurt, West Germany confirmed Dr. Verny's results. She studied 2,000 pregnant women and found that a woman's relationship with her husband "was equal or almost equal in importance to the attitude toward her unborn child in determining the emotional and physical health of the child." Dr. Dennis Scott studied 1,300 children and found that "a woman who regarded her marriage as relatively unhappy had a 237% greater risk of bearing a psychologically or physically damaged child than a woman who felt she was in a secure marriage relationship."[304]

The roles of the conscious and unconscious mind

The Austrian neurologist and founder of psychoanalysis, Sigmund Freud, used the iceberg analogy to describe the two main aspects of the human personality: the conscious and the unconscious mind (see Figure 5 below). In these two aspects, there exists memory, our ability, knowingly or unknowingly, to encode, store, retain and later recall coded information and past events and experiences which influence our present behavior. Memory can have impact on our spiritual or faith life, that is, our relationship with God. Saint Augustine said in *The Confessions*: "The power of memory is great, very great, my God. It is a vast and infinite profundity. Who has plumbed its bottom? This power is that of my mind and is a natural endowment, but I myself cannot grasp the totality of what I am" (*Conf. *10.8.15).

The conscious mind comprises all that is inside our awareness, the things we can rationally think and talk about ourselves. It includes our feelings, thoughts, fantasies, sensations, desires, perceptions, and so on. The preconscious mind is a subsection, and is closely associated with the conscious mind. It includes the things we can easily bring into our awareness, but which we are not thinking about presently. It also includes the dream state. The conscious and preconscious minds are important for our normal human functioning.

The unconscious mind appears to be of greater importance. It contains information hidden from our awareness but which deeply influence our personalities and behaviors.

The experiences of our lives beginning from the moment of conception are stored in our memories. As we develop and mature and accumulate more experiences, the memories of events in the womb and early childhood, which are located in the deeper memory sites relative to the more recent events, become less accessible to us. These memories are more difficult to access than more recent memories. What is remembered or not remembered will depend on the unique interior make up of a person: psychological, physical, spiritual, emotional, biological, environmental, relationships, and so on.

Traumatic and painful memories of events in utero, during birth and early childhood, will tend to be hidden away as a protective mechanism by the body. These may not be remembered, or may be remembered with difficulty, or they may be mixed up or confused, again depending on a person's interior dynamics, and other factors which are beyond the scope of this book. The event itself for which a memory exists may not be remembered, but the code or belief associated with the event remains with us, and can be detected, felt, or acted out in a human way.

What is important for us when an event occurs is the meaning (the code or the belief) the child associates with the event at the time it happened. This code is held in the memory and can be triggered by series of both the internal dynamics of the person and the external interactions in life. Unhealed memories of painful events can filter through and manifest, and can disrupt or influence a person's life negatively. The presence of painful emotional memories of childhood creates negative and distressful feelings, sensations, dispositions, perceptions, thoughts and desires. The sum total of these negative experiences, when they distress and burden our faith life, is called spiritual desolation. In this case, we need further investigation to understand them (see Chapter 4). We may have to address our desolation in spiritual direction. In addition, inner healing may be needed.

Dealing with emotional wounds

Emotional wounds and traumas, unlike physical wounds, are difficult to heal for various reasons. As part of the process of healing physical wounds, they may be monitored, examined, cleaned, anointed with balm, and bandaged. Christians and people of faith in God may even be inspired to pray for the healing of physical wounds. In the face of pain and suffering, the Christian faith encourages patience and acceptance, and prayers for the grace to bear the inconveniences. Catholic spirituality even encourages us to acquire the spiritual attitude of uniting their sufferings to the Passion of Jesus Christ to console His Most Sacred Heart and the Immaculate Heart of Mary, to make reparation for the sins of humanity, as well as offer our sufferings for the salvation of souls. All these we may elect to do in union with Jesus Christ, and out of love for Him, that the Father may be glorified and praised and loved in this world.

Emotional wounds, on the other hand, present a somewhat different and more difficult scenario. Though they are not in our immediate consciousness, somehow, we are aware of them. Although they are hidden and buried in our unconscious mind, the pains associated with them are very real to us. Since many persons, especially men, who are known to be emotional evaders, do not like to talk about emotional wounds; they tend to treat the pains emanating from these hidden wounds by avoiding them. They turn a blind eye to them and, as it were, sweep them under the rug. They neglect them and move on with life as if the wounds do not exist. They naively think the pains would go away. But unfortunately, that is not normally the case.

The pains coming from emotional wounds cry out for healing; only Jesus Christ can heal them. He created us and knit us together in our mothers' womb (Ps 139:14); He knows all our sufferings. It is by the wounds of His Passion that we are healed. Jesus invites all who are burdened and distressed in any way to come to Him and receive healing in His sacred Humanity (Mt 11:28).

Unfortunately, some of us treat emotional pains by numbing ourselves with self-gratifying means. Some resort to substance abuse or indulge in addictive behaviors that lead to eating disorders, overdependence on prescription medications, gambling, excessive watching of TV shows and movies, excessive alcohol use (alcoholism), excessive work (workaholism), retail therapy, daydreaming, and preoccupation with the body (cult of the body) and sex; others may engage in acts of self-destruction and self-gratification through masturbation, pornography, sexual immorality with others, anger and a host of other destructive behaviors that are embraced. These negative self-destructive actions can cause stress and discouragement that lead to depression and suicidal thoughts. The root of these problems may be located in the unconscious mind. If so, it is there that the problem will have to be resolved.

Voices of the unconscious mind

In the iceberg illustration of the mind shown below, the water level separates the conscious mind from the unconscious mind. The unconscious mind constitutes most of the body mass of the mind, while the conscious mind comprises only the tip of the iceberg. Most of our life's experiences are buried in the unconscious mind. It holds our deepest beliefs, which influence and drive our thoughts, feelings, words, urges, and our behavior—personal and relational. Because we are mostly unaware of how the embedded belief systems impact our lives, it is possible to be trapped and held in bondage in the unconscious mind.

As a Microbiologist and a Medical Laboratory Technologist, I liken the problem of the unconscious to the experience of early medical practice, when physicians refused to acknowledge that bacteria, viruses, and parasitic pathogens cause infection. This ignorance may be excusable, since science at that time in the history of medicine was not yet equipped to demonstrate the presence of these pathogenic microbes, because of their microscopic nature; the microscope had not yet been invented. As a result, medical science tended to deny the reality of the presence of these pathogenic or disease-causing microbes, which were invisible to the human eye. Since the contents of the unconscious memory influence us more heavily than those of the conscious memory, I will address its role in our personal and generational issues.

A medical doctor once explained to me that more than 90% of all mental activities are not immediately visible to the conscious mind. Our earliest memories of experiences, which occur in this order: moment of conception, in the womb, time of birth, and early childhood, are located in the deep memory section (see Figure 5).

Sigmund Freud, understandably, was more interested in the unconscious mind. As a neurologist and psychoanalyst, he suspected it held clues to the interior dynamics in his patients.

The Iceberg Analogy of the Mind

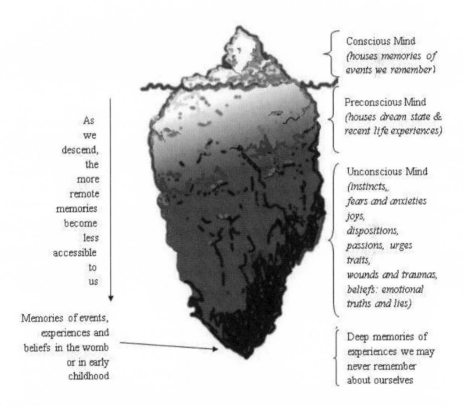

Figure 5: *Freud's iceberg analogy of the conscious and unconscious mind*

To access the memories housed deep in the unconscious mind, we need time of silence and solitude. More importantly, we need God's grace and the light of the Holy Spirit to help us see or notice our deep memory contents. We get in touch with the coded information in our memories through monitoring our thoughts, feelings, words, desires, urges, dispositions, behaviors and actions, body reactions, instincts, and dreams that we notice about ourselves.

When processing these movements in prayer, as a rule of thumb, we are encouraged to stay with our experiences and to talk to Jesus about them. If the experience is one of desolation, we stay with it and not run from it. This staying-with helps us to take a closer look, as if to magnify it, so we can understand the affective movement, and then take necessary corrective action for our health and well-being and for the good of our faith. The affective moments we notice in prayer, whether they are spiritual consolation or spiritual desolation, are privileged moments of encounter with God.

When we are in consolation, we want to stay with the experience to receive more of what God has for us, since true spiritual consolation always comes from God. As stated earlier, when we are in desolation, we also want to stay with the experience, and from there, we cry out for help. It is there that Jesus, who hears the cry of the poor, will come to touch and rescue us with His healing love,[305] just as He rescued Peter as he cried out, "Lord, save me" (Mt 14:30).

The great Saint Augustine had a checkered past, possibly influenced by his upbringing or culture. His rise to glory began when he turned inward in personal self-reflection. This inward journey enabled him to experience the beauty of God within him. He also saw the reality of the misery of his sins. As he recollected, pondered and listened in self-reflection, he grew in self-knowledge and in God-knowledge, and he became the saint he was created to be. In his *Confessions,* he wrote:

> Urged to reflect upon myself, I entered under your guidance into the inmost depth of my soul. I was able to do so because you were my helper. On entering into myself I saw, as it were with the eye of the soul, what was beyond the eye of the soul, beyond my spirit: your immutable light... This light was above me because it had made me; I was below it because I was created by it. He who has come to know the truth knows this light... Late have I loved you, O Beauty ever ancient, ever new, late have I loved you! You were within me, but I was outside, and it was there that I searched for you.[306]

God dwells within us. Times of prayer and personal self-reflection constitute the contemplative approach that prepares us for the intimate encounter with God. The fruits of this encounter are always peace, freedom, joy, liberation, conversion, healing and restoration, and ultimately, salvation.

The smoke analogy of feelings

Two fundamental beliefs, truths and lies, influence our thoughts, words, feelings, actions, and desires. They determine whether we have a habit of accusing or encouraging people, whether we have interior peace or turmoil within ourselves, and they influence our dreams and inner dispositions as well.

When we believe truth about ourselves, we have peace and reflect peace. But if we believe lies, we lack peace and experience division in ourselves. To understand how our emotions arise, let us use the smoke analogy in Papal elections to explain this.

When a Pope dies or resigns, the *Cathedra* of Saint John Lateran, the Cathedral Church of the Bishop of Rome, becomes vacant (*Sede Vacante*). The College of Cardinals will take over the administration of the Holy See and the Universal Church. They will gather in the Sistine Chapel in Vatican City for the conclave to elect a new Pope. At this, the eyes of the world will be turned on the chimney above the Sistine Chapel for evidence of election results: the black smoke or white smoke.

Once the conclave begins, the smoke emissions tell the outside world whether a pope has been elected or not. Black smoke means "no pope;" white smoke means *Habemus Papam,* "We have a pope."

The smoke, black or white, represents our emotions, which may be either good (consolation) or bad (desolation). The smoke is produced when ballot papers are burnt in a furnace deep down below the chimney after each voting. The smoke color, black or white, depends on which chemicals were added to the ballot papers during the burning. The furnace represents our memory, and the chemicals represent truths or lies.

When there is a *fumata nera* (dark smoke), it is because the chemicals: potassium perchlorate, anthracene and sulphur were added to the burnt ballots. When there is *fumata bianca* (white smoke), it is because the chemicals: potassium chlorate, lactose / milk sugar and colophony / pine rosin were added to the burnt ballots.[307]

I worked with a woman who had struggled with fear for most of her life. She did not know the origin of her fear. After several months of spiritual direction and praying with the Scriptures, one day she came for direction as usual. As soon as we began the session, she said, "Father, my fear is gone." My response was, "Really." She then related how, while praying with the Scriptures, Jesus had shown her an image. In the image, He held her heart in water cupped in His hands, and was rocking it back and forth. At that moment, the fear left her.

As we prayed, the Lord also showed her the root of her fear. At the moment of her pre-mature birth, she did not have contact with her mother. In that moment of separation, she experienced fear, which had remained with her until Jesus healed her of it.

The memory holding the coded information about the fear was resolved when Jesus, who is Truth and God's perfect love to us, came into that wounded memory and dispelled the darkness of fear. This was a miracle. Jesus Christ desires to give anyone suffering from childhood wounds and traumas miracles, like He did for this woman. Only Jesus Christ can heal such wounds. He is the light that came into the darkness and defeated the darkness (Jn 1:5). It is as if Jesus is saying again: "Let there be light!" (Gen 1:3). For this woman, the miracle of the healing of her fear happened in the contemplative prayer experience with Jesus. If we are finding it difficult to stop being angry, unforgiving, impatient, fearful, or suffering from addiction, let us go to Jesus for the answer in the silence of our hearts and hear Him say to us: I have called you out of darkness into My own wonderful light (1 Pet 2:9). He wants us to let go of anger, to forgive, and to be humble. No one who holds unto anger in his heart against another should expect God's healing (Sir 28:3).

How emotional wounds can be open doors

Emotional wounds created in preborn infants and children can be open doors to spiritual contamination, which in turn can lead to spiritual bondage. Emotional wounds are created as explained above when children are exposed to abuses and traumas or subjected to situations in which they do not experience God's love. In these situations, they may believe emotional lies about themselves based on the abuse. Emotional lies or vows are not sins, since they are not acts of the will. However, they can compromise our interior integrity making it possible for evil spirits to attach to these compromised areas of our interior life and threaten our peace by putting us in bondage.

Evil spirits behave very much like bats or flies. Bats prefer dark places as their hide outs to avoid detection; they flee when light is introduced into their hideout. Flies are easily attracted to open wounds on our bodies and to rotten smell. These emotional wounds represent the *dark* and the *wounds* of our spiritual nature that attract evil spirits, and they attach to these areas. Preborn infants and children cannot rationally process events and traumas they experience. These signals affect them emotionally and in other ways.

Children are always the fruit of love. They are created by God to be loved and to love. They can sense and respond emotionally to signals that speak of love. John the Baptist in the womb leaped for joy when his mother heard the greeting from Mary, the Mother of God. Preborn infants can also sense and respond to signals that do not correspond to love. They react to these with fear and insecurity. In those groups of children who are deprived of love, abandonment issues, unforgiveness, anger, self-hatred, shame, resentment, or a distorted self-image get coded into their memories. If these are not addressed and resolved, they linger and fester and can cause distress in the life of the individual. Memories of such wounds of childhood are retained deep in the unconscious memory (see Figure 5).

This situation should not cause parents, grandparents, or guardians to hold themselves or anyone else to blame for either their parenting styles or the problems their children may suffer. It is never the intention of any loving parent to inflict wounds on their children. The goal of this author is not to place the burden of responsibility for their children's hurts on the parents. For those of us who may not be familiar with the problems of the unconscious, this section may shed some light on the root lies and false belief systems behind problems in the behaviors of children and adults, so we can gain the necessary knowledge on how to address and resolve them. There are no perfect parents anywhere on this earth, except of course the parents of Jesus Christ—Joseph and Mary.

The effects of original sin on us are far-reaching; we lost sanctifying grace. The effects of our own upbringing, native cultures and various life experiences are also far-reaching. John tells us that if we claim we do not have sin, we make God a liar (1 Jn 1:10). We all came into this world wounded by sin, and without the grace of God, but thank God for our baptism in Christ. The way a child is raised will influence the child's perception of reality. It will also affect the way he/she will raise his/her own child. With God's grace and by paying close attention to the interior movements of our hearts, we can gain self-knowledge and receive the healing that Christ desires for us.

Children are weak, open, and dependent, and they trust the adults around them. Their motives are pure and simple. Children are real; they are what you see—no masks and no hidden agenda. They are not complicated; they are free of intellectual blocks. This is why Jesus commands that we all become like little children, because Heaven is for the childlike (Mt 18:3). Because of their innocence, simplicity and openness, children do not know how to hide or disguise their feelings. They are like sponges that soak in whatever is exposed to them. Most of their experiences are hidden in the unconscious mind. As children mature into adulthood, the childhood experiences buried deep in their memories seep out and influence thoughts, words, feelings, actions and desires. The beliefs, truths or lies, associated with memories of past events are carried through life. These beliefs are felt and acted out in real life. If we believe lies about ourselves, we feel and act out lies. If we believe truths about ourselves, we feel truths and act out truths.

Inner healing may be needed if we become aware of deep-rooted negative beliefs manifesting in some distressful observable way. Through our thoughts, words, feelings, and desires, we become aware of these deep-rooted beliefs. We do not need inner healing when we become aware of deep-rooted positive beliefs, because we are uplifted and feel good and loved and confident about ourselves. The negative beliefs distort our perception of reality and can adversely affect our spiritual lives, distorting our image of who God is in Himself. They can adversely impact the way we relate with God, with others, and with ourselves.

Saint Ignatius of Loyola refers to these interior movements or experiences: feelings, thoughts and desires, as spiritual consolation or spiritual desolation. They are spiritual, because they affect our relationship with God; that is, they cause an increase (consolation) or decrease (desolation) in faith, hope and love. There are also non-spiritual movements that can be noticed; these are called psychological movements. They do not affect our relationship with God (Chapter 4 deals with these heart movements).

The significance of thoughts, words, feelings and desires

Spiritual consolations are interior movements, often associated with thoughts, feelings and desires, which build us up and make us have healthy self-worth; and they give us confidence about ourselves. When we encounter events that cause us joy, peace, etc., we feel loved and uplifted, and we consider ourselves the most precious of all creatures. Spiritual desolations are contrary to spiritual consolations. Their effects are also contrary to those of consolation. They cause us to feel depressed, lost, abandoned, shame, guilt, separated from God, and alone (see Appendix II). We may blame ourselves and others for our sadness and misery, impatience and lack of interior peace. We may feel that God does not care, or maybe He has taken a vacation on the beaches of the Bahamas enjoying Himself, while we are here suffering.

The truth is, none of these assumptions are true; but we may feel that way. We may even get angry at God, and wrongly accuse Him of doing a poor job as a Father. It will be helpful to remember, that our image of God is mostly a projection of what we experienced of our parents or some person who strongly influenced us as children. If our relationship with our fathers is sour, we may project that on the Fatherhood of God, the perfect and All-Holy Father. If our relationship with our mothers is strained, we may project that on the Father's motherly qualities; or we may project that on our Most Blessed Mother and refuse to speak with her, whom Jesus gives us as our mother (Jn 19:27).

Desolation experiences should be addressed with a spiritual director, or one who is spiritually matured and knowledgeable to guide us. These experiences need to be understood so that appropriate action can be taken to resolve them. The director can help the directee dialogue these issues with Jesus, who alone can bring the directee to experience and rest in God's peace.

Hurtful events of childhood can fester and breed anger, resentment, unforgiveness, self-hatred, and so on, which can disrupt a person's spiritual life. They can lead to addictions to sex and related immoral activities and behavioral anomalies, such as scrupulosity, perfectionism, impatience, abnormal or unnatural attraction tendencies, and relationship problems.

A child in her mother's womb can experience violent abuses when her mother is battered or abused. The child may in turn become violent as an adult based on her preborn experience, without external causes. A child in the womb may "hear" the mother and/or father talk about how they might abort their child. That child may turn out to be filled with anger, rage and hatred, based on that experience, without any external cause.

Preborn and childhood wounds and the beliefs associated with them can distort our image of our true identity. Such distortions and their accompanying effects can block our openness to receive God's love through those in our lives. They can stunt our spiritual growth, orient us toward worldly things, and create negative dispositions. They can cause tepidity and laziness and make us not take our faith life seriously, causing us to adopt a casual attitude toward our salvation. It is important to emphasize; when we become aware of these desolating interior movements, we should seek spiritual counsel.

Prayers for the healing of secondary open door (I) begin on page 335.

Chapter 15

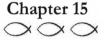

Secondary Open Door II:
Unholy Soul-Ties, Personal Choices, Affections and Addictions

Walk with wise men and you will become wise, but the companion of fools will fare badly (Prov 13:20).

God created us in His image and likeness. He made us for Himself (Gen 1:26–27); God gave the man a partner so that he is not alone (Gen 2:18). He placed them (Adam and Eve) in the garden so He can have a direct relationship with them. He even walked with "blameless" patriarchs: Abraham (Gen 17:1), Noah (Gen 6:9), and Enoch (Gen 5:21–24). By faith, we walk with God (Heb 11:5) in a relationship of love. Jesus calls us to love one another as He first loved us (Jn 15:12; 1 Jn 4:19). God created us to live always in the warmth of His love, hence the Incarnation—"I am with you always, until the end of the age" (Mt 28:20). God who is Trinity: Father, Son and Holy Spirit, is relational in His Being. He created us for relationship with Him and with one another.

Healthy loving relationships make us mature to our fullest capacity as humans; we live happy and fulfilled lives glorifying God. Human relationships create bonds that are physical and spiritual, because we are body and spirit beings. Our deepest and lasting relationships are spiritual; we are most like God in our spirit. God is spirit (Jn 4:24), and eternal life is our destiny. Saint Paul says that of God's three gifts of faith, hope and love, the greatest is love (1 Cor 13). God is love. We call this spiritual bond 'soul-tie,' or soul-relationship. If our relationship is holy, healthy and life giving, it is a *holy soul-tie.* If it is sinful, unhealthy and poisonous, it is an *unholy soul-tie.* Soul-ties affect us positively or negatively.

Holy soul-ties

Scripture tells us that David and Jonathan struck a deep bond of friendship. "Jonathan made a covenant with David, because Jonathan loved him as his very self" (1 Sam 18:1–4). Early Church history tells us of the covenant friendship between the Cappadocian Fathers: Saints Basil the Great (329–379) and Gregory Nazianzen (329–389). Their deep friendship inspired them to greatness so that they became Bishops and Doctors of the Church, and above all, Saints (feast day, January 2). Saints Cornelius and

Cyprian (feast day September 16) were also good holy friends, as well as Saints Cyril and Methodius (feast day February 14), the Apostles of the Slavs, who were brothers. Saints Francis of Assisi and Clare had a similarly close friendship. All these saints had common friendship in Christ, and were spiritually bonded with each other, while supporting one another in their journey and hunger for holiness.

Because of our body and spirit being, to which Scripture testifies, "Did he not make one being, with flesh and spirit?" (Mal 2:15). Human relationships engage both our bodily and spiritual dimensions. The fruits of holy soul-ties witness to the relationships themselves. A tree is known by its fruit. A good and holy relationship is known by its fruit, namely, peace, patience, confidence, mutual respect and trust, purity, joy, friendship, love and holiness. All these glorify God.

God created the family precisely to foster a relationship of holy love among members. Spouses, parents and children, brothers and sisters, as well as extended families, friends, and indeed all of humanity are called to live and share in this communion of love that exists between the Father and the Son and the Holy Spirit, where holy soul-ties flourish. Jesus said to Philip, "Whoever has seen me has seen the Father" (Jn 14:9). "The Father and I are one" (Jn 10:30). Cultivating holy soul-ties make saints flourish in our families and in the world. When Jesus walked the face of this earth, it was known to all that He was a holy Man. But He was more than a holy Man. He loved people and did good works. "He did all things well" (Mk 7:37). Holy soul-ties among families create the civilization of love that Pope Saint John Paul II hoped for us in his *Letter to Families* in the year of the Family 1994.

As a former member of the Intercessors of the Lamb community for over eleven years, until its suppression in October 2010, I experienced the joy of holy soul-ties with people of different cultures, nationalities and backgrounds who, responding to God's call, joined the Intercessors. In our intercessory ministry, we developed holy soul-ties among ourselves because of our love of Jesus. Jesus fostered a holy soul-tie with His Twelve Apostles and with the seventy-two disciples whom He sent out two by two to preach and heal. Our Savior Jesus Christ desires that we have a holy soul-tie with Him. He said, "I no longer call you servants, because a servant does not know his master's business..." I have called you My friends, for I have made known to you everything that I heard from my Father (Jn 15:15, NIV). The slave-master relationship is one of fear, not love. Fear is never of God. Relationships based on fear are unhealthy, and very easily lead to unholy soul-ties between master and slave.

Holy soul-tie with Jesus?

Jesus does not want us to be afraid of Him; He calls us His friends. Jesus is the sum total of the Father's love for us. In Jesus, we are the sum total of the Father's love for us. We are God's delight (Is 62:4). One might even boldly say that the Father exists to love us and to be in relationship with us. This is absolutely amazing! We are the Father's delight. To seal this soul-bond with us, Jesus gives us His very Spirit, "Receive the Holy Spirit" (Jn 20:22); He also gives us His Precious Body and Blood in the Most Holy Eucharist to forge a deeper covenant soul-tie with us in an unbreakable bond of love (Jn 6). He said, "Remain in me as I remain in you." As a branch is to the vine, so you must be to Me (Jn 15:4–5). To have a soul-tie relationship with Jesus is to enter into a soul-tie relationship also with the Father (Jn 12:44). Jesus declared that to see Him is to see the Father. He also said, "Those who love me will keep my word, and my Father will love them, and we will come to them and make our home with them" (Jn 14:23, NRSV).

The Church unites the community of believers under the one Lordship of Jesus Christ. In Him, everything is held together as one (Col 1:17). Jesus is the bond that holds the mystical body together uniting the Church Victorious, the Church Suffering, and the Church Militant as one. To the Church Militant, the believers, the Apostle Paul offers encouraging words, to live blamelessly according to their vocation in life. He wants them to accept each other lovingly and to strive to grow in the oneness of the Holy Spirit and hold together in peace in one body and one spirit (Eph 4:1–4). Holy soul-ties lead to interior freedom among those bonded by them. By exercising their free will rightly, persons in holy soul-tie create the space for the Holy Spirit to operate. When the Holy Spirit is present, there is always freedom and joy of the Lord (2 Cor 3:17).

Unholy soul-ties

Unholy soul-ties can develop in relationship with authority figures:[308] superiors, employers, people in leadership, bosses, and pastors of Churches, who impose, disrespect, intimidate, maltreat, abuse, and lord things over those under them. This can create uneasy tensions that are unhealthy for all sides. Gang members, drug rings and mafia groups are soul-tied by evil bonds. These evil bonds result in conflicts among members and between groups, because they are based on alliances of evil and sin. Not surprisingly then, initiates to these gangs experience much violence and abuse. The violence is much when rival gangs and cults clash for dominance. Since these unholy relationships are acts of free will, they attract demonic activity, which can lead to bondage. Spiritual bondage is the complete opposite of everything that is freedom; it is slavery in the true sense.

Human relationships based on sin create unholy spiritual bonds. These bonds can predispose us to spiritual contamination. A lady named Kia came to me seeking help because she and her children were experiencing strange phenomena in their house. Three figures or shadows she said move about freely in the house. She claimed that sometimes she smells fresh food being cooked in her kitchen while no one was physically cooking. These frightening occurrences caused them to flee the house. She also claimed that at her current temporary residence, a different "spiritual visitor" was clinging around her. She requested I come and bless her troubled house. I went. Before the rite of blessing of her house, she informed me and my prayer partner that she is a single mother of five children; each has a different father; none of them live morally sound lives. I understood her situation. It was clear to me as we prayed and chatted that multiple open doors to contaminations exist, primarily through her choices: lust, sloth, pride, unholy soul-ties with multiple sexual partners, lukewarmness in the practice of her Christian faith, predisposing factors and unresolved childhood wounds, besides previous occult involvement. She and her children were easy prey to demonic attacks.

We know that the most intimate union between two persons on earth is the conjugal union of man and woman oriented toward procreation and marital love. This is the exclusive purpose of the gift of sexuality, to be experienced only between a man and woman who are in a flesh bond of marriage. Scripture says, "God created man in his image; in the divine image he created him; male and female he created them" (Gen 1:27). He blessed and commanded Adam and Eve to "be fertile and multiply; fill the earth and subdue it. Have dominion…" (Gen 1:28). No other human relationship can fulfill this Divine command except the union of man and woman. This command is the basis of the human family as envisioned by God. Jesus reechoed this Divine teaching and command in His response to the question on divorce by the Pharisees: "Have you not read that from the beginning the Creator 'made them male and female'" (Mt 19:4). Scripture also records that God commanded Noah to populate the ark with various animals and birds, males and females, in preparation for the flood (Gen 7).

The male-female exclusive relationship is for spouses in the one-flesh bond of marriage for the propagation of humanity. Any other form of sexual relationship apart from the marriage of man and woman violates God's Sixth Commandment as commanded in Sacred Scripture (Ex 20:2–17). Such ungodly relationships can and do create unholy soul-ties that open the door to spiritual contamination and subsequent demonic bondage.

The genius of Saint John Paul II's teaching in the *Theology of the Body* is that our bodies, which share in God's image and likeness, are meant to speak and act in truth. When we fail to live the truth in our bodies but rather live lies by engaging in sinful acts, we open the door of our hearts to spiritual bondage by the father of lies and the prince of iniquity—Satan. Human relationships by which our bodies speak lies include fornication, abortion, contraception, heterosexual activities outside of marriage, lifestyles of homosexual relationships and acts of sodomy, prostitution, pornography, masturbation, bestiality, and so on (see 1 Cor 6:8). Other relationships of interest to our discussion are those that cause pain and suffering, those opposed to God's values, and which are contrary to Gospel standards.

For the youth especially and others as well, the Internet, Facebook, chat rooms, and other electronic gaming and social media have become snares to draw souls into unhealthy and dangerous relationships. Some of these have led to serious demonic contamination, and sometimes even possession. Plenty of evidence abounds to testify to the reality of these dangers. Occult and evil-minded individuals use the electronic media outlets to recruit members into their realm so as to destroy their faith in God and then ruin their lives and their future. Through engaging in these activities we can develop unholy soul-ties with other people involved. We can develop unhealthy and poisonous ties and affections with ourselves, as in masturbation, etc., which open doors to spiritual bondage.

Family relationships involving parents and children, siblings, and spouses, as well as friends and peers and authority persons in our lives, can generate unhealthy tensions that lead to unholy soul-ties. We know that a child's deepest wounds come from those who are supposed to love him/her the most—parents or guardians, etc. When children fail to receive the love they deserve, in all the scenarios in which these can happen, serious problems can develop later in the child's life in her perception of her true identity and in her relationships. Spouses in abusive relationships, and relationships where persons in authority over others abuse such privilege through intimidation, bullying, anger, rage and impatience, can cause unholy soul-ties to develop between them. Also membership in criminal and drug gangs, and engaging in intrinsically immoral behaviors and lifestyles can be open doors to spiritual contamination. All these promote demonic activity that can lead to spiritual bondage.

Participants who attend the Family Healing Retreats are encouraged to examine and log past and present awkward relationships in the *Investigation Sheet III* provided (see Appendix I), in preparation for the prayer ministry to close the doors to bondage, and open them to Christ and freedom. The unholy soul-ties entered into in these relationships must be renounced and repented of, and severed in the name of Jesus Christ. The persons involved in these relationships are challenged and encouraged to make lifestyle changes where necessary. They are to leave the past behind and cultivate new and holy friendships. If these efforts are neglected, the doors to bondage may remain open, and the situation may worsen, creating unnecessary hardships under the slavery of demons. More importantly, it may put our relationship with God the Father at risk.

Once the evil ties are broken during prayer ministry, the Cross of Christ is invoked and placed between the liberated persons and the sources of contamination to prevent future re-contamination. It is important that those in unholy soul-ties renounce all such relationships and recommit to live holy Christ-like lives.

Prayers should be offered unceasingly in the spirit for the healing of spiritual wounds. This is done most effectively through the invocation of the Holy Spirit, the Balm of Gilead. He is God's healing Rays who heals wounds in our souls. The holy sacrifice of the Mass is absolutely necessary for the breaking and healing of unholy soul-ties and all other healings. The name of Jesus—Lord and Messiah—, is the name above all names. Jesus' name is the source of healing and salvation for all. It is important that holy soul-ties be established with people in a supportive faith community. The Church is a community of believers seeking oneness in Christ. We are one body in Christ! Jesus prayed that the Church may be one (Jn 17:22). When believers in holy soul-ties unite in prayer, the power of the Holy Spirit is present, and the Church comes alive (Mt 18:20).

Unholy personal choices, not necessarily relationship related, can also open doors to bondage. Our fallen nature is capable of developing inordinate affections for lesser creatures, situations, institutions and nations such that the resulting attachments limit our interior freedom. The case of the rich young man who was held captive by his possessions and attachments that he could not obey and follow Jesus' invitation to become His disciple illustrates the threat and the danger affections and addictions can pose to our quest for eternal salvation (Mk 10:17–23). Understanding the dynamics of these affections within us can help us resist them. God's grace, our personal self-reflection and spiritual direction are effective remedies for dealing with bondage caused by unholy affections and addictions (Mk 10:26–27). These can help us avoid becoming functioning addicts.

Created things and situations should serve only to move us on the path to Heaven; that is the only reason they have been allowed in our lives. Rather than feed these affections and addictions, we should starve them. We should deny ourselves, carry the cross, and follow Jesus.

Prayers for the healing of secondary open door (II) begin on page 338.

● ● ●

Chapter 16

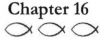

Secondary Open Door III:
Denial of God and Rejection of the Church's Doctrines,
Morals and Practices

Understand this, you who forget God, lest I attack you with no one to rescue
(Ps 50:22).

The Church: the means of our salvation and knowledge of God

Jesus Christ established the Church by the authority of His Father as the means of salvation for all people. We read that Jesus went up the mountain, and He spent the whole night in prayer to God. At daybreak, He called His disciples, and from them He chose His Twelve Apostles (Lk 6:12–16). To Simon, whom He named Peter, He said, "I say to you, you are Peter, and upon this rock I will build my church" (Mt 16:18). Jesus further said: "I will give you [Peter] the keys of the kingdom of heaven; whatever you bind on earth will be bound in heaven, and whatever you loose on earth will be loosed in heaven" (Mt 16:19, NIV; also see Jn 20:19–23, the Doctrine of Infallibility). Through the Church, by baptism, the door to salvation is opened to all. Upon His glorious resurrection from the dead, Jesus revealed Himself to His Apostles to confirm and invest His authority on them: "As the Father has sent me, so I send you." "Receive the Holy Spirit." "Go...make disciples of all nations, baptizing them in the name of the Father, and of the Son, and of the Holy Spirit, teaching them to observe all that I have commanded you...I am with you always, until the end of the age" (Jn 20:21–22; Mt 28:19–20).

The Church's faith is founded on the risen Lord. Saint Paul taught that if Christ was not raised, our preaching and our faith are empty; "Your faith is vain" (1 Cor 15:14, 17). But Jesus Christ truly rose from the dead. He appeared to the Eleven, ate with them, and breathed and empowered them: "Receive the Holy Spirit. If you forgive the sins of any, they are forgiven them; if you retain the sins of any, they are retained" (Jn 20:22–23, NRSV).

On Pentecost day, the Holy Spirit descended like tongues of fire and rested on one hundred and twenty persons gathered in prayer in the Upper Room (Cenacle). He empowered them to take the Good News of the Father's love in Christ to the entire world. Jesus had promised: "...you will receive power when the Holy Spirit has come upon you, and you will be my witnesses in Jerusalem and in all Judea and Samaria, and to the end of the earth" (Acts 1:8, ESV). For two thousand unbroken years, the Church has remained ever faithful to this mandate to bear witness to the world that the Lord Jesus is risen.

The Holy Spirit is the soul of the Church. He guides her on the path of faith and obedience to God's commandments. The Spirit helps us to discern the truth and to remain in the truth of our faith.

Pope Saint John Paul II taught that faith is based on Divine Revelation. Because of faith, man can say, "I believe." He said that Sacred Scripture, both the Old Testament and the New Testament, which is a source of Divine Revelation teaches:

That man is capable of knowing God by reason alone. He is capable of a certain "knowledge" about God, even though it is indirect and not immediate. Therefore, alongside the "I believe" we find a certain "I know." This "I know" concerns the existence of God and even, to a certain extent, his essence. This intellectual knowledge of God is systematically treated by a science called "natural theology," which is of a philosophical nature and springs from metaphysics, that is, the philosophy of being. It focuses on the knowledge of God as the First Cause, and also as the Last End of the universe.[309]

Saint John Paul II continues,

The sources of Christianity speak of the possibility of a rational knowledge of God. Therefore, according to the Church, all our thinking about God, based on faith, also has a "rational" and "intellective" character. Even atheism lies within the sphere of a certain reference to the concept of God. If it denies the existence of God, it must also know whose existence it is denying.[310]

It is clear that knowledge through faith differs from purely rational knowledge. Nevertheless God would not have been able to reveal himself to the human race if it were not already naturally capable of knowing something true about God. Therefore, alongside and in addition to an "I know," which is proper to man's intellect, there is an "I believe," proper to the Christian. With faith the believer has access, even if obscurely, to the mystery of the intimate life of God who reveals himself.[311]

It is mysterious and maybe unfortunate that sometimes we encounter people who deny or question God's existence or do not acknowledge Jesus Christ as Lord. It is unclear why some of our brothers and sisters who did not create themselves sometimes adopt a violent and morbid hatred of anything that has to do with God. Some go to extremes to wipe out every trace of God they can found. These children of God, for whom Christ died and rose from the dead, may go by different terms, but they reveal levels of unbelief and Godlessness: atheists, agnostics, deists, theists, feminists, empiricists, theism, adevism, paganism, satanism, secularism, relativism, materialism, apostates, heretics, etc. No one judges them, for Jesus commands us not to judge. But we must pray and love them unconditionally, while acknowledging that their unbelief and actions against God are spiritually unhealthy. The truth is that these states of belief, since to deny God is a belief, can open these persons or their families and descendants to spiritual contamination and bondage.

In discerning spirits: good spirits, bad spirits, and human spirit, Saint Ignatius said that the 'good spirits' or the 'bad spirits' act in a person depending on the direction the person freely chooses to go. If the choice is from one mortal sin to another, the evil spirits would normally propose attractive pleasures. They fill the person with sensual delights and gratifications to make him/her remain and increase in their unbelief and sinful habits till they become spiritually numb and blind to reality. Such blindness and the consequences thereof may not be easily apparent to the casual observer. Such a person may flourish in the eyes of the world. This is so, only because he or she is already in bondage and captivity to evil (Mk 10:17–23). In such a person, the good spirits work contrary to the bad spirits; they use the light of reason to rouse and sting his/her conscience, filling them with remorse to make them change for good (# 314).[312]

But if the person strives to live a sinless and holy life and grow in perfection, the evil spirits harass with anxiety, afflict with sadness, and raise obstacles to prevent his/her growth in holiness. The good spirits encourage and strengthen, and fill the person with consolations, tears, inspirations and peace. The path is cleared for this soul to become free and grow in doing good (# 315).[313] Here the person becomes a new creation in the risen life of Christ.

The Church: the body of Christ and the bride of Christ

For Saint Paul, the Church is the bride of Christ and the body of Christ (Eph 5:23; Col 1:24). Christ loved the church and laid down His life to sanctify her (Eph 5:25–26). The Blood and Water from the pierced side of Christ are the living streams of the Church's Sacraments, washing us clean, and giving us salvation.

On April 23, 2013, in the Pauline Chapel in the Apostolic Palace, Pope Francis said in his homily, "You cannot find Jesus outside the Church." To reject the Church is to reject Christ. "Christian identity is belonging to the Church, because all [the apostles] belonged to the Church, the Mother

Church [the bride of Christ, Eph 5:25–27] …finding Jesus outside the Church is impossible."[314] Jesus established the Church so that through her, all may experience the Father's merciful love. Jesus is the one and only Mediator between God and man; only through Him are we saved. Only through Him do we come to know and enter into a most intimate relationship with the Father. The Church is the gate that leads to Jesus, and Jesus is the Gate to the Father.

The open door to all bondage is the violation of our friendship with God in Christ; when we break His commandments (Jn 14:15). Alienation from the Church makes us vulnerable to spiritual attacks. The Church is the new Israel. Moses spoke to the Israelites and set before them a blessing and a curse: a blessing, if they obey God's commandments, and a curse, if they disobey them (Deut 11:26–28). If the old law had power to bring down blessings or curses when the people obeyed or disobeyed them, how much more effective will the New Covenant in the Blood of Christ be in these regards, since we are moral and free agents. John says, no one begotten by God sins (blessing); whoever sins belongs to the devil (curse) (1 Jn 6–10). Only in the Church and through her are we protected from Satan's effects (Mt 16:18). Jesus assures us, "My sheep listen to my voice; I know them, and they follow me. I give them eternal life, and they shall never perish; no one will snatch them out of my hand" (Jn 10:27–28, NIV). The sheep that stray from the Church become prey to the wolves (Jn 10). The seriousness of the danger of separating oneself from Christ and His Church is best exemplified by Judas Iscariot as an extreme case. He was intent on betraying and destroying Jesus, and by extension, His Church, even after multiple warnings: "Woe to that man by whom the Son of Man is betrayed. It would be better for that man if he had never been born" (Mt 26:24), "None of them was lost except the son of destruction" (Jn 17:12). At the Last Supper, the beloved disciple leaned on Jesus' chest and asked: "Master, who is it" (Jn 13:25) who would betray You? He said: "It is the one to whom I hand the morsel after I have dipped it" (Jn 13:26). He handed the morsel to Judas. "After he took the morsel, Satan entered him" (Jn 13:27).

The rejection of Christ and His Church must be a conscious act of the will for one to be affected negatively (curse). I knew a Catholic woman who suffered mental illness. She was tricked by her friend to come to her Protestant church against her husband's advice, where she was re-baptized. I was surprised to learn at the time that a Catholic could be re-baptized in a Protestant denomination. Did Paul and the Church Fathers, especially Saint Augustine, not teach that there is one faith, one Lord, and one baptism? (Eph 4:5). I inquired about the circumstances of this 'baptism.' The woman recalled that her mental suffering began soon after this unbiblical and ungodly ritual. She celebrated the Sacrament of Penance, and we prayed together. I strongly discouraged her from returning to that church.

Jesus stated, "If you love me, you will keep my commandments" (Jn 14:15). His commandments also mean we should obey the Church He formed and placed in the care of the Apostles. That Church, the One, Holy, Catholic and Apostolic Church subsists only and always in the Catholic Church under the successor of Saint Peter, the Pope. A faithful Catholic is obliged to obey all the teachings of the Church without exception as revealed in Sacred Scripture, Tradition, and the Magisterium. Saint John Fisher said, "He who disbelieves even a single article of the faith is justly held guilty of disbelief in the whole faith."

Juan Donoso Cortés, Marqués de Valdegamas, a Spanish author and Catholic conservative political theorist and diplomat, who was influenced by Saint Thomas Aquinas among others, in *Essays on Catholicism, Liberalism, and Socialism,* said: "Catholicism is the law of life. The life of the intelligence, the solution to all problems. Catholicism is the truth, and everything that departs from it one iota is disorder, deception, and error."[315] Jesus founded the Church on the rock of Peter; the Church gave us the Canon of the Scriptures. The Church's mission is to proclaim the Gospel so that all people might believe and be saved. Christ has given us His word from the Father; we must preserve what we have received, witness to it, and teach and communicate it to others so that God's joy in us might be complete.

The Church is holy

The Church is holy, essentially because God is holy. The Church is a school for training in holiness. All in the Church, the clergy and faithful, must witness and exude holiness, since we are a consecrated and chosen race. As such, the desecration of persons, especially clergy, religious, sacred objects and places, can be open door to spiritual contamination that might in turn lead to spiritual bondage. Demons operate freely where God's laws are violated. Such violations offend God and distance us from Him (see Jer 7:1–20). Demons hate God, so wherever sin reigns, demons reign. Sin is the authority and sting of demons, and it is always the abuse of our free will. Demons can and do tempt us, but cannot force us to obey them.

When desecrations occur affecting church buildings, sacred vessels and objects, Tabernacles, the Bible or holy books, the Blessed Sacrament, and in some cases consecrated persons, the Bishop or priest would normally perform a rite to re-claim or re-consecrate such places or object for sacred use. This action restores the order and spiritual integrity of the places or objects. The act of re-consecration banishes the activity of evil spirits, and renders the places or sacred objects ready for sacrificial use and the worship of God.

We read in the Book of Judith that while the Assyrians were about to attack Israel, Judith prayed for God's intervention saying: "For they intend to defile your sanctuary, and to pollute the tabernacle where your glorious name resides, and to break off the horns of your altar with the sword" (Jud 9:8). Judith moved by faith, rose and went into the enemy camp, charmed them with her beauty, and came back with the head of Israel's enemy Holofernes, the commander of the Assyrian army (Jdt 9–14). The following Scriptures concern the restoration of the temple and sacred vessels (1 Chron 34:8; Jer 28:3).

Mission of the Church

In order that we may not be ravaged by sin and be lost, our Lord commanded His disciples to preach repentance that sins may be forgiven. Zechariah's prophecy contains the seed of the Church's mission: "You, child, will be called the prophet of the Most High; for you will go before the Lord to prepare his ways," to give His people the experience of salvation by forgiving their sins (Lk 1:76–77, ESV).

Salvation means upholding the dignity of the human person as created in God's image, so that it transcends the present life. It is liberation from the evils that hold us captive. Sin, especially grave and intrinsically sinful lifestyles, more than any other reality, defaces and destroys our true dignity; it makes us less free, leaves us empty and fearful of God, and makes us God's enemies. But holiness of life promotes our freedom and enriches our dignity. So the Church is sent to preach repentance for the forgiveness of sin (Acts 5:31; 11:18; 20:21; 26:20; Rom 2:4; 2 Cor 7:9–10; 2 Tim 2:25; Heb 6:1; 2 Pet 3:9).

Secular humanism promotes human welfare and dignity to the exclusion of Christ in whose image and likeness we were created. Our authentic identity and dignity come from Christ. He calls us through His Church to rediscover our true dignity and vocation as God's children in the Holy Spirit. This dignity finds its fullest meaning in the freedom of a holy life. "For freedom Christ set us free; so stand firm and do not submit again to the yoke of slavery" [of sin] (Gal 5:1).

When Jesus entered the region of Caesarea Philippi with His disciples, He asked them: "Who do you say that I am?" (Mt 16:13). Peter's profession of the Christ prompted Jesus to announce His mission for the Church, "I tell you that you are Peter, and on this rock I will build my church, and the gates of Hades will not overcome it. I will give you the keys of the kingdom of heaven; whatever you bind on earth will be bound in heaven, and whatever you loose on earth will be loosed in heaven" (Mt 16:18–19, NIV).

The Church's mission to loose sinners from the bondage of sin and the legal claim of Satan (Col 2:14), finds fulfillment as she calls sinners to repentance and conversion of heart, so that the gates of Hell do not overwhelm the beautiful and precious work of God's hand—humanity. The Church must rediscover her mission anew as she celebrates God's great love and gift in her liturgies, and rejoices with the sinless Virgin, Mother and Prototype of the Church, the Virgin of Nazareth, and all the Saints, in God our Savior.

Prayers for the healing of secondary open door (III) begin on page 340.

Chapter 17

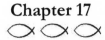

Secondary Open Door IV:
The Danger of Occult, Freemasonry and New Age

Do not turn aside to idols, nor make molten gods for yourselves. I, the LORD, am your God (Lev 19:4).

There is one God

Christianity professes the worship of three Persons in one God: Father, Son and Holy Spirit. In the Christian economy of salvation, God sent His only begotten Son, Jesus Christ in the likeness of human nature to redeem us from our sins by His death on the Cross and His Resurrection from the dead. By this Paschal event, the death and resurrection and glorification of Jesus, fallen humanity is reconciled to the Father, is established in the reign of grace, and is destined for the beatific vision. In Exodus 3:15, God identified Himself to Moses as "The Lord God of your fathers, the God of Abraham, the God of Isaac, and the God of Jacob..." (NKJV). Under this name and title, all generations will experience the power and liberation of God. No other god is able to reveal his name; only the true God, the Christian God, reveals His name. Other gods are given their names by human beings, because they are idols made by human hands of gold, silver, and wood; they cannot see, hear, or walk (Rev 9:20).

God gave this commandment to His people:

'I am the Lord your God, who brought you out of Egypt, out of the land of slavery.' 'You shall have no other gods before me. You shall not make for yourself an image in the form of anything in heaven above or on the earth beneath or in the waters below.' 'You shall not bow down to them or worship them; for I, the Lord your God, am a jealous God, punishing the children for the sin of the parents to the third and fourth generation of those who hate me' (Ex 20:2–5, NIV).

Any form of occult or pagan activity violates God's commands and carries with it serious consequences that affect persons and generations. The Israelites offended God by worshipping idols. God was displeased and threatened to destroy them because they were stiff-necked; they built and worshipped the Golden Calf, and claimed it saved them (Ex 32:8–9). God later made a covenant with His people, and He warned them not to make a covenant with the people whose land they were entering to occupy; they would be trapped and corrupted if they do (Ex 34:12). God rather commanded them: "Break down their altars, smash their sacred stones and cut down their Asherah poles" (Ex 34:13, NIV).

Jesus reiterated the teaching against idol worship when He said that one cannot serve two masters (Lk 16:13). The greatest commandment Jesus said, is to love God with one's whole heart, one's whole soul, and one's whole mind and strength (Mk 12:30). When tempted by Satan in the wilderness, Jesus said, "The Lord, your God, shall you worship and him alone shall you serve" (Mt 4:10).

God wants us to know and trust Him. He wants us to depend on Him for all we need. God wants to give us Himself as our possession and inheritance. We need to trust God. Adam and Eve did not trust God. Instead of receiving true wisdom from God, who is Wisdom, they chose to receive poisoned wisdom from the devil. Every time we sin, we choose the devil over God; we choose Satan's poisoned 'apple' and not the holy Wisdom that God gives. Every sin we commit is the 'fall' of Adam and Eve repeated in the now.

Our blessed weakness

God created human beings weak so we can depend on Him for all our needs. Our weakness was to avail us of all the blessings of God. In our weakness, we are blessed. New born infants and children are helpless, but their helplessness places them at a great advantage before their parents. They receive all the attention and love available. We cannot but love children in their total dependence; theirs is a blessed weakness. All a child needs to do to get attention and receive love is cry. Jesus reminds us, "If you, then, though you are evil, know how to give good gifts to your children, how much more will your Father in heaven give good gifts to those who ask him!" (Mt 7:11, NIV). What a blessed weakness!

The true wisdom Adam and Eve desired by eating the forbidden fruit could only come from God Himself. By disobeying God, they lost the chance to be truly wise. By obeying Satan, they acquired a darkened and corrupted wisdom that says, "I will not serve" (Jer 2:20). This false wisdom boasts to scale the heavens, and rise beyond the stars to establish its throne contrary to God's design. This corrupted wisdom boasts: "You said in your heart, "I will ascend to heaven; I will raise my throne above the stars of God; I will sit on the mount of assembly on the heights of Zaphon; I will ascend to the tops of the clouds, I will make myself like the Most High" (Is 14:13–14, NRSV).

To those who have this wisdom, God says: "Down to the nether world you go to the recesses of the pit!" (Is 14:15). Of this wisdom, the Blessed

Virgin speaks in her song: He has "dispersed the arrogant of mind and heart. He has thrown down the rulers from their thrones" (Lk 1:51–52). The greatest wisdom available to us is obedience. This obedient Wisdom is revealed fully in the life of Jesus Christ, who completely emptied Himself, not clinging to His oneness and equality with the Father. He became a slave in His human nature, and by the death He suffered, He humbled Himself and received power and riches, wisdom and strength, honor, glory and every blessing (Phil 2:7–8; Rev 5:12). The total dependence of Jesus on the Father is a model for our imitation.

Satan: god of the occult

The occult realm is the domain of Satan and the demons. The human heart is created for God. It is able to reach out and cling to God and be fulfilled in God alone—saved. The human heart also is able to reach out and cling to things and evil entities that bring it to destruction. In its weakness, our embodied spirit in the attempt to reach out to God can be deceived and cling instead to evil entities. Because of this, we need to discern things in our lives; especially, spiritual things. This is why Jesus said to His Apostles: "Watch and pray that you may not undergo the test. The spirit is willing but the flesh is weak" (Mk 14:38). To discern is to seek the Truth, to seek Jesus in all things.

Satan attacks us at our weakest points. Satan is an opportunist; a roaring lion looking around for souls to destroy. We must be alert and fight back strong in faith (1 Pet 5:8–9). Pope Leo XIII said Catholics are born for combat. If so:

- Are we ready for combat?
- Are we trained and strong in faith as warriors waging a victorious battle with the Lamb?
- What spiritual exercises are we engaged in to strengthen our drooping hands and weak knees for battle (Heb 12:12)?
- Have we resisted sin to the point of shedding our blood (Heb 12:4)?
- As baptized Christians, are we ready for the mission of saving souls?
- What are your strengths for this warfare?

There are two main levels of demonic spiritual power: cardinal spirits and ministering spirits. Cardinal spirits or high-powered spirits are mostly associated with occult and satanic rituals and activity. Occult involvement spans a wide range of activities. In the extreme cases people look up to Satan and his demons for power, authority, wealth and influence. Some others enter into pacts with the devil and actually consecrate themselves to it, and the pacts are sometimes sealed in blood. Such persons come under the reign of Satan and his demons, and this can sometimes lead to demonic possession, where Satan becomes their lord and master. As often as such consecrations are renewed, such persons become demonic strongholds, since their action involves the deliberate misuse of their free will.

Satan has been defeated and condemned forever. On its own, Satan has no power to enslave a child of God, since it has been hopelessly crushed in the humble Humanity of Jesus. In Him, we too are able to crush Satan. Unfortunately, the power Satan has over any Christian is the power that Christian has given over to it through sin. When we disobey God's commandments, we make ourselves slaves of Satan. Satan enjoys being a slave master, and it knows how to torture its slaves. The true nature and wickedness of Satan is seen in the Pharaohs and their task masters, who subjected the Israelites to cruel slavery for 430 years (Ex 1–5).

Pope Saint Leo XIII on September 25, 1888 in the presence of fellow bishops at the Vatican experienced a moment of trance in which he heard a conversation between Satan and Jesus. Here are the words of the exchange:

Satan boasted: "I can destroy Your Church"

Jesus replied: "You can? Then go ahead and do so."

Satan: "To do so, I need more time and more power."

Jesus: "How much time? How much power?"

Satan: "75 to 100 years, and a greater power over those who will give themselves over to my service."

Jesus: "You have the time. You have the power. Do with them what you will."

Such is the power that Satan has over those who obey and serve it. Satan asks from Jesus power to torture its slaves. This exchange inspired Pope Leo XIII to compose the Saint Michael's Prayer which many of the faithful pray for the effective protection of Saint Michael the Archangel against the devil and its cohorts (see Appendix V for the Chaplet of Saint Michael).

Saint Michael the Archangel, defend us in battle
Be our protection against the wickedness and snares of the devil
May God rebuke him we humbly pray
And do thy O prince of the Heavenly Host
By the power of God, cast into hell Satan and all evil spirits
Who wander throughout the world
Seeking the ruin of souls. Amen.

Apart from making deliberate pacts with the devil, people can and have come under occult bondage in other ways, such as eating and drinking consumables contaminated with occult power designed to cause harm in the targeted individual. A brilliant and lively young man was reported to me who suddenly was struck dumb for more than a year. His life went downhill as if a light bulb inside of him was suddenly switched off. No one knew exactly what happened to him. Members of his family informed me this young man had travelled to his home country. Upon his return, he suddenly stopped speaking. He grew hostile and angry and isolated from his family, dropped out of school, and lost his job. His family was concerned for him. I asked if I could speak with him, but he would not come.

I had a prayer team lift him up in intercession. We asked the Holy Spirit to show us how to pray for him. He revealed to us that unknown to this fellow, a cup of juice beverage that was contaminated with occult/witchcraft material was given to him to drink. Instantly, a deaf and dumb spirit, and a spirit of death entered him and held him bondage, and he stopped speaking. Curses (especially the curse of death) were inflicted on him. When we had gathered enough information, the Lord directed us to proceed with deliverance ministry (the young man was not present). I proceeded to break all curses and bondages on him in the name of Jesus and completed the ministry as the Spirit led us.

I then prayed for a new baptism in the Holy Spirit for him, and commended him to the powerful and unfailing intercession of our Most Blessed Virgin Mary, the holy Angels, and the Saints. Three days after we did this ministry, I got a jubilant phone call saying that the young man spoke for the first time in one and a half years. Truly all things are possible with God, our Refuge and Deliverer.

The bondage of curses and spells can be inflicted instantly on those who meddle with the occult. People can and have been afflicted with occult bondage through unnecessary curiosity and obsession with occult objects, movies, games, and books, and through friendships, or by consulting with occult and witchcraft practitioners, or entering buildings where such things are practiced. Some people have come under demonic bondage by being initiated, consecrated or 'sold' in the womb, at birth or in childhood by their parents or guardians for various reasons. Some victims of the occult have experienced "Satanic Ritual Abuse" (SRA). These rituals performed on victims are designed to interiorly fracture and 'program' them so they can be remotely controlled.

A woman was directed to me who was 'marked' and 'followed' (Targeted Individuals or TI) by certain persons in the occult. They had diabolically or surgically implanted 'electronic spiritual chips' into her to monitor her movements. She claimed she could tell in her mind that they were tracking her and could pin-point her whereabouts at any time. I was ministering to her once, and she stopped strangely and told me they were trying to 'log' into her mind. A man shared a similar experience with me in which he claimed the *hell angels* (a motorcycle group) were tracking him with their occult computer. In these two cases mentioned above, I found that there were some levels of the free consent of the will in occult activity by these persons.

As a general rule, for occult or demonic power to affect an individual so severely, there is some consent of free will (open door) in that person, or someone of authority over that person that allowed demons to gain access. Either the person knowingly or unknowingly allowed this to happen, or the person has not taken his/her faith in Jesus Christ very seriously. It is somewhat difficult to explain how sometimes persons experiencing demonic bondage have traced their affliction back to the womb or early childhood. I have encountered cases like these. But Jesus Christ has power over all demonic bondage, and He sets us free from them.

The supremacy and the Lordship of Jesus Christ

Our goal in life is to be in intimate friendship with our Lord and Savior, Jesus Christ, the Lion of Judah and the Victorious Lamb of God. It is to Jesus that the whole heaven, day and night, never stops praising: "Holy, holy, holy is the Lord God almighty, who was, and who is, and who is to come" (Rev 4:8). In worship, many angels around the throne with all the living creatures and elders exclaimed: "Worthy is the Lamb, who was slain, to receive power and wealth and wisdom and strength and honor and glory and praise!" (Rev 5:12, NIV). To Jesus, every knee must bend and every mouth must confess that He is Lord of lords and the King of kings. To Jesus belongs all power in Heaven and on earth, and under the earth, and all creation must acknowledge Him as Lord to the praise and glory of God the Father (Phil 2:11; Mt 28:18).

Freemasonry:[316] "Their god is the devil"

Modern freemasonry has its roots in the Enlightenment movement that began in Europe led by the French man Voltier. The Enlightenment had as its goal to change society and rid it of all religious principles, namely, faith, revelation, and tradition as taught by the Catholic Church.

Freemasonry was initially a Christian organization. In the 1600s, it was known to have used prayers which acknowledged and honored the Most Blessed Trinity. Soon after the Grand Lodge of England was formed and, subsequently, the United Grand Lodge of England on November 25, 1813, all began to change for the worse. Freemasonry can be confusing because it masquerades as a non-religious social organization, but behind the curtains, in the inner chambers of its lodges, secret oaths and beliefs, and all kinds of evil go on with impunity.[317]

Papal condemnations of freemasonry

The U.S. President John Quincy Adams said in *Letters on the Masonic Institution,* T.R. Maruin Press, Boston, 1847: "Masonry ought forever to be abolished. It is wrong—essentially wrong—a seed of evil, which can never produce any good." Pope Pius VIII in his Encyclical *Traditi Humilitate* (1829) said of freemasonry and the other clandestine sects that it had the same characteristics. Pope Leo the Great said of the Manichees in the fifth century, "Their law is untruth; their god is the devil; and their cult is turpitude."[318] In his Apostolic Constitution *Providas,* Pope Benedict XIV condemned Masonry for five reasons: (1) Its secret (2) Its oaths (3) Its propaganda of Indifferentism (4) Its opposition to Church and State, and (5) Its immorality. According to Fisher, none of these characteristics of the Masonic Fraternity have changed.[319]

Freemasonry has received more condemnations and bans than any other issue plaguing the Church up to the papacy of Pope Emeritus Benedict XVI. Pope Clement XIII in 1738 was the first to condemn freemasonry, saying, "We have resolved and decreed to condemn and forbid such societies, assemblies, reunions, conventions, aggregations or meetings called either Freemasonic or known under some other denomination."[320] He said it forces candidates to serve two masters, a clear violation of the command of Jesus Christ (see Lk 16:13). Pope Leo XIII, in his Encyclical, *Humanum Genus* (April 20, 1884, the same year he composed the Leonine Prayer (the Saint Michael the Archangel prayer)), said,

> Freemasons... strive, as far as possible, to conceal themselves, and admit no witnesses but their own members... to enroll, it is necessary that the candidates promise and undertake to be... strictly obedient to the leaders and masters with utmost submission and fidelity, or, if disobedient, to submit to the direst penalties and death itself.[321]

Leo XIII also wrote in his encyclical on Masonry, "Possessed by the spirit of Satan—whose instruments they are—they burn like him with a deadly and implacable hatred of Jesus Christ and His work; and they endeavor by every means to overthrow and fetter it."[322] Pope Pius XII at a pastoral conference on May 23, 1958, said: "The root of modern apostasy lay in scientific atheism, dialectical materialism, Illuminism, and Freemasonry—which is the mother of them all." Pope Gregory XVI in *Mirari Vos,* (1832) said that Masonry is, "...the principle cause of all the calamities on earth and in the kingdoms...the cesspool of all preceding sects," in which are "congregated all the sacrileges, infamy and blasphemy which are contained in the most abominable heresies." Finally, for our purposes, Leo XIII, in his Apostolic Letter to the Catholic hierarchy in

1902, stated, "Filled with the spirit of Satan, who knows how to transform himself as an angel of light, freemasonry puts forward as its pretended aim the good of humanity." Speaking against the insidious attack of the Masons on the clergy, Leo XIII further wrote in *Dall'alto Dell'apostolico Seggio,* "To soften the opposition of the clergy with their promises, Masons wish to win over the clergy by cajolery; once the novelties have confused them, they will withdraw their obedience to legitimate authority. Far too many of our compatriots, driven by the hope of their personal ambition, have given their hands to the sect."

The Code of Canon Law (1917–1983) stated in regards to membership or affiliation with Masonic or similar Societies: "Those who join a Masonic sect or other societies of the same sort, which plot against the Church or against legitimate civil authority, incur *ipso facto* an excommunication simply reserved to the Holy See" (c. 2335, p. 924). This position of the 1917 Code of Canon Law which explicitly states that membership in Freemasonry entails automatic excommunication, differs from the 1983 Code of Canon Law, which expressly avoids mention of the subject. In responding to this lack of clarity or omission in the 1983 Code, the Prefect for the Sacred Congregation for the Doctrine of the Faith, Joseph Cardinal Ratzinger (later Pope Benedict XVI), on 26 November 1983, with the approval and at the order of the Supreme Pontiff, Saint John Paul II, published the "Declaration on Masonic Associations" (cf. *AAS* LXXVI [1984], 300). The declaration reaffirmed the consistent teaching of the Church on the subject: "Therefore the Church's negative judgment in regard to Masonic association remains unchanged since their principles have always been considered irreconcilable with the doctrine of the Church and therefore membership in them remains unlawful and forbidden. The faithful who enroll in Masonic associations are in a state of grave sin and may not receive Holy Communion." This conclusion was reached after more thorough study led by the S.C.D.F. confirmed its conviction of the basic irreconcilability between the principles of Freemasonry and those of the Christian faith. The Declarations of 17 February 1981 (1917 Code c. 2335) and 26 November 1983 maintain that local ecclesiastical authorities lack the competence to make any judgment on the nature of Masonic associations, since the Apostolic See had already ruled on the matter.[323]

The perversion of Freemasonry

Firstly, Masonic candidates are deceived to accept a vague and generic concept of a supreme being, The Grand Architect of the Universe, and a rival magisterium of beliefs which are designed to parallel Christianity, namely, brotherly love, charity for others and mutual aid for fellow masons (that is, they may lie with impunity to protect other masons). They twist and pervert Christianity; for example, the cross is stripped of its salvific/religious significance and becomes a mere symbol of nature and eternal life without Jesus Christ and His redemptive sacrifice for sin. Since Masons are not permitted to mention the name of Jesus inside their lodges, they replaced the inscription: *"Jesus of Nazareth King of the Jews,"* on the Cross of Jesus with, *"The Fire of Nature Rejuvenates All."*[324] Everything about freemasonry is a distortion of Christianity. Brother Masons are instructed to remove Saint Michael, the Protector of the Catholic Church, from every prayer, and are instructed to remove his statues as well.[325]

Pope Leo XIII wrote in his encyclical *Humanum Genus* (1884), "We wish it to be your rule first of all to tear away the mask from freemasonry, and to let it be seen as it really is." He cautioned, "Let no man think that he may for any reason whatsoever to join the masonic sect, if he values his Catholic name and his eternal salvation." Monsignor George F. Dillon declared: "I believe the secret Atheistic organization [freemasonry] to be nothing less than the supreme conflict between the Church and Satan's followers."[326] It is either we are with God or we are not; there is no middle ground. Jesus declared: "Whoever is not with me is against me, and whoever does not gather with me, scatters" (Mt 12:30).

Freemasons do not worship the one God and Father of our Lord Jesus Christ. Rather, they worship Lucifer.[327] Albert Pike, a famous American masonic writer and freemason, wrote: "Yes, Lucifer is God..." "The Masonic Religion should be... maintained in the purity of the Luciferian Doctrine." The ritual that elevates Masons to the Knights Kadosh 30th degree involves a platform on which rests three skulls, one of which is surmounted by a Pope's triple crown. Soon after taking the first of four oaths, the candidate upon the example and instruction of the Thrice-Puissant Grand Master stabs the skull crowned with the Pope's crown and cries out, "Down with imposture, down with crime." The "imposture" always refers to the Pope as Vicar of Christ.[328] It is significant to note that masons take their oaths in the presence of a representative of Satan. Not surprisingly then, Saint Maximilian has referred to freemasonry as "the head of the serpent."[329]

The Saint who confronted Freemasonry

Saint Maximilian Kolbe's direct confrontation with freemasons led him to initiate his movement of renewal and evangelization—the *Militia Immaculatae*. The trigger for this was an event that occurred in Rome in 1917. At their bicentenary commemoration, freemasons chose Rome as the theater of their sacrilegious demonstration. "In their hatred for the Church, they marched right up to the doors of Saint Peter's [Basilica], where the Pope was a voluntary prisoner. Boldly they displayed their banners: "Satan must reign in the Vatican. The Pope will be his slave."[330] At this, the zeal and militant spirit of Friar Maximilian was stirred up, and he responded with this challenge: "In the face of such attacks of the enemies of the church of God, are we to remain inactive? Is that all we can do—complain and cry? Everyone of us has a holy obligation to personally hurl back the assault of the foe."[331]

This and similar events led the militant Saint Maximilian to single out Freemasonry from the very beginnings of his *Militia Immaculatae* (October 16, 1917) as the principal enemy of the Catholic Church and of Christianity to battle with our rosaries and Marian consecrations, and our lives, if necessary. He believed that masonry is the very "head" of the serpent which must be crushed by the foot of the Immaculata in her prophetic, historic, certain and ultimate triumph.[332] Friar Maximilian stated that freemasons have spread their deceit throughout the world in different disguises, but their objective remains the same, religious indifference and the weakening of morality; these accord with their basic principle—"We will conquer the Catholic Church not by argumentation, but rather by moral corruption."[333]

Saint Kolbe's assessment of the damage caused by Freemasonry on the Church and in the world is becoming evident in our time. Far back in 1917, Friar Maximilian recognized the subtle and insidious nature of masonry, the damage caused by promoting a secularist, humanist, anti-supernatural society and culture. As a result, today religious freedom is threatened; God and the open practice of Christianity in particular and religious beliefs in general are excluded from the private and public lives of the average American. The pervasive culture of death which manifests as anti-life, anti-God, anti-good, anti-family, anti-marriage, and the anti-morality rulings of the US Supreme Court are powerful reminders of the evils perpetrated by Freemasonry. These *antis* have led to spiritual paralysis, moral compromise, and furthered secular humanism that has dominated the Western world these days.[334]

The immutable word of God in Genesis 3:15 had promised victory to the woman and her seed: "I will put enmity between you [Satan] and the Woman, between your seed and hers [Jesus]. You will lie in wait for her heel and she will crush your head."[335]

I have gone to great lengths to speak about Freemasonry so that no one gets hoodwinked into believing what it is not. Precisely because Freemasonry attacks God, this makes Masons and all those associated with them subjects of satanic attacks and bondage.

New Age - a "green-snake-in-a-green-grass" spirituality

New Age is a Western spiritual movement which began in the second half of the twentieth century. It draws its beliefs from both the Eastern and

Western spiritual and metaphysical traditions, infusing them with influences of self-help and motivational psychology, holistic health and parapsychology. Its aim is to create "a spirituality without borders and confining dogmas."[336] "The term *New Age* refers to the coming astrological Age of Aquarius."[337] "The Age of Aquarius is conceived as one which will replace the predominantly Christian Age of Pisces."[338]

But what exactly is New Age? According to Barbara Curtis, it is almost impossible to narrow "new age" down to anything specific. It "is actually a vast smorgasbord of beliefs and practices. Each New Ager fills his tray with whatever assortment fits his appetite. All is liberally seasoned with self-centeredness. It's really a have-it-your-way religion—thus its modern appeal."[339] Barbara believes that the roots of the New Age tree spread around the world from India. The typical New Ager beliefs are the following:

- God is in everything (pantheism).
- All things are one (monism).
- Man is God.
- Mind creates reality.
- One's own experience validates the truth.[340]

It is not uncommon in our societies, in Christian churches, and even in Catholic parishes to encounter people who are under the diabolical effects of the rising cases of witchcrafts, Wicca, and other New Age outfits, such as the proliferation of spiritism, yoga, reiki, Pilates (pronounced pɪˈlɑːtɪz), tai chi, Zen, Harry Potter, transcendental meditations, and so on.[341] These effects include murder, rape, pornography, and other evils. New Age is occult; it is demonic. Could the New Age infestation be by your door?

"A Chicago parish hosts a professional astrologer to lecture on the stars and inform parishioners where they can go for further astrological consultations."[342] "A Campus Chaplain at a Catholic university recommends crystals, the energy source of Atlantis, for personal help."[343] "A catechist objects to her required textbook because it uses the term 'mantras' for Catholic aspirations. The pastor demands that she call these prayers mantras or else be fired. She is fired."[344] "Fr. Justin Belitz, OFM, advertises on the *Tao Te Ching* to teach 'passive meditation,' the 'most valuable and important kind of mental prayer.' The retreat promises to help one come 'in contact with the Divine Presence in you, so that infinite peace, deep joy, all knowledge and wisdom, can flood your life and give it true meaning.'"[345] "Several Carmelite religious offer retreats combining Carmelite spirituality with Theravadan Buddhist traditions of vipassana (insight) meditation, which are 'compatible with any religious affiliation' and 'require no belief commitments.'"[346]

Father Pacwa writes, "Catholic retreat houses and parishes nationwide offer enneagram workshops conducted by priests and nuns." Then he poses the following question: "What are Catholics to make of all these New Age practices at parishes, retreat houses, universities, and colleges? Why are they attracting so many Catholics today, specially clergy and religious? Are these practices legitimate expressions of spirituality for Catholics? Or do they run counter to the Catholic faith?"[347]

Father Pacwa makes it abundantly clear that New Age is dangerous and destructive to an authentic Catholic spirituality. But he cautions that the anger and sense of betrayal expressed by faithful Catholics over the presence of New Age foolishness, the introduction of false teachings and rites into Catholic churches, institutions and parishes, even though legitimate, should not be allowed to dominate their responses. He says we must display the virtue of hope, and strive to love as Jesus commanded us, even to love those involved in New Age. Saint Paul challenges us not to allow anger to take root in our hearts (Eph 4:26-27).[348] In loving those who are corrupted and are the agents of corruption of the true faith handed down to us by the Apostles, we must also intercede for them before the throne of the Lamb of God for the renewal of the gift of supernatural faith in their hearts.

Another term that has come out of the new age database is "spiritual but not religious." This is a clever and deceptive attempt by its practitioners to avoid any sort of responsibility to anyone. They have made themselves into gods, with the right to operate however they choose, following their own commandments, and worshipping themselves as supreme spirits. At best, they worship an imaginary god which does their bidding and obeys their rules.

As Paul said to the men of Athens, so he says to all new agers:

I see that you are very religious in all respects. For as I went around and observed closely your objects of worship, I even found an altar with this inscription: "To an unknown god." Therefore what you worship without knowing it, this I proclaim to you. The God who made the world and everything in it, who is Lord of heaven and earth, does not live in temples made by human hands, nor is he served by human hands, as if he needed anything, because he himself gives life and breath and everything to everyone (Acts 17:22–25, NET).

The true God, Paul continues:

Has given them the seasons of the year and the boundaries within which to live. He has done this so that they would look for God, somehow reach for him, and find him. In fact, he is never far from any one of us. Certainly, we live, move, and exist because of him. As some of your poets have said, "We are God's children." So if we are God's children, we shouldn't think that the divine being is like an image made from gold, silver, or stone, an image that is the product of human imagination and skill. "God overlooked the times when people didn't know any better. But now he commands everyone everywhere to turn to him and change the way they think and act. He has set a day when he is going to judge the world with justice, and he will use a man he has appointed to do this. God has given proof to everyone that he will do this by bringing that man back to life" (Acts 17:26–31, GW).

The negative effects and consequences of occult, masonic and New Age involvement can be serious. They can lead to the corruption and loss of faith, death of parishes, vocational crises, sicknesses, disruptions in healthy relationships, behavioral delinquencies and societal violence, and possibly, eternal separation from God if people do not repent from deliberate occult practice. These evil practices can be open doors to demonic contamination and bondage. The deleterious effects of practicing these unholy and false spiritualities can in turn be transmitted along generational lines and create misery for generations. In preparing for the Family Healing Conference, it is important to investigate our family trees for possible ancestral occult, masonic or new age involvements.

The truth we must proclaim here and now is that *Jesus Christ is Lord* of all! "Through him all things were made; without him nothing was made that has been made. In him was life, and that life was the light of all mankind" (Jn 1:3–4, NIV). "For in him all things were created: things in heaven and on earth, visible and invisible, whether thrones or powers or rulers or authorities; all things have been created through him and for him. He is before all things, and in him all things hold together" (Col 1:16–17, NIV).

Criteria for distinguishing the Christian faith from "New Age" deception[349]

▸The spiritual life for Christians is about growing in intimate relationship with God who is love, through His Son Jesus, and with all men and women everywhere. God desires this relationship and gives the grace for it to be realized in His precious human creatures. *New Age* spirituality is about experiencing states of consciousness dominated by fusion with the Whole. There is no acknowledgment or desire to meet a transcendent God, who loves, but only to experience an exhilarating sense of letting oneself sink into the great ocean of Being.

▸The core of the Christian faith is that God comes to His creatures. He never abandons them. He seeks them to save them. He comes to the humble, the weak and the rejected of the world. Spiritual techniques are contrary to the invitation to surrender and to spiritual childhood that the Gospel of Christ proclaims. Christian mysticism is God's gift and cannot be achieved through personal effort alone. We are nothing; God is everything. *New Age* mysticism is achieved through self-effort, involving an "ascent" on the level of consciousness to what is understood to be a liberating awareness of "the god within." The benefit of these techniques is limited to a few who have access to them.

▸Christian conversion is about turning back to God, through His Son, in the power of the Holy Spirit. This movement is God's gift. The more we make progress, the more we turn away from sin, spiritual myopia and self-infatuation, all of which obstruct genuine self-surrender and love of God and openness to others. All meditation techniques are to be purged of presumption and pretentiousness. Christian prayer is not a focus on the self, "but a dialogue of love one which 'implies an attitude of conversion, a flight from "self" to the "You" of God.'" *New Age* is completely contrary to all Christianity stands for.

▸The Christian God is the Creator of all, the Maker of heaven and earth, and the source of all personal life. *New Age* concept of God is diffused; their god is an impersonal energy, an extension of the cosmos, the life-force or soul of the world; divinity is found in everything; god is a Great Consciousness; humans are to think of themselves as gods; god is to be sort deep within oneself not outside of the self; and if there is a "God" outside of self, it is there to be manipulated.

▸Christian Tradition teaches that Jesus Christ is the Jesus of Nazareth, who is the central character in the Gospels and who is the Gospel of God. He is Son of God and Son of Mary; He is God; the Way, the Truth, the Life, and the Savior of the world: "for our sake he was crucified under Pontius Pilate; he suffered, died and was buried. On the third day he rose again in fulfillment of the Scriptures; he ascended into heaven and is seated at the right hand of the Father." In *New Age,* Jesus Christ is one among many wise men, an avatar. He is not the only Christ; His death on the cross is denied; extra-biblical documents (like the neo-gnostic gospels), which are not part of the canon of the Scriptures are considered authentic sources of knowledge of Jesus' life. Entities, spirit guides, ascended masters, and *Akasha* Chronicles are sources of *New Age* christology.

▸Christian doctrine is rooted in Sacred Scripture, which teaches that men and women are created in the image and likeness of God. "The human person is a mystery fully revealed only in Jesus Christ (cf. GS 22) and in fact becomes authentically human properly in his relationship with Christ through the gift of the Spirit." *New Age* techniques claim to produce mystical states at will, as if manipulating the spiritual life to produce specific results. "We are authentic when we 'take charge of' ourselves, when our choice and reactions flow spontaneously from our deepest needs, when our behavior and expressed feelings reflect our personal wholeness." There is a conviction that humans are divine, or contain in them divine sparks.

▸In Christianity, we are saved by our participation in the passion, death and resurrection of Christ, through a personal relationship with God. Sin offends God. The saving work of Christ—God and Man and the one Mediator between God and man—is the source of forgiveness of our sins, and our redemption. In *New Age,* "we save ourselves by our own actions... [the] Key words are self-fulfillment and self-realization, self-redemption. *New Age* is essentially Pelagian in its understanding of human nature."

▸In Christianity, Jesus Christ is "the way and the truth and the life" (Jn 14.6). There is an objective knowable truth that governs the life of believers, and all are required to abide by them. That truth is written in human hearts; to deny it is to be blind to reality itself. There is no objective truth in *New Age* beliefs. It is all "about good vibrations, cosmic correspondences, harmony and ecstasy, in general pleasant experiences." Religious and ethical truths are determined by whatever makes you feel good.

▸*New Age* practices are not prayer; they are merely introspection or fusion with cosmic energy through personal effort. If there is a link with Universal Energy, which *New Agers* may call "God," his functions are to supply human needs. This shows the selfishness at the heart of *New Age.* Christian prayer involves introspection and an encounter with God. It is a dialogue which "implies an attitude of conversion, a flight from 'self' to the 'you' of God." The Christian, whether praying alone or in secret, is aware "he prays always for the good of the Church in union with Christ, in the Holy Spirit, and together with all the saints."

▸*New Age* does not accept the concept of sin, but only an imperfect knowledge. All one needs is enlightenment requiring some psycho-physical techniques that fits one's liking. The *New Age* dogma is "Trust yourself. Authority has shifted from a theistic location to within the self." The most serious problem in "*New Age* thinking is alienation from the whole cosmos, rather than personal failure or sin." The remedy for this is fusion with Universal Energy. For Christians, Divine Revelation helps us recognize sin for what it is—"an abuse of freedom that God gives to created persons so that they are capable of loving him and loving one another," and not merely a mistake, or developmental flaw or psychological weakness. "Sin is an offense against reason, truth and right conscience;" a failure of humans to the love of God and neighbor arising from disordered attachments. "Sin is thus 'love of oneself even to contempt of God.'"

▸Reincarnation is a necessary element in *New Age* spirituality, because it allows "people to realize their full potential." One life is not enough. Reincarnation is a stage in progressive spiritual evolution which began before our birth and will continue after our death. Some *New Agers* see suffering as self-imposed or as bad karma; others teach methods of achieving success and wealth (e.g., Deepak Chopra, José Silva, *et al.*). Christianity says that "a human person is a distinct being, who lives one life, for which he or she is fully responsible. Christ, though sinless, accomplished human redemption from sin through the suffering of His cross. "Believers are called to share in that suffering through which… all human suffering has also been redeemed." Through His suffering, Christ "raised human suffering to the level of the redemption. Thus each man in his suffering can also become a sharer in the redemptive suffering of Christ."

▸*New Age* is about self-promotion; it focuses on self-actualization through the fusion of individuals into the cosmic self, relativization, or abolition of difference and opposition in a cosmic harmony. Christian love involves the other (a different person), with whom union is achieved through a free expression in love of one's "yes" or "no." Christian union in love is communion, and is oriented toward community.

▸The coming *New Age* era will be "peopled by perfect, androgynous beings who are totally in command of the cosmic laws of nature." Here, Christianity will be no more; it will "give way to a global religion and a new world order." Christian hope calls for vigilance as we wait for Christ's return. Jesus of Nazareth ushered in the true New Age two thousand years ago at Christmas; the Word of God made man who dwelt among us. His Holy Spirit, the Gift of God, is our Advocate, our guide and our teacher on our pilgrim journey home to Heaven. "We live in the last times."

Prayers for the healing of secondary open door (IV) begin on page 343.

Chapter 18

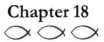

Secondary Open Door V:
Generational or Ancestral Bondage (or Curses)

You continue your kindness through a thousand generations; and you repay the fathers' guilt, even into the lap of their sons who follow them (Jer 32:18).

Original Sin and Adam's generational descendants

The primordial and universal bondage on humanity is "Original sin" committed by Adam and Eve as recorded in Genesis 3. "Revelation gives us the certainty of faith that the whole of human history is marked by the original fault freely committed by our first parents."[350] By this sin, the devil has gained a certain dominion over man, even though man remains free.[351] "Original sin entails 'captivity under the power of him who thenceforth had the power of death, that is, the devil.'"[352] This human captivity Saint John speaks of in clear terms: "the whole world is in the power of the evil one" (1 Jn 5:19).

How did the sin of Adam affect us, his descendants? The whole human race is in Adam "as one body of one man." By this "unity of the human race,"[353] all men are implicated in Adam's sin, just as all are implicated in Christ's justice. Saint Paul explains it succinctly, as in Adam all have died, so in Christ, all have been brought to life again (1 Cor 15:22). Still, the transmission of original sin is a mystery beyond our full understanding. We know by Revelation that Adam received original holiness and justice not for himself alone but for all humanity; just as Abram received blessings, not for himself alone but also for all his descendants: "All the communities of the earth shall find blessing in you" (Gen 12:3). By yielding to the tempter, Adam committed a personal sin with a universal negative effect, which can now be transmitted in the fallen state. It is a sin transmittable by propagation to all mankind, that is, by the transmission of a human nature deprived of original holiness and justice. That is why original sin is called "sin" only in an analogical sense: it is a sin "contracted" and not "committed"—a state and not an act.[354]

This book does not deal with the transmission of generational bondage as it affects all of humanity through original sin. Rather, it addresses the subject as it affects individual ancestry. The bondage, or woundedness, in the natural powers proper to human nature, manifested as ignorance, limitation, deprivation, suffering, the dominion of death, and an inclination to sin and evil that is called "concupiscence"[355] of sin, affected humanity due to the personal sin of our first parents. Scripture says, "All have sinned and are deprived of the glory of God" (Rom 3:23). Similarly, bondage can and does affect individual generational lines due to the personal sins of our ancestors.

The understanding of the mystery of original sin is seen in the revelation of Christ's redemptive sacrifice. The Apostle Paul taught that, by the sin of one man, death began to reign in all persons through the one man, Adam. But we who have been redeemed and filled with God's grace and have received the grace of justification have abundant life through the one Man, Jesus Christ. Paul concludes:

> For if, because of one man's trespass, death reigned through that one man, much more will those who receive the abundance of grace and the free gift of righteousness reign in life through the one man Jesus Christ. Therefore, as one trespass led to condemnation for all men, so one act of righteousness leads to justification and life for all men (Rom 5:17–18, ESV).

Paul contrasts the universality of sin and death with the universality of salvation in Christ.[356] He went on to say that because of one man's disobedience, many became sinners; by the obedience of one man, the gift of holiness has been granted to many (Rom 5:19).

Baptism imparts the divine life of Christ on Christians, also called sanctifying grace; it erases original sin and orients us toward God as His beloved sons and daughters. But "the consequences for nature weakened and inclined to evil, persist in man and summon him to spiritual battles."[357]

Generational blessings and bondages

Why generational?

Through propagation, human beings are equipped to fulfill God's command to "be fertile and multiply" (Gen 1:22). This blessing of the Creator helps man perpetuate human earthly existence until the Lord comes. God intended human generational capacity for good purposes only, since He creates only the good. Through it, we pass on God's blessings of nature for the happiness of our descendants. The disobedience of Adam poisoned this innate human capacity to transmit only the good of our nature. Evil, the result of sin in our human nature, can now be passed down the generations. Sin, the misuse of our free will, alienates us from God. It introduced misery, bondage, and death into human genealogy, so that even the ancestors in the genealogy of Jesus—the God-Man—were not free of the poison of sin (Mt 1). Only Mary, the Virgin Mother of God, was free from sin, original or actual, by the grace of her Son, Jesus. Jesus Christ, who is God, and also the Son of God and Son of David, was not affected by the sins of His own genealogy. For it is impossible for God to sin; Jesus is impeccable. In God, there is no darkness (1 Jn 1:5). Through His Humanity and His death on the cross, Christ brought redemption not only to His own genealogy, but also to all human genealogies. Paul taught that all things were reconciled and made peaceful in His human nature, and by the blood of His cross, He removed all the reproaches and blemish that are the result of our evil deeds (Col 1:19–23.

What are generational blessings or bondages?

Generational blessings refer to the good effects or traits that promote the health and well-being of individuals and families which are passed down the family bloodlines. The fruits of these blessings are many; among them are freedom, unity, peace, etc. When we are experiencing generational blessings, we bubble with life in the Holy Spirit; we honor and glorify God and are joy-filled, hope-filled, restful, and full of life.

Generational bondages, on the other hand, are the negative effects or traits that are transmitted through the family bloodlines. They produce effects in individuals and families contrary to those of generational blessings, such as discontent, distress, misery, hopelessness, restlessness, and death. Generational blessings and the effects they produce correspond to the experience of consolation. God alone gives true consolation. Generational bondages and their effects on the other hand correspond to desolation experiences. God never causes desolation; He permits it for our good (see Appendix IV, Ninth Rule). Consolation and desolation experiences will need to be discerned and investigated, especially when we struggle with bondage (see Appendix II: vocabulary of consolation and desolation feelings).

Are the transmission of blessings and bondages limited to bloodlines?

Certainly not! The transmission of blessings and bondages transcend the biological limitations imposed by blood relationships. First, and most importantly, God is spirit; spiritual realities cut across blood relationships. We are created in God's image and likeness; we are embodied spirits, that is, spirits with flesh and blood.

The Christian life is a supernatural life, not a natural one. For this reason, Paul would remind us that we should be led by the Spirit of God, because we are children of God (Rom 8:14, 16; 1 Jn 3:1–2). As Christians, our hope is to attain a spiritual destiny—Heaven. It is for this reason that the Anointed Son of God, Jesus Christ, true God and true Man, died on the cross and rose from the dead.

The blessing bestowed on Adam and Eve to increase and multiply is both physical and spiritual, and is shared by all humanity. Similarly, the curse incurred by Adam and Eve because of original sin, is both physical and spiritual; it is also shared by all humanity. In Genesis 12:1–3, God said to Abram: "Go from your country, your people and your father's household to the land I will show you. 'I will make you into a great nation, and I will bless you... and you will be a blessing... and all peoples on earth will be blessed through you'" (NIV).

This promise of God to Abram easily reveals a spiritual dimension to ancestral transmissions. Abraham believed God, and his faith went in his favor as righteousness (Rom 4:9). By this faith-based righteousness, he would have descendants who would inherit the world (Rom 4:13). By faith, Abraham became the father of many nations (Rom 4:16, 17). Even Saint Paul claimed descent from Abraham by faith (2 Cor 11:22). Those who have faith are children of Abraham (Gal 3:7), and they along with Abraham, are blessed (Gal 3:9).

In the natural order, blood is thicker than water. But in the spiritual order, the reverse is the case; water is thicker than blood. The waters of Baptism that bind us to Christ and to one another are far thicker than blood relationships.

A woman once praised Jesus saying: "Blessed is the womb that carried you and the breasts at which you nursed" (Lk 11:27). But Jesus replied: "Rather, blessed are those who hear the word of God and observe it" (Lk 11:28). Again, Jesus was informed that His mother and brothers were outside wishing to speak with Him. Stretching out His hands toward the disciples, He said: "Here are my mother and my brothers! For whoever does the will of my Father in heaven is my brother and sister and mother" (Mt 12:47–50, NRSV).

By the waters of Baptism, we have been inserted into the family of God as His sons and daughters. The implication of this is that, if we disobey God by sinning, the consequences are equally spiritually grave and far-reaching and do harm to the mystical body of Christ. The bondage that results can be transmitted to those within our circles of spiritual influence and relationships. The evidence of such connections can be brought to our awareness through dream experiences, visions or images of troubled spirits, disturbing apparitions in homes, or "by a simple spiritual intuition of a deceased person's need in one's family background"[358] and beyond. It is important to point out that dreams should be discerned by talking to the Holy Spirit in prayer and asking for His light to understand them. Bringing our dreams to spiritual direction is a valid discernment step, especially if the director is knowledgeable in such matters. We should never seek dream interpretation by consulting "dream readers." It is superstitious to do so, and may even border on the occult.

Discerning generational issues

Understanding the differences between consolation and desolation can help us discern generational issues. The experiences of consolation or desolation follow the biblical principle that every tree produces its own type of fruit. A good tree will produce good fruit, and a bad tree will produce bad fruit. A farmer who plants mango trees cannot harvest the deadly English yew (*Taxus Baccata*) from them. A farmer who plants tomato seeds cannot gather castor beans at harvest time. In the same way, a person with a good and pure heart can only say and do good and pure things. A person with an evil and rotten heart will say and do evil and rotten things; no good can come out of that person's heart (Lk 6:44–45).

In discerning generational issues, we may ask, "Do the fruits experienced in the family speak of consolation (blessings) or desolation (bondages, curses)?" Often, when people attend generational healing retreats, they do so because they are in throes of personal or family distress. During these retreats, I make some effort to encourage and invite participants to a deeper personal reflection and to conduct some generational excavations to ascertain if a distressing situation has multiple occurrences among family members, living or deceased, for example, if cancer runs in the family or if heart disease affecting a family member also caused the death of another.

When we make a doctor's visit, often we are subjected to a litany of questionnaires about our family medical history. The principle is that a present medical situation may be better treated or managed if a connection can be established with a deceased and living family member.

Generational bondage, which is a spiritual reality, manifesting as physical ailment or spiritual limitation, should similarly be investigated. In fact, it is even more necessary that such investigation be conducted, because a spiritual contamination resulting from sin may be involved which medical science often neglects or denies and, more importantly, is not equipped to handle. The power of Jesus Christ—the Divine Physician, is able to restore perfect health, physically and spiritually, to those under the yoke of intergenerational bondage.

The discernment process is part of the healing. It includes investigating personal and family history where possible. We learned to use this tool as we followed the healing ministry of Doctor Jesus. Before healing the boy who was possessed by a spirit, Jesus questioned his father, "How long has this been happening to him?" (Mk 9:21). He replied, "Since childhood. It has often thrown him into fire and into water to kill him" (Mk 9:22).

The advantages of conducting an investigation of the family tree are many: we gain valuable knowledge about our ancestry; we come to know things about ourselves and family members which otherwise would remain hidden; we learn to intercede more effectively for our family trees, because we have informed knowledge; and it generates hope and confidence to fight the good fight in the trials and sufferings of bondage.

Such was my experience when I was directed by Monsignor John Esseff, a priest of the Diocese of Scranton, who was knowledgeable in generational healing issues, to conduct an investigation of my family tree. For years, I had been experiencing bondage due to occult/pagan practice in my culture, as well as some issues that affected me while in the womb. I had no clues what was going on, nor did I know where to turn for help. My investigation revealed a lot more than I expected. I am grateful to Almighty God that I followed Msgr. Esseff's advice. This was how the Lord began to teach me about generational healing in a concrete and experiential way. The Scriptures have a lot to teach us about this mysterious suffering and reality, which was first brought into the light by the clinical psychologist, Dr. Kenneth McAll.

The evidence of Sacred Scripture

Among the core Scriptures that will anchor our discussion of the reality and dynamics of generational blessings and bondages are Deuteronomy 30:1–20 and 20:17–19, Exodus 34:6–7, and Ezekiel 18.

See, I set before you today life and prosperity, death and destruction. For I command you today to love the Lord your God, to walk in obedience to him, and to keep his commands, decrees and laws; then you will live and increase, and the Lord your God will bless you in the land you are entering to possess. But if your heart turns away and you are not obedient, and if you are drawn away to bow down to other gods and worship them, I declare to you this day that you will certainly be destroyed. You will not live long in the land you are crossing the Jordan to enter and possess. This day I call the heavens and the earth as witnesses against you that I have set before you life and death, blessings and curses. Now choose life, so that you and your children may live (Deut 30:15–19, NIV).

The Lord passed in front of Moses, proclaiming:

The Lord, the Lord, the compassionate and gracious God, slow to anger, abounding in love and faithfulness, maintaining love to thousands, and forgiving wickedness, rebellion and sin. Yet he does not leave the guilty unpunished; he punishes the children and their children for the sin of the parents to the third and fourth generation (Ex 34:6–7, NIV).

The bondage Adam and Eve incurred due to their disobedience did not nullify the blessings God first bestowed on them at the time of creation. God's greatest blessing is the promise of eternal life in Christ. Sin is a denial of the truth and the attempt to destroy Christ's life in us. This book deals with the healing of personal and generational evils that plague our lives and families: sinful habits and negative behaviors—anger, anxiety, hatred, rage, resentment, substance addictions (drugs, alcohol), behavioral addictions (sexual, work, food), deep seated relationship difficulties, violence, and all kinds of perversion. God resists these evils which are the result of the misuse of our free will.

I have become aware that some do not suspect their ancestry as a possible source of the evils and bondage that oppress them. The reality is that several cases have turned out to be exactly so. Scripture confirms it. We cannot claim, however, that every bondage has ancestral roots.[359] Scripture says that "God stores up punishment for a man's sons" (Job 21:19). In warning the children of Israel of the danger of idolatry, God pronounced a consequence and a blessing:

> You shall not bow down to them or worship them; for I, the Lord your God, am a jealous God, punishing the children for the sin of the parents to the third and fourth generation of those who hate me, but showing love to a thousand generations of those who love me and keep my commandments (Ex 20:5–6; also see Ex 34:7 and Num 14:18, NIV).

On the basis of this injunction given through Moses, the descendants of Korah, Dathan and Abiram suffered extinction for their evil actions (Num 16:27–34).

Generational bondage features severally in the Book of Lamentations: "Our ancestors sinned; they are no more, and we bear the weight of their guilt" (Lam 5:7, NRSV). The people experienced this guilt in the following ways: they were ruled by slaves, had shriveled skin, their wives ravaged by the enemy, and had lack of respect for elders. In addition, they lacked joy; there was suffering; they had sick hearts (heart diseases); their eyes are dimmed (eye diseases); "our dance has turned into mourning;" "woe to us, for we have sinned" (Lam 5:8–16). The negative effects of ancestral bondage were not limited to defaulting families; in fact, it led to the destruction of whole nations, such as the Amalekites (1 Sam 15:2). God even used this principle to free the world of descendants of wicked leaders to prevent them from ruling the earth (Is 14:21).[360]

Scripture also teaches that every soul bears responsibility for her choices. It is the soul that sins that dies. Children shall not suffer for the sins of their fathers, and the father shall not suffer for the sins of their children. The righteous deeds of the righteous person shall accompany him, and the wicked deeds of the wicked shall follow him (Eze 18:20). Aquinas helps us to better understand this phenomenon. He wrote:

> According to Saint Augustine in his letter to Avitus, children are never inflicted with spiritual punishment on account of their parents, unless they share in their guilt, either in their origin or by imitation, because every soul is God's immediate property. Sometimes, however, by Divine or human judgment children receive bodily punishment on their parents' account, since the child, as to its body, is part of its father.[361]

Saint Thomas Aquinas insists that actual sins of ancestors are not transmitted to their offspring, because they are solely personal.[362] However, the effects of the sins of the ancestors can be passed down the generations because of reproduction (nature). The Hebrew Scriptures—Torah—, already upheld the principle of individual responsibility in matters of God's law: "Parents shall not be put to death for their children, nor shall children be put to death for their parents; only for their own crimes may persons be put to death" (Deut 24:16, NRSV; cf. Eze 18:25–28). The consequences of the father's sins can be visited on the children, just as the primordial and universal human bondage, original sin, is contracted, but not committed by Adam's descendants. Again Aquinas explains:

> It is impossible for the sin of the nearer ancestors, or even any other but the sin of our first parents to be transmitted by way of origin. The reason is that a man begets his like in species but not in individual. Consequently those things that pertain directly to the individual, such as personal actions and matters affecting them, are not transmitted by parents to their children: for a grammarian does not transmit to his son the knowledge of grammar that he has acquired by his studies. On the other hand, those things that concern the nature of the species are transmitted by parents to their children, unless there be a defect of nature: thus a man with eyes begets a son with eyes, unless nature fails. If nature is strong, even certain accidents of the individual pertaining to natural disposition, are transmitted to the children, e.g. fleetness of body, acuteness of intellect, and so forth.[363]

Role of Baptism in generational transmissions

Baptism effectively takes away the guilt of original sin, but its effects, Aquinas says, still remains:

> As regards the '*fomes*' which is the disorder of the lower parts of the soul and of the body itself, in respect of which... man exercises his power of generation. Consequently those who are baptized transmit original sin: since they do not beget as being renewed in Baptism, but as still retaining something of the oldness of the first sin.[364]

"Just as Adam's sin is transmitted to all who are born of Adam corporally, so is the grace of Christ transmitted to all that are begotten of Him spiritually, by faith and Baptism: and this, not only unto the removal of the sin of their first parent, but also unto the removal of actual sins, and the obtaining of glory."[365]

This means that in spite of Baptism, the effects of the sins of our ancestors can still affect "children and grandchildren to the third and fourth generations." Baptism is the first of the Seven Sacraments necessary for our salvation. It brings us into our first encounter with the Most Blessed Trinity—Father, Son, and Holy Spirit. Through the Seven Sacraments, we experience the redemption of Christ here and now. Baptism accomplishes three things in us: it washes away original sin; it makes us members of the mystical Body of Christ, the Church; and it incorporates us into the family of God, as sons and daughters of the Father. We become children of God by virtue of the indwelling Trinity. By Baptism, we regain sanctifying grace.

There is an exorcism rite integral to the Baptismal Rite. It is important that ministers of this Sacrament not omit this rite. It is an exorcism rite, which means, it expels evil spirits that may be transmitted through the generational line, or may have attached themselves to emotional wounds and traumas, which may have been created in preborn infants or in early childhood before Baptism.

I participated at an Exorcism and Healing Conference where it was reported of a case of a newly born baby who was possessed by the devil. The baby performed strange postures and growled like a beast. He was set free after a priest prayed over him. So while the Exorcism Rite of Baptism does expel evil spirits, and while Baptism itself washes away original and personal sins effectively, the effects of these sins, which may remain, can still be transmitted down the generational line. This is so, Aquinas explains, because the effect of sin that remains is a disorder of the lower parts of the soul and of the body itself, in respect of which man exercises his power to reproduce.[366]

The Eucharist in generational healing

The Holy Eucharist is the fulfillment of Jesus' promise to be with us until the end of time. The Eucharist is Jesus Christ Himself—true God and true Man. In the Eucharist, Jesus continues His saving mission to all humanity. The Holy Eucharist is the sacrament of God's love for the human race. The Eucharistic sacrifice is "the Source and Summit of the Christian life."[367] It is effectively, the source of spiritual life as well; for all the other Sacraments flow toward the Eucharist, and issue from the Eucharist. In the Eucharist, Jesus makes Himself available to heal and console us. In the Eucharist also, we have the opportunity to make reparation to His Sacred Heart for sins, personal and generational.

Saint Paul teaches that the Christian life is life lived in the Holy Spirit; it is a supernatural life. In Romans 8:14, he says, "Those who are led by the Spirit of God are children of God." The Eucharist is a spiritual food. It is the Bread of eternal life. The Christian life is a Eucharistic life. Saint Thomas Aquinas taught that:

> No other sacrament has greater healing power [than the Eucharist]; through it sins are purged away, virtues are increased, and the soul is enriched with an abundance of every spiritual gift. It is offered in the Church for the living and the dead so that what was instituted for the salvation of all may be for the benefit of all.[368]

In generational healing prayers, we address both spiritual and physical bondage. The Holy Eucharist is the most real of all spiritual realities. It is the greatest miracle God works in our world every day upon every Catholic altar at Holy Mass. It is the source of every healing possible in this life. The celebration of the Sacrifice of the Holy Eucharist is central in the *Family Healing Retreats*. Baptism issues from the Eucharist and flows back into the Eucharist. The grace of Christ given to us at Baptism reaches its summit in the Eucharistic celebration. This grace flows backward into our ancestry, and forward to our offspring to bring healing to our family trees. It is the timeless sacrifice of Jesus Christ, who "is the same yesterday, today, and forever" (Heb 13:8). Of the Eucharist, Paul says: "For as often as you eat this bread and drink the cup, you proclaim the death of the Lord until he comes" (1 Cor 11:26). It is Christ's death that set us free.

Transmission of generational bondage

Generational bondage or curse is an evil that afflicts families. It deprives us of peace and may affect our relationship with God. Sin is at the root of all generational bondage. Every sin is an act of disobedience to God's commands. Where sin exists, demons thrive; but we do not blame demons for our sins, even though Satan is the mastermind behind all sin and sinful tendencies. He is the undisputed CEO of all sin-related industries and products. He is the one who keeps God's children in bondage.

Scripture narrates that, as Jesus and His disciples passed by, He saw a man blind from birth. The disciples asked Him, "Rabbi, who sinned, this man or his parents, that he was born blind?" (Jn 9:1–2). The question of the disciples evokes a Jewish belief that physical deformities, illnesses, and evil spirit possession have their root in personal and generational sins. This is also evidenced by the accusation the Pharisees levied against the blind man: "You were born totally in sin?" (Jn 9:34).

The Jews knew that the Book of the Law states that children and grandchildren do experience the consequences of their fathers' sins. They knew Exodus 20:5, which said, "For I, the Lord your God, am a jealous God, punishing the children for the sin of the parents to the third and fourth generation of those who hate me" (NIV). Other relevant Scripture texts in the Law of Moses include Exodus 34:7, Numbers 14:18, and Deuteronomy 5:9.

Jesus' response that, "Neither he nor his parents sinned; it is so that the works of God might be made visible through him" (Jn 9:3), shows that not all bondage can be attributed to the sins of the individual or the ancestors. Such would be the result of the effect of the sin of Adam. A person or family may be in bondage as a result of sins committed, or according to the ordinance of God, who permits all things for the salvation of all. Whatever may be the source of bondage, Jesus Christ has supreme power over sin and the forces of evil that cause bondage. He is able to manifest the mighty works of God through His healings, even to raising the dead.

The crippled woman

Luke's Gospel tells us that on the Sabbath, Jesus healed a woman, who for eighteen years was crippled by an evil spirit. "She was bent over, completely incapable of standing erect" (Lk 13:11). The leading synagogue official, angry that Jesus healed the woman on the Sabbath, protested and yelled at the people to come for healing only on the six days on which faithful Jews were permitted to work and not on the Sabbath. Jesus said to them, "And ought not this woman, a daughter of Abraham whom Satan bound for eighteen long years, be set free from this bondage on the sabbath day?" (Lk 13:16, NRSV).

The text does not state clearly that the woman's bondage is generational. However, the mention of "daughter of Abraham" might suggest a reference to her descent from the line of Abraham, father of those who worshipped the true God, the covenant people. The allusion to "daughter of Abraham" gives a clue of the possible ancestral origin of her bondage. Jesus had said to her, "Woman, you are set free from your ailment" (Lk 13:12, NRSV). While the origin of her infirmity was not disclosed, is it likely that her bondage was not rooted in her sin, but rather, may be generational?

When Jesus healed the paralytic, He said to him, "Child, your sins are forgiven" (Mk 2:5). When Jesus healed the man at the pool called Bethesda, who had been ill for thirty-eight years, He said to him, "Rise, take up your mat, and walk" (Jn 5:8). Jesus later found him and said, "Look, you are well; do not sin anymore, so that nothing worse may happen to you" (Jn 5:14).

It was necessary for Jesus to remind those He healed of the danger of sin as the open door to demonic contamination, ailments and bondage. Obedience to His words guarantees health, freedom and peace, and the avoidance of the evil consequences of sin—bondage, sickness, demonic contamination, death and eternal damnation. It is precisely for this reason that Jesus was sent, to destroy Satan, sin and death; and to seek out and save the lost (Lk 19:10). Jesus said to the adulterous woman, "Go, (and) from now on do not sin any more" (Jn 8:11). This woman, believed to be Saint Mary Magdalene, obeyed Jesus, and was rewarded for her faith with the first vision of the risen Lord, according to the Scriptures (Jn 8:11; Lk 8:2; Mk 16:9). Saint John writes: "Everyone who commits sin is a child of the devil; for the devil has been sinning from the beginning. The Son of God was revealed for this purpose, to destroy the works of the devil" (1 Jn 3:8, NRSV).

In the cases mentioned above, it is evident that personal sins plunged the paralytic and the man at the pool of Bethesda into bondage. This does not appear to be the case with the crippled woman, because Jesus did not alert her about her sin. Her bondage may be generational, since in all fairness to the Good Teacher, Jesus would have cautioned her as He did the paralytic and the man at the pool of Bethesda to sin no more, not only out of compassion and love for her, but also as a warning, so that the bondage may not return should she sin again. In her regard, Jesus said nothing about sin.

The man born blind

The healing of the man born blind presents an unusual and exceptional case, as well as a pedagogical moment in the healing ministry of Jesus. We learn from it that there is more to suffering and bondage than simply pain, inconvenience and suffering, when viewed from God's perspective. Suffering has greater value in that it reveals God's glory when His power is made visible as the bound are unbound and the dead are raised to life. Since the man's bondage of blindness had no apparent cause, it raises hopes that we too can be healed by Jesus, even when the cause of our bondage is unknown.

Jesus restored sight to the man born blind, because it was impossible for Him not to heal the blind, raise the dead, and give life in abundance, since these are actions of the compassionate Father (Jn 5:17). They are signs of the manifestation of God's Kingdom here and now. In healing the blind man, Jesus revealed the power and glory of God shining on the face of His Beloved. It is possible that we too might be experiencing bondage with unknown origin, but which God has allowed to reveal His glory. If such is the case, we may never know, but we still pray and ask in faith that the Lord Jesus would intercede for the healing necessary for our wellbeing and wholeness.

How do demons cause bondage?

From the Fall of Adam and Eve, we learn that Satan's main tactics are lies and deception, which it uses to create confusion and half-truths, in order to trick us into agreements with it. Satan's goal is to divide and separate us from God. Human generational bondages, in a general sense, are rooted in Adam's failure to protect himself and Eve, as well as God's promises through him to all humanity before the deceiver as recorded in Genesis 3. It is possible that the bondage experienced in our families can be traced back to someone in our ancestry, who knowingly or unknowingly, may have been tricked into an alliance with the devil through its lies. In its intent to deceive, Satan sometimes disguises itself as an angel of light (2 Cor 11:14). We need God's light, and truth to expose Satan's deceptions and lies. We need faith to resist the devil's machinations.

Jesus tells us that Satan is a thief and the robber who enters the sheepfold not through the gate, but climbs over elsewhere (Jn 10:1). It enters through cracks and crevices, wounds, ignorance, disobedience, weaknesses, and vulnerabilities in our lives. It climbs over to steal our identity and destroy the divine image and likeness in us, leaving us dazed and confused about who we are as God's precious children. This often happens when we practice superficial Christianity and a false spirituality of feelings. The devil sneaks in and roams around like an angry beast looking for lukewarm, tepid, unsuspecting, and sleepy souls to devour. Satan is a master at the lying craft. When it lies, it speaks in character, because it is a liar and the father of lies (Jn 8:44). Lying is Satan's native tongue, which it shares with its demons and human agents. Scripture says that it is impossible for God to tell a lie (Titus 1:2; Heb 6:18). Truth is our formidable weapon against demonic lies. Truth is a Person, Jesus Christ, the Word of the Father.

When Satan gains a foothold in a person or family tree through deception, it claims rights over them. By these rights, it has freedom to operate as it chooses. Since its mission is to steal, slaughter, and destroy, it is able to inflict misery and bondage as it pleases, until it is stopped. The degree of its power over a person or generational line will depend on how much human free will has been surrendered to it. The gravity of the sinful choice will determine the degree of bondage. The more serious the sin, that is, the offense against God, the greater the bondage demons can exercise over people. All these happen only within the permissive will of Almighty God. Satan, irrespective of how vicious and malevolent it can be, cannot exceed the limit of action on a soul permitted it by Jesus Christ. The case of Job serves to illustrate this principle clearly for our understanding (Job 1:11; 2:6). Here we learn that the suffering of bondage can have an educational value for us (Job 6).

Jesus said to his seventy-two disciples, "See, I have given you authority to tread on snakes and scorpions, and over all the power of the enemy; and nothing will hurt you" (Lk 10:19, NRSV). In the face of the onslaught of the evil one in our lives and families, we must resist in the name and power of the Lord. The realities of generational and personal bondages call us to spiritual warfare. Scripture says we must put up resistance to the devil and it will flee from us. But first, we must submit to God, draw near, and know Him through prayer (Jam 4:7, NRSV). We must lament and repent of our sins and distance ourselves from the evil actions of our ancestors, which may have opened the doors to bondage. So that when healed, we may live peaceful holy lives (see Jam 4:7–9).

Every contamination with evil spirits, from the moment of our conception, can potentially create in us physical, emotional, psychological, genetic, and most especially, spiritual wounds; since we are spirit-body beings. God is Spirit. We are most like Him in our spiritual nature. The wounded areas become the platform for evil spirit's activity to inflict bondage. Hampsch believes that families that have a history of occultism or witchcraft have a much higher percentage of physical abnormalities than families that have never experienced the occult. He says there is strong pastoral and clinical evidence which suggests that the production of defective genes, or at least the activation of a defective gene, opens the door to spiritual contamination, which in turn can be generationally transmitted.[369] The reason for this theory, Hampsch argues, is that the celebration of deliverance prayer within the context of the Eucharist has with "remarkable consistency" alleviated disorders whose origin appears to be genetic.[370] According to him,

The medical use of recombinant DNA can change material substructure, but the use of prayer and repentance for one's own sins and those of the ancestors (Lev 26:40) can bring about an interruption in the overall transmission of the disorder to oneself and one's offspring. The healing effect of this family healing prayer is even more dramatic when it cures otherwise intractable disorders.[371]

Transmission of the effects of sin in the ancestry

When God blessed Adam and Eve saying, "Be fertile and multiply; fill the earth and subdue it. Have dominion," He invested them with authority over all creation. This authority extended to their offspring through their generative capacity. We see this authority in the influence man has over material creation. This meant that the words and actions of Adam and Eve had consequences beyond themselves. As long as they remained obedient to their Creator, their authority would produce effects similar to God's authority, but limited to the degree that they are human. As God had authority over Adam and Eve, so parents have authority over their children. This idea of authority by extension can be applied in every area of human life, namely, politics, society, religion, and so on.

Jesus of Nazareth stood trial before Pontius Pilate, who threatened Him: "Do you not answer me? Don't you know I have power to crucify you" (Jn 19:10)? Jesus answered: "You would have no power over me if it had not been given to you from above" (Jn 19:11). The authority of God invested on Adam and Eve has implications at every level of human activity. Those who exercise religious, educational, political, administrative authority, and so on, have a responsibility to care for their subjects, to provide for their needs, to feed them with spiritual food, to govern and enact morally just laws that protect and respect human life and dignity, and to advance the knowledge of the Supreme God among men.

Religious leaders have an obligation to spiritually feed their people. Jesus was a spiritual leader, and the model of all spiritual leaders. He took seriously the mission of feeding the poor. He fed the hungry multitude (Mk 6:34–43), travelled from place to place doing good works and healing the oppressed (Acts 10: 38), went in search of the lost sheep (Lk 15:4), was anointed to set the captives free (Lk 4:18), loved and protected those the Father gave Him (Jn 17:12), and proclaimed the Kingdom of God (Mk 1:15). After He rose from the dead, He commanded Peter: "Feed my sheep" (Jn 21:17). Peter becomes the model of every leader in taking care of the spiritual and material needs of God's people, irrespective of who they are or their religious loyalty. The truth is, everyone belongs to Jesus, and will ultimately be accountable to Him. As Jesus prayed for Peter not to fail, so He prays for us not to fail (Lk 22:32).

Adam failed to feed his offspring with the food of God's word through his disobedience. He lost the privilege of being called the "prince of this world" through his unfaithfulness. By feeding on Satan's poisonous wisdom, he fed his offspring with death, allowing Satan to be "the prince of this world" (Jn 12:3; 14:30; 16:11). Satan is the spirit that is now at work in the disobedient (Eph 2:2). We must resist this spirit. It is the spirit of the world (1 Cor 2:12). We must confront and fight it as a matter of life and death. This evil spirit comes to steal the word sown in our hearts; the Word made flesh that is our very life, the beginning and end of our identity. It comes to destroy the image and likeness of God in us, and to slaughter our spiritual lives and render us spiritually dead. It comes to poison our life in the Holy Spirit; to hold us in bondage and divide us within, and divide our families, parishes, and communities, our nations, and all that God created and made very good. We must stop it!

Saint Louis Marie de Montfort dedicated the first twelve days of the 33-Day preparation for total consecration to Jesus through Mary, to ridding ourselves of the spirit of the world, which consists essentially in the denial of the supreme dominion of God, manifested in practice by sin and disobedience.[372] The seven capital sins constitute the spirit of the world: anger, envy, lust, greed, avarice, pride, and sloth. This spirit stunts and kills our spiritual growth, and blocks our call and movement toward transforming union with Jesus Christ. Adam, contaminated with the spirit of the world, passed it down to his offspring: Cain and Abel; the consequence of this reality is the first murder ever committed. Today, murders are committed with impunity daily all around us. Adam, through disobedience, not only lost his friendship with God, but also his authority over his children.

Personal guilt for sin is not transmitted, only the effects of sins are capable of being transmitted through the generations. To transmit or pass on a sin is equivalent to putting a "curse" upon one's descendants.[373] These curses or bondage make us subject to Satan's power and influence. As distressing as the captivity confronting us and our families may be, we have at our disposal the power of the holy name of Jesus who does not want us, His little ones, to be afraid. Jesus assures us that the Father is pleased to share His kingdom with us (Lk 12:32). Jesus has the victory.

The presence of generationally transmitted defects within families should be no reason for anyone affected to blame himself or herself, or others. Parents should not be blamed, nor should they blame others for the tragedies caused by generational curses. We should be assured that all things happen only within the permissive will of God who alone is able to bring good out of evil. Paul assures us: "And we know that in all things God works for the good of those who love him, who have been called according to his purpose" (Rom 8:28, NIV). Generational bondage from God's perspective is always a blessing in disguise. God is greater than all human problems of all generations put together. So, do not be afraid!

What of adopted children?

In praying for healing for an adopted child, it is important, if possible, to have some knowledge or to investigate the family trees of the natural parents, and also the adopting parents. This should not come as a surprise to the adopting parents, since adopted children do have different parental, religious and cultural backgrounds that can affect their physical and spiritual wellbeing. Adopted children are known to carry within them the seeds of personal and generational bondage which develops in adulthood to present discernible symptoms. These symptoms can be traced back to the children's birthparents, or they can come from the adopting parents through association (refer to Chapter 15).[374] But more importantly, the children may carry within them the seeds of personal or generational bondage from their biological parents with roots in their ancestry. Whether or not historical or background information is available on the biological parents, careful observation will be helpful in spotting signs of distress that might point to bondage. Most often, adoptions are done without thought or consideration for these situations. When diagnosed, they can easily be dealt with through the celebration of prayer and the Sacraments.

What can be transmitted inter-generationally?

The effects of sin, personal or generational, can be passed down the generational line. In the state of original innocence, Adam and Eve did not have sin, and could not transmit the effects of sin. In the fallen state, the defects of sin were now transmissible. Hampsch classified generationally transmissible defects as follows:

- Inherited spiritual defects: anything from prayerlessness to atheism
- Inherited physical defects: anything from dandruff to diabetes
- Inherited emotional defects: anything from shyness to suicide tendencies
- Inherited psychological defects: anything from poor inter-spouse communication to psychopathic murder
- Inherited societal defects (defects common to entire families, and even nations or ethnic groups): anything from in-law aloofness to Mafia families.[375]

The transmission of these defects can occur from our ancestors to us their descendants, and from us to our offspring, both present and future.

However, the generational transmission of the effects of sin (bondage) does not necessarily have to occur. It can be prevented, mitigated, resolved, and healed in all directions by the power of God, through intercession, or the life of righteousness within families. We should seek the light of the Holy Spirit in discerning what and how to pray and intercede for the healing of the root causes of bondage in persons and families. It is necessary that such prayers be celebrated in the context of the Eucharistic sacrifice to break the bondage, stop the transmission of evil, and restore wholeness to families. Generational intercession invokes the healing power of the Precious Blood of Jesus' sacrifice. By His death and resurrection, Jesus ransomed us from the curse of the law of death by taking it on Himself as He hung on the tree; He destroyed the bond against us, nailing it to the cross; and He despoiled demons of their power and led them away in triumph (Gal 3:13, Col 2:14–15). Jesus Christ, always the same, yesterday, today and forever He lives.

Prayers for the healing of secondary open door (V) begin on page 344.

Part IV

Chapters 19–20

Celebrating the Healing Power of Christ

Glory be to Jesus; honor to Mary and Joseph!

Chapter 19

∝ ∝ ∝

Prepare the Way of the Lord for Healing

Rescue me from death, God, my saving God, that my tongue may praise your healing power (Ps 51:1).

Preparing our hearts to receive healing

It is necessary that we prepare and open our hearts to receive healing during the Family Healing Retreats. Every healing is a gift from God, and it has to be received freely. When God heals, He intervenes to free and save us. God is able and willing to intervene whenever, and as He pleases, to cause healing in our lives (Mk 1:41). Healing is always the fruit of Jesus' excellent ministry of intercession at the right hand of the Father. He is always able and willing to heal and save those who come to God through Him, because He lives forever making effective intercession for us (Heb 7:25). Jesus Christ came to heal the sick and raise the dead. There was no one who came to Jesus who was not healed (Lk 6:19). Each time Jesus heals, He pours out His life as power goes forth from Him (Mk 5:30); He gives His flesh and blood for the life of the world (Jn 6:51); He dies and rises to share with us His life in the Spirit. We need Doctor Jesus. Only the sick need a physician; those who are well do not (Mt 9:12).

To continue His healing work, Jesus commanded the Twelve, and by implication and extension, all the baptized, to "Cure the sick, raise the dead, cleanse the lepers, cast out demons. You received without payment; give without payment" (Mt 10:8, NRSV). The principles suggested in this book for healing are designed to make us interiorly open to receive the healing God desires to give us. They provide opportunities for prayer and reflection, and help us prepare spiritually for God's healing. Paul gives us the perfect recipe for interior openness for healing: "Rejoice in hope, endure in affliction, persevere in prayer" (Rom 12:12), and be grateful in all situations.

Conditions necessary for healing

Faith

Healing is always the fruit of a relationship with God; it is a gift to be received. Jesus came to heal us in the deepest possible way, and to give us abundant life here and now, and then eternal life. "For God so loved the world that He gave His only begotten Son, that whoever believes in Him should not perish but have everlasting life" (Jn 3:16, NKJV). Healing is an experience of salvation. One condition for receiving it is that we believe in Jesus Christ.

Jesus often demanded faith before He pronounced healing. To the blind man, He asks, "Do you believe that I can do this?" (Mt 9:28); to Martha, who was mourning the death of her brother, Lazarus, Jesus also asks, "Do you believe this?" (Jn 11:26). In other situations, the manifestation of faith was necessary for healing to occur. Even when our Lord did not explicitly demand it, He confirmed its presence and necessity in those He healed. We see this dynamics in the healing of the centurion's servant (Mt 8:5–13), the Canaanite woman (Mt 15:22–28), and the woman suffering from hemorrhages (Mk 5:25–35). To stress the necessity for healing-faith, Jesus did not perform healings in His native place, because they lacked faith (Mt 13:58).

Faith is an openness that receives God's gift of healing. Healing is never the result of any human manipulation, method or technique; it is always a gift to be received with and in faith, and with gratitude. Faith is the receptivity gift given to us at Baptism in the Holy Spirit. It is one of the three Theological Virtues (given directly by God): Faith, Hope and Charity, without which we cannot be saved. Through faith, God initiates a relationship with us, and makes us open to His love. "These are the beginning and end of life: faith the beginning, love the end. When these two are found together, there is God… No one professing faith sins; no one professing love hates."[376]

True faith manifests itself by perseverance in trials (Acts 14:22, Rom 12:12), gratitude for favors (Lk 17:18–19), persistence and humble boldness (Mt 15:22–28), and surrender (Mt 8:8), witness (Acts 5:41). Concerning faith, there are no quick routes and no short cuts. Endurance is a true test of faith. The faith that endures to the end is the faith that heals and saves. Faith gives us access to all the possibilities of God in this world (Rom 5:2–5; Mk 9:23).

In Mark's Gospel, Jesus' rebuke of the Apostles for their lack of faith is striking. He wanted them to know that it was both important and necessary, if they are to further the mission He would entrust to them and their successors. They cannot delegate this responsibility to anyone else; they must grow in faith through persevering prayer and spiritual exercises. Every baptized Christian, in his or her own way, is called to a lived demonstration of living faith. "For just as the body without the spirit is dead, so also faith without works is dead" (Jam 2:26, NET). Someone might say, "You have faith and I have works." Show me your faith without works and I will show you faith by my works… faith without works is useless?" (Jam 2:18, 20, NET).

By faith in Jesus, we are justified; by faith in Jesus Christ we are healed. To pray correctly then we must pray with faith; all things are possible for those who have faith (Mk 9:23). Without faith no one can please God (Heb 11:6). No bondage, whether personal or generational, can stand the power of the prayer of faith. Part of life's spiritual formation is to fan into flame the gift of faith we received at Baptism. Let us join the Apostles in their supplication to the Lord and humbly pray: **Lord Jesus Christ, Son of the living God, "increase our faith!"** (Lk 17:5).

The goal of faith is the acknowledgement of the Lordship of Jesus Christ, and its fruit is our salvation. This acknowledgement glorifies the Father. True faith reveals itself in the harmony of our thoughts, words, works and actions. Faith must bring us to witness to the identity of the Father's only Son, Jesus. When this happens, the words of Jesus come true in our lives: "your faith has saved you." Thomas manifested this faith exclaiming: "My Lord and my God" (Jn 20:28); Peter confessed it, "You are the Messiah, the Son of the living God" (Mt 16:16); Martha yielded, "Yes, Lord. I have come to believe that you are the Messiah, the Son of God, the one who is coming into the world" (Jn 11:27); and Nathanael proclaimed, "Rabbi, you are the Son of God; you are the King of Israel" (Jn 1:49). For Paul, the faith that heals and saves is the faith that confesses with the mouth that Jesus is Lord and believes in the heart that God raised Jesus from the dead (Rom 10:9).

Humility

Humility is total openness and submission to God. Only humble souls receive God's favors. Humility reveals itself in obedience. Jesus is our model in perfect humility and receptivity, because He showed perfect obedience when He humbled Himself, and in our place, accepted the humiliating death of the cross in obedience to the Father, for our salvation. Our Blessed Mother teaches us how to imitate the humble obedience of her Son when she gave her Fiat to be the Mother of Jesus: "I am the handmaid of the Lord, may it be done to me according to Your word" (Lk 1:38). This is what our response to God should always be, "Yes Lord. Your will be done." She lets us know that God throws down the mighty from their thrones of pride, but He lifts up the lowly and exalts them in His presence. In humility, we must empty ourselves of the false-self, in order to be filled with God's-self, which is our healing. Humility defines the contemplative approach to healing. It is God's approach, since it fosters union and communion with God, which He desires so much. Union with God brings healing to the creature united to Him.

Forgiveness

To forgive unconditionally is to love unconditionally. Forgiveness opens our hearts to receive God's healing. The First Words of Jesus on the Cross opened the door to our healing: "Father, forgive them, for they know not what they do" (Lk 23:34, ESV). In these words, Jesus exercised for the last time on earth the power of His Priesthood and obtained for us from the Father remission of sin and healing from bondage. Throughout His earthly ministry, Jesus forgave sins: "Your sins are forgiven" (Mt 9:2; Lk 7:48); "Go, and from now on do not sin any more" (Jn 8:11, NET); "Look, you are well; do not sin any more" (Jn 5:14); etc.

Jesus invested His Priestly power to forgive sins on the Church through His Apostles (priests) in the Holy Spirit: "Whose sins you forgive are forgiven them" (Jn 20:23). This power is exercised in the Church in the Sacrament of Penance only by the ordained priesthood. However, all the baptized: laity and ordained, are called to forgive the daily offenses of others. This was why as a baptized "seminarian," Peter, who was not yet ordained priest, asked Jesus how often he must forgive his brother if he sins against him, "As many as seven times?" But Jesus replied: "I say to you, not seven times, but seventy-seven times" (Mt 18:21–22).

The highest authority/power a person can exercise on this earth is the power to forgive others, that is, to release them from bondage, and help them to be saved; this power essentially and strictly speaking, belongs only to Jesus Christ Crucified. Those who are priests by baptism (laity) and the ordained priests (Priests and Bishops), in their own name, and in their daily encounters, can exercise this priestly act in the words: "I forgive you," when "my brother sins against me." This is why Jesus said: "…if you do not forgive others, your Father will not forgive you your sins" (Mt 6:15, NET). To say with our whole heart, "I forgive you," unites us with the forgiveness Jesus offers to all humanity, and in the name of all humanity. When we can forgive others this way, the Father embraces us with His Divine Mercy and healing, and makes us administrators and ambassadors of His merciful healing love.

My God, I believe, I adore, I trust and I love Thee! I beg pardon for those who do not believe, who do not adore, Who do not trust and who do not love Thee.[377]

Desire

To desire is to hunger and thirst for that which will satisfy us. The sick goes in search of the doctor's cure, and the sinner goes in search of God's mercy. Jesus does not assume that those who came to Him had the intention to be healed. He required and waited for the sick to manifest their desire for healing. Jesus asked the blind Bartimaeus: "What do you want me to do for you?" Jesus saw clearly that he was blind, but He still asked the question. Jesus seemed to disregard the plea of the Canaanite woman, but she did not give up (Mt 15:22–28).

In manifesting our desire for healing, we should take care to be specific. The specificity of our desire is a sign of healthy self-knowledge, which comes from a deep place of our true identity and need within us. How many people who, when asked what they asked for in prayer would not know what to say, because they do not know what they need, or what to ask for.[378] "It is self-deception to go to the altar and ask something merely at random."[379] Prayer is truly the food of the soul only when we pray according to our spiritual wants.[380]

The process of acknowledging, investigating and relating to God all our bondage issues, helps us to present specific needs to our Heavenly Father in prayer for healing. "The object of our prayer, then, must be lawful, and conducive to our spiritual welfare."[381] "God will not hear our prayer if we pray to be delivered from a particular temptation or cross which God knows to be useful to our advancement in humility and other virtues."[382]

Repentance

God constantly calls us to return to Him with our whole heart to receive mercy and healing (Joel 2:12; Haggai 2:17; Jer 24:7). Our response to this call, namely, repentance, must be a free choice. According to Pope Saint Clement's Letter to the Corinthians, a review of various ages of history shows "that in every generation the Lord has offered the opportunity of repentance to any who were willing to turn to Him."[383] The power of repentance opens our hearts to God's forgiveness and healing. In Isaiah 1:18, the Lord invites us to settle matters with Him: "Though your sins are like scarlet, I will make them as white as snow. Though they are red like crimson, I will make them as white as wool" (NLT). The following accounts illustrate the power of repentance.

Noah preached God's message of repentance and all who listened to him were saved.[384] The Prophet Jonah preached repentance and conversion to the sinful nation of Nineveh. At this, they proclaimed a fast and covered themselves in sackcloth and ashes as a sign of interior change. For the king's decree said, "Let man and beast be covered with sackcloth, and let them call out mightily to God. Let everyone turn from his evil way and from the violence that is in his hands" (Jonah 3:8, ESV). When God saw *by their actions* how they turned from their evil way, He relented and forgave them, and Nineveh was spared from peril (Jonah 3:9–10).

Repentance consists of two movements, a turning away from sin, and a turning toward God and embracing the Gospel. Let us ask for the grace to repent of our sins, and to be freed from the consequences of the sins of our ancestors, through some practical actions that reveal our interior renewal and change of heart. In this way, we are disposed to receive God's healing love.

Prophet Isaiah recommends to us practical acts of repentance: releasing those bound unjustly (forgiveness), setting the oppressed free, breaking every yoke, sheltering the homeless, sharing our bread with the hungry, clothing the naked, satisfying the afflicted, not turning our backs on our own; and removing from our midst oppression, false accusations and malicious speech. Then, light shall shine for us in the darkness, gloom shall be gone, God will renew our strength and give us plenty, and we shall be like watered gardens. Our ancient ruins will be rebuilt, and the "Restorer of ruined homesteads" we shall be called (Is 58:6–12).

Bearing witness to the truth

Faithfulness to the truth releases us from bondage rooted in lies (Jn 8:32). The Christian faith is founded on the truth that Jesus Christ lived, suffered, was crucified, and was buried; on the third day, He rose from the dead. It is also founded on all that Jesus taught and revealed of the Eternal Father and His Kingdom; on the truth handed down to us by the Apostles through Sacred Tradition, contained in Sacred Scripture, and taught by the Magisterium. The Church therefore is at the service of the Gospel of truth and the deposit of the doctrine of the faith, and she has the mission to preach and witness to that truth without fear or favor, and without compromise.

Jesus said, "I am the way and the truth and the life. No one comes to the Father except through me. If you really know me, you will know my Father as well. From now on, you do know him and have seen him" (Jn 14:6–7, NIV). Lies, falsehood and the distortion of the Gospel alienate us from Jesus and ally us with the devil, who is a liar and murderer from the beginning; in him there is no truth (Jn 8:44).

The Church's doctrine and pastoral practice (discipline) must always conform and witness to truth if we are to remain faithful to Christ. Pastoral practice flows from the Church's beliefs or doctrines, and doctrine informs pastoral practice. Pastoral practice not based on truth will sooner or later pull down the doctrine on which it stands. Without the light of faith rooted in the truth, those who walk do so in darkness and gloom and captivity. As this early Christian tradition says, *Lex orandi, lex credendi, lex vivendi.* As we worship, so we believe, so we live.

Speaking in defense of the truth, Pope Emeritus Benedict XVI, reaffirmed that the Church's supernatural mission is to preach the truth of Christ. He said that to renounce or abandon the truth in an attempt to compromise with the world "is nonetheless lethal to the faith."[385] In his

* * *

Letter to priests, Pope Saint John Paul II mentioned points of extreme importance for the Church and the world at this historical moment. He said the Church, "will be able to carry out her mission to the world only if—in spite of all human weakness—she maintains her fidelity to Christ."[386] The truth lived in love helps us to mature in the likeness of Christ. In this way, the Church also matures to the fullness of Christ as God desires (Eph 4:15–16).

We know that "the whole world is under the power of the evil one" (1 Jn 5:19), who puts us in bondage. When the Church proclaims the truth, she brings the faithful into the experience of salvation and healing by dispelling the darkness of sins. This is because Jesus, our Lord, has conquered the world with its precepts and standards that are rooted in compromise, confusion, lies and sin (Jn 16:33). The Church must resist the attempt to compromise with the world if she is to fulfill her mission to save souls for Christ. God will never violate His covenant, and His truth will never fail (Ps 89:34).

Conformity to God's will

A leper approached Jesus and kneeling before Him, begged: "'If you will, you can make me clean.' Moved with pity, he stretched out his hand and touched him and said to him, 'I will; be clean.' And immediately the leprosy left him, and he was made clean" (Mk 1:40–42, ESV). John the Evangelist, whose Gospel and three Letters focus on developing an intimate and contemplative relationship with Jesus assures us that "we have this confidence in him, that if we ask anything according to his will, he hears us. And if we know that he hears us in regard to whatever we ask, we know that what we have asked him for is ours" (1 Jn 5:14–15).

Praying according to God's will is like trying to listen to a favorite radio program. It does not matter how sophisticated our radio receivers may be, if we do not tune-in to the correct wavelength or channel, we will not enjoy that program. Jesus taught us to pray: "Father...your will be done" (Mt 26:42). In His agony in the garden of Gethsemane, Jesus prayed, "Abba, Father... everything is possible for you. Take this cup from me. Yet not what I will, but what you will" (Mk 14:36, NIV). Every prayer patterned on Jesus' prayer of conformity receives the Father's hearing. We must tune-in and listen on God's FM radio through obedience.

Obedience, patience and reverence for God are the recipe for Divine conformity in prayer. The prayers of Jesus Christ, the Eternal High Priest, were heard because of His reverence; suffering taught Him obedience and patience, and made Him perfect (Heb 5:7–8; 10:36). All Jesus' disciples must also imitate His reverence, be trained in obedience and patience, and be perfected and healed by the crosses God allows in our lives.

The signs of our lack of conformity to God's include: getting angry at God, resentment, complaining, sin, disobedience, impatience and rebellion, lying, blaming and accusing others for our troubles. Besides, the many inordinate desires and attachments that fill our lives, which manifest as one or more of the seven capital vices (see chapters 7–13), show lack of conformity. They also show lack of gratitude when we don't accept ourselves as we are, and much more. These deprivations deny us of interior peace, and reveal our resistance to God's will. They show we do not see reality from God's perspective, and are not surrendering to His Divine will. Jesus' whole earthly life was one of total surrender. He prayed: "Your will be done" (Mt 26:42). Our Blessed Mother's Fiat is our perfect model in imitating Jesus' obedience and surrender: "May it be done to me according to your word" (Lk 1:38).

Come Holy Spirit! Come by means of the powerful intercession of the Immaculate Heart of Mary, Your well beloved spouse.[387]

Our Blessed Mother Mary in personal and generational intercession

God mightily blessed humanity in the gift of the Virgin with Child (Is 7:14; Mt 1:23). Through her, God's Son took flesh and became the one Mediator between God and the human race (1 Tim 2:5). Through her, who is "Full of grace," all humanity has access to God's grace in the fullest possible way. Through her also, all humanity entered into spiritual warfare in league with Jesus against the ancient serpent to whom God said, "And I will put enmity between you and the woman, and between your offspring and hers; he will crush your head, and you will strike his heel" (Gen 3:15, NIV).

In her canticle of praise and joy to the Lord God, the Virgin with Child prayed: "For he has looked on the humble estate of his servant. For behold, from now on all generations will call me blessed; for he who is mighty has done great things for me, and holy is his name. And his mercy is for those who fear him from generation to generation" (Lk 1:48–50, ESV).

Mary's song is one of hope and intercession for all generations. It is God's desire that all generations call *The Woman of Genesis*[388] – Blessed. Any of our generations that do not call Mary "Blessed," is not yet healed. In calling her "Blessed," we are in perfect harmony with God's will who first honored her most eminently in calling her to be the mother of His Son, and bestowing on her the plenitude of grace in the total overshadowing of the Holy Spirit. In calling her "Blessed," we unite with her in her song of joy, and so experience the mystery and grace of the Magnificat: our souls in union with hers, proclaim God's greatness, and our spirits rejoice with her spirit in God who saves. By this grace, we are led by the spirit of Blessed Mary, so that as she was overshadowed and led by the Holy Spirit from the first moment of her Immaculate Conception, we too may be led by the Spirit to union with Jesus.

Saint Louis Marie de Montfort says that, those who are led by the spirit of Mary are children of Mary.[389] The Blessed Virgin in her holiness and co-redemptive graces prays for all generations as the specific charism she received from her Son at the Foot of the Cross: "Woman, behold, your son" (Jn 19:26); and as the specific charism in which she was confirmed on Pentecost as she devoted herself to prayer with the Apostles, and the men and women in the Upper Room (Acts 1: 14).

At the wedding feast of Cana in Galilee, she interceded with her Son for the wedding guests for the new wine of joy. Today, she continues to intercede for us, her children, for a new Pentecost. She is indeed the mother of all generations by virtue of her spiritual motherhood of all the elect until the Kingdom of God comes in its fullness. May all our generations call Mother Mary, Blessed! Amen.

The royal road to healing

Acknowledge the reality of bondage

The first step to receiving healing is to be aware of the sickness and to acknowledge it. Spiritual healing begins with spiritual awakening. The Holy Spirit began to teach me about this spiritual awakening through my association with Fr. Emmanuel Edeh, CSSp[390] and his Eucharistic adoration ministry. I began to experience an inner awakening that was totally new, as if I received a new pair of glasses, a spiritual "aha" moment you might say, a heightened spiritual awareness that I tried to understand. Saint Paul said that God's children are led by His Spirit (Rom 8:14); we are children of the light and of the day, not of darkness (1 Thess 5:5).

Sensitivity and knowledge of heavenly things is a gift of the Holy Spirit (Jn 3:12; Dan 2:24 –49). We know readily when we are physically hurt. But spiritual wounds are not readily obvious. We need to pay closer attention to be aware of them; in this way, we can seek healing. Time of silence and solitude may be necessary to allow the hurts of anger and unforgiveness, for example, housed in our deep memories to rise up to the surface, so we can notice them. We can then make a choice how to respond: either to forgive or to hold on to anger and unforgiveness or to repent and allow ourselves to be embraced by God's love and mercy or to be closed in and be held in bondage. Spiritual awakening empowers us to be more effective intercessors for our families and for souls.

Bondage creates distress. To deal with it effectively, it's important that we try to understand it. Once we acknowledge bondage, we should investigate its roots, where possible. Jesus taught this approach when He questioned the father of the boy with an unclean spirit: "How long has this been happening to him?" (Mk 9:21).

To facilitate the process of generational investigation in preparation for Jesus' healing, I have provided the *Investigation Sheets I–VI* (Appendix I) to help log our findings. This process exposes the enemy and its hidden tactics. It disarms the evil one and equips us with the knowledge of the extent of the problem, whether other family members, living or deceased, may have been affected.

I was privileged to struggle with generational bondage for almost thirteen years. At that time, I was totally ignorant of this reality. Besides, the subject of intergenerational bondage was beyond the scope of those around me. It was Monsignor John Esseff, a staff of the "Institute for Priestly Formation," Omaha, who pointed me in the right direction. He indicated that I was dealing with a generational situation, and he encouraged me to conduct an inquiry into my family tree. It turned out to be a fruitful exercise for me; I was amazed at my finding. Much information about my family tree came to light for me, which were at the root of my distress. The knowledge I gained not only armed me for battle but also equipped me to pray and intercede in an informed way for my family tree.

The investigation process involves observations. We may visualize it as an experience of lifting a rock that had remained untouched for years. As the rock is moved, light falls on the exposed areas, forcing the bugs underneath to try to escape for safety to new hideouts. They may then be eliminated. Similarly, when we investigate our family trees, the evil that had remained hidden for generations are exposed to the light of Christ through our faith as we pray and investigate our family tree. In this way, we are able to intercede more effectively for the healing our families need.

It is not pretty for us human beings to identify with other peoples' evils. Generally, we recoil and try to distance ourselves from them. Only God, willingly and without shame, identifies with human evils in order to bring us healing. Our human miseries are a fragrant aroma to His Divinity; God is attracted by our sufferings. God so loved the world that He sent Jesus to seek out and save those who were lost. He went everywhere doing good. He was a great and trusted friend of sinners. He took joy to stoop down and wash Peter's messy and smelly feet. Jesus humbled Himself, even to dying on the Cross. But sinful Peter was so uncomfortable and embarrassed that Jesus washed his feet. Are we different from Peter?

When we identify willingly with the suffering and evil of our ancestors, we become powerful intercessors with Jesus mediating God's healing graces to them. Just as we like to identify with the goodness and achievements of our families for our benefit, we should also identify with their failings for their spiritual benefit and ours. Bondage is distressful; but in acknowledging and accepting it, we create the openness for healing to occur.

Saint Ignatius of Loyola placed the act of "Becoming Aware" as the first step in discerning interior or affective movements. We are in the truth if we have a headache and acknowledge we have a headache. If we deny we have a headache, when actually we do, we deny a reality about ourselves. Living under a lie can be harmful. If someone does not know he/she is sick, no effort will be made to seek healing. If an alcoholic denies her alcoholism, treatment will not be sought. Once the truth of bondage is acknowledged, only then can we freely and fruitfully investigate and deal with it.

Acknowledging and accepting the reality of bondage help us to identify with it in ourselves and in others. If the bondage is generationally transmitted, accepting and identifying with it makes us privileged intercessors for the healing of our generations, past, present, and future. If our hearts are blocked through unforgiveness, resentment, anger, hatred, and so on, we cannot be effective instruments of God for healing. The great value of this book is that it helps us prepare our hearts to receive healing.

Jesus, our Savior, gave us the perfect model of acceptance and identification with sin for the salvation of all through His Incarnation. He accepted and identified with human nature and human sinfulness in many ways: He is the Word made flesh. He was baptized. He was weak, hungry, and thirsty. He cried and suffered. Jesus was crucified. He was buried. Through His suffering, Jesus was made perfect (Heb 2:10); and through the wounds of His Passion, He became the source of healing and eternal life for those who choose Him as Lord (Heb 5:7). Saint Paul speaks powerfully of Christ's identification with us that brings about our healing. He said that Jesus though sinless in His Divine nature became sin, so that we, the sinners, might be made whole (2 Cor 5:21).

It is certain that nothing happens outside of the permissive will of God, who alone is able to bring good out of evil. This truth is a source of courage to help us persevere in the midst of our suffering, so we can glorify the Eternal Father. God is greater than our hearts and all human suffering. Saint Padre Pio's wise counsel tells us to surrender and accept all that happens to us as if they have come directly from the hand of God. This attitude will help us deal peacefully and victoriously with the suffering that comes with bondage.

Let us examine carefully the prayers of three Old Testament intercessors: Tobit, Esther, and Daniel, to learn how we can better intercede for the healing of our families.

The intercession of Tobit

Tobit makes a claim that is not disputed in the Book of Tobit. He says, "All my life I have been honest and have tried to do what was right. I often gave money to help needy relatives and other Jews who had been deported with me to Nineveh, the capital of Assyria" (Tob 1:3, GNT). Then he adds, "Later, I was taken captive and deported to Assyria, and that is how I came to live in Nineveh. While we lived in Nineveh, all my relatives and the other Jews used to eat the same kind of food as the other people who lived there, but I refused to do so" (Tob 1:10–11, GNT).

The righteous Tobit, in spite of his goodness, became blind. In his grief-stricken spirit, he prayed to God for himself and his ancestors saying: "I beg you, treat me with kindness. Do not punish me for my sins, not even for sins of which I am unaware. My ancestors rebelled and disobeyed your commands, but do not punish me for their sins" (Tob 3:3–4, GNT). Tobit was distressed that the Lord allowed His people to be ravaged, held captive, disgraced, killed, and held in contempt by other nations. But Tobit's prayer was heard, and God sent Archangel Raphael to heal his blindness and to bless him.

The intercession of Esther

Esther is presented in the Book of Esther as "beautifully formed and lovely to behold" (Esth 2:7). This can be a metaphoric way of saying that she was righteous. The people of Israel were threatened with extermination by wicked leaders. Queen Esther, seized with mortal anguish, prayed to the Lord: "But now we have sinned in your sight, and you have delivered us into the hands of our enemies, (C:18) because we worshipped their gods" (Esth 4:16). Esther prayed for the deliverance of Israel from the hands of the wicked. Her prayers were backed by action, and God saved the Israelites from destruction.

The intercession of Daniel

Daniel belonged to the righteous breed of the Israelites. He was taken captive early as a young boy into Babylon with all of Israel. The suffering of the people weighed heavily on him, and he turned to the Lord God in prayer, with fasting, sackcloth, and ashes, pleading for deliverance. He prayed, "We have sinned! We have done what is wrong and wicked; we have rebelled by turning away from your commandments and standards" (Dan 9:5, NET). Daniel's prayer of repentance and identification with the sinfulness of his people continued: "While I was still speaking and praying, confessing my sin and the sin of my people Israel and presenting my request before the Lord my God concerning his holy mountain" (Dan 9:20, NET), God sent the Archangel Gabriel to assure Daniel that his prayer has been answered.

A likely temptation that may arise when confronted with generational and personal bondage is to think that our situation is hopeless and irredeemable. This is not the case at all. The truth is that God is able to rescue us from any situation of bondage, if it will be for our ultimate good. All we need to do is trust in Jesus; fear is useless. Fear is a powerful weapon of the evil one to keep us in perpetual bondage. Fear immobilizes us so that we do not act in faith to help our situation. We might erroneously think that God cannot help us, or that He is punishing us for some evil we committed in the past or even worse, that we are damned. These kinds of thoughts are not of God; their origin is from the evil one, and we should reject them. God is love. He desires our freedom more than we do.

The positive effect of the Family Healing Retreats is that it builds confidence; participants feel empowered and hopeful in their situation. Almost always, they leave the retreats inspired in faith and equipped to embrace their trials with new zeal. They are ready for battle to take back what the evil one had stolen from them. In this warfare for freedom, the Christian soldier is called to stand fast and hold his ground, knowing that the battle always belongs to the Victorious Lamb of God.

Relate your findings to Jesus in prayer

The next step is to share with Jesus our struggles, concerns, and sufferings and our findings, expectations, and desires, as patients would talk to their doctors about their sicknesses in order to be diagnosed and treated. This step is important in family healing as it demonstrates trust in the Divine Physician, who alone delivers and heals us from bondage. Like a good doctor, Jesus listens attentively to our problem; He may ask us questions as He diagnoses our situation, with a view to finding a unique cure, based on our faith relationship with Him. This relating to (or sharing with) Jesus our distress informs the contemplative approach emphasized in this book.

Jesus loves us infinitely. By embracing suffering and death, He shares intimately with our sufferings. When we talk to Jesus about our bondage, we imitate Martha's example at the death of her brother Lazarus, when in Saint Luke's Gospel she dialogues with Jesus:

- ✠ "Lord," Martha said to Jesus, "if you had been here, my brother would not have died. But I know that even now God will give you whatever you ask."
- ✠ Jesus said to her, "Your brother will rise again."
- ✠ Martha answered, "I know he will rise again in the resurrection at the last day."
- ✠ Jesus said to her, "I am the resurrection and the life. The one who believes in me will live, even though they die; and whoever lives by believing in me will never die. Do you believe this?"
- ✠ "Yes, Lord," she replied, "I believe that you are the Messiah, the Son of God, who is to come into the world" (Jn 11:21–27, NIV).

In our dialogue with Jesus about our situation, He may challenge us as He did to Martha. This was a teaching moment for Martha as Jesus assured her He is the resurrection and the life. Martha was challenged that if she believed, she will witness the glory of God. Martha's profession of faith that Jesus is the Messiah, the Son of God, whose coming was expected, was the necessary human faith-condition for the miracle of raising Lazarus from the dead (Jn 11:20–45).

It is important that we converse with Jesus about our situation. The Divine Physician is the only One who can set us free and give us abundant life. He makes no mistakes nor does He engage in guess work. This is His specific mandate from the Father: that all who have faith in Him would receive healing and life. Jesus' specialty is to set the captives free. It is for this reason that He was anointed by the Holy Spirit (Lk 4:18). When we relate our problems to Jesus, we are responding to His invitation to come to Him with our burdens and sufferings to receive His healing and rest (Mt 11:28).

As we dialogue with God, we listen attentively to what He might say. This dialogue helps us to see the situation from God's perspective. God's perspective is the right perspective. When we see from God's point of view, we will never be afraid or discouraged. In relating to our Lord, listening is crucial for us. This is the contemplative approach; it inspires in us the faith necessary to receive healing.

Faith, Paul says, comes through hearing God's Word (Rom 10:17). Listening is receiving. Listening opens the door of our hearts to healing, life and wholeness. "Listen, that you may have life" (Is 55:3). As we acknowledge, investigate and talk to Jesus, we are discerning and gaining deeper understanding about our bondage at the same time. Jesus in the process encourages and gives us hope. It is greater suffering when, in our suffering, we know not why we suffer, because we are in the dark.

Receive God's love through repentance

Repentance opens our hearts to receive God's healing love. Jesus is full of grace and truth (Jn 1:14), and the fullness of divinity resides in Him (Col 1:19). Through Jesus, God desires to give us everything if only we are open to receive Him.

There is an emphasis on receptivity in our journey of family healing; it is the necessary condition for healing. Receiving from God is the highest and most fruitful human activity. For this reason, repentance is crucial in the healing process. Jesus preached repentance (Mk 1:15), and He sends us out to preach repentance also. The fruitfulness of the New Evangelization depends on our commitment to preach, and our response to the call to repentance. Repentance is the key to interior spiritual renewal and healing. Jesus gathered His Twelve Apostles and, after investing them with authority over unclean spirits, sent them out two by two. They went everywhere and preached repentance; they drove out many demons and healed the sick by anointing them with oil (Mk 6:7, 12–13).

The Archangel Gabriel said to Mary, "Hail, full of grace" (Lk 1:28). In her sinlessness, Mary received all that God gave her. The Blessed Virgin is a sign of receptivity for all of us. She is the sign prophesied in Isaiah 7:14. She shows us how to receive God's gifts as Virgin, i.e., humble and open.

Sin blocks our hearts from receiving God's life and healing. Generationally transmitted bondage can also block our hearts from receiving healing, since at some level, human free will is involved. Hurts and painful memories of early childhood, which can create deep within us belief systems of unforgiveness, self-hatred, anger, and inherited negative dispositions that hinder our ability to receive God's unconditional love, can also block our hearts. To deepen the grace of receptivity in us, our Lord enjoins us to "Come away by yourselves to a deserted place and rest a while" (Mk 6:31). Silent retreats are highly beneficial in addressing these interior blocks that limit our ability to listen and receive God's love. The commonest symptom that shows we are not receiving God's love in prayer is that we are not hearing God's voice. Jesus said His sheep hear His voice, and they follow Him (Jn 10:27). We need the receptive spiritual disposition of Samuel: "Speak, LORD, for your servant is listening" (1 Sam 3:9).

Saint John says, "Those who received him, who believed in his name, he gave power to become children of God" (Jn 1:12). It is important that we invest ourselves in receiving God's love. God's love empowers us to pursue the truth in the process of healing, and be witnesses of the truth. By it, we boast only in the Cross of our Lord Jesus Christ, and have strength for everything. It is in God's love that we are fulfilled in our true identity as sons and daughters. This identity of ours as the Father's adopted children is received. It is a gift to be cherished. We are created to receive God until we are filled to capacity and become saints. Jesus said, "If you knew the gift of God… you would have asked him, and he would have given you living water" (Jn 4:10). To have this receptive disposition is to choose the better part like Mary, who sat at Jesus' feet and listened to His words (Jn 10:39, 42).

Before His Ascension into Heaven, Jesus promised the Apostles: "You will receive power when the Holy Spirit has come upon you, and you will be my witnesses in Jerusalem and in all Judea and Samaria, and to the end of the earth" (Acts 1:8, ESV). We need the power of the Holy Spirit to take the necessary remedial action when faced with bondage. This power comes through prayer, the power to fight and take back what the enemy has stolen from us—our identity and freedom. We cannot draw back.

Repentance: turning away from sin, and turning toward God

Sin opens the door to bondage and puts us under the slavery of Satan and the demons. Healing and release from bondage comes when we repent from evil and choose the truth. Bondage occurs by an act of the will; repentance leading to healing is also an act of the will. True repentance means we resolve to move away from the source and occasions that exposed us to sin, and embrace God's mercy through the Gospel.

Repentance reconnects us with the compassionate love of the Father. The Father is always open to the sinner; He draws close to the burdened sinner through Christ's Passion and offers His gift of mercy and freedom. Through repentance, the sinner reciprocates the Father's compassionate love in his openness to receive Divine Mercy. In repentance, the sinner is lifted up in Christ to the degree of the Father's descent in love to the sinner, because by it, he demonstrates humility—the principal virtue that defines the legacy of the saints. "The LORD supports all who fall and raises all who are bowed down" (Ps 145:14).

Repentance brings with it the fruit of conversion of heart. As the Father is defined by His compassionate love, the sinner is defined by his repentant love. This is the positive and negative encounter of love that makes us saints, the marriage of the Almighty with the weak sinful humanity which produces a synergy of Paschal life giving union. Paschal love, which unites God and man in Christ, generates the energy of merciful love that heals wounded souls.

Life giving repentance breeds self-confidence, which is free of the side effects of self-pity or shame. Here, the soul knows that God is greater than her heart and sins (1 Jn 3:20). Repentance inspires courage and faith that conquers the world. God's power to forgive the sinner is matched by the sinner's capacity to receive His mercy. When this happens, the sinner is healed, God is glorified, and the angels of God rejoice that a sinner has come to salvation (Lk 15:10).

Sin, a free act of the will, is always opposed to God. It breeds fear and produces guilt. It cuts our friendship with God and the life of grace we have in Christ Jesus. Repentance brings forgiveness of sins; it reconciles and restores our friendship with God. Jesus forgives our sins in the Confession. But the punishment due to sin may still have to be paid for. Contrition or sorrow for sin is required for absolution to be validly granted and for the forgiveness of our sins. When a penitent has perfect contrition, that is, moved by love for God, venial sins are remitted, and mortal sins as well, only if the penitent has the firm resolve to have recourse to sacramental confession as soon as is possible,[391] and also firmly resolves not to sin again. The priest, in the Sacrament of Confession, grants us absolution by which God through the Church infuses our souls with sanctifying grace turning us back to God. But God's grace is effective in us and bears fruit when we cooperate with it; God's grace does not force our will. The story of the sinful woman who washed Jesus' feet with her tears illustrates this point (Lk 7:36–8:3). Imperfect contrition does not obtain the forgiveness of grave sin, because it is motivated by the ugliness of sin, and the fear of Hell.[392] It is emotion-based and so does not restore our friendship with God.

The desire to love God which is at the heart of contrition must find expression also in the desire to love our neighbor, more so, our own family. John the Evangelist reminds us that a true test of God's love is how much we love our fellow human beings. To profess to love God without loving our neighbor is false. Charity must always be the first law on earth; it is the first law in Heaven. Every person is a living image of God. To love everyone is to acknowledge the Creator of them all (1 Jn 4:20–21). On the issue of love and forgiveness of neighbor, the Lord Jesus allows no compromise (Mt 6:14–15; 18:21–35; Mk 11:25–26). Let us strive to love unconditionally.

When we have repented and experienced the grace of conversion, we become a new creation, and we can say with Paul, it is no longer I but Christ living in me (Gal 2:20). A heart totally converted and immersed in Christ ceases to be a conduit for the transmission of the evil effects of sin and bondage across generations (Eze 18:14). Such a heart becomes rather an instrument of healing of the bloodlines from which it takes its root. Such is the power of repentance in generational and personal healing. In his Catechetical instructions, Saint Cyril of Jerusalem stresses the point on repentance: "Like a dry tree which puts forth shoots when watered, the soul bears the fruit of holiness when repentance has made it worthy of receiving the Holy Spirit."[393]

In family healing ministry, we can speak of two responses to the presence of two kinds of evil, which create bondage. The first is a personal *repentance* directed at personal sins. Jesus began His public ministry of preaching and healing by calling us to freedom through repentance: "The time is fulfilled, and the kingdom of God is at hand; repent and believe in the gospel" (Mk 1:15, ESV). The personal sin for which we need to repent corresponds to the first kind of evil mentioned in the Lord's Prayer: "Forgive us our trespasses, as we forgive those who trespass against us." *Deliverance* is the second response to the presence of evil entities—Satan and the demons. This evil requires that we pray for deliverance as Jesus taught us to pray: "Father, deliver us from evil."[394]

It is important to Jesus that we be free of spiritual contamination and bondage. He emphasized this in His priestly prayer to the Father on the eve of His Passion: "My prayer is not that you take them out of the world but that you protect them from the evil one" (Jn 17:15, NIV). Jesus does not want our unnecessary meddling with evil spirits. Evil spirits are wicked and nasty creatures. They are committed to our eternal destruction, and they are sworn enemies of God. Evil spirits are attracted to us by negativity and spiritual pollution—sin. In the Family Healing Retreats, we pray for forgiveness and freedom from sin and evil by invoking the holy name of our Lord and Savior Jesus Christ, our Commander-in-Chief. We also use the double-edged sword of repentance and deliverance to wage spiritual war against the enemy of our souls.

When we celebrate the Sacrament of Penance, our personal sins are forgiven. As part of the Family Healing Retreats, I encourage participants to celebrate this healing Sacrament as often as they can. In addition, they can relate to Jesus through the priest, any generational sins and evils they have become aware of through the investigation process, and how these might be affecting them or tempting them to sin. The effect of the power of the sacrifice of the Lamb at Calvary during Mass affects families and generations and the Church, because it is the action of "God, our savior, who wills everyone to be saved and come to the knowledge of the truth" (1 Tim 2:3–4).

We belong to the Mystical Body of Christ. If a member of this body suffers, all members are affected (1 Cor 12:18–27). When we celebrate the Sacraments, their effects transcend our personal spiritual space. When we offer the Holy Sacrifice of the Mass, the graces of the Mass affect in some positive way, all who are redeemed by Christ. The words of Saint Padre Pio say more: "It is easier for this world to exist without the Sun than without the Mass."

At every Mass, the faithful pray in reparation for any sins of our ancestors. We do this in imitation of several Old Testament figures, who made confessions and intercessions employing God's mercy for "our fathers." Among them were Daniel, Tobit, and Esther. Jesus knows our hearts; He only can respond to our heart's deepest cry in such intercessions.

Generational intercession for the sins of our ancestors can be seen in the larger context of enriching the spiritual blessings of our generations, living and deceased. During the Eucharistic Sacrifice of the Mass or the praying of the Holy Rosary, the Chaplet of Divine Mercy or in our private prayer petitions to God, we should do whatever we deem necessary to besiege God's mercy for our families. We can be creative in responding to situations of this nature, remembering that God counts on us to pray for our ancestors, who may not yet have reached their home in Heaven. We can offer indulgenced prayers of the Church for them or draw on the treasury of prayers of holy mother Church for the benefit of our ancestors. We are the ambassadors of our ancestors; let us represent them well here by commending them to God. And may the Holy Spirit open to us new frontiers of intercession for ourselves and our generations.

Sin and evil spirits block personal and family healing. When that is the case, they must be removed for healing to be received: sin, through repentance and confession, and evil spirits, through prayer and deliverance. Evil spirits obey only Jesus; they do not obey people. However, Jesus has given us authority over them, as the Scriptures make it clear: to the twelve (Lk 9:1), to the seventy-two (Lk 10:19), and to all believers (Mk 16:17). The Church's ministers are able to bind and cast them out in the name of Jesus from those under their grip. In this way, we are able to live out the new life of the Resurrection in Christ, where, as Paul says, the old order has passed away and all is now new (2 Cor 5:17).

Sin, spiritual contamination, and bondage disrupt our relationship with God, and make our journey to perfection unfulfilled, but only if we do not repent. In his treatises on Christian perfection, Saint Gregory of Nyssa says: "Christian perfection consists in sharing the titles which express the meaning of Christ's name; we bring out this meaning in our minds, our prayer and our way of life."[395] The Christian life with its three distinguishing aspects: thoughts, words and deeds, must reflect this perfection.[396] Spiritual contamination and bondage affect all three aspects, and can potentially roll back our progress in perfection.

Take action (faith demands action)

A critical stage in family healing ministry is when we have to take action. Faith demands we do something, and we need courage to do it. We need the same strength and courage that was given to Daniel when the Lord's servant visited him and said: "Fear not, beloved, you are safe; take courage and be strong" (Dan 10:19). We need to take the kind of action that God demanded of Moses as he led the Israelites out of slavery in Egypt. As they were stranded by the Red Sea, Moses got busy preaching to the Israelites: "Do not be afraid. Stand firm and you will see the deliverance the Lord will bring you today. The Egyptians you see today you will never see again. The Lord will fight for you; you need only to be still" (Ex 14:13–14, NIV). But the Lord interrupted Moses' pep talk and said: "Why are you crying out to me? Tell the Israelites to move on. Raise your staff and stretch out your hand over the sea to divide the water so that the Israelites can go through the sea on dry ground" (Ex 14:15–16, NIV). This is God's power in action, and at its best. Our God is the God of action. He is the God of power and might!

In Genesis 1:3, God said, "'Let there be light;' and there was light." The Gospels reveal Jesus as a Man of action. He said to the man with a withered hand, "Stretch out your hand" (Mt 12:13). He did, and his hand was restored. To the unclean spirit in a man, Jesus said, "Be still, and come out of him" (Mk 1:25), and it happened. To Lazarus who had been dead for four days, Jesus "cried with a loud voice, 'Lazarus, come out!' The dead man came out" (Jn 11:43).

We need action in the Church today and not just theological talk. Our God is not a talkative God. He is the God of power and might. Paul showed God's power in his ministry. He said,

> For I determined not to know anything among you except Jesus Christ and Him crucified. I was with you in weakness, in fear, and in much trembling. And my speech and my preaching were not with persuasive words of human wisdom, but in demonstration of the Spirit and of power, that your faith should not be in the wisdom of men but in the power of God (1 Cor 2:2–5, NKJV).

Christians today are called to this demonstration of God's power by their lives of faith. Generational and personal healing demands faith-based action. We are called to exercise this faith-power in our daily lived experience of Christianity. Because of the mystery of the Incarnation, we have a formidable baptismal-priestly identity that is able to draw down God's healing power and destroy the strongholds of darkness and evil in our families. This power is in the name of Jesus Christ. It is in the name of Jesus that we renounce and repent of our sins, destroy any pacts with the evil one, break bondages, bind and cast out demons, and are healed. We should call on the assistance of the Archangels Saint Michael—Prince of the Heavenly Hosts, Saint Raphael—Medicine of God and Defender of Family Life, and Saint Gabriel—Herald of the Incarnation and Strength of God; our holy Guardian Angels and all the Angels and Saints. We need to invoke the unfailing and maternal intercession of the Blessed Virgin Mary, the Immaculate Conception. Demons cannot bear her presence, because her holiness is a crushing defeat for them.

Sin, which occurs through the deception of the devil, leads to bondage. As a rule of thumb therefore, it is normal in dealing with spiritual contamination, addictions, and other bondage situations, that we renounce any agreements we or our ancestors may have made with the evil one. In renouncing these agreements, it is customary to do so three times to render them null and void. We renounce them three times because evil spirits act to mock the Blessed Trinity. Things that can be renounced include: agreements/pacts, death-wishes, occult or new age involvement of any kind; thoughts, words and actions that are done against God and His truth, denial of the true faith. We may use these or similar words:

In the name of Jesus Christ, I renounce any pacts, death-wish, the occult, etc. that I (or any members of my family and family trees) have made with the evil one in any way (pray three times).

Every agreement or pacts we make with the evil one through deception is binding until voided (see Col 2:14). This is because our free will is involved. Such pacts compromise our covenant relationship with our loving Father, which is ratified in the Precious Blood of Jesus Christ. By this blood covenant, we belong to God exclusively as His treasure, and the apple of His eye. Baptism confers on Christians a fundamental indelible identity and character that grounds us in God as His beloved children. At baptism Christ's light destroys the darkness of sin in us. Through Baptism, "He rescued us from the power of darkness and transferred us into the kingdom of his beloved Son, in whom we have redemption, the forgiveness of sins" (Col 1:13).

By renouncing any agreements with the evil one, we distance ourselves from our past errors and choose anew to submit to the Lordship of Jesus Christ. Through this renunciation, we agree with Paul that: righteousness and lawlessness, light and darkness, Christ and Beliar, a believer and an unbeliever, the temple of God and the temple of idols, have nothing in common. We are the living temple of the Holy Spirit who is within us; God has chosen/consecrated us as His people and pledged to be our God (2 Cor 6:14–16; Jn 15:16).

Jesus is the one who reveals the identity and mission of Satan. He said Satan is a liar. He comes to steal our identity, to destroy the image and likeness of God in us, and slaughter our spiritual lives so that we become empty, worthless and miserable victims, cut off from the vine and ready to be cast into the fire, like the withered branch that is gathered and thrown into the fire (Jn 15:6).

Renunciation may also happen as part of repentance. If we are in bondage and have made any pacts with the evil one, this must first be renounced. Next, we should renounce any agreements our ancestors may have entered into with the evil one which allowed him to keep us in bondage (if we are not sure, it is safe to renounce them anyway).

In the first case of renouncing personal pacts with the evil one, we are following the biblical principle that what we sow is what we reap. Adam and Eve made a grave choice in obeying Satan rather than God. Similarly, we can make choices that bring either death and doom or life and prosperity (Deut 30:15). In the second case of renouncing possible pacts made by our ancestors with evil, we are applying the biblical principle that our actions can free our dead relatives from the bondage of sin. The Church encourages us to pray for the dead that they may be loosed from their sins. In the Book of Maccabees, Judas and his army prayed to the Lord that the sinful deed of his associates might be blotted out completely (2 Mac 12:42). The sinful deed committed in this case was that his fallen comrades had made a pact with false gods. Found under the tunic of each of the dead, were amulets sacred to the idols of Jamnia, which the law forbids Jews to wear (2 Mac 12:40). It is important to state that this renunciation cannot be merely lip service. It must be made in faith and from the heart, in the name of Jesus, for it to void any pacts with demons.

Once pacts have been renounced, we must break any armor the demons often use to protect themselves against expulsion. Demonic armor may include: *seals, curses, covenants, consecrations, hexes, spells, (and all demonic bondage)*, and so on.

In 1 Samuel 17:5–7, we read the story of the Philistine—Goliath of Gath, who represents Satan. He was dressed in armor from head to toe: his head covered in a bronze helmet, he wore a heavy bronze corselet of scale armor and bronze greaves, and had a bronze scimitar slung from a baldric. The shaft of his javelin was like a weaver's heddle-bar with a heavy iron head. The little David on the other hand, depended on God for his protection; he would not wear any human armor. He showed his faith in God in these words: "The Lord who delivered me from the paw of the lion and from the paw of the bear will deliver me from the hand of this Philistine" (1 Sam 17:37, ESV). David concluded, "You come to me with a sword and with a spear and with a javelin, but I come to you in the name of the Lord of hosts, the God of the armies of Israel, whom you have defied" (1 Sam 17:45, ESV). David hurled one of his five stones with his sling which tore through Goliath's armor and killed him (1 Sam 17:49). Demonic armor must always be broken three times in the name of Jesus as explained earlier. We may use these or similar words to break all demonic armor; which should only be prayed for and by oneself, and not over another person:

In the name of Jesus Christ, I break all seals, curses, covenants, spells, hexes and any other demonic armor or bondage present on (silently mention manes)(pray three times).

I worked with a young man who made a pact with a demonic spirit disguising itself as a friend when he was a young boy. He became familiar with this spirit and regarded it as a true companion. But the spirit was making his life very miserable; he had been deceived into entering into agreements with this demonic spirit. The Holy Spirit revealed that over the years, the demons had built a fortress inside this person to protect themselves. When I began breaking the demonic armor around him silently, the demon(s) reacted and spoke angrily and sharply through the man and said, "Stop that!" Well, but I do not obey demons; I obey only Jesus Christ. So I had to silence the demon(s) as I continued the ministry, and they obeyed. Demons have no choice but to obey Jesus.

Demons will always back down whenever they encounter the power of God in a person; they have no choice but to back down. They are completely helpless when they encounter God's power in a person. You may be tempted to doubt whether anything really happened during the breaking of demonic armor. Well! Be assured that faith does not fail; Jesus Christ is truly Lord of all. He said, "All power in heaven and on earth has been given to me" (Mt 28:18). Something truly does happen! The Holy Spirit is at work, and He is faithful. If we are observant we may see some signs that something really did happen, but it is not necessary that you see. Just believe it! This is faith—to believe without seeing and without doubting.

After breaking the demonic armor, we proceed to call on Saint Michael the Archangel to bind the evil spirits and to render them inactive, and to cast them out in the name of Jesus. We can also do this ourselves if we are equipped and empowered to do so. As was stated earlier, the Church forbids the laity to take action directly against evil spirits when praying over others. Please refer to Chapter 5 to learn more about basic spiritual warfare.

We receive power when the Spirit of the Lord comes upon us

It is not enough to silence, bind, and cast out evil spirits; the job is not finished yet. It is far more important to pray for the infilling of the Holy

Spirit to restore wholeness and heal us. The Holy Spirit is the Lord who brings freedom (2 Cor 3:17). We invoke the Spirit to fall afresh on us and our families and to renew us in body, mind and spirit. It is important to call on the Spirit to fill areas and aspects of us and our families vacated by evil spirits. Healing happens when the Spirit of Jesus comes upon us. The Spirit is the Life Giver; the flesh means nothing (Jn 6:63). Spiritual contamination and bondage create spiritual wounds in us, and the Holy Spirit is the Balm that heals these wounds. He gives new life and makes us new creation in Christ.

The Holy Spirit is the Lord and Giver of life. This is an article of our Christian faith. The exercise of life-giving repentance by which our sins are forgiven fundamentally opens the door of our hearts to the in-filling of the Holy Spirit. Sin, the basis of all human suffering and bondage[397] blocks the sanctifying graces of the Holy Spirit from being experienced in our lives. This in-filling with the Holy Spirit is like a homecoming for the families set free from bondage. The Holy Spirit, the *Ruah*—the life-breath of God in us, comes to rest in us, so that we can now live and move and have our being in God again (Acts 17:28). Freedom in the Holy Spirit makes us docile and faithful listeners to God, so that we can attain the perfection of Christ Jesus. Paul said, "Those who are led by the Spirit of God are children of God" (Rom 8:14). When we are filled with the Spirit, we no longer listen to the lies and deceptions of the devil that lead us astray, but only to the truth that is from God, which sets us free.

The Holy Spirit does not force His presence upon us. He always seeks our consent and never violates our free will. We have to pray and invite Him to fall afresh on us as the Apostles, united with our Blessed Mother, did after the Ascension of the risen Lord Jesus. Nothing in our Christian life is automatic. We have to freely invoke the Holy Spirit. The gift of free will is a sign of God's committed love and openness to us. Humanity did not lose the power of free will after the fall of Adam and Eve, so that we might exercise it and choose God anew and be healed and be saved.

The evil one, on the other hand, never seeks our free consent. Rather, he looks for ways to violate our free will with brute force whenever he can. Most times his actions are subtle and deceptive; he customizes his temptations and attacks us depending on who we are, our strengths and weaknesses, and our likes and dislikes. The destruction or distortion of our true identity and dignity as God's beloved children is the principal goal of demons. If the enemy succeeds, he leaves us empty and confused; we are filled with guilt and shame, and we may even question the existence of God and challenge His Commandments; we even question the teachings and authority of the Church. But we must realize that the Church is the mystical Body of Christ.

When we are filled afresh with the Promise of the Father, the Holy Spirit, we know we are at home within ourselves and at peace with God. We experience the peace that surpasses understanding (Phil 4:7), and we begin to enjoy the honor of truly being called children of God.

Pope Emeritus, Benedict XVI after the Mass of Pentecost in 2008, called on the faithful to rediscover the value of being baptized in the Holy Spirit. He said, "In effect, Jesus' whole mission was aimed at giving the Spirit of God to men and baptizing them in the 'bath' of regeneration." The Holy Father continued, "The Spirit of God was poured out in a super-abundant way, like a waterfall able to purify every heart, to extinguish the flames of evil and ignite the fire of divine love in the world."[398] The Pope concluded, "This baptism in the Holy Spirit [has] personal and communal dimensions..."[399]

The presence of the Holy Spirit in generational healing restores family unity. He repairs the altar and sanctuary of the family as God's dwelling place where holiness can again begin to flourish. Family prayer in the Holy Spirit, practiced in silence and solitude, fosters a genuine *Contemplative Approach to Generational Healing,* as it trains our focus and attention on Jesus Christ. We learn to surrender to Him in all things, and make Him the Lord of our families. We are called as a family to surrender and die to ourselves so that Christ may live in us. When we listen and submit to Jesus, we become more open to the inspiration and infilling of His Spirit.

Saint John the Baptist yielded and submitted to Jesus and allowed himself to baptize the Savior and the Author of Life. His surrender gave Jesus the full freedom to be the God that He is. The result was that the Holy Spirit descended like a dove, and the Father spoke in testimony about His Son.[400] When we submit to Jesus, we experience the fullness of God as Trinity.

Here is a traditional prayer of invocation of the Holy Spirit:

Come Holy Spirit, and fill the hearts of your faithful; and enkindle in them the fire of your love. Send forth Your Spirit and they shall be created. And You shall renew the face of the earth.

Let us pray:
O, God, whom by the light of the Holy Spirit, did instruct the hearts of Your faithful, grant that in the same Spirit we may be truly wise and ever rejoice in His consolations. Through the same Christ Our Lord. Amen.

When we receive the Holy Spirit we rejoice in God as our Blessed Mother did. Her soul proclaimed the Lord's greatness, and her spirit rejoiced in her Savior (Lk 1:46–47). The Virgin Mary proclaimed and rejoiced in God always, because her soul and spirit were never wounded by sin, even from the first moment of her conception. Nothing in her limits God's greatness from being manifested through her. She is full of grace. She is the Immaculate Conception. She lived and reached the fullest expression of God possible for a human creature. Her union with God was so intense that Duff, the founder of the Legion of Mary, wrote: "May we not validly reason that Mary is made and meant to display to us a likeness to the Holy Spirit analogous."[401] By baptism, we are not only called to this same likeness to God, it has been given to us. Frank Duff says that our Blessed Mother can be seen, in a far inferior sense relative to the Incarnation of the Son of God, as the incarnation of the Holy Spirit, just as Jesus is, in the fullest sense, the incarnation of the Second Person of the Blessed Trinity.[402]

When we have invoked and received the Holy Spirit, our rejoicing will witness to the fruit of the Spirit in us and in our families: charity, joy, peace, patience, kindness, goodness, generosity, gentleness, faithfulness, modesty, self-control, and chastity (Gal 5:22–23).

Gratitude and praise

It is a great virtue to be grateful for all things. Every gift, every healing, and every grace received, begs for gratitude. We owe God gratitude not only for everything, but especially for our lives. *God is good!* Healing should never be taken for granted; it comes at the great cost of the life of the Son of God.

Jesus teaches us the value of giving thanks for God's favors in the story of the ten lepers who were cleansed. Only one of them, the Samaritan, returned giving thanks and glorifying God. Jesus said, "Has none but this foreigner returned to give thanks to God?" Then he said to him, "Stand up and go; your faith has saved you" (Lk 17:18–19). Faith motivates us to give thanks and praise. Faith saves. Gratitude is faith. Many Psalms help us cultivate this attitude of gratitude. These are the Thanksgiving Psalms: 18, 30, 33, 100, 116, 118, 138, and 147. By His personal example, Jesus invites us to give praise and thanks to the Father for all things. "I give praise to you, Father, Lord of heaven and earth" (Mt 11:25).

Gratitude fosters a deeper healing experience and opens our hearts to receive more of God. God is grateful when we respond to His call; His generosity knows no limits. Jesus' ultimate thanksgiving to the Father was His sacrifice on the Cross for our salvation. *Eucharistia,* which is Greek for Thanksgiving, is at the heart of the Christian celebration of the mystery of

Christ. In the Holy Eucharist, Christ places His life in the Father's hands that all creation might be renewed in Him. To give thanks and praise for God's gifts is a sign of deep humility and surrender to God. Paul lived a life of gratitude, constantly giving thanks in all his letters (Rom 1:8; 6:17; 7:25; 1 Cor 1:4; 14:17; 2 Cor 2:14; Phil 1:3; Col 1:3). We do not need to see the fruit of our prayers of healing before we give thanks to God the Father. True and unconditional gratitude is a sign of great faith and a trust that God is always pleased to confirm in His own time to those who believe.

To live out the thanksgiving of Jesus to the Father, the sacrifice of the Holy Mass is always celebrated as the central mystery and event during Family Healing Retreats. There is no healing for anyone in this world apart from this ultimate sacrifice of Jesus Christ. Every healing comes from the Cross of Jesus Christ, even the healing of those who do not acknowledge Jesus Christ as Lord. He is their Lord anyway, only that they are in denial or are ignorant. Everyone belongs to Jesus Christ, because all things were created through Him and for Him (Col 1:16). "All things were made through him, and without him was not anything made that was made. In him was life, and the life was the light of men. The light shines in the darkness, and the darkness has not overcome it" (Jn 1:3–5, ESV).

Now let us "give thanks to the Lord, for he is good, for his mercy endures forever" (Dan 3:89).

Reparation

When we conclude the family healing retreats and resume our normal lives, we are reminded that the journey of faith continues; we are not finished yet. We make amends for the harm done by sin which opened the door to bondage. Atonement for sin is made by prayer and penance. By these same means, we make repairs for sins done to others by restoring to the other what was damaged. Reparation and satisfaction are essential when we have been forgiven by God for our sins.[403] "For a total repentance, it is not enough to be sorry and to receive the remission of faults. It is also necessary that reparation be made for the disorder provoked by sin, a disorder that usually continues after the sin."[404]

Spiritual wounds, just as physical wounds, take time to heal. The human spirit cannot stand alone; it seeks to attach to a higher spirit power. The human spirit finds itself sandwiched, as it were, between two spiritual beings: the Spirit of God together with the Angelic spirits, and the evil spirits. We are created for God and for God alone. We came from God and are destined to return to God. Because the human spirit seeks to unite with a higher spirit—God's Spirit, it can be deceived and become attached to demonic spirits, hence the need for discernment in the spiritual life.

John the Evangelist cautions us not to trust every spirit. We must discern every spirit to know which ones are of God (1 Jn 4:1). Jesus said the evil one comes to steal, slaughter and destroy. So we must be vigilant. It is healthy, healing and necessary for our spirit to attach and be possessed by the Holy Spirit. But the human spirit becomes wounded, damaged, and sick when it makes contact with or is affected by evil spirits. When this happens, the human person needs healing, because the human person is created both body and spirit. If the damage or wound to our spirit is deep, just as when we sustain deep physical wounds or injuries, healing will take time depending on the seriousness of the wound. It follows that the deeper one is immersed in false spirituality or evil behavior, such as New Age, occult, immoral lifestyles, etc., the deeper the damage to one's spirit.

Reparation opens the door of our hearts for the healing of the wounds of sin. The importance of this act of faith was stressed in the Fatima apparitions in 1917. In addition to asking the visionaries to pray the holy Rosary daily, our Lady requested that they bear sufferings and hardships in *reparation* for the many offenses committed against her Son and her Immaculate Heart. Two popular Fatima prayers carry this message:

Most Holy Trinity—Father, Son and Holy Spirit—I adore Thee profoundly. I offer Thee the most precious Body, Blood, Soul and Divinity of Jesus Christ, present in all the tabernacles of the world, in *reparation* for all the outrages, sacrileges, and indifferences by which He is offended. By the infinite merits of the Most Sacred Heart of Jesus and the Immaculate Heart of Mary, I beg of Thee for the conversion of poor sinners.[405]

The second prayer: "Oh my Jesus, I offer this for love of Thee, for the conversion of sinners, and in *reparation* for the sins committed against the Immaculate Heart of Mary."[406]

Our Lady also asked for the Communion of Reparation on the First Saturdays to avert the spread of error and much suffering. She wants people to stop offending God. And she promised, "In the end, My Immaculate Heart will triumph."

God's peace plan for the healing of the world as revealed through the Fatima apparitions, and our personal and generational healing, involves making reparation to the Sacred Heart for sins.

Obstacles to receiving healing

Unbelief

Unbelief is contrary and opposed to faith; it works against our prayer and healing. We must believe in God as a disposition of the interior life to receive His gifts. Elizabeth praised Mary's faith in these words: "Blessed are you who believed that what was spoken to you by the Lord would be fulfilled" (Lk 1:45). Mary's faith opened the door for God's Word to become flesh in her. Unbelief makes impossible and fruitless all of God's possibilities in a soul. God is generous and does not ration His graces on those who ask Him for favors. After all Jesus promised, whatever we ask in His name, "I will do it" (Jn 14:13–14; 15:7; 16). Ask and you shall receive. But we must ask in faith, believing that what we ask for we will receive, "for the one who doubts is like a wave of the sea that is driven and tossed by the wind" (Jam 1:6, ESV).

Because of unbelief, Jesus did not work miracles in Nazareth, His home town (Mt 13:57). He stressed the importance of believing to His disciples: "Therefore I tell you, whatever you ask in prayer, believe that you have received it, and it will be yours" (Mk 11:24, ESV). To reinforce this further in the hearts of His disciples, Jesus appeared to them and rebuked them for not believing the reality of His resurrection (Mk 16:14). When we struggle with unbelief, we can pray with the Centurion: "I do believe, help my unbelief" (Mk 9:24).

Unforgiveness

God desires to heal us more than we desire to be healed. He desires our freedom in the deepest possible way, if only we are open and free from the blockage of unforgiveness. Jesus wants our joy to be complete, and for us to have fullness of life. It is impossible for God to hold back His love from us. The love the Father has for Jesus is the same love He has for us. Our journey with God is one of freedom. Love is about being totally free in God. Saint Augustine tells us to love God, and do all things.

Peter, concerned with the problem of unforgiveness, asked Jesus how often he must forgive his brother, "As many as seven times?" (Mt 18:21). Jesus said, "Not seven times, but seventy-seven times" (Mt 18:22). By His response, Jesus taught that we should not keep count of how often we forgive others. We simply keep forgiving until He comes back. We have been forgiven immeasurably by God. We should forgive; else, the Father will not forgive our offenses (Mt 6:15).

Forgiveness is a choice we must make; it is not a feeling. It cannot be forced or imposed on another. It must be given freely for it to bear the fruit of freedom. Unforgiveness is also a free act that can potentially block our hearts to receive God's love and healing; it can create bondage. Unforgiveness wraps itself around our hearts and blinds us spiritually to the reality of God's love.

I directed a woman on retreat. She was in deep pain because her heart was blocked. She was connected and hearing the Lord. But unforgiveness laid buried deep in her heart. As a little girl she had been abused by a father-figure in her life, and he had long passed on to eternity. Seeing her pain, I asked if she had forgiven him. She replied, "Oh yes! Several times." I then invited her to pray for him so he can have peace and go to heaven. Instinctively, she replied, "Oh no!" I repeated the question in a different way, to make sure she understood me. She replied the same: "Oh no!

This is how stubborn and deadly unforgiveness can be. It can wrap itself around our hearts and drains us of divine life. I had to intercede for this woman for the grace to let go of past hurts. The Lord Jesus in His mercy did grant her the grace of freedom.

I had a dream on one of my retreats some years ago. In it, I was sitting opposite my father in a discussion. My mother was seated on one side between us. Suddenly, I stood up and charged at my father (he passed on many years ago). My mother got up and stood in my way; she held me. When I awoke, I was shocked by this dream, because in real life I could never imagine myself doing such a thing.

I took it to prayer and journaled with Jesus about it. It was clear to me I had anger, resentment, and unforgiveness deep in my heart toward my father for various hurtful experiences of childhood. Childhood memories of hurts and unforgiveness were surfacing in this dream that needed to be resolved. I was thankful to God for showing them to me. My religious formation during this time as an Intercessor of the Lamb in the area of inner healing, equipped me to know what to do. I was faced with a choice: to forgive and be free, or to hold onto unforgiveness and remain in bondage. This was a moment of decision, and God will not decide for me. I began the process of unconditionally forgiving my father for all the memories of painful events as far as I could recall.

Forgiveness is not an option; it is not a feeling either. It is a command from our Lord Jesus Christ to us. Not to forgive is to fail in charity. Love is at the heart of the Commandments. "Love the Lord your God with all your heart, with all your soul, with all your mind, and with all your strength" (Mk 12:30, NET). Jesus said, "Love one another just as I have loved you" (Jn 15:12, NET). "If you love me, you will keep my commandments" (Jn 14:15). Jesus loves and forgives us always and unconditionally. Jesus does not only forgive us, He also makes excuses for us before the Father: "Father, forgive them, they know not what they do" (Lk 23:34). We are called to forgive others and to excuse their faults.

Our Blessed Mother reiterates Jesus' teaching on love and forgiveness in a recent alleged message from her:

I know that you desire consolation and hope from me because I love you and intercede for you. I ask of you to unite with me in my Son and to be my apostles. For you to be able to do so, I am calling you, anew, to love. There is no love without prayer - there is no prayer without forgiveness because love is prayer - forgiveness is love. My children, God created you to love and you love so as to forgive. Every prayer that comes out of love unites you with my Son and the Holy Spirit, and the Holy Spirit illuminates you and makes you my apostles - apostles who will do everything they do in the name of the Lord.[407]

Fear

Fear can be a debilitating experience. It can prevent us from fulfilling our mission as disciples of Christ. Unhealthy and sickening fears arise from within us. When we are afraid, the right place to look for the answer is within ourselves, not outside of us. If we complain and blame and accuse others, or become angry and frustrated and fearful, we may harm ourselves and cave in under emotional distresses, while the underlying problem remain unresolved. We may also be looking in the wrong place for an answer. The truth is, when the person we blame for causing our fears and anger is gone, something else will trigger the fear in us, and we can be stuck in the bondage of blaming others. Even to the point that a fly buzzing around can cause us to snap and be fearful and angry, all because we never dealt with the root problem inside us. Such behavior can degenerate into a vicious circle of "everybody hates me," and so on.

All human beings are subject to certain innate fears: danger of falling (fear of heights), loud noises, and not being loved. These types of fears are caused by factors external to us. All other fears arise from within us. They come from memories of belief systems embedded in our subconscious mind (Chapter 14, Figure 5). Fear deprives us of interior freedom and peace, and keeps us in bondage.

Fear is a powerful weapon of the evil one to hold us captive. Whatever we are afraid of has power over us. God is not a God of fear (Rom 8:15; 1 Cor 2:12). Fear is never of God. Jesus constantly told His disciples, "Do not be afraid." God is love! John says that no one who is afraid is yet full of God's love (1 Jn 4:18). The antidote to fear is receiving God's love. The fullness of God's love in us drives all fear away (1 Jn 4:18).

Every fear in us is ultimately the fear of dying. We do not want to die. Only Jesus Christ came into this world to die. "The Son of Man did not come to be served, but to serve, and to give his life as a ransom for many" (Mt 20:28, NIV). Isaiah prophesied that the servant of God would suffer; He will be led to the slaughter, and He will be silent and will not open His mouth (Is 53:7). But by His wounds and His death, our fears will be healed (Is 53:5). Fear and anxieties will prevent us from saying yes to God; they will make us grow cold in our faith, and will choke God's word in us so that they bear no fruit (Mk 4:19). We must fight fear and not allow it to take root in our hearts. Fear will make us lukewarm and compromise with the world. It will turn us into cowards, who will not stand up for the truth of the Gospel of Jesus Christ, when He gives us the opportunity to witness (Lk 21:13).

Emotional wounds sustained in the womb and childhood can predispose us to a life of constant fear. We should investigate our fears by bringing them to Jesus in prayer, and allow Him to speak and minister to us. It is also important that we try to identify what we are afraid of. In prayer we should try to listen to our thoughts, feelings and desires. These three markers will alert us to the memories buried in our subconscious mind. Our dreams can help us identify our fears. In processing these dreams, we should reflect on how we felt both in the dream and when we awoke. We may want to keep track of what makes us afraid so we can pray to understand their roots, and then invoke the healing of the Holy Spirit. A knowledgeable spiritual director can be very helpful in dealing with our fears.

Negative emotions generally result from memories of past hurts where we have believed lies about ourselves. When we become aware of these desolating affective movements, we are encouraged to bring them to spiritual direction. Knowledgeable Spiritual guides can help directees resolve fear issues through inner healing in the Holy Spirit. We are encouraged to pray and journal with the Lord about these interior movements, as we try to understand their root causes, and through them grow in self-knowledge. We should strive for greater humility and allow God to love us unconditionally, by disposing ourselves properly to receive the Sacraments worthily and regularly, especially Penance and the Holy Eucharist.

Healthy friendships can be helpful in healing our fears, because they provide outlets to share and talk about our fears; they can be inlets to receive God's love and build up confidence in us. But some of us are terribly afraid that we would do all in our power to avoid letting others come too close to us, lest they see the skeletons in our closets that we don't want them to see. Such attitudes can be self-defeating and can 'stabilize' us in a state of perpetual bondage, and we may blame other things for our problems. A rediscovery of the value of regular Eucharistic adoration might help us seek and allow God's face to gaze upon us. We can join the psalmist now in prayer:

One thing I ask from the Lord, this only do I seek: that I may dwell in the house of the Lord all the days of my life, to gaze on the beauty of the Lord and to seek him in his temple. For in the day of trouble he will keep me safe in his dwelling; he will hide me in the shelter of his sacred tent and set me high upon a rock. Then my head will be exalted above the enemies who surround me; at his sacred tent I will sacrifice with shouts of joy; I will sing and make music to the Lord. Hear my voice when I call, Lord; be merciful to me and answer me. My heart says of you, "Seek his face!" Your face, Lord, I will seek (Ps 27:4–8, NIV).

Self-hatred

Self-hatred poses a serious block to healing, because people who hate themselves do not forgive themselves. Self-hatred manifests in its most serious and damaging form through our actions, by self-condemnation, self-abuse of different forms, and not seeing the goodness of God in ourselves and in others. It is not uncommon to find that sometimes our problems are rooted in self-hatred. You see, God is good. He made us very good, and gave us our beautiful bodies as gifts to care for. Our bodies are beautiful indeed. We should thank God daily for the gift of our bodies. The Second Person of the Blessed Trinity became a human being (Heb 2:14, 17). The Word became flesh and lived in our midst (Jn 1:14). Oh! What a gift to be human like Jesus. It is a tremendous privilege we have to be human; our humanity has been integrated into the very being of God because of the mystery of the Incarnation. God's love has been poured into human nature through the God-Man, Jesus Christ.

One time in my prayer, I heard these two words spoken directly into my heart by the Eternal Father: "sacred humanity." These words remained with me for several months as I contemplated them with amazement. I began to marvel at the depth of the Father's love for me, and for all His children. Saint Augustine said that God became man, that man might become God. We are destined to reproduce in our bodies the image of the Son of God. We are called to be holy and perfect in and through our bodies.

Unfortunately, sometimes we are so consumed and focused on ourselves that we even try to destroy ourselves. When someone is involved in the hatred of self-abuse, one can legitimately ask: "Why is he/she doing that?" Very often, this question startles us. But the answer that normally comes back is "I don't know!" This response shows a deep lack of self-knowledge. It is like someone ingesting cyanide and yet turns a blind eye to what will happen—death. Saint Paul would challenge us and remind us that our body is a temple to the Holy Spirit God gave us at Baptism. He warned that a person who destroys this temple of God, will in turn be destroyed by God who built it (1 Cor 3:17). Actions that show self-hatred also show a lack of self-knowledge. If we are in touch with our true identity as God's children, we will not engage in self-destructive behavior, because we will see ourselves as God sees us, and love ourselves as God loves us (Song 1:13–14). We should constantly pray for the grace to forgive ourselves and to love ourselves as God loves us. We cannot fulfill God's Commandments if we do not forgive and love ourselves as God forgives and loves us.

Lack of self-knowledge

This can result from and lead to spiritual blindness to the point that a person rationalizes sin and lives it as a lifestyle without the slightest remorse in offending God. Lack of self-knowledge can render someone insensitive to their real desires and needs, so that they do not know what they want, or what to ask for. Jesus asked Bartimaeus: "What do you want me to do for you?" (Mk 10:51). The blind man did not lack self-knowledge; he asked for the gift of sight, and he got it. If we do not know what we want, or what to ask for, because we are spiritually blind and lack self-knowledge, then we get nothing. Jesus said, "Ask and you shall receive." "Whatever you ask the Father in my name he will give you" (Jn 16:23). For more on self-knowledge see Chapter 4.

Self-will

Self-will is opposed to God's will; hence, it is not open to receive healing that only God gives. Self-will breeds unhealthy self-love, and it is motivated by pride. It always leads to disobedience and a lack of interior peace and freedom. Self-will comes from a false identity of who we truly are. In its grip, we become closed and locked in within ourselves and are unable to surrender to another, not even to God.

Healing requires that we surrender and be emptied, and to lower our defenses, so that we can experience the miraculous catch of fish. Jean-Pierre de Caussade says: "If we are truly docile, we will ask no questions about the road along which God is taking us." "God's action is boundless in its scope and power, but it can only fill our souls if we empty them of all false confidence in our own ability."[408] "If we do not concentrate entirely on doing the will of God we shall find neither happiness nor holiness, no matter what pious practices we adopt, however excellent they may be. If you are not satisfied with what God chooses for you, what else can please you?"[409]

Self-will renders us blind to the needs and gifts of the present moment, because we are too focused on attaining our own interests and not that of Christ. Self-will manifests as perfectionism, unnecessary and oppressive control over others and situations, imposing and bullying of others, and unhealthy monitoring and sniffing around to find fault with people, which creates distraction and restlessness; anger, rage, intimidation, and false accusations. Self-will can be subtle and deceptive; it can lie hidden behind a mask of "goodness," which when exposed to the light of truth, is not goodness at all. Self-will is humility with a mask, a false humility. A patient and careful process of discernment will reveal the reality behind the mask—pride.

People with this problem most often do not have spiritual directors, because they cannot submit to another person's direction. Jesus warned His disciples that Gentile leaders impose on others, and powerful people abuse authority, but they are to stay away from these practices. Those who aspire to greatness must learn how to serve others, and those who want to be first should dispose themselves as slaves (Mt 20:25–27). Jesus, Teacher and Master, taught by His own example; He washed the feet of His disciples, and taught them to wash one another's feet. "I have given you a model to follow, so that as I have done for you, you should also do" (Jn 13:12–15).

Saint Padre Pio of Pietrelcina reminds us that "the life of a Christian is nothing but a perpetual struggle against self; there is no flowering of the soul to the beauty of its perfection except at the price of pain." The Cross of Jesus is a sure medicine to cure self-will. "If anyone wishes to come after me, he must deny himself and take up his cross daily and follow me" (Lk 9:23).

Victim mentality syndrome
For the detailed treatment of VMS, refer to Chapter 6.

Sin
Sin is disobedience and opposition to God which separates us from Him. Sin is always a willful act. The bases of sin are the Ten Commandments, the Beatitudes and teachings of Jesus Christ, as well as the precepts of the Church. Sin must be feared and resisted. When we separate ourselves from God by sin, we make ourselves impervious to His love and graces; we block out all God's favors. This causes hopelessness and sadness. Sin is always a choice to place oneself above God; it is opposition to God's reign in our hearts. Sin is in the intention; to persist in it is to choose to remain separated from the life-giving friendship of God. Sin destroys all God's beautiful works, and turns us into allies of the demons. Scripture says that "the wages of sin is death" and the loss of eternal life (Rom 6:23).

Healing the bondages

Healing of spiritual illnesses, including bondage, requires discernment. This means relying heavily on the help of the Holy Spirit to reveal to us the root of our problems, and to show us how to resolve them. We do not know exactly how many combinations of bondages may be involved in our situation, or how the bondages interact to produce spiritual illnesses in us. The prayers that follow in Chapter 20 are designed to address all the open doors to bondage so that we can close them, and then open the doors to the Holy Spirit, the Lord and the Giver of life, so that the promise of Jesus our Savior for an abundant life might be fulfilled is us (Jn 10:10). If the conditions necessary for healing are present (see Lk 5:17), God's Word can be trusted that we will receive the healing He desires for us, not the healing we want at all cost, but what He desires for our salvation. God's will is always the best for us in every situation. To possess God is the greatest healing!

Scriptural prayer of surrender and healing Isaiah 53:4–12

Scriptures and questions for self-reflection and journaling

   1)   Revelation 22:1–7
2)   Isaiah 53:5
   3)   Isaiah 42:6–13

✗   Am I holding unforgiveness, grudges, anger, hatred, or resentment in my heart against anyone, myself or God?
✗   How am I allowing God to love healing into me?
✗   What do I really want Jesus to heal the most in me today?

Chapter 20

⊂✕ ⊂✕ ⊂✕

Celebrate Christ's Healing Love

Raphael said, "Take courage! God has healing in store for you; so take courage!" (Tobit 5:10).

These prayers are offered to prepare our hearts to be open to receive Christ's healing. They do not necessarily address our personal sins, but situations with our generations who may have been involved in evils acts that may be affecting us negatively which we do not know.

The Church emphasizes the importance of the worthy celebration of the Sacraments. It is most important and highly recommended that the celebration of the Eucharistic Sacrifice and the Sacrament of Penance take precedence over, and if possible, be part of the following suggested prayers. The Sacraments are efficacious signs of grace, and are the principal means of healing and salvation for all humanity. Either separately or as part of the family healing prayers, the faithful are encouraged to pray the holy Rosary and/or the Chaplet of Divine Mercy and/or other devotional prayers of choice. These prayers help foster a deeper relationship with Jesus Christ—who inspires and perfects the faith necessary for healing (Heb 12:2).

If the priest is to celebrate the Holy Eucharist as part of the healing prayers, he can alter and adapt the format of these prayers to give central place to the Mass. These prayers are not intended to replace, or be used as part of the Liturgy of the Eucharist. It is a violation to do so.

Please have your Bibles handy in preparation to celebrate these healing prayers.

Prayer of protection over the venue of meeting
(Holy water and/or blessed salt may be sprinkled in the place of meeting and on participants.)
*P/... In the name of Jesus, and by His Most Precious Blood, I take authority over Satan and all evil spirits in the air, ground, water, and the elements that may interfere with our presence now and after. By the power of the Victorious Cross of Jesus, I strike deaf, dumb, and blind all demons that will interfere with our gathering in any way, and I cut all communications between them all. Depart! And go immediately and

directly to the Foot of the Cross of Jesus Christ, and never return to us again.

**All/... All-powerful Father! Cover us in the Blood of Jesus Christ, and anoint us in the power of the Holy Spirit. Protect all our families wherever they may be at this time; protect our friends and loved ones; protect this property where we are gathered, and all those who live and work here; protect all of us from all danger or demonic retaliation. Send Mother Mary, the Immaculate Conception, to cover us in her mantle of love and intercession. Send the Archangels: Saint Michael, Saint Raphael, and Saint Gabriel and the holy Angels to surround and protect us this hour, as we resist the attacks of the enemy. Our battle is not with flesh and blood, but with evil powers of darkness. The battle belongs to Jesus, the Victor Ever-Glorious. Amen.

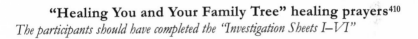

"Healing You and Your Family Tree" healing prayers[410]

The participants should have completed the "Investigation Sheets I–VI"

We call upon the Angels and the Saints to intercede with us and for us. We ask our Immaculate Virgin Mary, Mother of God, under whose mantle we gather, to obtain for us and our families, freedom from all bondage, and that all our generations would truly call her Blessed.

Note: P/... indicates Priest. (N.B. *Some of these prayers can only be prayed by a priest.*)

1) Opening prayer and repentance

*P/... +In the name of the Father, and of the Son, and of the Holy Spirit.
**All/... Amen.

*P/... The Lord be with you.
**All/... And with your spirit

*P/... To dispose ourselves to celebrate this prayer session, we humbly acknowledge our personal sins and how generational sins have affected us, and we ask our merciful Father for healing and peace *(brief silence)*.
**All/... Most merciful Father, we have sinned against You in thought, word, and deed, by what we have done, and what we have failed to do. We have failed to love You with our whole heart and mind, soul and strength, and we have not loved our neighbor as ourselves. We repent of our sins.

For the sake of the sorrowful passion of Jesus Christ, have mercy on us and our family trees. May Your Spirit purify our hearts to love You alone. Renew our faith to live the truth with love, and to praise and glorify You always. Through Christ Jesus our Lord. Amen.

*P/... May Almighty God have mercy on us, and by the Blood of the Lamb wash away our sins. May the Holy Spirit sanctify and strengthen us in holiness. We make our prayer in the name of Jesus Christ our Lord.
**All/... Amen.
**All/... Glory to God in the highest and on earth peace to those on whom his favor rests. Hosanna to the Son of David; "Holy, holy, holy is the Lord God almighty, who was, and who is, and who is to come;" blessed is he who comes in the name of the Lord; hosanna in the highest (Lk 2:14; Rev 4:8; Mt 21:9).

*P/... *Let us pray:*
Almighty and ever-living God! Your love never fails. You restore all things through faith in Jesus Christ. Mercifully grant that the families gathered here to intercede, and all families who seek Your healing from the bondage imposed on them by sin and its consequences, be set free by the Blood of the Lamb. Grant all our families new life and make us the beauty of the ages and a joy from generation to generation in the risen Christ. He lives and reigns with You, in the unity of the Holy Spirit, one God, forever and ever.
**All/... Amen

*P/... Let us praise and glorify the majesty of God as we sing *(worship songs may be played or sung that uplifts hearts and spirits to God).*

2) Scripture readings
(Select the texts of choice from the following options from your Bible)

2.a/... First Reading:

A Reading from the Book of Tobit (Tobit 3:1–4)
   (Options: Daniel 9:2–11, 15–23; Hebrews 2:14–18)

2.b/... Psalm Reading: Psalm 51 *(options: Ps 27)*

**All/... R/. A clean heart create for me, Oh God, renew in me a zealous and steadfast spirit

Side 1: Psalm 51: 3–8   Side 2: Psalm 51: 9–14
Side 1: Psalm 51: 15–18   Side 2: Psalm 51: 19–21

2.c/... *Gospel Reading:*

*P/... *A reading from the Holy Gospel according to Luke*
(Lk 4:16–21)
(Options: Jn 1:1–18; Mk 2:1–12; Lk 13:10–17)

*P/... The Gospel of the Lord.
**All/... Praise to You, Lord Jesus Christ.
(A brief homily may follow or silence if the priest prefers)

3) Prayer to desire the grace of healing

**All/... Almighty Father, Jesus commands us to ask and we shall receive; to seek and we shall find; to knock and the door will be opened to us. Give us hearts that long for You, and a thirst for the Holy Spirit as the deer longs for running water. May we thirst for the healing graces of Your love as the dry land begs for rain. Help us to believe in Jesus, whom You sent, that the rivers of living water He promised may flow from within us and give life to the world (Jn 7:38). Amen.

4) Ministry and spiritual warfare prayers

*P/... We entrust ourselves and persevere in prayer with the Mother of God that through her unfailing and maternal intercession, we may be freed from all bondage of body, soul, and spirit:
**All/... *Remember, O most gracious Virgin Mary, that never was it known that anyone who fled to thy protection, implored thy help, or sought thy intercession was left unaided. Inspired with this confidence, I fly unto thee, O Virgin of virgins, my mother; to thee do I come, before thee I stand, sinful and sorrowful. O Mother of the Word Incarnate, despise not my petitions, but in thy mercy hear and answer me. Amen.*

*P/... Our help is in the name of the Lord.
**All/... Who made heaven and earth.

*P/... All-powerful Father, we come to You in the name of Jesus our Lord, and in the power of the Holy Spirit, as we celebrate these healing prayers for ourselves and our generations. We dwell in the shelter of Your Godhead and abide in the shadow of the Your Almighty power. You are our Lord, our refuge, and fortress. Oh Lord our God, we trust in You.

*All/... "Blessed be the LORD, my rock, who trains my hands for battle, my fingers for war; My safe guard and my fortress, my stronghold, my deliverer, My shield, in whom I trust, who subdues [enemies] under me" (Ps 144:1–2).

---

5) Shutting secondary open door I: preborn infants and childhood emotional wounds

*(Use "Investigation Sheet II")

Unforgiveness, fear, anger, self-hatred, etc. can block us from receiving God's healing love. Wounds of childhood can affect the way we perceive ourselves, others, and God. We pray for the desire and the grace to forgive and be healed.

*P/... *Let us surrender to Jesus and let go of hurtful memories of childhood— thoughts, words, actions, anger, unforgiveness, etc. (Pause for a moment and reflect.)*

Prayers to heal the wounds of false images of self, others and God

5.a/... False self-image

**All/... Loving Father, You created my inmost being in Your image and likeness. You knit me together in the womb with a great love. I am precious in Your eyes. You chose me in love to bear fruit that will remain. I praise You Father, for I am the wonderful work of Your hand (Ps 139). In the Child Jesus, You embrace my weakness; and in the Holy Spirit, I am Your adopted child. Praise be to You, God and Father of our Lord Jesus Christ. You chose me in Him before the world began to be holy and blameless in Your sight (Eph 1:3–4).

Some distressful events of my life in the womb and childhood, over which I had no control, have led me to believe lies about myself and others. These lies have caused me to have a false self-image, and burdened me with the slavery of unforgiveness, fear, anger, bitterness, resentment, impatience, and hatred. I do not see myself as You see me. I renounce all the lies and vows I may have believed. I repent of all sinful thoughts, words and actions of self-hatred, self-condemnation, complaint, judgment and blame; and for not accepting and loving myself as I am. In Jesus' name, I forgive myself for the lies that I am of no good, rejected, not good enough, abandoned, unwanted and unworthy of Your love, ruined, a failure, and all lies. I forgive unconditionally anyone against whom I hold an evil wish, unforgiveness, anger, resentment, malice and hatred in my heart. Especially, I forgive family members: parents, siblings, spouse, children, relatives, and friends who have hurt me in any way. Trusting in the Lord's mercy, I surrender to Jesus all the negativity I hold against myself and others, and against You, dear Lord; and for any mishaps, tragedies, sickness, deaths and trials that have come upon my family for which I may carry unhealthy grief.

In the name of Jesus, I renounce these lies and forgive myself unreservedly (pray three times).

My humble Jesus, You love me more than I love myself. I give You permission to heal all the wounds and bondage of my heart, mind, memories, senses, emotions, faculties, spirit, soul and body, and my whole being, and anything that blocks me from receiving Your merciful love. Grant me Your peace and consolation. By Your death and resurrection, set things right in me. You promised that if my sins be like scarlet, You will make them white as snow. If they be crimson red, You will make them white as wool (Is 1:18). Restore my true self-image and self-esteem. Grant me the humility and confidence of a child. Create in me, O God, a clean and new heart. Breathe into me the Spirit of peace You gave Your Apostles (Jn 20:19, 20). Make me faithful and obedient to Your covenant of love always, for without You I can do nothing. I invite You Father, Son, and Holy Spirit, into all the painful memories of my life. Let Your *love, light,* and *truth* dispel the *fear, darkness,* and *lies* these memories contain. Grant me the freedom to see reality as You see them, and to glorify Your Majesty; for You created all things very good.

In the name of Jesus, I renounce and repent of any sins which may be the effect of the sins of my ancestors; I pray in reparation for them. I plead the Divine Mercy of the pierced Heart of Jesus upon my family trees. By the Wounds of Jesus' Passion, Father heal the lack of charity, division, hatred, anger, and negativity in words, thoughts and actions, and deliver us from the evils of my entire generational lines. I pray with gratitude for answering my prayers. May I witness to the love of the risen Christ present and active in my life and in my family trees.

Glory be to the Father and to the Son and to the Holy Spirit. Forever and ever. Amen!

5.b/... False image of others

**All/... Loving Father, through Jesus You call me to love and forgive as You love and forgive me. I repent for my failures in charity. I forgive unconditionally all who have hurt and caused me pain by their words and actions, causing me to harbor unforgiveness in my heart. May I see them through the eyes of Jesus, and not through my negativity and woundedness. Through pride rooted in lies, I have judged and blamed others. You are the merciful Judge who knows our hearts. Father, grant me all the spiritual blessings of the humble Heart of Jesus. Renew in me the Spirit's gifts of Knowledge, Understanding, Wisdom, Counsel, Fortitude, Piety and Fear of the Lord, for Your greater glory. I let go of the past, and I embrace the present moment in freedom and hope. Amen.

5.c/... False image of God

**All/... All Holy Father, Your love is everlasting. Every good and perfect gift comes from You. You are the Father of lights and the Creator of all (Jam 1:17). Every good in me is from You. I repent I may have ignorantly blamed You for the painful events of my life, because I believed the lie that You were not there to care and protect me or I did not deserve Your attention. I belong to You, and You love me with an enduring love. In Christ, You espouse me to Yourself. You spoke to me through Prophet Isaiah: "Before I formed you in the womb I knew you, before you were born I dedicated you, a prophet to the nations I appointed you" (Jer 1:5). The lies I believed distorted my true image of You as my loving Father. I take responsibility for my distorted beliefs, and I exonerate You completely. I ask for Your pardon and healing in the Blood of Jesus my Lord.

Father, forgive me for any pains I have caused You. Pains that are so evident in the suffering of Jesus, whom You sent to save me from my sins. Thank You for Your love for me. Heal my unbelief that I may trust Jesus' love for me. You are the Comforter of Zion, my Healer and Stronghold, my Deliverer, my God in whom I have my being. Heal every wound in me from the moment of my conception until now. Deliver me from my fears and sins, and from all bondage by the Blood of the Lamb. Make me open to receive Your love, and to see myself as the apple of Your eye (Zach 2:12). You said it is impossible for a mother to forget her infant, and not tenderly love her child. But even if she forgets, You will never forget me. My name is written in the palms of Your hands (Is 49:15–16). Father, may I never forget this truth that I belong to You. May I dwell in Your house all the days of my life with Jesus, the Holy Spirit, our Blessed Mother, and the Angels and Saints. Amen.

*P/... *In the name of Jesus Christ, I break all seals, curses, spells, hexes, covenants, strongholds, vows and any bondage holding you captive from the moment of conception until now (pray three times).*

In the name of Jesus, I take authority over all evil spirits associated with these devices. Depart! Satan, and all spirits of fear, lies, deception, death, poor self-esteem, self-hatred, the seven capital sins, unforgiveness, abandonment, isolation, condemnation, resentment, rejection, and all evil spirits! Go immediately and directly to the Foot of the Cross of Jesus Christ, and never return! *(Pause.)*

**All/... Come, Holy Spirit! Pour out the healing rays of Your truth and dispel on all lies, fear, darkness, and death in all my unhealed memories. Restore me to freedom and peace as Your temple, in the name of Jesus Christ our Lord. Amen

*"Jesus I love You, all I have is Yours,
Yours I am and Yours I want to be,
Do with me whatever You will"*[M11] (pray three times).

6) **Shutting secondary open door II: unholy soul-ties, personal choices, and affections**
   (Use "Investigation Sheet III")
Unholy soul-ties and bonds are formed when we use our God-given ability for relationships to inordinately attach to persons, living or deceased, or things, places, or situations, which compromise our total dependence on God. Such unholy bonds can open doors to bondage.

6.a/... Renouncing and cutting unholy soul-ties

**All/... Lord Jesus Christ, thank You for all my holy relationships by which You allow me to live out Your command to love as You love me. Sometimes I have abused this grace and used my ability for good relationship in unhealthy ways.

In Jesus' name, I forgive all who have influenced me negatively through their words and actions, especially all uncharitable and abusive authority persons. I forgive all who have used, manipulated, intimidated, dominated, and controlled me. I bring to You any inappropriate and immoral relationships and abuses, unholy soul-ties formed through reading and viewing pornography, violence, and all depressive and unhealthy grieving of loved ones. I renounce forever, any agreements, promises, and immediate or remote influences that exist between me and anyone with whom I have had any negatively charged relationship, living or deceased. I renounce, and I cut any links between me and any evil spirit being, such as *incubus and succubus,* attached to me or harassing me in any way in dreams, emotionally, physically, sexually, spiritually, and psychologically, or that attack me through day-dreaming, idleness, fantasy, and drowsiness. I renounce and repent of any times in my life I made a death-wish (by thought, word, action or desire), wishing that I was dead or did not exist, or want to die or disappear, or to harm myself, or thinking my life is a waste, or questioning why God made me.

In Your Precious Blood, dear Lord Jesus, forgive and cleanse me of every sin, guilt, shame, hurts, or damage resulting from my choices. This day, and for all eternity, I choose life. I choose God as my Father; I choose Jesus Christ as my Lord and Savior; and I choose the Holy Spirit as my Advocate and Companion and Friend, now and for all eternity. Amen.

In the name of Jesus, I renounce and repent of these unholy relationships. With the Cross of Jesus, I severe all unholy soul-ties and affections that link me to anyone and anything in my past or present (pray three times).

*P/... In the name of Jesus Christ, I break any seals, curses, covenants, strongholds, spells, hexes, and all bond that links you with the forces of darkness to which you may be exposed through any of these relationships (pray three times).
In the name of Jesus, I take authority over Satan and all evil spirits associated with these evil devices: spirits of fear, lust, death, addictions, anger, infirmity, resentment, hatred, spirit of the world, and all evil spirits. Depart! And go immediately and directly to the Foot of the Cross of Jesus Christ! Never return to us again! (*Pause briefly!*).

**All/... Come, Holy Spirit! Breathe life into the deadness in my relationships. As You put life into the dry bones when Prophet Ezekiel prophesied to them in the Spirit (Eze 37), so heal the wounds of my relationships; unite me in a holy soul-tie with Jesus, our Savior, and with God the Father. Amen.

• • •

In the name of Jesus, I loose myself from all unholy soul-ties and bondage on me from any relationships contaminated by evil spirits and their human agents in any way. I consecrate my whole being: spirit, soul and body, heart, memory, intellect, emotions, senses, and all my faculties to my Savior Jesus Christ, as a living sacrifice, holy and pleasing to God (Rom 12:1). I accept Christ's consecration of Himself for me to the Father (Jn 17:19), and His death for me on the Cross. Jesus has made me a living stone to build His spiritual temple and house of prayer, to be a holy priesthood offering spiritual and acceptable sacrifices to God through the High Priest, Jesus Christ (1 Pet 2:4–5, GNT). Amen.

6.b/... *Prayer of restoration*
(Unholy soul-ties and contacts with evil injure and fragment our spirit, just as physical wounds do. This prayer aims to restore our interior or spiritual integrity and well-being.)

*P/... Oh Holy Spirit, the Lord and Giver of life, "from the four winds come" (Eze 37:9; Mk 13:27); breathe life, unity, and wholeness into all parts of your persons wounded through unholy relationships or contact with evil. *Be healed by the wounds of Jesus, the Lamb once slain, who lives forever* (Rev 1:17, 18). Compassionate Father, breathe Your life-giving *Ruah*—the Holy Spirit, into us. Fill us anew with the Spirit of the risen Lord, who said: "Receive the Holy Spirit" (Jn 20:22). Your Spirit gives us life, human power is nothing. We pray this with the humble assurance of faith:
+*In the name of the Father, and of the Son, and of the Holy Spirit.*
**All/... Amen.

---

7) Shutting secondary open door III: the occult, Freemasonry, and New Age
(Use "Investigation Sheet IV")

7.a/... *Renouncing occult, Freemasonry and New Age involvement*

**All/... Father of our Lord Jesus Christ, for our good You commanded: "I am the Lord your God who brought you out of the... house of bondage. 'You shall have no other gods before Me.' 'You shall not make for yourself a carved image—any likeness of anything that is in heaven above, or that is in the earth beneath, or that is in the water under the earth" (Deut

5:6–8, NKJV). We have been unfaithful and served other gods: self, others, knowledge, wealth, possessions, prestige, honor, power and influence, immortality, health, friendships and spouses, children and the world. We repent of our unfaithfulness and beg Your mercy on behalf of our past and present generations.

Merciful Father, pardon us for the evils of the occult, satanism, freemasonry, witchcraft, paganism, new age, and the false spirituality that we may have practiced, and protect us from the consequences of these evils, which any member of our generations may have done that violated Your covenant love with us, and opened the door to the evil one to wreak havoc and keep us in bondage. We renounce and repent of these evils in the name of Jesus our Savior. May the Precious Blood of the Lamb make null and void any pacts the deceiver may have made with any family members. Destroy all curses passed down to us, and cleanse our families of all spiritual contamination. We reject all demonic entities affecting our family trees, and we take back any rights Satan and the demons have over anyone in our families to hold us in bondage.[412] We surrender all our generations to the Lordship of Jesus Christ.

Lord God, You promised to match ahead of us to straighten the crooked paths; to shatter the bronze gates and snap the iron bars; to give us treasures out of the darkness and gifts that are hidden in secret places, so that we may know and trust Your love for us (Is 45:2–3, NLT). Fulfill these promises for us today; bless our generations with abundant graces; You alone can bring good out of evil. "Better is one day in your courts than a thousand elsewhere; I would rather be a doorkeeper in the house of my God than dwell in the tents of the wicked" (Ps 84:11, NIV). Restore us in Christ, O God our savior; withdraw Your wrath against us. Please give us life that we may rejoice in You. Let us know Your love; give us the experience of Your salvation (Ps 85:5–8).

P/… In the name of Jesus Christ, I break any covenants, seals, curses, strongholds, spells, hexes, voodoo, witchcraft, and any other occult or other demonic bondage on you and your family trees (pray three times).

In the name of Jesus, I take authority over all the evil spirits contained in these devices or attached to you and your family trees: Satan, spirits of fear, antichrist, occult, ancestral spirits of the dead, death, addictions, anger, resentment, unforgiveness, hatred, spirit of the world, and all evil spirits in our various cultures. Be-gone! Satan and all demons – inventors of all evil; go immediately and directly to the Foot of the Cross of Jesus Christ Crucified, and never return to any of us again (*take any occult objects in our possession or in the house to the priest for destruction*) Pause.

● ● ●

*P/... Come, Holy Spirit! Fill Your people with new life and healing. May Saint Michael the Archangel stop all powers and principalities and all demonic forces from harassing us. May he bind and cast them out from us. We ask our Blessed Mother to cloth us in her protective mantle of love and intercession, and may the Angels and Saints intercede for our freedom from all bondage.

Merciful Father, You love us so much that You sent Jesus Christ, Your Son, who, by His death and resurrection, has set us free from Satan, sin, and death. Look with favor upon our repentant hearts and forgive us who cry to You for mercy. You delivered Your people Israel from slavery in Egypt by the blood of lambs, deliver us today by the Blood of the Lamb.

**All/... We praise You, Oh Lord, God Almighty, who is and who was. The reign and saving authority of Your Anointed One has begun. Our accuser is defeated and cast down and out by the Blood of the Lamb (Rev 11:17). In faith, we confess with our tongue that Jesus is Lord and believe in our hearts that You, Father, raised Him up from the dead. Our help shall come from You, who created heaven and earth (Ps 121:1–2).

*P/... Brothers and sisters, soldiers of Christ, from this moment, "Draw your strength from the Lord and from his mighty power. Put on the armor of God so that you may be able to stand firm against the tactics of the devil. For our struggle is not with flesh and blood but with the principalities and powers, with the world rulers of this present darkness, with the evil spirits in the heavens. Therefore, put on the armor of God that you may be able to resist on the evil day and, having done everything, to hold your ground. So stand fast with your loins girded in truth, clothed with the breastplate of righteousness, and with the footgear of zeal in readiness for the Gospel of peace. In all circumstances, hold faith as a shield, to quench all the flaming arrows of the evil one. And put on the helmet of salvation and in your right hand, take the sword of the spirit, which is the word of God. With all prayer and supplication, pray at every opportunity in the Spirit... be watchful with all perseverance... for all the holy ones" (Eph 6:10–18), and fight for the salvation of souls.

**All/... "Worthy is the Lamb that was slain to receive power and riches, wisdom and strength, honor and glory and blessing" (Rev 5:12). We join all creation to proclaim: "Holy, holy, holy is the Lord God almighty, who was, and who is, and who is to come" (Rev 4:8), and we cry out in adoration with "every creature in heaven and on earth and under the earth and in the sea, everything in the universe... "To the one who sits on the throne and to the Lamb be blessing and honor, glory and might, forever and ever...Amen" (Rev 5:13–14) *(Pause for silent adoration.)*

Blood of Jesus, we trust in You (pray three times)

Most Sacred Heart of Jesus, may Your Kingdom reign in us and in our family bloodlines (pray three times)

---

8) **Shutting secondary open door IV: rejection of Christ's one true Church, her doctrines and morals**
*(Use "Investigation Sheet V")

Denial or rejection of Jesus Christ, His Church and her teachings, abandonment and luke-warmness in the faith, profaning the Saints, desecrating holy persons, objects and places: the Bible, the Cross, the Blessed Sacrament, the Ten Commandments, anger at or cursing God, apostasy, agnosticism, atheism, etc.

**All/... Almighty Father, thank You for the gift of the Church born from the redemptive sacrifice of Jesus Christ and the outpouring of the Holy Spirit. Through the Church, You call us daily to repentance and conversion, and to experience salvation anew in the Eucharistic mystery. Through the Church, You adopt us as Your children in the Spirit by the waters of baptism; You purify us in the Blood of the Lamb, and nourish us with the Sacraments, which flows from the pierced Heart of the Savior.

We confess the ways that we ourselves have rejected the Church and her teachings and have not believed in You, our God; and have broken Your commandments and dishonored the values You hold dear for our happiness in this life; the ways we have out rightly denied the faith and believed the lies and deceptions of the devil or failed to take seriously our life of grace in Christ as Christians; or have cursed and been angry at You or in our blindness have denied Your existence through words and actions, all to our detriment.

Father, forgive our unbelief. Pardon us who have offended You in any way through acts of desecration of sacred persons, places or things, or the Blessed Sacrament, for violations of Your holy days, and other evils by which the evil one gained a foothold to cause misery and bondage in our lives and families. O Lord, hear us. O Lord, pardon us. O compassionate Father, be merciful to us. You do not punish us as our sins deserve. The Scriptures speak of Your high regard for us: "God proves his love for us in that while we were still sinners Christ died for us" (Rom 5:8).

In the name of Jesus, we renounce these evils and we take back any rights the devil claims over us. We make null and void pacts that we or anyone in our family trees may have made with the evil one through his lies and deception, which brought us under his captivity. We repent with our whole heart for offending You, Lord.

*P/... *In the name of Jesus, I break any covenants, seals, curses, spells, hexes, strongholds, and other bondages causing deadness in our faith resulting from the forces of darkness that may be affecting our families (pray three times).*

I take authority over all the evil spirits associated with these evil protective devices, and all evil spirits involved: Satan, spirit of the world, antichrist, rebellion, disobedience, blasphemy, freemasonry and occult, jezebel, etc. I command all evil spirits involved to depart and go immediately and directly to the Foot of the Cross of Jesus Christ and never again return to us! *(Pause.)*

**All/... Come Holy Spirit! Fill our hearts with the fire of Your love, heal our wounds and renew our faith in Jesus Christ, our Savior. Convict, convert and consecrate us anew in the truth to the Father as His children confident to call Him, *Abba,* Father. Fill every part of our being vacated by evils keeping us in bondage; make us alive to the Word of God. Grant us the grace of perseverance in carrying our crosses as we follow Jesus to Calvary. We unite ourselves with the sacrifice of Jesus, our Eternal High Priest through all the Masses celebrated throughout the world, in union with the Immaculate Heart of Mary and the holy Choirs of Angels. Amen.

---

9) **Shutting secondary open door V: family / ancestral / generational bondage (curse)**
   *(Use "Investigation Sheet VI")

9.a/... Thanksgiving for all generations

**All/... God of glory and might, You blessed Adam and Eve to be fruitful and to fill the earth (Gen 1:28), and so gave them the gift of many generations until the end of time. You chose Abraham, our father in faith, to be the father of a great nation. Through him, You bless all our generations in Your love (Gen 12:2). By faith in Christ we share in all the spiritual blessings You bestow on Your holy people (Rom 4:16). By Your Divine favor, You have adopted us in the Holy Spirit as Your children; in the Blood of Christ we have redemption and forgiveness of our sins (Eph 1:3–7); forever You have made us a blessing to You and to one another.

9.b/... Generational healing

*P/... You do not punish us for the sins of our ancestors. In our solidarity with them, the effects of their sins affect us to the third and fourth generations. Your Divine Goodness multiplies the good effects of their virtuous deeds on us their descendants down to a thousand generations (see Deut 5:9–10), making Your glory shine on earth through Christ to all ages.

**All/... We bring to You the offences of our past generations who in their ignorance and disobedience were pagans, and may have practiced occult and satanic worship. We pray for those who committed suicide, murder, and abortions and those who died in a state of unforgiveness, anger, hatred, and every action that offended charity that was committed. We also pray for any family members who died by acts of violence, murder, wars, tragic accidents by land, sea, or air; natural disasters, and diabolical attacks. We pray for those who may have been killed by wild beasts, and those who died suddenly without adequate preparation to meet their Creator (*brief silence*).

In the power of Your Divine Mercy, Oh Jesus, we forgive all who have hurt members of our families and caused us unnecessary suffering. We forgive any family members who have hurt others and caused them unnecessary suffering. Be merciful to our present generations who follow in the footstep of our ancestors by their disobedience, unfaithfulness and vain living. Grant them conversion graces, Oh Lord, we pray, to abandon immoral lifestyles, acts of wickedness, abomination and violence, and attachment to the passing things of this world. Lord, sprinkle clean water upon us and cleanse us from our impurities. Renew our hearts and spirits; restore to life any dead and dry bones within us. Open our graves, Oh Lord, raise us up from our deadness (Eze 36:25–26, 37). "Be exalted, O God, above the highest heavens! May your glory shine over all the earth" (Ps 57:5, NLT). Wash us clean in Your Divine Blood, and make us whiter than snow.

We beg for Your mercy for the unfaithfulness of our past and present generations, and for our ungodly choices that opened the door to our bondage. Break these bondages, and deliver us, heal us and set us free in Your great mercy. Remove the misery and pains these sins have caused our family bloodlines. In Your mercy, deliver us and heal us from these evils. Give us victory over them by the Precious Blood of the Lamb. May only goodness and love follow us all our days to dwell peacefully in Your house forever (Ps 23:6).

*P/... We pray for all children and parents who died through miscarriages, abortions, and stillbirths, and their families. We present to the Father in the name of Jesus, all those who died without the grace of baptism through no fault of theirs. Lord Jesus, grant them salvation and count them among the blessed in Heaven. We invoke upon them the graces of all the Masses celebrated world-wide. Father, You take no pleasure in the death of sinners, but that they repent and be converted that they may have life. There is no condemnation for those covered in the Blood of the Lamb. Bless them Father in the name of the Holy Family of Jesus, Mary and Joseph. By His death and resurrection, Jesus has consecrated them to You forever in truth. *+In the name of the Father and of the Son and of the Holy Spirit.*

9.c/... Healing negative generational predispositions

**All/... Jesus, our Divine Physician, we pray for the healing of negative predispositions, vices, weaknesses, sicknesses, evil traits and inclinations, compulsions, and bondages that have come down to us and our siblings and relatives through our parents and grandparents, down to the very origin of our family bloodlines. By the power of the Holy Spirit and the Sword of the Spirit, release me and my family trees from these evil influences *(pause and reflect)*. Lord, heal these dispositions and fill me with saintly dispositions and attitudes, strength, health, virtues, traits, and freedom. Fill me with the Spirit's gift of self-control, confidence, courage, fortitude, generosity, chastity, faith, reverence, hope, interior freedom, discernment, and all the gifts of the Spirit to cancel the negative traits that deny me interior peace and limit my freedom. Lord Jesus, You said, "If you then, who are evil, know how to give good gifts to your children, how much more will the heavenly Father give the Holy Spirit to those who ask him!" (Lk 11:13, ESV). Father, we ask You in the precious name of Jesus that You fill us with the Gift of the Holy Spirit. Amen!

*P/... Compassionate Father, look with mercy upon all our generations; free us from any evils that cling to us. Shine the light of Your love to dispel every darkness in our generations causing suffering and misery in any form. You are the light that broke through our darkness and overcome it to set us free (Jn 1:5). We take back what the evil one has stolen from us, and may God rebuke him, we humbly pray. We ask Saint Michael the Archangel to bind and cast him into the bottomless pit, never to return to any of us again. We pray this with confidence in the victorious name of Jesus. ****All//...** Amen.

9.d/... Breaking generational bondage
Generational bondage may be: seals, covenants, curses, strongholds, spells and hexes and other demonic entrapments that shield evil spirits from expulsion, allowing them to inflict suffering on us.

**All/... *In the name of Jesus Christ, we stand in the place of our whole family bloodlines, and we break all seals, covenants, inner vows, curses, contracts, hexes, spells, strongholds, or pacts and all other demonic armor placed upon us and our family bloodlines, and all those associated with us, bodily, spiritually, emotionally, and in any other ways (pray three times).*

**All/... In the name of Jesus Christ, we take authority over all the evil entities associated with these demonic devices: Satan, evil spirits of fear, death, jezebel, and all other evil spirits; depart from us and our whole family bloodlines and all those bodily and spiritually connected to us, and go immediately and directly to the Foot of the Cross of Jesus Christ, and never return to us or any members of our family bloodlines.

In the power of the glorious Cross of Jesus Christ, we bind all evil spirits mentioned, including powers and principalities; world rulers of this present darkness; evil spirits in the high places; all demonic forces and strongholds; all satanic powers, attributes, clusters, endowments, and thrones; all evil spirits of all ranks; and all the disobedient spirits defeated by Saint Michael the Archangel, the Prince of the Heavenly Host. We bind these spirits from outer space, air, water, fire, the ground, and all evil forces of nature and all other evil spirits involved. Saint Michael, please bind them and cast them out from us that they go immediately and directly to the Foot of the Cross of our Lord Jesus Christ and never to return to us or our family bloodlines (Pause!)

*P/... We praise You, the Lord God Almighty, for You have conquered. You routed Pharaoh's army in the Red Sea when they threatened the lives of Your chosen people. Rout the evil forces bent on dominating us, and free our whole ancestry from all evil bondage.

**All/... By the Blood of the Lamb, and the sword of the Spirit, the word of God; You have led us from darkness and gloom and broken to pieces the chains that held us captives. You have broken down the prison gates of bronze and snapped the iron bars over all our families. We thank You, Lord, for Your kindness, and Your wondrous loving deeds for us.

*P/... The Lamb of God is our Shepherd. We have nothing to fear, because the battle belongs to the Lord. He leads us to fresh restful springs of water to revive our drooping spirit and strengthen our weak knees to reclaim our family trees for the Kingdom of God.

**All/... Surely, Your goodness and generosity shall be with us always. You turn deserts into pools of water and parched lands into flowing springs, where You bless and settle Your people. We shall dwell in the Father's house for ever and ever (Ps 107).

*P/... Even if I should walk in the valley of darkness, I will fear no evil, because God's perfect love casts out all fear in me. Lord, You are there with me with Your staff of authority that gives me confidence, comfort, and healing.
**All/... The Lord God is our Light and Victor. The Lord's right hand has triumphed. You are my God; I thank You. My God, I praise You. Give thanks to the Lord who is good, because His love endures forever (Ps 118:27–29). I am your servant, you have broken my bondage. I will offer to you the sacrifice of thanksgiving, and call on the name of the Lord. Alleluia (Ps 116: 16–17).

───────────────

10) Renewal of Baptismal promises and profession of Faith

*P/... We have been consecrated to the Father forever at our Baptism by the self-consecration of Jesus that we may be consecrated in truth (Jn 17:19). We are children of God. We now renew this covenant consecration as we pledge our obedience and dedication to God, who knew us before we were formed in the womb, and consecrated and chose us before we were born (Jer 1:5). We repent for the times we failed to believe that God exists, or were lukewarm in our faith, or failed to acknowledge His goodness. We repent for the times we rejected God in our relationships and choices, and denied His sovereignty and holiness by meddling with the occult. We repent for the times we broke His Commandments or denied His true Church founded on the Rock of Peter, and inaugurated on Pentecost Day. We repent for the failings of our generations, past, present and future. We now renew our fundamental covenant identity with the Father in the Blood of the Lamb, as His beloved sons and daughters:

Renunciation of Satan and its works.

**All/... In the name of Jesus Christ, I renounce Satan, and all his works, and all his empty show.

Act of Faith in God
**All/... I believe in God, the Father Almighty, Creator of Heaven and earth *(pause).*

**All/... I believe in Jesus Christ, His only Son Our Lord, Who was conceived by the Holy Spirit, born of the Virgin Mary, suffered under Pontius Pilate, was crucified, died, and was buried. He descended into Hell; the third day He rose again from the dead; He ascended into Heaven, and sitteth at the right hand of God, the Father Almighty; from thence He shall come to judge the living and the dead *(pause)*.

**All/... I believe in the Holy Spirit, the holy Catholic Church, the communion of saints, the forgiveness of sins, the resurrection of the body, and life everlasting.   Amen.

*P/... Almighty and Ever-Living God, bless Your children who have renewed their covenant love with You in the death and resurrection of Jesus Christ, Your Son. Through Him and in Him, Satan, sin and death are conquered; captives are set free; and we are reconciled to You. By the grace of Your Spirit, seal and bind us to You forever, never to be separated. Deepen our self-knowledge as Your children confident to call You, Father. You are our Helper, our Stronghold, and our Refuge. Deliver us from every evil by the sword of the Spirit – Your Anointed Word, and protect us from the evil one. Give us strength by Your Spirit to be humble and obedient to the Victorious Lamb. By experiencing Your freedom, may we witness to our brothers and sisters the fruit of healing, joy and peace of Your Kingdom. Grant this through our Lord Jesus Christ Your Son, who lives and reigns with You, in the unity of the Holy Spirit, one God, forever and ever.
**All/... Amen.
**All/... Beloved Jesus, You offered Yourself completely for our sins, and are seated forever at God's right hand interceding for us. In fulfillment of Scripture, we now place all Your enemy and ours, and every evil bondage beneath Your Feet (Heb 10:13–14). We place Your Victorious Cross between us and our ancestry and future generations; we renounce and cut ourselves free of all bondage, and put a stop to all bondage transmission in our generations, in the name of Jesus Christ. Lord Jesus, You are the Way, the Truth and the Life; the Mediator between God and us; the Eternal High Priest, who reconciles us to the Father by the Blood of Your Cross. Let Your word that is spirit and life be fulfilled in us who believe: "I will give the victor the right to sit with me on my throne, as I myself first won the victory and sit with my Father on his throne" (Rev 3:21). Amen.

11) Prayer-hymn of the humility and victory of Jesus

*P/... "Though He was in the form of God, Jesus did not deem equality with God something to be grasped at. Rather, He humbled Himself and took the form of a slave, being born in the likeness of men. He was known to be of human estate, and it was thus that he humbled himself, obediently accepting even death, death on a cross! (Phil 2:6–8).

All/... Because of this, God highly exalted him and bestowed on him the name above every other name, so that at Jesus' name, every knee must bend in heaven, on earth, and under the earth, and every tongue proclaim to the glory of God the Father: **Jesus Christ is Lord! (Phil 2:9–11).

*P/... "One thing I ask from the Lord, this only do I seek: that I may dwell in the house of the Lord all the days of my life, to gaze on the beauty of the Lord and to seek him in his temple. For in the day of trouble he will keep me safe in his dwelling; he will hide me in the shelter of his sacred tent and set me high upon a rock" (Ps 27:4–5, NIV).

**All/... "Let those who fear the Lord say, God's love endures forever. In danger I called on the Lord; the Lord answered me and set me free. The Lord is with me; I am not afraid; what can mortals do against me? The Lord is with me as my helper; I shall look in triumph on my foes... All the nations surrounded me; in the Lord's name, I crushed them. They surrounded me on every side; in the Lord's name I crushed them. They surrounded me like bees; they blazed like fire among thorns; in the Lord's name I crushed them. I was hard pressed and falling, but the Lord came to my help. The Lord, my strength and might, came to me as savior. The joyful shout of deliverance is heard in the tents of the victors: "The Lord's right hand strikes with power; the Lord's right hand is raised; the Lord's right hand strikes with power" (Ps 118:4–7, 10–16).

12) Empowerment of the Holy Spirit

This prayer of anointing is for the healing of all the wounds and open doors to evil contamination in ourselves and generations

All/... ***Come, Spirit of renewal!* Renew and fill all aspects of our being and generations with Your healing love. Renew the graces of that first Pentecost in us. You are the Lord, the Giver of Life. Heal and restore to wholeness all our wounds and brokenness, and all places of bondage in us. Give us new hearts and new spirits to love God with healed hearts. We welcome You into our inmost being; touch our minds, hearts, bodies, senses, spirit and soul. Recreate and make us whole again in Christ. Give us a renewed hunger to see and hear God; to thirst for the Word of life and overflow with love and sentiments for Jesus Christ.

Come, Spirit of blessings! Bless us with Your gifts of Wisdom, Knowledge, Understanding, Piety, Fortitude, Fear of the Lord, and Counsel. Manifest in us the fruits of Your divine presence: peace, patience, love, joy, charity, humility, sympathy, forgiveness, kindness, generosity, courage, faithfulness, unity, gentleness, goodness, discipline, relinquishment, holiness, freedom from shame and guilt, good self-image, prosperity, obedience, a sound mind, order, fulfillment in Christ, truth, acceptance of self and others, trust, self-control, freedom from addictions and control, wellness, health, and light, life and love of Jesus Christ, Victor Ever Glorious. Amen.

Come, Spirit of consolation! Console and gladden us in our sorrows and sufferings. Turn our misery into joy. Shut the doors to bondage in our families that may still be open for any reasons; when You shut no one can open (Rev 3:8). Remove from us all the unnecessary sufferings that burden us, and cast out all servile fear. May we carry joyfully the crosses You have prepared for us for our salvation. Strengthen us in our temptations and struggles by Your divine power and mercy, and increase our faith, hope and love. Be the Advocate in our trials, the Companion and the Resistance in our temptations, and the Strength in our weakness. Bring unity, forgiveness, reconciliation, and peace in the divisions that distress our families, for only Your Divine help can save us. Lavish Your choice portions upon us and fill us with Your blessings. Have pity on us, most merciful Father and shower Your favors on us, that our enemies may see to their confusion that You are with us as the God who never fails.

Come, Spirit of holiness! Cloth us in Your armor of light and holiness, and dispel all our darkness. As You did for the Prophet Jeremiah, do now for us: make us into a fortified city, a pillar of iron, and a wall of brass against the whole kingdom of darkness (Jer 1:18). As You made Isaiah the prophet, so now make us, into sharp-edged sword, concealed in the shadow of Your arm, a polished arrow hidden in Your quiver (Is 49:2). Help us to fight the battles of the Christian life without fear, for the battle belongs to the Lord, who has conquered the grave.

Come, Spirit of love! Grant our families an active and fruitful love of God and neighbor. Make us receptive to Your love. You first loved us and have made us living stones to build up God's Kingdom of love here on earth. Inspire us to heroic lives of virtue; empower us to witness to the redemptive love of Jesus, the Lamb of God, who lives and reigns world without end. Amen.

● ● ●

Come, Lord Jesus! Maranatha! You promised that those who drink the water You will give will not thirst again, because it will give them eternal life (Jn 4:14). Lord, give us this water of the Holy Spirit always, the water of grace and conversion and healing. We want to drink "Jesus' water" to make us obedient to the Father's will always as His beloved children.

---

13) The intercession of the Blessed Virgin Mary

**All/... Dear Blessed Mother, Mother of Jesus and our Mother, Spouse of the Holy Spirit, the Immaculate Conception, Mother of the Cross, we thank you for interceding for us before the throne of your Son, Jesus Christ. Help us to imitate your humble discipleship and obedience to God's word, and to ponder it. Teach us to love and imitate Jesus, as you did, and to do all that He tells us. Cover our family bloodlines in your mantle of grace; we invoke your power as the Mother of God, that you crush the head of the proud serpent beneath your humble feet.

**P/... Litany of praises of the Blessed Virgin Mary*

Holy Mary, Mother of God ...	*Pray for us.*
Holy Mary, Spouse of the Holy Spirit ...	*Pray for us.*
Holy Mary, The Immaculate Conception ...	*Pray for us.*
Holy Mary, Virgin and Mother ...	*Pray for us*
Holy Mary, Refuge of sinners ...	*Pray for us.*
Our Lady of Guadalupe ...	*Pray for us.*
Holy Mary, Mediatrix of all graces ...	*Pray for us.*
Holy Mary, Queen of the Most Holy Rosary	*Pray for us.*
Holy Mary, Queen of the Holy Angels ...	*Pray for us.*
Holy Mary, Queen of all the Saints ...	*Pray for us.*
Holy Mary, Health of the sick ...	*Pray for us.*
Holy Mary, Comforter of the afflicted ...	*Pray for us.*
Holy Mary, Help of Christians ...	*Pray for us.*
Our Lady of the Miraculous Medal ...	*Pray for us.*
Holy Mary, Mother and Queen of families	*Pray for us.*

*P/... We fly to your patronage,
**All/... O holy Mother of God; despise not our petitions in our necessities, but deliver us from all dangers, O glorious and blessed Virgin. Amen.

*P/... We ask the protection of the Archangels: Saint Michael, Saint Raphael and Saint Gabriel, and all the Angels and Saints for all our families; may they keep us safe and sound and guide us home to Heaven. Amen.

14) Enthronement of our families to the Sacred Heart of Jesus and Immaculate Heart of Mary
You may use the prayer of consecration on Appendix VIII as an alternative

**All/... O Most Sacred Heart of Jesus, You revealed to Saint Margaret Mary Your desire to rule over all Christian hearts and families; I enthrone You in my heart and in my whole generations to be the Alpha and Omega, the Beginning and End, the Prince of Peace. Together with the Pure and Immaculate Heart of Mother Mary, may Your Kingdom come; Your Divine will be done in us. May Your Divine Mercy reign victorious over all our sins and failings to be the salt of the earth, and the light of the world.

*P/... With confidence and simplicity of heart, we pray to our Father, as the Church prays:
**All/... Our Father..., Mail Mary..., Glory be... (pray three times)

15) Final blessing and dismissal

*P/... Gracious and Merciful Father, You make all things new in Christ, Your Son. You have brought us safe and sound to this hour in our journey to find You and have freed our families from all evil bondage. Seal us and our generations with the seal of Your Spirit and bind us forever to You, Lord our God, never to be separated. Grant our brothers and sisters who are not here with us—peace, joy, and the healing of Your love. Grant the deceased members of our families eternal happiness with You and fellowship with all the Saints. We ask this through Jesus Christ our Lord.
**All/... Amen.

*P/... *Bow your heads and receive God's blessing (optional).*
*P/... The Father of all consolations has given you new life through the Holy Spirit. In His great love, may He keep and bless you with faith, hope and charity in His Son, Jesus Christ!
**All/... Amen.

*P/… As you seek the Lord's face, may you find Him, and in finding Him may He be gracious to you and bless you with forgiveness and peace. To your deceased families, may he grant eternal rest in Heaven.
**All/… Amen.

*P/… May God's peace and favors rest upon you and overshadow you as you believe that Jesus died and rose from the dead, and lives forever to intercede for us. May you be a witness of His mercy and life-giving love to the world.
**All/… Amen.

*P/… May Almighty God bless you, +the Father, and the Son, and the Holy Spirit.
**All/… Amen.

*P/… Go in the peace and joy of the Risen Christ.
**All/… "Thanks be to God, who always leads us in triumph in Christ" (2 Cor 2:14).

Appendix I

Seven Capital Sins: the primary open doors

You may use extra sheets if necessary (the seven capital sins are the primary open doors to all bondage)

Anger: a desire to seek revenge for a wrong done

Envy: sorrow/grief/inordinate desire for another's good

Sloth: inordinate love of rest which leads us to neglect our duties

Lust: inordinate craving/indulgence of the carnal pleasures, it affects all our 5 senses

Pride: a person aiming higher than he/she is, or wishing to appear above what one really is. Love of one's own excellence which competes with God's excellence.

Avarice (Greed): inordinate desire and love of riches and worldly goods

Gluttony: excessive/inordinate love of eating and drinking

Preborn infants and childhood wounds

Unforgiveness, fear, self-hatred, etc. prevent us from receiving healing. They can destroy our relationship with God and keep us locked in a vicious circle of bondage. These wounds result from past painful events that are remote from us (i.e. not in our immediate consciousness), but can be accessed through self-reflection as we monitor our thoughts, feelings, desires, and actions that speak of desolation.

Investigation Sheet III   *HealingYouandYourFamilyTree©*

Unholy soul-ties, choices and affections

Name relationships that have negatively affected you (unholy soul-ties); relationships where God's Commandments have been violated (i.e., false love); true love always obeys God. Have you made death-wishes, suicide attempts, etc? "No one whose actions are unholy belongs to God" (1 Jn 3:10).

Investigation Sheet IV   HealingYouandYourFamilyTree©

The occult, Freemasonry and New Age involvement

Name memories of experiences and involvement in these areas (findings may overlap with information on sheets II, III, IV, V, and VI). If so, include them also. Occult activities include New Age, superstition, Eastern religions, blood pacts, witchcraft, voodoo, etc.

Rejection of God's Church, her teachings, and morals

Denial or rejection of Jesus Christ, His Church and her teachings, abandoning the faith, profaning the Saints, desecrating holy persons, objects and places: the Bible, the Cross, the Blessed Sacrament, the Ten Commandments, invoking Satan's help, anger at God, cursing God, apostasy, atheism, etc.

Family and generational bondage

Name known or suspected issues and concerns in your biological (or adopted) family background (both parents) as much as you know and can find out.

Appendix II

Vocabulary of feelings

Words that convey consolation (positive or healthy emotions):

absorbed	energetic	merry
acceptance	enchanted	mirthful
affection	engrossed	moved
amazed	enjoyment	open
amused	enlivened	optimistic
animated	easy-going	overjoyed
anticipation	ecstatic	overwhelmed
alert, alive	enthusiastic	peaceful
ardent	excited	pleased
aroused	exhilarated	pleasant
assured	expansive	pure
astonished	expectant	proud
attached	exultant	quiet
attracted	fulfilled	radiant
awe	free	refreshed
blissful	friendly	relaxed
buoyant	fascinated	relieved
calm	generous	sacred
carefree	glad	satisfied
caring	glowing	secured
cheerful	good-humored	sensitive
cherished	grateful	self-assured
closeness	gratified	serene
comfortable	glorious	spellbound
comforted	gleeful	splendid
compassion	happy	stimulated
complacent	helpful	surprised
concerned	holy	tender
consoled	hopeful	thankful
contented	inspired	thrilled
cool	intense	touched
curious	interested	tranquil
confident	intrigued	trusting / trusted
composed	invigorated	triumph

delighted
desired
eager
ebullient
effervescent
elated
encourage

involved
joyful
jubilant
kind
keen
loved
mellow

upbeat
uplifted
vigilance
warm
wanted
wonderful
zeal

Words that convey desolation (negative or unhealthy emotions):

afraid	envious	pissed-off
agitated	envy	placid
aggressive	enraged	pride
aggravated	enraptured	pulled apart
agony	enthralled	puzzled
alarmed	evil	rage
aloof	fatigued	rancorous
alienated	fear	rejected
angry	fearful	reluctant
anguished	fidgety	remorse
annoyed	forlorn	repulsed
anxious	frightened	resentment
apathetic	frustrated	restless
apprehensive	furious	revulsion
ashamed	fury	raptured
bewitched	gloomy	ruined
bitter	guilty	sad
blah	harried	scared
blue	helpless	shame
blocked	hesitant	shocked
bored	horrible	skeptical
boredom	horrified	sleepy
brokenhearted	hostile	sorrowful
burdened	hot	sorry
chagrined	humiliated	spiritless
cold	hurt	split
confused	hate	spite
contempt	heavy	startled
concerned	hysteria	surprised
crabby	impatient	suspicious
crushed	imprisoned	stingy
damaged	indifferent	suffering
dazed	insulted	tepid
dead	insecurity	terrified
defeated	irate	terror
dejected	irritated	tired
depressed	isolated	tormented
disappointed	jealous	tense
disapproved	jittery	troubled
disconnected	laid back	threatened

discontent	lazy	timid
disenchanted	listless	unhappy
disgusted	lonely	unnerved
disheartened	loneliness	upset
disillusioned	lulled	uptight
disliked	lust	uncomfortable
dismayed	mad	unconcerned
displeasure	mean	uneasy
disquieted	miserable	used, I feel
dissatisfied	mournful	vain
distracted	neglected	vexed
distressed	nervous	violated
disturbed	nettled	vengeful
divided	nothing	wall/walled
downcast	numb	wary
downhearted	overwhelmed	weary
dragging	outraged	withdrawn
dread	oppressed	woeful
dull	panic	worried
edgy	pity	wrathful
embarrassed	passive	wretched
embittered	pensive	
exasperated	perplexed	
exhausted	pessimistic	
empty		

This vocabulary of feelings helps us to clearly and specifically identify and name interior (affective) movements so we can talk to Jesus about them, and also share them in spiritual direction. It helps us also to be in touch with our true inner self, so that we can express ourselves in concrete terms, and seek ways of resolving interior conflicts and deepening our relationships.

Appendix III

Novena to Our Lady of the Miraculous Medal

Immaculate Mary (Lourdes Hymn)

Immaculate Mary, your praises we sing.
You reign now in splendor with Jesus our King.

Chorus:
Ave, Ave, Ave, Maria!
Ave, Ave, Maria!

In heaven the blessed your glory proclaim,
On earth we your children invoke your sweet name (repeat Chorus)

Opening prayer:
In the name of the Father and of the Son and of the Holy Spirit. Amen.

Come, O Holy Spirit, fill the hearts of Your faithful, and kindle in them the fire of Your love. Send forth Your Spirit, and they shall be created. And You shall renew the face of the earth.

Let us pray:
O God, whom by the light of the Holy Spirit, did instruct the hearts of the faithful, grant that in the same Spirit to be truly wise, and ever to rejoice in His consolations.
Through Jesus Christ our Lord. Amen.

O Mary, conceived without sin, pray for us who have recourse to thee (*pray three times*).

O Lord Jesus Christ, who have vouchsafed to glorify by numberless miracles the Blessed Virgin Mary, immaculate from the first moment of her conception, grant that all who devoutly implore her protection on earth, may eternally enjoy Your presence in heaven, who, with the Father and Holy Spirit, live and reign, God, for ever and ever. Amen.

O Lord Jesus Christ, who for the accomplishment of Your greatest works, have chosen the weak things of the world, that no flesh may glory in Your sight; and who for a better and more widely diffused belief in the

Immaculate Conception of Your Mother, have wished that the Miraculous Medal be manifested to Saint Catherine Labouré, grant, we beseech You, that filled with like humility, we may glorify this mystery by word and work. Amen.

Memorare:

Remember, O most compassionate Virgin Mary, that never was it known that anyone who fled to your protection, implored your assistance, or sought your intercession was left unaided. Inspired with this confidence, we fly unto you, O Virgin of virgins, our Mother; to you we come; before you we kneel sinful and sorrowful. O Mother of the Word Incarnate, despise not our petitions, but in your clemency hear and answer them. Amen.

Novena prayer:

O Immaculate Virgin Mary, Mother of Our Lord Jesus and our Mother, penetrated with the most lively confidence in your all-powerful and never failing intercession, manifested so often through the Miraculous Medal, we your loving and trustful children implore you to obtain for us the graces and favors we ask during this Novena, if they be beneficial to our immortal souls, and the souls for whom we pray. (*Here, privately form your petitions.*)

You know, O Mary, how often our souls have been the sanctuaries of your Son who hates iniquity. Obtain for us then a deep hatred for sin and that purity of heart which will attach us to God alone so that our every thought, word and deed may tend to His greater glory. Obtain for us also a spirit of prayer and self-denial that we may recover by penance what we have lost by sin and at length attain to that blessed abode where you are the Queen of Angels and of men. Amen.

Act of Consecration to Our Lady of the Miraculous Medal:

O Virgin Mother of God, Mary Immaculate,

we dedicate and consecrate ourselves to you under the title of Our Lady of the Miraculous Medal. May this Medal be for each one of us a sure sign of your affection for us and a constant reminder of our duties toward you. Ever while wearing it, may we be blessed by your loving protection and preserved in the grace of your Son. O most powerful Virgin, Mother of our Savior, keep us close to you every moment of our lives. Obtain for us, your children, the grace of a happy death; so that, in union with you, we may enjoy the bliss of heaven forever. Amen.

O Mary, conceived without sin, pray for us who have recourse to you (*pray three times*).

Appendix IV

Rules for the Discernment of Spirits[413]

———————

Rules to help discern, recognize, and understand spiritual movements in our soul.
If they are good (of God), we accept them.
If they are bad (not of God), we reject them.

* These 14 Rules (#313–327) apply to the First Week of the Spiritual Exercises of Saint Ignatius of Loyola.

First Rule
Those who live sinful lives from one mortal sin to another:
- The evil spirit -
  o Suggests gratifying pleasures and sensual delights
  o Corrupts the imaginations to keep us sinning and increase our sins
- The good spirit uses a reverse method -
  o Using the light of reason, he stings our conscience so we can change direction for good
  o Fills us with remorse for our sins, and helps us decrease our sins

Second Rule
Those who strive to live holy lives and serve God:
- The evil spirit -
  o Will inflict anxiety, sadness, and inspire false thoughts to obstruct and block us
  o Will want to stop us from moving forward in the love of God
- The good spirit -
  o Will encourage and strengthen, inspire, console, and fill us with tears and peace
  o Will remove obstacles, give joy, and make things easy for our growth in holiness

* Rules 3–14 below apply only to those in the "Second Rule" above.

Third Rule
Spiritual consolation

- The soul is filled with zeal, and is on fire for God. It loves God dearly; it loves other creatures only for God's sake and not for their own sake.
- Sheds tears out of love and praise of God, for sins committed, or for Christ's suffering.
- Every increase of faith, hope, and love. Interior peace and joy drawing us to heavenly things, to the salvation of our souls. Our soul is calm and resting in God's love.

Fourth Rule
Spiritual desolation
- The soul is in darkness and troubled; there is heaviness of spirit. There is attraction to worldly and earthly things, and restlessness caused by temptations.
- The soul lacks faith, hope, and love; it is slothful, tepid, and sad as if separated from God.
- Thoughts are negative in every way, and are contrary to the thoughts in consolation.

Rules 5–9 help to guide us through times of desolation.

Fifth Rule
- If in desolation, do not make a change to the former decision you made before the desolation, or the decision you made when you were in consolation, that is, never turn the ship in the midst of a storm.
  o In consolation, the good spirit surely directs and counsels us.
  o In desolation, the evil spirit also directs and counsels us, but we will be lost if we obey him.

Sixth Rule
- When in desolation, Resist it! Fight it! Pray more, meditate on Scripture, do self-reflection and self-examination. Do some penance; mortify yourself.

Seventh Rule
- When in desolation, it is because God has left us to our natural powers to resist the devil's attacks and trials. But God's grace is never totally withdrawn, only that we don't feel it. God has withdrawn intense favors and overflowing love, but leaving us with enough grace to be saved.

Eight Rule

- When in desolation, be patient and persevere as a way to overcome any anger in us. Consider that consolation will return. As in the "Sixth Rule" above, we must diligently resist the desolation.

Ninth Rule

Three reasons why we suffer desolation:

- It is our fault. We are tepid and slothful; we are not serious with our spiritual lives.
- It is a test of our faithfulness. God is testing us to see if we truly love Him (seeking the God of consolation) or if we only want to get something out of Him (seeking the consolation of God).
- God wants us to have true self-knowledge, so that we realize that by our own ability, we cannot make spiritual progress. All is a grace and a gift. We cannot claim any credit for what God is doing in our spiritual lives.

* Rules 10–11 teach us what to do in times of consolation.

Tenth Rule

- Get ready for the desolation that will follow by storing up strength. Consider and plan what you will do when desolation returns.

Eleventh Rule

- Remain humble and lower yourself as much as possible. Recall how weak we are in desolation.
- If in desolation, we recall that sufficient grace was given to resist the enemy. Trust God and find strength in Him.

* Rules 12–14 teach us three dangerous tactics of the devil.

Twelfth Rule

- The evil one behaves like a woman quarrelling with a man. If the man proves strong, resolute, and fearless, the woman is discouraged and runs away.
- If he proves weak and flees, the woman's anger and aggression mounts; she gets tougher.
- Similarly, the evil one is weakened and flees when we, alive in the Holy Spirit, boldly resist his temptations.
- But if we are afraid and become discouraged, the devil becomes wild, fierce, and deadly, and can destroy us.

Thirteenth Rule

- The evil one acts like a false lover. He wants the soul being tempted with lies and deceptions to keep everything secret. If we tell our confessor or a person who is alive in the Holy Spirit (who understands his tricks), he gets angry because he is sure to fail
- Learn to bring things into the light by consulting with a spiritual director or trusted friend.

Fourteenth Rule

- The evil one acts like an army commander who wants to seize his enemy's territory or stronghold. First, he explores the area, and then attacks at the weakest point.
- Similarly, the devil studies every aspect of our lives: spiritual and moral, the virtues we practice, and how we live in the flesh. Then he attacks and storms the areas where we are weakest with regard to our eternal salvation.

Rules to help discern, recognize and understand spiritual movements in our soul[414]

These 8 Rules (#329–336) are for more accurate discernment of spirits; they apply to the Second Week of the Spiritual Exercises of Saint Ignatius

Rules 1–2 concern consolation.

First Rule

- God and His Angels give true happiness and spiritual joy; and dispel sadness and disturbances.
- The evil one fights and tries to destroy our consolation by false reasoning; he sows doubts and deception to make us fall.

Second Rule

- God alone gives consolation without any previous cause; that is, we cannot attribute our peace, joy and love for God to our thoughts or actions, that are spurious.

Rules 3–6 help us deal with deceptive consolation.

Third Rule

- If our consolation had a previous cause, both the good angels and the bad spirits can cause it, but for different goals.
- The key in this rule is to watch for the fruit!
- The good angels console to move the soul to become more perfect in holiness like Jesus.
- The bad spirits console to lead the soul to follow its own perverse intentions and evil desires, causing the soul to fall from grace and depend on itself rather than on God.

Fourth Rule

- The evil spirit can disguise himself as an angel of light, he suggests thoughts that we agree with, and later adds his own.
- He suggests holy thoughts that agree with the sanctity of the soul, then in little subtle steps draws the soul to his own evil plans.

Fifth Rule

- Carefully note the whole path of our thoughts and experiences: the beginning, the middle and the end. If they lead to what is right, good, and holy, they are from the good angel.
- But if they end in some evil, or distraction, or less good than previously planned, or weakens and disquiets our soul, if we lose our peace and tranquility, they are from the evil one.
- If what started good ends up in confusion, desolation, and negative spirituality, it is from the evil spirit.

Sixth Rule

- If we realize we have been deceived due to the trail of evil and bad fruit, we should carefully review the stages of our thoughts: how it began, how the evil one crept in to take away our peace, and how we ended in enemy territory. This will help us guard against future attacks, since we now have knowledge of his tricks.

* Rules 7–8 help us to understand more the dynamics of consolation.

Seventh Rule

- As we grow in perfection, the good spirits act in a delicate, gentle, and delightful way, as drops of water penetrating a sponge.
- The action of the evil spirits is violent, noisy, and disturbing, as drops of water falling on a stone.

- If we are going from bad to worse, the evil spirits act in a reverse way.

The state or disposition of our soul determines how the good or evil spirits enter and act.
  - o If we are well disposed (open) to the good or evil spirits, they enter quietly without disturbance.
  - o If we are not well disposed (not open) to the good or evil spirits, they enter with noise and commotion, and we know it.

Eight Rule
- When consolation is directly from God, no deception can be involved.
- The one who experienced the consolation must be attentive and distinguish the consolation itself from the after effects of the consolation.
- In the actual consolation, we are still fervent and favored with the graces God gave in it.
- After the consolation itself, we often make resolutions which are not from God.
  - o These may come from our reasoning, interpretations or judgments.
  - o They may come from the good or evil spirits.
  - o So, they must be examined carefully and approved before we apply them to our lives.

Appendix V

The Chaplet of Saint Michael the Archangel

Prayer for assistance and protection against Satan and its demons

A) *Begin the Chaplet with this invocation on the medal:*

V/. O God, come to my assistance.
R/. O Lord, make haste to help me.

V/. Glory be to the Father, and to the Son, and to the Holy Spirit.
R/. As it was in the beginning, is now and ever shall be, world without end.

Recite one Our Father and three Hail Marys after each of the following nine salutations in honor of the nine Choirs of Angels

B) *On the first separate bead of the Chaplet, recite:*

1– By the intercession of St. Michael and the celestial Choir of the **Seraphim**, may it please God to make us worthy to burn with the fire of perfect charity. Amen. *(Our Father. 3 Hail Marys).*

2– By the intercession of St. Michael and the celestial Choir of the **Cherubim,** may God in His good pleasure grant us the grace to abandon the ways of sin and follow the path of Christian perfection. Amen. *(Our Father. 3 Hail Marys).*

3– By the intercession of St. Michael and the celestial Choir of the **Thrones,** may it please God to infuse into our hearts the Spirit of true and sincere humility. Amen. *(Our Father. 3 Hail Marys).*

4– By the intercession of St. Michael and the celestial Choir of the **Dominions,** may it please God to grant us grace to have dominion over our senses and overcome our unruly passions. Amen. *(Our Father. 3 Hail Marys).*

5– By the intercession of St. Michael and the celestial Choir of the **Virtues,** may it please God to preserve us from falling into temptation, and may He deliver us from evil. Amen. *(Our Father. 3 Hail Marys).*

6– By the intercession of St. Michael and the celestial Choir of the **Powers,** may God vouchsafe to keep our souls from the snares and temptations of the devil. Amen. *(Our Father. 3 Hail Marys).*

7– By the intercession of St. Michael and the celestial Choir of the **Principalities,** may it please God to fill our souls with the true and sincere spirit of obedience. Amen. *(Our Father. 3 Hail Marys).*

8– By the intercession of St. Michael and the celestial Choir of the **Archangels,** may it please God to grant us the gift of perseverance in faith, and in all good works, in order that we may attain the glory of Heaven. Amen. *(Our Father. 3 Hail Marys).*

9– By the intercession of St. Michael and the celestial Choir of the **Angels,** may God vouchsafe to grant us their guardianship through this mortal life, and after death a happy entrance into the everlasting glory of Heaven. Amen. *(Our Father. 3 Hail Marys).*

C) *On the four remaining beads, recite one Our Father in honor of each of the Archangels:* **Saint Michael, Saint Gabriel, Saint Raphael** *and our own* **Guardian Angel.**

Anthem: O glorious prince, St. Michael, chief and commander of the heavenly hosts, guardian of the souls of men, conqueror of the rebel angels, steward of the palace of the Divine King and our worthy leader, endowed with holiness and power, deliver us from every evil. With full confidence we have recourse to you, that by your gracious protection we may be enabled to make progress every day in the faithful service of God.

V/. Pray for us, O most glorious St. Michael, Prince of the Church of Jesus Christ.
R/. That we may be made worthy of the promises of Christ.

Let us pray: Almighty and Everlasting God, Who, by a prodigy of goodness and a merciful desire for the salvation of all men, has appointed the most glorious Archangel, St. Michael, Prince of Your Church, make us worthy, we beseech You, to be delivered by his powerful protection from all our enemies, that none of them may harass us at the hour of death, but that we may be conducted by St. Michael into the august presence of Your Divine Majesty. This we beg through the merits of Jesus Christ Our Lord. Amen.

Saint Michael the Archangel's Prayer

St. Michael the Archangel, defend us in battle. Be our protection against the wickedness and snares of the Devil. May God rebuke him, we humbly pray, and do thou, O Prince of the heavenly hosts, by the power of God, cast into hell Satan, and all evil spirits, who wander throughout the world seeking the ruin of souls. Amen.

The Holy Bible is the source of the nine choirs of angels that are revealed to us by God (Gen 3:24; Is 6:2; Col 1:16; Eph 1:21; Rom 8:38). Saint Michael the Archangel desires that we honor him through this Chaplet. He appeared in a vision to a devout Servant of God, Antonia d'Astonac, requesting that he be honored by nine salutations to the nine Choirs of Angels. He promised to the devotees of this Chaplet that they would have an escort of nine Angels from each of the nine Choirs when approaching Holy Communion. He promised in addition that those who would recite the Chaplet daily would receive his continuous assistance and that of the holy Angels during this life and after.[415]

Appendix VI

Occult and new Age Vocabulary

Crystal ball, palm-reading, handwriting analysis, psychic hotlines, yoga, horoscope, astrology, pirates, transcendental meditations or Eastern spirituality (often disguised as good),

Ouija board, fortune-telling, New Age, séance, Santeria, medium, Harry Potter, dungeon and dragon, occult games, casting spells, witchcraft, animal sacrifice, telepathy, kabala, mind control, charms, magic, sorcery, divination, wicca, blood rituals, holism, reiki. Have you entered a masonic temple or lodge, willingly witnessed or entertained New Age performance, any one practiced occult or New Age in your family tree?

Levitation, clairvoyance, astral projection/communication, visited/entered masonic/pagan temples/shrines, freemasonry and associated sororities, death-wish, rage within, feel like killing someone, metallic music, evil presence, visited by demons, hears voices, experienced nightmares, cutting, acupuncture (according to Taoism method).

Have rituals been done on you, or participated in rituals? Do you, or have you belonged to or taken part in the following: gangs, hate groups, terrorism, satanic initiation and worship, Halloween, drugs, addictive and crippling sexual bondage in any form, superstition, fascination with evil, spiritism, bibliomancy, druidism, spiritual-but-not-religious, crystals, electromagnetic healing, music therapy, therapeutic touch, psychic surgery, psychics, psychonautics, pyramid power, macrobiotics, homeopathy, palmistry, reflexology/iridology, polarity therapy, naturopathy, I ching, tarot card, tasseography, chiromancy, Nostradamus, water witching, astrology, biorhythms, auras, dreamwork, runes, voodoo, trance, pentacle, mantras, mutilation, mediumship, juju, incantation, kundalini energy, baphomet, alchemy?

Appendix VII

Prayer to Release from Masonic Oaths and Bondage

If you were once a Mason or are a descendant of a Mason(s), it is recommended that the following prayers be prayed from the heart. Masons make their obligations and oaths one line at a time and without prior knowledge of the requirements, like zombies; do not be like them. Where possible, first read through the prayers so you know what is involved, and to familiarize one-self with the words, some of which are difficult to pronounce. Then pray it aloud preferably in the presence of an official representative of the Church (priest or deacon) as witness who understands Freemasonry and the dangers associated with secret societies to undo the oaths. (Note: Masons make these oaths in the presence of a representative of Satan in a masonic lodge or temple). Observe a brief pause following each paragraph to allow the Holy Spirit to work in us, as a way of paying attention, and for the power of this prayer to permeate and irradiate us with divine glow. If possible, it should be prayed in the presence of our Eucharistic Lord.

~ ~ ~ ~ ~

God our Father, Creator of heaven and earth, I come to you in the name of Jesus Christ your Son. I come as a sinner seeking forgiveness, cleansing and healing of sins committed against you and against our neighbor. I honor my earthly father and mother, all my ancestors, and all your adopted children in the Spirit. I ask forgiveness for their sins and mine against You. I forgive them for their evil choices that have affected our family in any way. I renounce and rebuke Satan and every other demonic power causing problems in my family.

In the name of Jesus Christ, I renounce and forsake all involvement in Freemasonry or any other 'Lodge' or 'Craft' by my ancestors and myself. I renounce witchcraft spirit, the principal spirit behind Freemasonry, and I renounce Baphomet, the Spirit of the antichrist and the curse of the Luciferian doctrine. I renounce the idolatry, blasphemy, secrecy and deception of Masonry at every level. I specifically renounce the insecurity, the love of position and power, the love of money, avarice (greed), and the pride that may have led any of my ancestors into Freemasonry. I renounce all the spirit of fear that held them in Masonry, especially the fear of death, of men, and the fear of trusting in Jesus Christ as our only Savior and Redeemer.

I renounce every position held in the 'Lodge' by any of my ancestors, including "Tyler," "Master", "Worshipful Master" and any others. I renounce the calling of any man "Master." Jesus Christ is my only Master and Lord. For He said, "Do not be called 'Master;' you have but one master, the Messiah" (Mt 23:10). I renounce the entrapping of others into Masonry, and observing the helplessness of others during the rituals. I renounce the effects of Masonry passed on to me through any female ancestors who felt distrusted and rejected by her husband as he entered and attended any 'Lodge' and refused to tell her of his secret activities.

1st (First) Degree:

In the name of Jesus Christ, I renounce the oaths taken, and I break the curses involved in the First or Entered Apprentice degree, especially their effects on the throat and tongue. I renounce the Hoodwink, the blindfold and its effects on the emotions and eyes, including all the confusion, fear of the dark, fear of the light, and fear of sudden noises. I renounce the secret word Boaz and all it means. I renounce the mixing and mingling of truth and error and the blasphemy of this degree of Masonry. I renounce the noose around the neck, the fear of choking and the evil spirits causing asthma, hay fever, emphysema and any other breathing difficulties. I renounce the compass point, sword or spear held against the breast, the fear of death by stabbing pain and the fear of heart attack from this first degree.

In the name of Jesus Christ I now pray for healing of (the throat, vocal cords, nasal passages, sinus, bronchial tubes, etc.) and for the healing of the speech area, and the release of the power of the Word of God in me and through me and my family.

2nd (Second) Degree:

In the name of Jesus Christ, I renounce the oaths taken, and I break the curses involved in the second or Fellow Craft degree of Masonry, especially the curses on the heart and chest. I renounce the secret words *Jachin* and *Shibboleth* and all that these mean. I cut off any emotional hardness, apathy, unbelief, indifference and deep seated anger in my family and me. In the name of Jesus I pray for the healing of the chest/lung/heart area and also for the healing of my emotions that I may be more sensitive to the presence and inspiration of the Holy Spirit.

3rd (Third) Degree:

In the name of Jesus Christ, I renounce the oaths taken, and I break the curses involved in the third or Master Mason degree, especially the curses on the stomach and womb area. I renounce the secret words *Maila Bone*, *Machabe-n*, *Machbinna* and *Tubal Cain*, and all that they mean. I renounce the spirit of death from the blows to the head enacted as ritual murder, the fear of death, false martyrdom, and fear of violent gang attack, assault or rape and the helplessness of this degree. I renounce the falling into the coffin or stretcher involved in the ritual of murder. I renounce the false resurrection of this degree. Jesus Christ is the Resurrection and the Life (Jn 11:25)! I also renounce the blasphemous kissing of the Bible in the witchcraft oath. I cut off all spirits of death, witchcraft and deception. In the name of Jesus I pray for the healing of the stomach, gall bladder, womb, liver and any other organs of my body affected by Masonry. I ask for the release of the Spirit of Compassion and Understanding upon my family and me.

Holy Royal Arch Degree:
In the name of Jesus Christ, I renounce and forsake the oaths taken, and I break the curses involved in the Holy Royal Arch Degree of Masonry, especially the oath regarding the removal of the head from the body and the exposing of the brains to the hot sun. I renounce the 'Mark Lodge' and the mark in the form of squares and angles which marks the person for life. I also reject the jewel or talisman that may have been made from this mark sign and worn at lodge meetings. I renounce the false secret name of God, *Jahbulon*, and the password, *Ammi Ruhamah* and all they mean. I renounce the false communion or Eucharist taken in this degree, and all the mockery, skepticism and unbelief about the redemptive work of Jesus Christ on the cross of Calvary. I break these curses and their effects on my family and me in the name of Jesus Christ, and I pray for healing of the brain, the mind, etc.

18ᵗʰ (Eighteenth) Degree:
In the name of Jesus Christ, I renounce the oaths taken, and I break the curses involved in the eighteenth degree of Masonry, the Most Wise Sovereign Knight of the Pelican and the Eagle and Sovereign Prince Rose Croix of Heredom. I renounce and reject the Pelican witchcraft spirit, as well as the occult influence of the Rosicrucians and the Kabbala in this degree. I renounce the claim that the death of Jesus Christ was a 'dire calamity', and also the deliberate mockery and twisting of the Christian doctrine of the Atonement. I renounce the blasphemy and rejection of the divinity of Jesus Christ, and the secret words *Igne Natura Renovatur Integra* and its burning. I renounce the mockery of the communion taken in this degree, which includes a biscuit, salt and white wine.

30ᵗʰ (Thirtieth) Degree:
I renounce the oaths taken, and I break the curses involved in the thirtieth degree of Masonry, the Grand Knight Kadosh and Knight of the Black and White Eagle. I renounce the password, *"Stibium Alkabar,"* and all it means.

31ˢᵗ (Thirty-First) Degree:

In the name of Jesus Christ, I renounce the oaths taken, and I break the curses involved in the thirty-first degree of Masonry, the Grand Inspector Inquisitor Commander. I renounce all the gods and goddesses of Egypt which are honored in this degree, including Anubis with the ram's head, Osiris the Sun god, Isis the sister and wife of 0siris and also the moon goddess. I renounce the Soul of Cheres, the false symbol of immortality, the Chamber of the dead and the false teaching of reincarnation.

32nd (Thirty-Second) Degree:

In the name of Jesus Christ, I renounce the oaths taken, and I break the curses involved in the thirty-second degree of Masonry, the Sublime Prince of the Royal Secret. I renounce masonry's false trinitarian deity *Aum*, and its parts, Brahma the creator, Vishnu the preserver and Shiva the destroyer. I renounce the deity of *Ahura-Mazda*, the claimed spirit or source of all light, and the worship with fire, which are an abomination to God, and also the drinking from a human skull in many rites.

York Rite:

In the name of Jesus Christ, I renounce the oaths taken, and I break the curses involved in the York Rite of Freemasonry, including Mark Master, Past Master, Most Excellent Master, Royal Master, Select Master, Super Excellent Master, the Orders of the Red Cross, the Knights of Malta and the Knights Templar degrees. I renounce the secret words of *Joppa, Keb Raioth*, and *Maher-Shalal-Hash-Baz*. I renounce the vows taken on a human skull, the crossed swords, and the curse and death wish of Judas of having the head cut off and placed on top of a church spire. I renounce the unholy communion and especially of drinking from a human skull in many Rites.

Shriners (America only - doesn't apply in other countries):

In the name of Jesus Christ, I renounce the oaths taken, and I break the curses and penalties involved in the Ancient Arabic Order of the Nobles of the Mystic Shrine. I renounce the piercing of the eyeballs with a three-edged blade, the flaying of the feet, the madness, and the worship of the false god Allah as the god of our fathers. I renounce the hoodwink, the mock hanging, the mock beheading, the mock drinking and the blood of the victim, the mock dog urinating on the initiate, and the offering of urine as a commemoration.

33ʳᵈ (Thirty-Third) and Supreme Degree:

In the name of Jesus Christ, I renounce the oaths taken, and I break the curses involved in the supreme Thirty-Third Degree of Freemasonry, the Grand Sovereign Inspector General. I renounce the secret passwords, *De Molay-Hiram Abiff, Frederick of Prussia, Micha, Macha, Bealim*, and *Adonai* and all they mean. I renounce all of the obligations of every Masonic degree, and all penalties invoked. I renounce and utterly forsake 'The Great Architect of the Universe,' who is revealed in this degree as Lucifer, and his false claim to be the universal fatherhood of God. I renounce the cable-tow around the neck. I renounce the death-wish that the wine drunk from a human skull should turn to poison and the skeleton whose cold arms are invited if the oath of this degree is violated. I renounce the three infamous assassins of their grand master, law, property and religion, and the greed and witchcraft involved in the attempt to manipulate and control the rest of mankind. In the name of God the Father, and Jesus Christ His only Son, and the Holy Spirit, I renounce and break the curses involved in the idolatry, blasphemy, secrecy and deception of Freemasonry at every level, and I invoke the Precious Blood of Jesus Christ to cleanse all the consequences of these oaths, curses and rituals in my life and on my family. I now revoke, and make null and void all previous consent given by any of my ancestors or myself to the devil to be deceived.

All other degrees:

In the name of Jesus Christ, I renounce all the other oaths taken in the rituals of every other degree, and I break the curses associated with them. I renounce all other lodges and secret societies such as Prince Hall Freemasonry, Mormonism, The Order of Amaranth, Oddfellows, Buffaloes, Druids, Foresters, Orange, Elks, Moose and Eagles Lodges, the Ku Klux Klan, The Grange, the Woodmen of the World, Riders of the Red Robe, the Knights of Pythias, the Mystic Order of the Veiled Prophets of the Enchanted Realm, the women's Orders of the Eastern Star and of the White Shrine of Jerusalem, the girls' order of the Daughters of the Eastern Star, the International Orders of Job's Daughters and of the Rainbow, the boys' Order of De Molay and their effects on me and all my family.

I renounce the ancient pagan teaching and symbolism of the First Tracing Board, the Second Tracing Board and the Third Tracing Board used in the ritual of the Blue Lodge. I renounce the pagan ritual of the 'Point within a Circle' with all its bondages and phallus worship. I renounce the occult mysticism of the black and white mosaic checkered floor with the tessellated boarder and five-pointed blazing star. I renounce the symbol 'G' and its veiled pagan symbolism and bondages. I renounce and utterly forsake the Great Architect of the Universe, who is revealed in the higher degrees as Lucifer, and his false claim to be the universal fatherhood of God. I also renounce the false claim that Lucifer is the 'Morning Star' and

'Shining One.' I declare that Jesus Christ is the Bright Morning Star of Revelation 22:16.

I renounce the 'All-Seeing Third Eye' of Freemasonry or Horus in the forehead and its pagan and occult symbolism. I renounce all false communions taken, all mockery of the redemptive work of Jesus Christ on the cross of Calvary, all unbelief, confusion and depression and all worship of Lucifer as God. I renounce and forsake the lie of Freemasonry that man is not sinful, but merely imperfect and so can redeem himself through good works.

I rejoice in the Biblical teaching that God is love, and that salvation is a free gift of God. No one can do anything to earn his/her salvation. "For God so loved the world that He gave His only begotten Son, that whoever believes in Him should not perish but have everlasting life" (Jn 3:16, NKJV). I can only be saved by the grace of Jesus Christ through faith and works (Jam 2:22, 24; Gal 5:6), and what He accomplished through His redemptive sacrifice at Calvary.

I renounce the fear of insanity, anguish, death-wishes, suicide and death in the name of Jesus Christ. Jesus Christ conquered death and He alone holds the keys of death and hell (Rev 1:18). I rejoice that He holds my life in His hands, and no one can take me away from Him (Jn 10:28). He came to give me life abundantly and eternally (Jn 10:10), and I believe His promises.

I renounce all anger, hatred, murderous thoughts, revenge, retaliation, spiritual apathy, false religion, all unbelief, especially unbelief in the Holy Bible as God's Word, and all compromise of God's Word. I renounce all spiritual searching into false religions and all striving to please God by our own effort alone. I rest in the knowledge that I have found my Lord and Savior Jesus Christ, because He first found me.

I will burn all objects in my possession which connect me with all lodges and or cultic organizations, including Masonry, Witchcraft and Mormonism and all regalia, aprons, books of rituals, rings and other jewelry. In the name of Jesus, I renounce the effects these objects of Masonry, such as the compass, the square, the noose or the blindfold, and other evil objects have had on me or my family.

All present are invited to *spiritually* perform the following actions as you feel comfortable (you may place the objects on the altar or at the Foot of the Cross of Jesus for disposal):

- ⊕ Symbolically remove the blindfold (hoodwink); the veil of mourning and give them to the Lord for disposal.
- ⊕ Symbolically cut and remove the noose from around the neck, gather it up with the cable-tow running down the body and give it all to the

Lord for His disposal.

- Renounce the false Freemasonry marriage covenant, removing from the 4th finger of the right hand the ring of this false marriage covenant, giving it to the Lord to dispose of it.
- Symbolically remove the chains and bondages of Freemasonry from your body.
- Symbolically remove all Freemasonry regalia and armor, especially the Apron.
- Repent of and seek forgiveness for having walked on all unholy ground, including Freemasonry lodges and temples, including any Mormon or other occult/Masonic organizations.
- Symbolically remove the ball and chain from the ankles.
- Proclaim that "Satan and his demons no longer have any legal rights to mislead and manipulate me because I have repented and proclaim Jesus as my Lord, my Savior and my only source of Truth."

Dear Holy Spirit please show me anything else that I need to do or pray for so that I and my family may be totally free from the consequences of the sins and effects of Masonry, Witchcraft, Mormonism and Paganism.

(Pause and listen inside to God in your heart; pray quietly as the Holy Spirit leads you).

Almighty God and Father of our Lord Jesus Christ, I humbly pray that cleanse me from all these sins which I have confessed, and all the evils I have renounced by the Blood of Your Son. Cleanse my spirit, my soul, my mind, my emotions and every part of my body affected in any way by these evils.

Father, deliver me from Satan's power and every other evil spirits associated with Masonry, Witchcraft and their other evil activities. I pray St. Michael the Archangel to bind and cast out all these spirits from me and members of my family affected by them, and touching or harming anyone, and that they go immediately and directly to the foot of the Cross of our Lord Jesus never to return to me or any member of my family again. By the Blood of Jesus, break all curses, spells, hexes and other evil bondage, and deliver us from the evil spirits of infirmity, affliction, addiction, and allergy associated with the evil of freemasonry which I have confessed and renounced. I surrender to the Lordship of Jesus Christ in the power of the Holy Spirit every area of my life.

I ask you Lord Jesus to baptize me anew in Your Spirit as You promised. I put on the Lord Jesus Christ (Rom 13:14) as my armor and protection from all evils, in the Spirit of holiness. I put on the armor of God and stand firm against the tactics of the devil, with the Helmet of salvation, Breastplate of righteousness, Belt of truth, Footgear of zeal, Shield of faith, the Sword of the Spirit and to pray always in the spirit without ceasing (Eph 6:12-18). I enthrone you, Lord Jesus in my heart for you are my Lord and my Savior, the source of living water, the Way the Truth and the Life of the world.

Thank You Father for Your love and mercy, and for Your forgiveness.

Through Jesus Christ our Lord. Amen.

(This prayer is adapted from "Unmasking Freemasonry: Removing the Hoodwink" by Selwyn Stevens who has extensively researched the subject of freemasonry)

Appendix VIII

Consecration to Jesus through Mary Immaculate[416]

O Virgin Mary, most powerful Mother of Mercy, Queen of Heaven and Earth, in accord with thy wish made known at Fatima, I consecrate myself today to thy Immaculate Heart. Reign over me, Mother of the Incarnate Word, that I may be thine in prosperity and in adversity, in joy and in sorrow, in health and in sickness, in life and in death.

Most compassionate Heart of Mary, Queen of Virgins, watch over my mind, senses and heart and preserve me from the impurity of sin which thou hast lamented so sorrowfully at Fatima. I want to be pure and holy like thee. Queen of Peace, make me thy instrument of goodness as thou art God's perfect instrument of peace.

I, a sinner, renew and ratify today in thy Heart, O Immaculate Mother, the vows of my baptism; I renounce forever Satan, his deceit and empty promises, and I give myself entirely to Jesus Christ, Incarnate Wisdom, to carry my cross after Him all the days of my life, and to be more faithful to Him than I have ever been before.

Queen of the Most Holy Rosary, in the presence of all the angels and Saints, I choose thee this day for my Mother and Intercessor. I consecrate to thee and to thy Immaculate Heart, as thy child and slave of love, my body and soul, all my possessions, tangible and intangible, and all my good works, past, present and future.

My dearest Mother, may I and all that belongs to me be at thy disposal without exception for thy good pleasure and for the greater glory of God, now and for all eternity. Amen.

Select Bibliography

Amorth, Gabriele. *An Exorcist Tells His Story* (San Francisco: Ignatius Press, 1999).

Augustine. *The Liturgy of the Hours. Vol. IV. Confessions Lib.7, 10* (New York: Catholic Book Publishing Co., 1975).

Aquinas, Thomas. *Summa Theologica I-II, 81.2.1* (New York: Benziger Brothers, Inc., 1947).

Aquinas, Thomas. *O Precious and Wonderful Banquet!* (New York: Catholic Book Publishing Co., 1975).

Benedict XVI. Papal address to the community of the Pontifical Theological Faculty Teresianum (Vatican City: May 19, 2011, Zenit.org).

Benedict XVI. Benedict XVI is encouraging the faithful to rediscover the beauty of being baptized in the Holy Spirit (Zenit.org, Vatican City: May 11, 2008).

Carrera, Norberto Rivera. *A Call to Vigilance (Pastoral Instruction on New Age)*, January 7, 1996.

Carroll, Joe. *The Unholy Trinity* (Palmdale: Christian Book Club of America, 1995).

Carroll, Warren H. *Our Lady of Guadalupe And the Conquest of Darkness* (Front Royal: Christendom Press, 1983).

Catechism of the Catholic Church (New York: Doubleday, 1699).

Catholiceducation.org (accessed on May 25, 2014).

Congregation for the Doctrine of the Faith. *Dominus Iesus.*

Congregation for the Doctrine of the Faith. *Christian Faith and Demonology* (2014).

Congregation for the Doctrine of the Faith. *INDE AB ALIQUOT ANNIS On The Current Norms Governing Exorcisms* (September 29, 1984).

Clement XIII. *"In Eminenti"* (1738).

Clement. *The Liturgy of the Hours. Vol. II. Repent* (New York: Catholic Book Publishing Co., 1976).

Clement I. *The Liturgy of the Hours. Vol. III.* (New York: Catholic Book Publishing Co., 1975).

Curtis, Barbara. *What is 'New Age' Religion, and Why Can't Christians Get on Board?* (crosswalk.com. accessed August 2011).

Cyprian. *The Liturgy of the Hours. Vol. II. He has given us life; he has taught us how to pray.*

Cyril of Jerusalem. *The Liturgy of the Hours. Vol. II. The Living water of the Holy Spirit.*

Cyril of Jerusalem. *The Liturgy of the Hours. Vol. IV. Catechetical Instruction. On the Creed* (New York: Catholic Book Publishing Co., 1976).

Dillon, George F. *Grand Orient Freemasonry Unmasked*, 1885.

Domenico Agasso, Jr. Francis: *"Pray with your heart, not like a parrot"*

(Vatican Insider, May 16, 2014).

Dorotheus. *The Liturgy of the Hours. Vol. III. The reason for all disturbance.*

Duff, Frank. *The Woman of Genesis.*

Edeh, Emmanuel C.S.Sp. Composed this signature prayer of the Center for Eucharistic Adoration, Elele, Nigeria.

Fisher, Paul A. *Their God is the Devil* (American Foundation Research, Inc., 1991).

Francis. Address to Diplomatic Corps, March 22, 2013 (radiovaticana.va, accessed April 28, 2014).

Gadium et spes.

Galaeazzi, Giacomo. Article reported in Vatican Insider, June 1, 2014.

Gregory of Nyssa. *The Liturgy of the Hours. Vol. III. Christ should be manifest in our whole life.*

Gustin, Marilyn. *You Can Know God* (Liguori: Liguori Publication, 1993).

Haffert, John M. *Her Own Words to the Nuclear Age* (New Jersey: 101 Foundation, Inc., 1993).

Hampsch, John H. C.M.F. *Healing Your Family Tree* (Huntington: Our Sunday Visitor Publishing Division, 1989).

Ignatius of Antioch. *The Liturgy of the Hours. Vol. III. Have Faith in Christ, and love.*

Kalvelage, Francis M. FI. *Kolbe Saint of the Immaculata* (New Bedford: Franciscans of the Immaculate 2001).

Kempis, Thomas à. *The Imitation of Christ* (Rockford: Tan Books and Publishers, Inc., 1989).

Jean-Pierre de Caussade. *Abandonment to Divine Providence* (New York: Doubleday, 1975).

John Paul II. *Salvifici Doloris.*

John Paul II. *Familiaris Consortio.*

John Paul II. *Novo Millennio Ineunte.*

John Paul II. *The Theology of the Body* (Boston: Pauline Books and Media, 1997).

John Paul II. Homily given during pilgrimage to Lourdes on the occasion of 150th anniversary of promulgation of the Dogma of the Immaculate Conception in Prairie de la Ribère Sunday, 15 August 2004 (Vatican.va accessed May 29, 2014).

John Paul II. From an interview given to Catholics of Fulda in 1980 when he had been pope for several years.

John Paul II. This statement was reported in the Wall Street Journal of November 9, 1976 from an address to the U.S. bishops before Cardinal Karol Józef Wojtyła became Pope John Paul II (See of Peter, October 16, 1978 to April 2, 2005).

John of the Cross. *The Collected Works of St. John of the Cross* (Washington D.C.: ICS Publications, 1991).

Kowalska, Faustina. *Divine Mercy in My Soul* (Stockbridge: Marian Press, 2008).

Larson, Bob. *Larson's Book of Spiritual Warfare* (Nashville: Thomas Nelson

Publishers, 1999).

Leo XIII. *Dall'alto Dell'apostolico Seggio,* (October 15, 1890).

Louis Marie de Montfort. *Preparation for Total Consecration according to St. Louis Marie de Montfort* (Montfort Publications, 2006).

Lumen Gentium.

Marchi, John de. *The True Story of Fatima A Complete Account of the Fatima Apparitions.*

McElhone, James F.C.S.C. *Particular Examen* (Harrison: Roman Catholic Books, 1952).

Mueller, Michael C.Ss.R. *Prayer the Key to Salvation* (Rockford: Tan Books and Publishers, Inc., 1985).

Medjugorje.org Our Lady's June 02, 2014 Message (accessed June 2, 2014).

Onuoha, Christopher N. *Lay Leadership as a Charism of the Holy Spirit* (Thesis presented as partial fulfillment for the degree of Master of Arts, Kenrick School of Theology, Saint Louis, November, 18, 2005).

Pacwa, Mitch S.J. *Catholics And The New Age* (Ann Arbor: Servant Publications, 1992).

Eymard, Peter Julian. *The Eucharist and Christian Perfection I* (Cleveland: Emmanuel Publications, 1948).

Eymard, Peter Julian. *The Eucharist and Christian Perfection II* (Cleveland: Emmanuel Publications, 1948).

Stravinskas, Peter M.J. *Catholic Dictionary* (Huntington: Our Sunday Visitor, Inc., 1993).

Pius VIII. *Traditi Humilitate* (May 21, 1829).

Puhl, Louis J.S.J. *The Spiritual Exercises of St. Ignatius* (Chicago: Loyola Press, 1951).

Legio Mariae. *The Official Handbook of the Legion of Mary* (Dublin: Concilium Legionis Mariae, 1993).

The Roman Missal. Thursday of Fifth Week of Lent, Year A.

Ratzinger, Joseph. Homily Monday 18 April, 2005. vatican.va/gpII/documents/homily (accessed 2010).

Rengers, Christopher. O.F.M. Cap. *Mother of the Americas. A Handbook on Guadalupe* (New Bedford: Franciscan Friars of the Immaculate 1997).

Scupoli, Dom Lorenzo. *The Spiritual Combat and a Treatise On Peace of Soul* (Rockford: Tan Books and Publishers, Inc., 1990).

Ssemakula, Yozefu B. *The Healing of Families* (2011).

Teresa of Avila. *The Interior Castle or The Mansions* (Rockford: Tan Books and Publishers, Inc., 1997).

Thecatholicspirit.com/special-sections (accessed May 8, 2014).

Voris, Michael. *Freemasonry* ChurchMilitant.TV

Westen, John-Henry. Pope Benedict speaks: Renunciation of truth is 'lethal to faith' (lifesitenews.com, accessed October 3, 2014).

Zeller, Hubert van. The Currents of Spirituality (Springfield: Templegate Publishers, 1970).

Prayer before the Crucifix

Look down upon me, O good and gentle Jesus
while before Thy face I humbly kneel,
and with burning soul,
pray and beseech Thee
to fix deep within my heart lively sentiments
of faith, hope, and charity;
true contrition for my sins,
and a firm purpose of amendment.

While I contemplate,
with great love and tender pity,
Your five most grievous wounds,
pondering over them within me
and calling to mind the words which David,
Thy prophet, said to Thee, my Jesus:

"They have pierced My hands and My feet,
they have numbered all My bones."

Amen.

Cover Design Inspiration

Theme: The Light came into the darkness, and the Light overcame the darkness (Jn 1:5).

The Cover Design—the light breaking through the thick cloud and giving life to our family tree and to all generations and the whole world—speaks of the triumph of Christ, the Light of the world, over darkness. It depicts specifically the ministry of the New Covenant which is enacted now on better promises (Heb 8:6).

This ministry of the New Covenant is the ministry of the Spirit of Light, which gives and restores Christ's life in us and our generations. It reflects the true character of God's holy people who will experience for a thousand generations the blessings that abound in God (1 Chron 16:15; Ps 105:8), so that we may dance and announce His praises; for He has brought us out of the darkness of bondage into His own wonderful light (1 Pet 2:9), and He has turned our mourning into dancing (Ps 30).

In this sign of the light breaking through the dark cloud, we conquer as we experience anew our true identity in Christ; and since we have hope through the resurrection of Jesus Christ from the dead, we act very boldly (2 Cor 3:12). For we know that "the Lord is the Spirit, and where the Spirit of the Lord is present, there is freedom. And we all, with unveiled faces reflecting the glory of the Lord, are being transformed into the same image from one degree of glory to another, which is from the Lord, who is the Spirit" (2 Cor 3:17–18, NET).

Disclaimer:
*All the proper names used in this book are not real names of people.
*Under no circumstances can this book be used as a tool to diagnose and treat any illnesses.

Endnotes

¹ Fatima prayer

² St. John of the Cross. *The Collected Works of St. John of the Cross* (Washington D.C.: ICS Publications, 1991), 388.

³ Pope Clement I. *The Liturgy of the Hours. Vol. III. From the first, faith has been god's means of justifying men* (New York: Catholic Book Publishing Co., 1975), 75.

⁴ Giacomo Galaeazzi. Article reported in *Vatican Insider* (June 1, 2014).

⁵ *Ibid.*

⁶ *Ibid.*

⁷ Ignatius of Antioch. *The Liturgy of the Hours. Vol. III. Have Faith in Christ, and love,* 85.

⁸ *Catechism of the Catholic Church,* no. 1699.

⁹ Catholicnewsagency.com Exorcist says there's a demon that targets the family (accessed April 21, 2018).

¹⁰ Newadvent.org/cathen/01792c.htm (accessed April 21, 2018).

¹¹ *Ibid.*

¹² Fatima prayer

¹³ Haggerty, Fr. Donald. *Magnificat. vol. 19, no. 13. Jesus Left for the Desert* (New York: Magnificat, 2018) 367-8.

¹⁴ Some of the information contained in this discussion of the four pillars of contemplation is taken from my unpublished notes during formation and studies at the Intercessors of the Lamb (1999-2010).

¹⁵ John Paul II. Homily given during pilgrimage to Lourdes on the occasion of 150ᵗʰ anniversary of promulgation of the Dogma of the Immaculate Conception in Prairie de la Ribère Sunday, 15 August 2004. (Vatican.va accessed May 29, 2014).

¹⁶ *Ibid.*

¹⁷ Haggerty, Fr. Donald. *Magnificat,* vol. 19.

¹⁸ *Ibid.*

¹⁹ *Ibid.*

²⁰ A song by an unknown artist.

²¹ Tertullian. *The Liturgy of the Hours. Vol. II. The spiritual offering of prayer* (New York: Catholic Book Publishing Co., 1976), 248.

²² *Agape,* is Greek for sacrificial love; *filio,* is Greek for brotherly love.

²³ Louis J. Puhl, S.J. *The Spiritual Exercises of St. Ignatius* (Chicago: Loyola Press, 1951), 12.

²⁴ Hubert van Zeller. *The Currents of Spirituality* (Springfield: Templegate Publishers, 1970), 63.

²⁵ *Ibid.*

²⁶ Louis J. Puhl, S.J. *The Spiritual Exercises of St. Ignatius,* 12.

²⁷ John Paul II. *Familiaris Consortio,* no. 9.

²⁸ *Ibid*

[29] John Paul II. General Audience March 20, 1985 *"One Can Know God by the Natural Light of Human Reason"* (vatican.va accessed October 30, 2014).

[30] *Catechism of the Catholic Church,* no. 400, 404.

[31] *Ibid,* no. 1021, 1022.

[32] Newadvent.org (accessed on January 22, 2015).

[33] *Ibid.*

[34] *Ibid.*

[35] *Ibid.*

[36] *Ibid,* no. 1035.

[37] *Ibid,* no. 362.

[38] *Ibid.*

[39] *Ibid,* no. 363.

[40] *Ibid,* no. 364.

[41] Saint John Paul II. *The Theology of the Body* (Boston: Pauline Books and Media, 1997), 300.

[42] *Ibid,* 299.

[43] *Ibid,* 299—300.

[44] *Gadium et spes,* no. 14.

[45] *Ibid.*

[46] *Ibid.*

[47] *Catechism of the Catholic Church,* no. 364-5.

[48] Emphasis mine.

[49] Louis J. Puhl, S.J. *The Spiritual Exercises of St. Ignatius,* 141.

[50] *Ibid.*

[51] *Ibid.*

[52] *Ibid.*

[53] *Ibid.*

[54] Louis Marie de Montfort. *Preparation for Total Consecration* (Montfort Publications, 2006), 55.

[55] Newadvent.org/cathen (accessed April 17, 2014).

[56] *Ibid.*

[57] Newadvent.org/cathen (accessed April 17, 2014).

[58] *Ibid.*

[59] *Ibid.*

[60] *Ibid.*

[61] Jesuschristsavior.net/Tradition

[62] *Ibid.*

[63] *Ibid.*

[64] *Ibid.*

[65] Congregation for the Doctrine of the Faith. *Dominus Iesus,* no. 1—2.

[66] *Ibid,* no. 13.

[67] Maximus the Confessor. *The Liturgy of the Hours. Vol. II. The mercy of God to the penitent,* 304.

[68] Domenico Agasso, Jr. *Francis: "Pray with your heart, not like a parrot."* Article reported in *Vatican Insider* (May 16, 2014).

[69] *Ibid.*

[70] *Ibid.*

[71] *Ibid.*

[72] Peter M.J. Stravinskas. *Catholic Dictionary* (Huntington: Our Sunday Visitor, Inc., 1993), 190.

[73] Peter Julian Eymard. *The Eucharist and Christian Perfection I* (Cleveland: Emmanuel Publications, 1948), 284.

[74] *Ibid,* 281.

[75] *Ibid,* 281—2.

[76] Peter Julian Eymard. *The Eucharist and Christian Perfection II,* 27—28.

[77] *Ibid,* 29.

[78] *Ibid,* 28.

[79] *Ibid.*

[80] *The Liturgy of the Hours. Vol. IV. The living Church is the Body of Christ,* 521.

[81] Teresa of Avila. *The Interior Castle or The Mansions* (Rockford: Tan Books and Publishers, Inc., 1997), 50.

[82] *Ibid.*

[83] *Ibid.*

[84] Marilyn Gustin. *You Can Know God* (Liguori: Liguori Publication, 1993), 42.

[85] *The Liturgy of the Hours. Vol. I. On humility and peace,* (New York: Catholic Book Publishing Co., 1975), 280.

[86] Dorotheus. *The Liturgy of the Hours. Vol. III. The reason for all disturbance,* 295.

[87] *Ibid.*

[88] *Ibid.*

[89] *Ibid,* 296.

[90] Dorotheus. *The Liturgy of the Hours. Vol. III. On False spiritual peace,* 299.

[91] Hubert van Zeller. *The Currents of Spirituality,* 63.

[92] *Ibid.*

[93] Marilyn Gustin. *You Can Know God,* 43.

[94] The italicized emphasis is mine.

[95] Louis Marie de Montfort. *Preparation for Total Consecration,* 21.

[96] Cyprian. *The Liturgy of the Hours. Vol. II. He has given us life; he has taught us how to pray,* 106.

[97] Louis J. Puhl, S.J. *The Spiritual Exercises of St. Ignatius,* 28.

[98] Benedict XVI. *Papal address to the community of the Pontifical Theological Faculty Teresianum.* Article reported in *Zenit* (Vatican City, May 19, 2011).

[99] *Ibid.*

[100] Jean-Pierre de Caussade. *Abandonment to Divine Providence* (New York: Doubleday, 1975), 73.

[101] Louis J. Puhl, S.J. *The Spiritual Exercises of St. Ignatius,* 141.

[102] John Horn, S.J. Institute for Priestly Formation (IPF) handout for training in Spiritual Direction.

[103] *Ibid.*

[104] *Ibid.*

[105] *Ibid.*

[106] *Ibid.*

[107] *Ibid.*

[108] *Ibid.*

[109] *Ibid.*

[110] *Ibid.*

[111] *Ibid.*

[112] *Ibid.*

[113] *Ibid.*

[114] *Ibid.*

[115] *Ibid.*

[116] The Institute For Priestly Formation. *Christian Anthropology of the Heart,* 2011.

[117] *Ibid.*

[118] *Ibid.*

[119] Louis J. Puhl, S.J. *The Spiritual Exercises of St. Ignatius,* 142.

[120] John Horn, S.J. Institute for Priestly Formation (IPF) handout.

[121] Louis J. Puhl, S.J. *The Spiritual Exercises of St. Ignatius,* 142.

[122] John Horn, S.J. Institute for Priestly Formation (IPF) handout.

[123] The discussion of the three steps are taken from my lecture notes during IPF Certificate Program in Spiritual Direction and Retreat Ministry at the University of St. Mary of the Lake, Mundelein, IL (May 2011-January 2014).

[124] Louis J. Puhl, S.J. *The Spiritual Exercises of St. Ignatius,* 145.

[125] Louis Marie de Montfort. *Preparation for Total Consecration According to Saint Louis Marie de Montfort,* 65.

[126] Louis J. Puhl, S.J. *The Spiritual Exercises of St. Ignatius,* 143—144.

[127] John of the Cross. *The Collected Works of St. John of the Cross* (Washington, D.C.: ICS Publications, 1991), 353.

[128] *Ibid,* 356.

[129] *Ibid.*

[130] *Ibid.*

[131] *Ibid.*

[132] *Ibid.*

[133] *Ibid,* 357.

[134] John Paul II. *The Theology of the Body* (Boston: Pauline Books and Media, 1997), 69.

[135] Louis J. Puhl, S.J. *The Spiritual Exercises of St. Ignatius,* 60-61.

[136] *Ibid, 61—62.*

[137] *Ibid, 62.*

[138] The Intercessors of the Lamb was a Public Association of the Christian Faithful founded in 1985 by a late former clustered Nun, Nadine Brown, in the Archdiocese of Omaha, NE. It was a religious community of priests, sisters and brothers (and lay companions), who lived Jesus Christ and His Cross in the charism of "communal contemplative intercession," under four vows: chastity, obedience, poverty and victim love. It was canonically suppressed in October 2010.

[139] en.wikipedia.org/wiki/Socrates

[140] en.wikipedia.org/wiki/Know_thyself

[141] Norberto Rivera Carrera. *A Call to Vigilance Pastoral Instruction on New Age,* January 7, 1996, ewtn.com/library/bishops/acall.htm (accessed April 15, 2014)

[142] Gabriele Amorth. *An Exorcist Tells His Story* (San Francisco: Ignatius Press, 1999), 53.

[143] *Ibid,* 32.

[144] *Ibid,* 56.

[145] *Ibid.*

[146] Thomas à Kempis. *The Imitation of Christ* (Rockford: Tan Books and Publishers, Inc., 1989), 29-30.

[147] *Ibid.*

[148] *Ibid,* 32.

[149] *Ibid.*

[150] Gabriele Amorth. *An Exorcist Tells His Story,* 33.

[151] *Ibid.*

[152] *Ibid.*

[153] *Ibid,* 56.

[154] *Catechism of the Catholic Church,* no. 1673.

[155] *Ibid,* no. 1667.

[156] *Ibid,* no. 1667—1670.

[157] *Ibid,* no. 1673.

[158] This prayer is from the Roman Missal

[159] This statement was reported in the Wall Street Journal of November 9, 1976 from an address to the U.S. bishops before Cardinal Karol Józef Wojtyła became Pope John Paul II (See of Peter, October 16, 1978 to April 2, 2005).

[160] From an interview given by St. John Paul II to Catholics of Fulda in 1980.

[161] http://www.catholiceducation.org/articles/civilization/cc0371.htm (accessed on May 25, 2014).

[162] Congregation for the Doctrine of the Faith. *Christian Faith and Demonology* (2014).

[163] *Ibid.*

[164] Congregation for the Doctrine of the Faith. *Inde Ab Aliquot Annis On The Current Norms Governing Exorcisms* (September 29, 1984).

[165] *Ibid.*

[166] Christopher N Onuoha. *Lay Leadership as a Charism of the Holy Spirit* (Thesis presented as partial fulfillment for the degree of Master of Arts, Kenrick School of Theology, Saint Louis, November, 18, 2005), 85.

[167] Gabriele Amorth. *An Exorcist Tells His Story,* 53.

[168] Dom Lorenzo Scupoli. *The Spiritual Combat and a Treatise On Peace of Soul* (Rockford: Tan Books and Publishers, Inc., 1990), 125.

[169] *Ibid.*

[170] *Ibid,* 126.

[171] *Catechism of the Catholic Church,* no. 1667.

[172] Cyril of Jerusalem. *The Liturgy of the Hours. Vol. IV. Catechetical Instruction. On the Creed,* 488-489.

[173] wikipedia.org/wiki/Six-Day War (accessed May 25, 2014)

[174] Joseph Ratzinger. Homily Monday 18 April, 2005 (vatican.va/gpII/documents/homily-pro-eligendo-pontifice).

[175] Pope Francis. Address to Diplomatic Corps, March 22, 2013. en.radiovaticana.va.

[176] Prayer on the Miraculous Medal

[177] Augustine. *The Liturgy of the Hours. Vol. IV. She who believed by faith, conceived by faith,* 1573.

[178] Cyril of Jerusalem. *The Liturgy of the Hours. Vol. I. On the twofold coming of Christ,* 142.

[179] John Paul II. *Redemptoris Mater On the Blessed Virgin Mary in the life of the Pilgrim Church, no. 47.*

[180] www.agapebiblestudy.com (accessed May 27, 2014)

[181] *Catechism of the Catholic Church,* no. 966.

[182] John de Marchi, I.M.C. The True Story of Fatima A Complete Account of the Fatima Apparitions, 28.

[183] Francis M. Kalvelage, FI. *Kolbe Saint of the Immaculata* (New Bedford: Franciscans of the Immaculate 2001), 33.

[184] *Ibid.*

[185] *Ibid.*

[186] Christopher Rengers, O.F.M. Cap. *Mother of the Americas. A Handbook on Guadalupe* (New Bedford: Franciscan Friars of the Immaculate 1997), 3.

[187] thecatholicspirit.com (accessed January 20, 2013).

[188] Warren H. Carroll. *Our Lady of Guadalupe And the Conquest of Darkness* (Front Royal: Christendom Press, 1983), 104.

[189] *Ibid,* 105.

[190] Louis Marie de Montfort. *Preparation for Total Consecration,* 37.

[191] Legio Mariae. *The Official Handbook of the Legion of Mary* (Dublin: Concilium Legionis Mariae, 1993), 132.

[192] The Roman Missal. Thursday of Fifth Week of Lent, Year A.

[193] A German Lutheran pastor and theologian who founded the "Confessing Church" is the author of *The Cost of Discipleship.* He strongly resisted the Nazi dictatorship in Germany. He was arrested on April 1943 by the Gestapo and hanged April 1945 for his plot to assassinate Adolf Hitler, the German leader who started WW II.

[194] John Paul II. *Salvifici Doloris,* no. 5.

[195] *Ibid.*

[196] *Ibid.*

[197] *Ibid,* no. 6.

[198] *Ibid.*

[199] *Ibid,* no. 7.

[200] *Ibid.*

[201] *Ibid,* no. 8.

[202] *Ibid,* no. 9.

[203] *Ibid.*

[204] *Ibid,* no. 10.

[205] *Ibid.*

[206] *Ibid.*

[207] *Ibid.*

[208] *Ibid.*

[209] *Ibid,* no. 11.

[210] *Ibid.*

[211] *Ibid.*

[212] *Ibid,* no. 11, 12.

[213] *Ibid,* no. 12.

[214] *Ibid.*

[215] *Ibid,* no. 14.

[216] *Ibid.*

[217] *Ibid.*

[218] *Ibid.*

[219] *Ibid,* no. 15.

[220] *Ibid.*

[221] *Ibid,* no. 16.

[222] *Ibid.*

[223] *Ibid,* no. 18.

[224] John de Marchi, I.M.C. *The True Story of Fatima A Complete Account of the Fatima Apparitions,* 14.

[225] *Ibid.*

[226] "Victim Mentality Syndrome" as used exclusively in this book does not refer to any known or unknown human diagnosis or illness.

[227] John H. Hampsch., C.M.F. *Healing Your Family Tree* (Huntington: Our Sunday Visitor Publishing Division, 1989), 47.

[228] *Ibid.*

[229] Some materials contained in this discussion of the Capital sins are taken from unpublished personal notes during my religious formation and studies with the Intercessors of the Lamb (1999—2010).

[230] Thomas Aquinas. *Summa Theologica II—II, 153. 4. 3* (New York: Benziger Brothers, Inc., 1947), 1812.

[231] *Ibid, I-II, 84, 4, 1,* 964.

[232] John Chrysostom. *The Liturgy of the Hours. Vol. IV,* 600.

[233] Congregation for the Doctrine of the Faith. *Christian Faith and Demonology* (2014).

[234] Second Vatican Ecumenical Council, Dogmatic Constitution on the Church *Luman Gentium,* 40.

[235] John Paul II. *Novo Millennio Ineunte,* 30.

[236] *Ibid.*

[237] *Ibid,* 32.

[238] *Ibid.*

[239] *Ibid.*

[240] Thomas Aquinas. *Summa Theologica, II—II, 36, 4,* 1341.

[241] James F. McElhone, C.S.C. *Particular Examen* (Harrison: Roman Catholic Books, 1952), 111.

[242] From a Novena to the Holy Spirit by an unknown author.

243 Louis Marie de Montfort. *Preparation for Total Consecration, 73.*

244 Thomas Aquinas. *Summa Theologica I—II, 84, 1*

245 James F. McElhone, C.S.C. *Particular Examen,* 69.

246 From a Novena to the Holy Spirit by an unknown author.

247 *Ibid,* 70.

248 *Ibid,* 72—73.

249 *Ibid,* 73.

250 Thomas Aquinas. *Summa Theologica II—II, 162, 1.*

251 *Ibid.*

252 *Ibid, II—II, 162, 5*

253 *Ibid.*

254 *Ibid, II—II, 162, 1, 2.*

255 *Ibid.*

256 *Ibid, II—II, 162, 2, 1.*

257 *Ibid.*

258 Newadvent.org/cathen (accessed on April 28, 2014).

259 James F. McElhone, C.S.C. *Particular Examen,* 47.

260 *Ibid.*

261 *Ibid,* 50.

262 *Ibid,* 51.

263 *Ibid.*

264 *Ibid,* 53.

265 *Ibid.*

266 *Ibid.*

267 Thomas Aquinas. *Summa Theologica II—II, 163, 1.*

268 From a Novena to the Holy Spirit by an unknown author.

269 Thomas Aquinas. *Summa Theologica II—II, 162, 2, 3.*

270 James F. McElhone, C.S.C. *Particular Examen,* 105.

271 Thomas Aquinas. *Summa Theologica II—II, 148, 4.*

272 *Ibid.*

273 James F. McElhone, C.S.C. *Particular Examen,* 106.

274 *Ibid.*

275 From a Novena to the Holy Spirit by an unknown author.

276 *The Liturgy of the Hours. Vol. I. On humility and peace,* 280.

277 Faustina Kowalska. *Divine Mercy in My Soul* (Stockbridge: Marian Press, 2008), 438.

278 Louis Marie de Montfort. *Preparation for Total Consecration,* 37.

279 James F. McElhone, C.S.C. *Particular Examen,* 187.

280 *Ibid,* 189.

281 *Ibid,* 121.

282 From a Novena to the Holy Spirit by an unknown author.

283 Thomas Aquinas. *Summa Theologica II—II, 158, I.*

284 *Ibid, II—II, 158, 2.*

285 *Catechism of the Catholic Church,* no. 1830.

286 From a Novena to the Holy Spirit by an unknown author.

287 James F. McElhone, C.S.C. *Particular Examen* 91.

288 Newadvent.org/cathen (accessed on April 28, 2014)

289 James F. McElhone, C.S.C. *Particular Examen,* 78.

290 *Ibid.*

291 *Ibid,* 79.

292 *Ibid,* 80.

293 From a Novena to the Holy Spirit by an unknown author.

294 Louis Marie de Montfort. *God Alone* (Bat Shore: Montfort Publications 1999), 300.

295 *Ibid,* 301.

296 John M. Haffert. *Her Own Words to the Nuclear Age* (New Jersey: 101 Foundation, Inc, 1993), 278.

297 Bob Larson. *Larson's Book of Spiritual Warfare* (Nashville: Thomas Nelson Publishers, 1999), 449-457.

298 Giacomo Galeazzi. *Francis: "Please stop! Enough with all these child deaths.* Article reported in *Vatican Insider* (August 7, 2014).

299 *Ibid.*

300 Hampsch, John H. C.M.F. *Healing Your Family Tree,* 129.

301 *Ibid.*

302 *Ibid,* 130.

303 *Ibid,* 130.

304 *Ibid.*

305 From my lecture notes taken at the Institute for Priestly Formation three year program in Spiritual Direction and Retreat Ministry at Mundelein Seminary May 2011 – Jan. 2014.

306 Augustine. *The Liturgy of the Hours. Vol. IV. Confessions Lib. 7, 10,* 1355-1357.

307 wikipedia.org/wiki/Papal_conclave (accessed April 17, 2014).

308 Yozefu – B. Ssemakula. *The Healing of Families* (2011), 133.

309 John Paul II. General Audience March 20, 1985 *One Can Know God By the Natural Light of Human Reason. vatican .va* (accessed November 22, 2014).

310 *Ibid.*

311 *Ibid.*

312 Louis J Puhl. *The Spiritual Exercises of St. Ignatius,* 141.

313*Ibid.*

314 catholicnewsagency.com/news/jesus-not-found-outside-the-church-pope-preaches/ (Accessed September 2014).

315 Gornahoor.net/library/CortesEssays.pdf (accessed January 2013).

316 Some of the information on freemasonry were compiled using video presentation by Michael Voris on *Freemasonry* on ChurchMilitant.TV program.

317 Michael Voris. *Freemasonry* ChurchMilitant.TV.

318 Pius VIII. *Traditi Humilitate* (May 21, 1829).

319 Paul A. Fisher. *Their God is the Devil* (American Foundation Research, Inc., 1991), 5—6.

320 Clement XIII. *"In Eminenti"* (1738).

321 Joe Carrol. *The Unholy Trinity* (CA: Christian Book Club of America, 1995), 3.

322 Pope Leo XIII. *Dall'alto Dell'Apostolico Seggio* (October 15, 1890).

323 L'Osservatore Romano (March 11, 1985).

324 Michael Voris. *Freemasonry* ChurchMilitant.TV.

325 Joe Carroll. *The Unholy Trinity* (Palmdale: Christian Book Club of America, 1995), 5.

326 George F. Dillon. *Grand Orient Freemasonry Unmasked,* 1885.

327 Francis M. Kalvelage, FI. *Kolbe Saint of the Immaculata,* 240.

328 *Ibid,* 240—241.

329 *Ibid,* 241.

330 *Ibid,* 31.

331 *Ibid,* 32.

332 *Ibid,* 33

333 *Ibid,* 32.

334 *Ibid, 33.*

335 *Ibid,* 33.

336 wikipedia.org. *The free Encyclopedia. New Age* (accessed April 18, 2012).

337 *Ibid.*

338 Pontifical Council for Culture Pontifical Council for Interreligious Dialogue. *Jesus Christ the Bearer of the Water of Life: A Christian reflection on the "New Age."* vatican.va (accessed November 20, 2014), no. 6.1.

339 Barbara Curtis. What Is 'New Age' Religion and Why Can't Christians Get on Board? crosswalk.com/faith/spiritual-life/what-is-new-age-religion-and-why-cant-christians-get-on-board (accessed December 7, 2012).

340 *Ibid.*

341 Gabriele Amorth. *An Exorcist Tells His Story,* 54.

342 Mitch Pacwa, S.J. *Catholics And The New Age* (Ann Arbor: Servant Publications, 1992), 11.

343 *Ibid.*

344 *Ibid.*

345 *Ibid,* 12.

346 *Ibid,* 11—12.

347 *Ibid,* 12.

348 *Ibid,* 191.

349 This section summarizes the Pontifical Council for Culture Pontifical Council for Interreligious Dialogue document: *Jesus Christ the Bearer of the Water of Life: A Christian reflection on the "New Age,"* on the differences between *New Age* and Christianity.

350 *Catechism of the Catholic Church,* no. 390.

351 *Ibid,* no. 407.

352 *Ibid.*

353 *Ibid.*

354 *Ibid,* no. 404.

355 *Ibid,* no. 405.

356 *Ibid,* no. 402.

357 *Ibid,* no. 405.

358 John H. Hampsch, C.M.F. *Healing Your Family Tree,* 84.

359 *Ibid*, 14.

360 *Ibid*.

361 Thomas Aquinas. *Summa Theologica I—II, 81.2.1* (New York: Benziger Brothers, Inc., 1947), 953.

362 *Ibid, 81.2.2,* 954.

363 *Ibid, 81.2,* 953.

364 *Ibid, 81.3.2,* 954.

365 *Ibid, 81.3.3,* 954.

366 *Ibid, 81.3.2,* 954.

367 *Lumen Gentium,* no. 11; cf. *Catechism of the Catholic Church,* no. 1324.

368 Thomas Aquinas. *The Liturgy of the Hours. Vol. III. O Precious and Wonderful Banquet!* 610.

369 John H. Hampsch, C.M.F. *Healing Your Family Tree,* 42.

370 *Ibid, 43.*

371 *Ibid.*

372 Louis Marie de Montfort. *Preparation for Total Consecration,* 1.

373 John H. Hampsch, C.M.F. *Healing Your Family Tree,* 55.

374 Yozefu – B. Ssemakula. The Healing of Families, 179.

375 *Ibid,* 62.

376 Ignatius of Antioch. *The Liturgy of the Hours. Vol. III.,* 84.

377 Fatima prayer

378 Michael Mueller C.Ss.R. *Prayer the Key to Salvation* (Rockford: Tan Books and Publishers, Inc., 1985), 99.

379 *Ibid.*

380 *Ibid.*

381 *Ibid,* 97.

382 *Ibid.*

383 Pope Clement. *The Liturgy of the Hours. Vol. II. Repent* (1976), 51.

384 *Ibid.*

385 John-Henry Westen. *Pope Benedict speaks: Renunciation of truth is 'lethal to faith'* lifesitenews.com/news/pope-benedict-speaks-renunciation-of-truth-is-lethal-to-faith (accessed October 27, 2014)

386 John Paul II. *Letter of His Holiness John Paul II to All the Priests on the Occasion of Holy Thursday 1979.* Vatican.va (accessed November 13, 2014).

387 Prayer by an unknown author

388 Frank Duff. *The Woman of* Genesis (Frank Duff is the founder of the Legion of Mary, a pious Christian organization devoted to promoting the honor of the Mother of Jesus).

389 Louis Marie de Montfort. *Preparation for Total Consecration,* 74.

390 Father Founder of the Pilgrimage Center of Eucharistic Adoration, Elele, Nigeria.

391 *Catechism of the Catholic Church,* no. 1452.

392 *Ibid.*

393 Cyril of Jerusalem. *The Liturgy of the Hours. Vol. II. The Living water of the Holy Spirit,* 967.

394 John H. Hampsch, C.M.F. *Healing Your Family Tree,* 63.